Effectiveness of Music Therapy Procedures: Documentation of Research and Clinical Practice

completely revised
Second Edition

EDITOR

Charles E. Furman
University of Minnesota
Minneapolis, Minnesota

CONSULTANTS

Patricia J. Flowers
Department of Music Education
Ohio State University

Amelia G. Furman
Minneapolis Public Schools
Minneapolis, Minnesota

MEDICAL
ADVISORS

T. Michael Tedford, M.D.
Minneapolis, Minnesota

Rebecca J. Thoman, M.D.
Minneapolis, Minnesota

PRODUCTION
ASSISTANT

Thomas M. Lee
University of Minnesota
Minneapolis, Minnesota

Effectiveness of Music Therapy Procedures: Documentation of Research and Clinical Practice

completely revised
Second Edition

Edited by Charles E. Furman

National Association for Music Therapy, Inc.

Published 1996

The National Association for Music Therapy, Inc.
8455 Colesville Road, Suite 930
Silver Spring, MD 20910

Printed in The United States of America

LIST OF CONTRIBUTORS

Mary S. Adamek, Ph.D.
Minneapolis Public Schools
Minneapolis, Minnesota

Alice-Ann Darrow, Ph.D.
University of Kansas
Lawrence, Kansas

Amelia G. Furman, M.Mus.
Minneapolis Public Schools
Minneapolis, Minnesota

Charles E. Furman, Ph.D.
University of Minnesota
Minneapolis, Minnesota

Kate E. Gfeller, Ph.D.
University of Iowa
Iowa City, Iowa

Judith A. Jellison, Ph.D.
University of Texas
Austin, Texas

Carol A. Prickett, Ph.D.
University of Alabama
Tuscaloosa, Alabama

Iris M. Shiraishi, Ph.D.
Reuben Lindh Learning Center
Minneapolis, Minnesota

Jayne M. Standley, Ph.D.
Florida State University
Tallahassee, Florida

Myra J. Staum, Ph.D.
Willamette University
Salem, Oregon

David E. Wolfe
University of the Pacific
Stockton, California

Dedication

To our clients and students

Acknowledgments

On behalf of the National Association for Music Therapy, we would like to thank the many dedicated professionals who made this monograph possible: the editor, the production editor, the contributors, the advisory reviewers and the editorial assistant.

CONTENTS

MUSIC RESEARCH IN MEDICAL/DENTAL TREATMENT: AN UPDATE OF A PRIOR META-ANALYSIS*

Jayne M. Standley

REVIEW OF RELEVANT LITERATURE

MUSIC has been associated with the treatment of disease since ancient times. In fact, the oldest known written account of medical practices, the Kahum papyrus, refers to the use of incantations for healing the sick (Light, Love, Benson, & Morch, 1954). While many cultures throughout history have relied on music to cure physiological or psychological ills, it was not until the end of the nineteenth century that researchers began to study these applications systematically. The effects of music on specific physiological processes such as cardiac output, respiratory rate, pulse rate, and blood pressure were originally reported by Dogiel of France in 1880, by Corning of America in 1899, and by Tarchanoff of Russia in 1903 (Light et al., 1954).

Physiological Laboratory Studies

Between the turn of the century and the present day, other studies have followed these pioneer efforts and examined the relationship between music and physiological responses. Many have been conducted in a laboratory rather than a clinical context. One of the first was by Hyde (1924), who examined the effects of different kinds of musical selections upon the cardiovascular system, specifically pulse rate, blood pressure, cardiac output, and electrical phenomena of the cardiac muscles. Hyde concluded that cardiovascular functions were "reflexly stimulated concomitantly with physiological effects of music" (p. 222). Vincent and Thompson (1929) studied blood pressure responses of musical and nonmusical subjects and concluded that the important variable was not the type of music, but rather the subject's interest in or appreciation of the selection.

Other such studies have reported the effects of music on respiration and heart rate (Ellis & Brighouse, 1952), galvanic skin response and heart rate (Zimny & Weidenfeller, 1963), heart rate during repetitive exposure to music (Landreth & Landreth, 1974), electromyographic muscle tension (Scartelli, 1984), and electroencephalographic alpha brain waves (Wagner, 1975). In

---

*Portions of this article are reprinted, with permission, from the *Journal of Music Therapy* (National Association for Music Therapy, Inc.), (Standley, 1986).

general, these studies have found that slow, quiet, nonvocal music lowers physiological responses usually associated with stress, while faster music heightens responses, though these changes have not always been statistically significant and widely disparate individual responses have occurred. It should be noted that Bason and Celler (1972) reported that unless an external auditory stimulus, i.e., audible click, occurred within a precise time in the cardiac cycle measured from each R-wave of the subject's EKG, the heart rate did not alter. It may be that widely disparate individualized responses occur because of failure to match individual heart rates with music tempi and beat location in the cardiac cycle, because of the individual's intense or total lack of interest in the music selection or because of other, undefined, intervening variables.

Audioanalgesic Laboratory Studies

Taylor's history of music in general hospital treatment (1981) credits Evan O'Neill Kane with the initial clinical use of music as an audioanalgesic. In 1914, Kane began using a phonograph in the operating room for calming patients prior to the application of anesthesia. Contemporary research has documented the therapeutic benefits of this idea.

In an effort to investigate the effects of music on pain and/or anxiety, many researchers have simulated clinical distress by use of mild pain stimuli in the laboratory. Robson and Davenport (1962) tested a painful thermal stimulus and found that neither music nor white noise altered pain threshold. Melzack, Weisz, and Sprague (1963) tested the effect of auditory stimulation on experimental pain due to subjects' fingers being immersed in ice water. They reported that only slowly rising pain intensity was amenable to "control" by subjects, and that auditory stimulation together with strong suggestion that the stimulation abolished pain provided an effective stratagem for achieving such "control."

Several laboratory studies using mild shock have reported differing effects of music and/or white noise on pain suppression. Morosko and Simmons (1966) applied shock to subjects' teeth and found that music and white noise were effective in increasing pain threshold and tolerance. Howitt (1967) used six groups of children, a total of 136 subjects, to isolate the variables of music alone, music combined with verbal suggestion, all three stimuli together, and a control group receiving none of the above. He measured pain and tolerance threshold, cardiac rate, and GSR response to electrical stimulation of a tooth, and concluded that audioanalgesia techniques produced real clinical effects that were apparent in cardiac rate, but not GSR, that the effects were on tolerance for pain rather than on the response threshold, and that the effects were largely due to suggestion.

In similar studies using mild shock, Carlin, Ward, Gershon, and Ingraham (1962) and Camp, Martin, and Chapman (1962) found no differences in pain responses when the auditory stimulus was white noise only. Jellison (1975) found no difference in physiological responses to mild shock using two types of music stimuli. Conversely, Lavine, Buchsbaum, and Poncy (1976) applied mild shock to subjects' forearms and found that music and suggestion increased tolerance.

The aforementioned studies dealt with the effect of sound stimuli on pain threshold responses to superficial or cutaneous pain stimuli. Moore, Browne, and Hill (1964) theorized that audioanalgesic effects might differ in conditions with deep or visceral pain, such as the pain of the uterine muscle during contraction, i.e., ischemic muscle pain. Therefore, they investigated the effect of white noise on visceral pain produced by contractions of ischemic muscle by obliterating circulation to the subject's arm. In this experiment, white noise failed to alter pain threshold.

Some patients find the anxiety about a medical procedure to be more debilitating than the procedure itself. Music's effects on stress and anxiety have been measured through a variety of self-report, physiological, and observational means with some variation in results according to the type of dependent measure (Hanser, 1985). An early study by Peretti and Swenson (1974) used GSR to measure anxiety induced through negative feedback to subjects during a written maze test. In this instance, music significantly reduced GSR responses.

Clinical Use of Music

After 80 years of study, the literature now contains many references to the clinical use of music in actual medical/dental treatment. Music as an audioanalgesic in dental procedures was one of the earliest and most thoroughly investigated areas. Cherry and Pallin (1948) combined music with nitrous oxide-oxygen anesthesia; they reported that the presence of music reduced struggling and delirium, reduced vomiting, enabled rapid emergence from the anesthetic state, and decreased chair occupation time. Jacobson (1957) surveyed mental hospital patients following dental treatment with music and obtained highly favorable self-report data. Gardner and Licklider (1959) reported favorable results with 387 office patients receiving a variety of dental treatments, including drilling and tooth extraction. Patients listened to music on the Audio Analgesia, a stereophonic machine with earphones for both patient and dentist. These initial studies with actual dental patients were followed by others with similarly favorable results (Atterbury, 1974; Corah, Gale, Pace, & Seyrek, 1981; Davila & Menendez, 1986; Foutz, 1970; Gardner, Licklider, & Weisz, 1960; Long & Johnson, 1978; Monsey, 1960; Schermer, 1960; Weisbrod, 1969).

A 1983 experiment in this area was conducted in Japan by Oyama, Hatano, Sato, Kudo, Spintge, and Droh. Using subjects as their own controls during identical dental procedures under conditions of anesthesia alone versus music/anesthesia combined, they reported statistically significant reductions in blood pressure and pulse rate for the music/anesthesia condition.

In general, these dental studies have identified several factors that may be contributing to the analgesic effect of music and white noise: Auditory stimuli may directly suppress pain neurologically, auditory stimuli may mask the sound of the dental drill removing a source of conditioned anxiety, music may have a conditioned relaxing effect, focus on the music may serve as a distraction from the dental operation, controlling the volume and mix of the music and white noise may allow the patient to feel more in control of an aversive situation, or all benefits may be due to a priori suggestion.

Applications of audioanalgesia moved from dentistry to medical practices with early emphasis on use in surgery. Padfield (1976) and MacClelland (1979) initiated music listening in the operating room. Chetta (1981) demonstrated that music could reduce anxiety in preoperative pediatric patients up to and during the time of the first anesthetic hypodermic. Locsin (1981) used music with postoperative obstetric/gynecologic patients and found decreased overt pain reactions during the first 48 hours following surgery. It has also been determined that postoperative patients awakening to music will require less pain-relieving medication and will wait longer for the analgesic medication to be administered (Heitz, Symreng, & Scamman, 1992). Under regional anesthesia, patients listening to music have demonstrated a reduced need for sedatives

(Walther-Larsen, Diemar, & Valentin, 1988). In surgery research, music consistently has been shown to reduce self-report measures of postoperative pain (Mullooly, Levin, & Feldman, 1988), stress (Kopp, 1991), and anxiety (Kamin, Kamin, Spintge, & Droh, 1982; Moss, 1987; Siegel, 1983; Steelman, 1990; Updike & Charles, 1987). Additionally, orthopedic, gynecologic, and urologic surgery patients have demonstrated suppressed stress hormone levels in blood analyses as a function of music listening (Oyama, Sato, Kudo, Spintge, & Droh, 1983; Tanioka, Takazawa, Kamata, Kudo, Matsuki, & Oyama, 1985). Livingood, Kiser, and Paige (1984) studied the effect of music listening on families waiting for the outcome of surgery on their immediate relatives. They reported that music listening seemed to reduce anxiety; however, results were not statistically significant.

St. Joseph's Hospital in New York installed a Muzak system in its six-bed intensive care unit in 1972. They noted a drop in myocardial infarction and a mortality rate 8 to 12% below the national average (Howitt, 1972). Bonny pioneered music therapy procedures for the use, selection, and application of classical and familiar music listening in intensive, coronary care units and demonstrated beneficial pulse and blood pressure results (1983). Subsequent studies have shown music to increase relaxation and decrease anxiety in myocardial infarction patients (Bolwerk, 1990; Davis-Rollans & Cunningham, 1987; Guzzetta, 1989; Updike, 1990; White, 1992; Zimmerman, Pierson, & Marker, 1988).

Music has proven to be particularly effective in obstetric and gynecology treatment, especially childbirth (Livingston, 1979). Burt and Korn (1964) found reduced drug use in obstetric patients using music compared to those without audioanalgesia. McDowell (1966) reported favorable psychological responses but no reduction in drug use. Later research studies in this area have shown that music paired with Lamaze exercises can reduce pain and length of labor while enhancing the euphoria of birth (Clark, McCorkle, & Williams 1981; Codding, 1982; Durham & Collins, 1986; Hanser, Larson, & O'Connell, 1983; Winokur, 1984). Music has also proven beneficial during epidural caesarean section (Goroszeniuk & Morgan, 1984; Stein, 1991), during painful in-office gynecology procedures such as punch biopsy (Davis, 1992), and with adolescent pregnancies (Liebman & MacLaren, 1993). Shapiro and Cohen (1983) performed suction curettage abortions on 500 women using a paracervical block anesthetic and music versus methoxyflurane analgesia self administered versus no analgesia; results indicated that the music group had significantly less observed pain responses than either of the other two groups.

A number of studies have dealt with music's effects upon hospitalized infants and pediatric patients. Chapman (1975) and Owens (1979) investigated the effects of lullabies in the neonatal nursery on weight gain and movement of newborns. Chapman found a 16% reduction for premature infants in total time to reach weight criterion for discharge. Owens found no significant differences in variables in her study with normal newborns from birth to age 3 days. Research has shown, however, that premature neonates benefit from music played in the intensive care isolette (Katz, 1971). These babies remain calmer, use oxygen more efficiently (Collins & Kuck, 1991; Standley & Moore, 1993), gain weight faster (Malloy, 1979), and require a shorter time to reach discharge criteria (Caine, 1991). Music may also be effective in stimulating developmental milestones and mother-infant bonding with premature or hospitalized infants (Standley, 1991a).

The music therapy literature contains many references to the benefits of music activities in reducing fear, distress, and anxiety of hospitalized infants, toddlers, and their families (Fagen, 1982; Hoffman, 1980; Lindsay, 1981; Marley, 1984; McDonnell, 1984; Miller, 1984; Robinson,

1962; Schwankovsky & Guthrie, 1982). These authors cite the capability of music to promote creative "wellness" attributes of the very ill child. Additionally, research has demonstrated that music activities can effectively increase verbalizations about the trauma of hospitalization (Froelich, 1984); can generally reduce crying in infants (Lininger, 1987); and can be used contingently to reduce the prolonged and frequent crying of infants with colic (Larson & Ayllon, 1990). Marchette, Main, Redick, Bagg, and Leatherland (1991) found that music was not effective in reducing infant distress during neonatal circumcision.

A unique study by Falb (1982) investigated the effects of music versus recorded heartbeat as a reinforcer for conditioned vasoconstriction in three multiple handicapped, profoundly retarded, nonresponsive infants. Results showed the infants were physiologically responsive to both heartbeat and music, with overt signs of sucking beginning to be displayed toward the end of the experimental period.

In recent years, clinical music therapy programs have been developed on hospital pediatric units (Brodsky, 1989; Cohen, 1984). Research has shown that pediatric patients have reduced anxiety when listening to music during cardiac catheterization (Gettel, 1985; Micci, 1984) with greatest effects for children less than one year of age and between 7–12 years of age (Caire & Erickson, 1986). Other beneficial music applications have occurred for respiratory distress (Ammon, 1968); for preoperative anxiety (Chetta, 1981); nonspecific pain (Clinton, 1984) and postsurgical pain (Steinke, 1991); for fear and pain of injections (Fowler-Kerry & Lander, 1987), bone marrow aspirations (Pfaff, Smith, & Gowan, 1989), and lumbar punctures (Rasco, 1992); for cystic fibrosis congestion (Kamps, 1992); and for increases in salivary IgA indicating reduced stress (Lane, 1991).

In 1979, Christenberry detailed therapeutic uses of music with burn patients, including: alleviation of aesthetic sterility in the patient's environment; distraction from constant pain from the injury and treatments such as hydrotherapy, intravenous fluid therapy, and skin grafts; elicitation of movement for maintenance of joint mobility and to reduce contractures; augmentation of respiratory exercises; and reduction of psychological trauma of permanent disability and scarring. Christenberry emphasized that a crucial role of the music therapist was to enable the patient to have a relationship with one member of the medical team that was based on pleasure rather than pain. She cited the following important variables in maximizing music's effectiveness as an audioanalgesic for painful medical treatment: (1) use patient's preferred music, (2) begin music prior to the beginning of the pain-inducing stimuli, (3) use earphone or a pillow speaker if possible, and (4) teach the patient to associate music with pain reduction. Research in this area has confirmed that music (Barker, 1991; Schieffelin, 1988) and music videos (Miller, Hickman, & Lemasters, 1992) provide analgesic distraction during debridement.

Literature in the field of music therapy has placed some emphasis on the possible uses of music with the terminally ill (Brown, 1992a, 1992b; Gilbert, 1977; Lochner & Stevenson, 1988; Munro, 1984), and with patients with traumatic diseases such as cancer (Bailey, 1984, 1986; Ridgeway, 1983). An Australian journal documented highly favorable patient responses to the use of background music during radiotherapy (Mowatt, 1967). Sedei (1980) obtained increased self-disclosure verbalizations of cancer patients through music therapy activities. Music listening has been shown to reduce nausea of cancer patients receiving chemotherapy (Frank, 1985; Standley, 1992a) and to reduce anxiety during betatron radiation (Cook, 1982). Curtis (1986) studied terminally ill cancer patients' responses to music as an audioanalgesic in the last 6 months of their lives; statistically significant differences in the four measures of self-report data were not found although the music conditions were somewhat better than the nonmusic conditions. Beck (1991) utilized music and found a significant reduction in cancer-related pain. Music has proven effective for reducing even the chronic pain associated with the latter stages of cancer (Zimmerman, Pozehl, Duncan, & Schmitz, 1989). Bailey (1983) evaluated the perceived anxiety of hospitalized cancer patients in fair to good condition, and reported that live group therapy activities reduced anxiety more than did taped music sessions. Phillips (1980) advocated music in the care of elderly persons in nursing homes to reduce pain, isolation, and feelings of insecurity. Munro (1984) and Wylie and Blom (1986) developed music therapy techniques in hospice care.

Other clinical research has demonstrated physiological and psychological benefits of music with patients having a variety of diagnoses and undergoing differing medical treatments. Bob (1962) and Ohlsen (1967) studied the use of music in podiatric treatment and found significant reductions in perceived pain. Judd demonstrated benefits during hemodialysis (1982). Schuster (1985) studied blood pressure fluctuation during kidney dialysis under music and no music conditions, and noted periods of benefit but failed to find statistical significance in overall results. Colgrove (1991) replicated this study with similar results. Behrens (1982) successfully used pianica performance to increase the respiratory ability of impaired toddlers. Goloff (1981) conducted a group music therapy session for adults admitted to a general hospital and found that patients demonstrated elevated mood and comfort perceptions. Music has been reported to reduce distress during bronchoscopy (Metzler & Berman, 1991) and to increase immune responses in patients (Lane, 1991) and in well college students (Tsao, Gordon, Maranto, Lerman, & Murasko, 1991). In a study with chronically ill patients in a long-term care facility, Levine-Gross and Swartz (1982) contrasted group music therapy sessions with group psychotherapy sessions; results indicated significantly less perceived anxiety following music therapy. Music has even been used in the emergency room to reduce anxiety during laceration repair (Menegazzi, Paris, Kersteen, Flynn, & Trautman, 1991).

As early as 1950, Snow and Fields reported the use of music in physical therapy procedures to reduce the neurological problems of cerebral palsied children. Several research studies have demonstrated music therapy techniques to be effective with patients with motor impairments resulting from trauma or disease (Kozak, 1968).

Music's myriad effects on pain have been thoroughly reviewed by Maslar (1986) and overall, the body of research demonstrates music's effectiveness as an audioanalgesic though techniques for this usage vary. Rider demonstrated principles of music entrainment and imagery for pain reduction in a group of spinal pain patients (1985) and with arthritis and lupus patients (Rider & Kibler, 1990). In a pain rehabilitation clinic, Wolfe (1978) paired music with exercises for persons with chronic pain, and demonstrated increased frequency and duration of exercises and decreased verbalizations about pain. Godley (1987) has described such application in a music therapy program for pain clinics.

Staum (1983) employed walking to music to improve gait length, width, and balance of motor impaired persons, including stroke victims and the cerebral palsied. Scartelli (1982) used music and biofeedback to reduce muscle tension in spastic cerebral palsied subjects. Wolfe (1980) designed mercury switches which activated and deactivated music playing as a result of movement to increase head balance in motor impaired children. Music has also functioned to increase physical exercise compliance of adolescents with insulin-dependent diabetes mellitus (Marrero, Fremion, & Golden, 1988).

An innovative study using music to increase overt motor responses to verbal directions of four adults who had been comatose due to trauma for 6 months or longer was conducted by Boyle and Greer (1983). Dramatic increases were evident with two patients and minimal increases with the remaining two. A high degree of variability was noted in the responses of all four subjects. Roberts (1986) played music for comatose patients and demonstrated reduced intracranial pressure. Continued investigation in this area seems warranted to refine clinical applications of music with comatose patients.

Other innovative music therapy techniques have been reported in the medical literature. Foremost among these is music paired with vibrotactile stimulation to increase the awareness of comatose patients (Grundy, 1989), to enhance physical therapy objectives (Skille, Wigram, & Weeks, 1989), or to reduce headaches (McElwain, 1993). This technique would seem to have great potential for medical treatment and further research is anticipated.

META-ANALYSIS OF MEDICAL/DENTAL STUDIES USING MUSIC

A comprehensive review of literature in the area of music and medicine reveals such diversity that it is difficult to analyze the results definitively through traditional means. There are a myriad array of variables combined with or compared to music; a variety of patient diagnoses; a wide continuum of clinical severity from the mild, temporary pain and anxiety due to dental procedures to the devastating pain and trauma of a terminal illness; inclusion of the entire gamut of age ranges from premature neonates to the elderly; and a variety of research designs, statistical analyses, and dependent measures. Meta-analysis was selected as the most viable means of integrating such diverse research results.

A meta-analysis is a procedure which provides quantitative synthesis of research data through formal statistical techniques. Specifically, it is the application of a variety of formulae to the results of a body of homogeneous research to compute effect sizes, i.e., quantitative summaries of the properties and findings of individual studies. Effect sizes can then be compared and contrasted across multiple variables (Glass, McGaw, & Smith, 1984) and these overall results, to some extent, generalized.

Glass, McGaw, and Smith (1984) differentiate primary analysis, the original analysis of data in a research study, from secondary analysis, the reanalysis of data for the purpose of answering the original research question with better statistical techniques or for answering new questions with the original data, and meta-analysis, the statistical analysis of the summary findings of many empirical studies. They describe meta-analysis as follows: "The approach of research integration referred to as a meta-analysis is nothing more than the attitude of data analysis applied to quantitative summaries of individual experiments. By recording the properties of studies and their findings in quantitative terms, the meta-analysis of research invites one who would integrate numerous and diverse findings to apply the full power of statistical methods to the task. Thus it is not a technique; rather it is a perspective that uses many techniques of measurement and statistical analysis" (p. 21).

According to *Science* magazine (Mann, 1990), the precedent has been set for the use of meta-analysis to endorse and reject medical procedures on the basis of research findings. This precedent has been set by the Oxford Medical publication, *Effective Care in Pregnancy and Childbirth* (1989) edited by Chalmers, Enkin, and Keirse. It is the most extensive collection of meta-analyses to date with quantified results which the editors claim have proven to be more objective than a traditional review of the literature and which justify definitive conclusions about the efficacy of specific, standard medical procedures in the practice of obstetrics.

The purpose of this paper follows that precedent and is threefold: to utilize the results of an updated meta-analysis of existing research in music and medicine to identify and to authenticate effective music therapy techniques and, further, to develop these techniques into clinical procedures which meet the criteria of standard medical protocol.

Procedures

Studies qualified for inclusion in the original meta-analysis and in this updated version by containing empirical data; by utilizing actual, not simulated pain stimuli; by utilizing music as an independent variable; by utilizing subjects who were actual patients with medical/dental diagnoses; and by reporting results in a format amenable to replicated data analysis. The procedures followed the three basic steps outlined by Getsie, Langer, and Glass (1985): (1) a complete literature search was conducted to find all possible members of the defined population of studies whether published or unpublished sources; (2) the characteristics and findings of the collected studies were identified, described, and categorized; and (3) the composite findings were statistically analyzed and converted to computed effect sizes. The population for this analysis was defined as all empirical studies reported in English of the effects of music in actual (not simulated) medical/dental treatment. The starting point for the literature search was a bibliography developed by the author in 1980 and two published bibliographies, the Taylor review (1981) and the monograph, *Music Therapy for Handicapped Children: Other Health Impaired* (Schwankovsky & Guthrie, 1982). A complete individual search of the two journals, *Journal of Music Therapy* and *Music Therapy*, was conducted from inception to the present, as was a search of *Dissertation Abstracts* from 1950 to the present. Also included was a search of the three indexes to music therapy/psychology literature edited by Eagle (1976, 1978; Eagle & Minter, 1984), a published review by Slesnick (1983), and a search via MEDLINE (1983–1992), the computerized database of the National Library of Medicine which contains references from the Index Medicus, Index to Dental Literature and the International Nursing Index.

The original meta-analysis identified 29 empirical studies on this topic (Standley, 1986). In 1989, additional updated references were reviewed and analyzed, resulting in a pooled meta-analysis of 54 studies utilizing 129 dependent variables (Standley, 1992b). The current update pools data from 92 studies and 233 dependent variables.

Estimation of Effect Size

The value of each dependent variable reported in the selected studies was converted to an estimated effect size (ES) according to procedures outlined by Glass, McGaw, and Smith (1984). The ES represents that proportion of a standard deviation which quantifies the experimental effect on the two conditions, i.e., an ES = + 1.00 would indicate that the size of the experimental group's benefit was one standard deviation greater than the control group. One means of determining the effect size of an experimental result is estimated via the contrast of the means of experimental (Exp) and Control (Con) conditions divided by within condition standard deviation (*SD*), with the *SD* of the control group usually being the most logical. Given the means and *SDs* of groups or conditions, the estimation is straightforward via the formula:

$$\frac{X_{Exp} - X_{Con}}{SD_{Con}} = ES \text{ (Estimated Effect Size)}$$

Data not reported in a format which includes means and/or *SD* are converted via a variety of published statistical formulae. This allows linear comparison of music's effects across all studies despite widely diverse individual characteristics.

Results

Table 1 gives a complete list of the 233 variables analyzed with computed effect sizes in order from greatest to least effect. Estimated effect sizes ranged from 10.90 to –1.53, meaning that the music condition was sometimes more than 10 standard deviations greater in desired effect than the control condition without music and in some cases was more than 1 standard deviation worse. A few of the 233 variables did have a negative value, indicating that for those dependent measures the music condition was less beneficial than the nonmusic one. It should be noted that all negative results were from studies where other dependent measures in that same study showed a positive reaction to music. Many medical studies have a tendency to report an array of physiological measures available to the researcher, some of which seem tangentially related to the primary purpose of the investigation. Not all physiological measures respond consistently for the same individual within the same treatment condition. Such information is valuable to help identify those physiological measures which are most responsive to the effects of music.

A primary dependent variable was identified from the title and stated purpose for each music medicine study (*N*=92) and an average effect size computed. The overall mean effect of music as measured by the primary dependent variables was 1.17; measured in this context, the average therapeutic effect of music in medical treatment was more than one standard deviation greater than that without music.

Once each dependent variable had a value on a linear scale, the impact of music could be characterized and to some extent generalized by cross comparisons. First, studies were grouped by date of publication/presentation. Those prior to 1980 reported a mean ES=.77 (*n*=35 dependent variables analyzed) while those since 1980 have reported a greater average benefit (ES=.91) and a greater number of experimental variables analyzed (*n*=198). These data demonstrate the great interest in music medicine research in the last decade and reveal that the design of more recent research is improving upon the benefits of music to the patient.

Tables 2 through 6 provide information about other comparisons that were developed with the effect size data and the analysis of the studies' independent and dependent variables, patient descriptions, and treatment procedures. Table 2 gives a summary of the generalized effects of music that may be ascertained through this meta-analysis and shows that women respond to music with greater effect than do men; that, by age, infants show the least effects; that music's effects

Table 1

Mean Music Effect Size for Each Dependent Variable Analyzed

Reference	Dependent Variable	Effect Size
Updike & Charles	Mean Arterial Pressure-Presurgical	10.90
*Bob	Pain-Podiatric	>3.28
*Aldridge	Presurgical Anxiety-Pediatric	3.28
*Goroszeniuk & Morgan	Pain-Obstetric	3.28
*Ammon	Respiration-Pediatric	3.15
*Oyama et al.	Pulse-Dental	3.00
Guzzetta	Music Helpfulness-Cardiac	2.92
*McElwain	Headache Relief	2.92
Updike & Charles	Blood Pressure DPI-Presurgical	2.92
*Updike & Charles	Systolic Blood Pressure-Presurgical	2.86
*Monsey	Use of Analgesia-Dental	2.49
*Martin	EMG (35 Min. of Music)	2.38
Standley & Moore	Oxygen Saturation: NBICU (Day1, 1st 10 min.)	2.37
*Gardner & Licklider	Use of Analgesia-Dental	2.36
*White	Anxiety-Cardiac	2.34
Updike & Charles	Heartrate-Presurgical	2.33
*Guzzetta	Apical Heartrate-Cardiac CCU	2.31
Oyama et al.	Blood Pressure-Dental Pts.	2.25
*Rider	Pain-(*Debussy*)	2.11
*Siegel	Medication-Pediatric Surgery	2.11
Martin	EMG (26-30 Min. of Music)	2.10
Updike & Charles	Diastolic Blood Pressure-Presurgical	2.09
Schuster	Distraction-Hemodialysis	2.08
*Larson & Ayllon	Crying-Infant Colic	2.08
*Liebman & MacLaren	Anxiety-Obstetric	2.07
*Zimmerman et al. (1988)	Anxiety-Cardiac	2.04
Rider	EMG (*Entrainment*)	2.03
*Chetta	Observed Anxiety-Pediatric Surgery	1.97
*Cofrancesco	Grasp Strength-Stroke	1.94
Rider	EMG-(*Metheny*)	1.90
*Tanioka et al.	Cortisol-Surgical Recovery	1.80
*Bonny	Perceived Anxiety-Cardiac	1.77
Budzynski et al.	EMG-Tension Headache	1.76
*Budzynski et al.	Pain Intensity-Headache	1.76
White	Heartrate-Cardiac ICU	1.72
Davis	Respiration Rate-Gynecology Punch Biopsy	1.71
*Davis	Observed Pain-Gynecology Punch Biopsy	1.57
Rider	EMG (*Crystal*)	1.56
Rider	Pain (*Reich*)	1.55
Rider	EMG (No Music)	1.52
*Barker	Pain- Burn Debridement	1.52
Rider	Pain (*Entrainment*)	1.51
*Locsin	Pain Postoperative	1.49
Standley & Moore	Oxygen Saturation: NBICU (Day 1, 2nd 10 min.)	1.47

Table 1
Continued

Reference	Dependent Variable	Effect Size
*Standley (1992a)	Nausea Onset-Chemotherapy	1.41
*Moss	Anxiety-Surgical	1.38
*McDowell	Attitude Toward Music	1.34
Tanioka et al.	Adrenalin-Surgery	1.33
Winokur	Relaxation-Obstetrical	1.32
*Collins & Kuck	Observed Behavior-NBICU	1.29
*Bolwerk	Anxiety-Cardiac ICU	1.28
Siegel	Pulse-Pediatric	1.28
Tanioka et al.	Anxiety-Surgical	1.28
*Schieffelin	Crying-Debridement	1.23
Bonny	Pulse-Cardiac	1.22
Martin	EMG (18-25 Min. of Music)	1.22
*Mullooly et al.	Pain-Surgical	1.21
*Roberts	Intracranial Pressure (Prefer. vs. Sedative Music)	1.21
*Walther-Larsen et al.	Anxiety-Surgical	1.21
*Jacobson	Perceived Pain-Dental	1.19
Rider	Pain (*Metheny*)	1.16
Bonny	Perceived Pain-Cardiac	1.15
Aldridge	Comfort-Pediatric	1.12
*Marrero et al.	Oxygen uptake-Diabetes (Aerobic Fitness)	1.12
*Spintge & Droh	Choice of Epidural Anesthesia-Surgery	1.12
*Standley & Moore	Oxygen Amount-NBICU	1.11
White	Respiration Rate-Cardiac	1.10
Marrero et al.	Hemoglobin-Diabetes (Aerobic Fitness)	1.07
*Stein	Anxiety-Cesarean Surgery	1.04
*Zimmerman et al. (1989)	Chronic Pain-Cancer	1.04
Sanderson (1986)	Anxiety-Preoperative	1.02
*Epstein et al.	Migraine Headache	1.00
*Winokur	Length of Labor-Childbirth	.99
Goloff	Perceived Satisfaction	.98
*Levine-Gross & Swartz	State-Trait Anxiety	.98
Winokur	Use of Medication-Obstetrical	.98
*Froelich	Verbalizations	.97
Rider	Pain (*Crystal*)	.96
Rider	Pain (No Music)	.96
*Shapiro & Cohen	Pain-Abortion (Music only)	.96
Davis-Rollans & Cunningham	Mood-Cardiac ICU	.95
Standley & Moore	Oxygen Saturation: NBICU (Day 2, 2nd 10 min.)	.95
*Beck	Pain-Cancer (Music & Sound)	.94
*Gfeller et al.	Helplessness-Dental	.94
Staum	Walking Speed-Stroke	.94
*Staum	Gait Improvement-Stroke	.94
Rider	EMG (Preferred Music)	.91

Table 1
Continued

Reference	Dependent Variable	Effect Size
Zimmerman et al. (1989)	Pain intensity-Cancer	.91
*Hanser et al.	Observed Childbirth Pain	.90
Pfaff et al.	Anticipated Fear Pediatric Bone Marrow Aspiration	.90
*Pfaff et al.	Observed Distress Pediatric Bone Marrow Aspiration	.90
Standley & Moore	Oxygen Alarm Frequency-NBICU	.90
*Sanderson (1986)	Pain Relief-Surgical	.89
Crago	Relaxation-Open Heart Surgery	.88
*Miller et al.	Pain Intensity-Burn	.88
*Standley (1991a)	Calmness-Premature Infants	.88
Steelman	Diastolic Blood Pressure-Surgery	.88
*Crago	Pain-Open Heart Surgery	.87
Miller et al.	Anxiety-Burn	.85
*Scartelli	EMG-Spasticity	.85
*Behrens	Exhalation Strength	.83
*Hoffman	Blood Pressure-Hypertension	.83
Mulloolly et al.	Pain 2 Days After Surgery	.83
Locsin	Blood Pressure-Surgical	.82
*Kamin et al.	Cortisol-20 Min. After Extubation	.80
*Davis-Rollans & Cunningham	Heartrate-Cardiac ICU	.77
Davis-Rollans & Cunningham	Respiration Rate-Cardiac ICU	.77
Pfaff et al.	Fear Experienced-Pediatric Bone Marrow Aspiration	.77
Tanioka et al.	Cortisol-1 hr. of Surgery	.75
Brook	Pulse-Obstetrical	.73
Brook	Neonate Apgar Score	.73
*Mandle et al.	Anxiety-Cardiac Angiography	.73
*Caire & Erickson	Anxiety-Pediatric Cardiac Catheterization	.72
*Lininger	Crying-Neonate	.72
Caine	Weight Gain-NBICU	.71
Guzzetta	Finger Temperature-Cardiac ICU	.71
Shapiro & Cohen	Pain-Abortion (Music vs. Anesthesia)	.71
*Schneider	Pain-Pediatric Burn Debridement	.70
Curtis	Contentment-Cancer	.67
Kamin et al.	Cortisol-at Anesthesia	.67
Roberts	Intracranial Pressure (Prefer. Music vs. Silence)	.67
Burt & Korn	Perceived Effect-Obstetrical	.66
*Chapman	Length of Hospitalization-Neonate	.65
Heitz et al.	Positive Recall-1 month-Surgery	.65
*Curtis	Perceived Pain-Cancer	.63
Frank	Anxiety-Chemotherapy	.63

Table 1
Continued

Reference	Dependent Variable	Effect Size
*Fowler-Kerry & Lander	Injection pain-Pediatric (Music/Suggestion)	.62
Kaempf & Amodei	Respiration Rate-Surgery	.61
Standley (1991b)	Attentiveness-Premature Infants	.61
*Codding	Perceived Pain-Childbirth	.59
Epstein et al.	Pain Intensity-Headache	.59
Rider	Pain-(Preferred Music)	.59
Heitz et al.	Positive Recall-1 day-Surgery	.58
Sanderson (1986)	Pain Verbalization-Surgical	.58
Armatas	Nausea-Surgical Postanesthesia	.57
*Caine	Length of Hospitalization-Neonate	.56
Locsin	Pulse-Surgical	.56
Sanderson (1986)	Blood Pressure-Surgical	.55
*Menegazzi et al.	Pain-Emergency Laceration Repair	.54
Mandle et al.	Pain-Cardiac Angiography	.53
*Brook	Cervical Dilation Time	.52
*Heitz et al.	Analgesia Delay-Surgery	.52
*Goloff	Physical Comfort	.51
Larson & Ayllon	Parental Distress-Infant Colic	.50
Rider	EMG (*Reich*)	.50
Sanderson (1986)	Analgesics-Surgical	.50
*Steinke	Pain Rating Intensity-Pediatric Scoliosis Surgery	.50
Barker	Pulse-Burn Debridement	.50
Guzzetta	Cardiovascular Complications-Cardiac ICU	.49
Roberts	Blood Pressure (Preferred Music vs. Silence)	.49
Barker	Perceived Pain- Burn Debridement	.48
Collins & Kuck	Heartrate-NBICU	.47
*Corah et al.	Autonomic Sensations-Dental	.47
*Davila & Menendez	GSR-Dental	.47
Frank	Emesis Intensity-Chemotherapy	.47
*Durham & Collins	Pain Medication-Obstetric	.46
Collins & Kuck	Mean Arterial Pressure-NBICU	.45
Crago	Music Listening-Open Heart Surgery	.45
Kamin et al.	Cortisol (15 Min. after Incision)	.44
*Sammons	Music Choice	.44
Bonny	Blood Pressure-Cardiac	.42
Crago	Sleep-Open Heart Surgery	.42
Kamin et al.	Cortisol (10 Min. Before Anesthesia)	.42
*Spintge	Epidural Anesthesia	.42
Crago	Anxiety-Open Heart Surgery	.41
Steinke	Pain Intensity Visual Analog Scale-Surgery	.41
*Colgrove	Pulse-Hemodialysis	.40
Miller et al.	Pain Rating Index-Burn	.40
*Burt & Korn	Use of Analgesic-Obstetrical	.39
Fowler-Kerry & Lander	Injection Pain-Pediatric (Music Distraction)	.39

Table 1
Continued

Reference	Dependent Variable	Effect Size
*Metzler & Berman	Pulse-Bronchoscopy	.39
Beck	Pain - Cancer (Music vs. Sound)	.38
Standley (1991b)	Crying - Premature Infant	.37
*Frank	Nausea Length-Chemotherapy	.36
Burt & Korn	Amount of Analgesic-Obstetrical	.35
*Bailey (1986)	Perceived Anxiety-Cancer	.34
Clark et al.	Perceived Anxiety-Obstetrical	.34
*Clark et al.	Perceived Pain-Obstetrical	.33
Frank	Emesis Length-Chemotherapy	.33
Rider	EMG (*Debussy*)	.33
Steinke	Present Pain Intensity-Pediatric Scoliosis Surgery	.33
Crago	Analgesics-Open Heart Surgery	.30
Armatas	Skin Response-Surgical	.29
*Roter	Perceived Benefit-Patients	.28
Lininger	Neonate Crying (Instrumental vs. No Music)	.26
Roter	Perceived Benefit-Families	.26
Colgrove	Peripheral Temperature-Hemodialysis	.24
Steinke	Anxiety-Pediatric Scoliosis Surgery	.24
*Livingood et al.	Perceived Anxiety-Families	.23
Menegazzi et al.	Respiration Rate-Emergency Laceration Repair	.23
Kaempf & Amodei	Pulse Rate-Surgery	.19
*Owens	Movement-Neonate	.19
Fowler-Kerry & Lander	Injection Pain-Pediatric (Suggestion)	.17
Lininger	Crying-Neonate (Vocal vs. Instrumental Music)	.15
Chapman	Movement-Neonate	.14
Clark et al.	Perceived Length of Labor	.14
Kaempf & Amodei	Diastolic Blood Pressure-Surgery	.13
*Lane	Salivary IgA-Cancer	.13
Standley & Moore	Oxygen Saturation: NBICU (Day 1, Post Music)	.13
Armatas	Excitability-Surgery	.12
*Armatas	Anesthesia Recovery Time-Surgery	.11
Mandle et al.	Pain Medication Request	.11
Clark et al.	Childbirth Attitude	.10
Collins & Kuck	Oxygen Saturation-NBICU	.10
*Kaempf & Amodei	Anxiety-Surgery	.10
*Schuster	Blood Pressure-Dialysis	.10
Standley & Moore	Oxygen Saturation: NBICU (Day 2, 1st 10 min.)	.10
Zimmerman et al. (1988)	Temperature-Pediatric Cardiac Catheterization	.09
Armatas	Anxiety-Surgery	.06
Owens	Crying-Neonate	.06
Caine	Relaxation-Neonate	.05
Armatas	Pain-Surgery	.04
Roberts	Blood Pressure (Preferred vs. Sedative Music)	.03
*Steelman	Anxiety-Surgery	.03

Table 1
Continued

Reference	Dependent Variable	Effect Size
Zimmerman et al. (1988)	Heartrate-Cardiac	.03
Armatas	Anesthesia Recovery Rate-Surgery	.02
Owens	Weight-Neonate	.02
Siegel	Respiration-Pediatric	.01
Frank	Nausea Intensity-Chemotherapy	.00
Zimmerman et al. (1988)	Systolic Blood Pressure-Cardiac	-.06
Kaempf & Amodei	Systolic Blood Pressure-Surgery	-.15
Standley & Moore	Oxygen Saturation: NBICU (Day 3, 2nd 10 min.)	-.17
Tanioka et al.	ACTH Level-Surgery	-.17
Menegazzi et al.	Heartrate-Emergency Laceration Repair	-.27
Menegazzi et al.	Blood Pressure-Emergency Laceration Repair	-.29
Corah et al.	Anxiety-Dental	-.39
Standley & Moore	Oxygen Saturation: NBICU (Day 2, Post Music)	-.39
Standley (1992a)	Finger Temperature-Chemotherapy	-.49
Crago	Hospitalization-Open Heart	-.51
Caine	Neonate Formula Intake	-.59
Corah et al.	Anxiety-Dental	-.39
Standley & Moore	Oxygen Saturation: NBICU (Day 2, Post Music)	-.39
Standley (1992a)	Finger Temperature-Chemotherapy	-.49
Crago	Hospitalization-Open Heart	-.51
Caine	Neonate Formula Intake	-.59
Standley & Moore	Oxygen Saturation: NBICU (Day 3, Post Music)	-.66
Standley & Moore	Oxygen Saturation: NBICU (Day 3, 1st 10 min.)	-.68
Standley & Moore	Apnea After 3 Days of Music: NBICU	-1.53

N=233
( )=Type of Music/Auditory Stimulus
Overall Mean Effect Size of Music for Primary Variables=1.17
*=Primary Variable for Each of 92 Studies

are greatest when the patient is experiencing some pain but these effects are reduced as the pain becomes severe; and that live music presented by a music therapist is far more powerful than is the use of recorded music. Studies utilizing patients' preferred music demonstrated the greatest effect (ES=1.40, *n*=30). The medical benefits of live music performance by musicians have yet to be documented in the research literature and were not included in this analysis.

The effects of music seem greatly differentiated according to patient diagnosis and related level of pain, anxiety, and prognosis. Table 3 gives a listing of specific diagnoses included in the analyzed studies in the order of greatest response to music. Such a listing has definite implications for music therapy programs developed in medical settings. Podiatry studies have reported the greatest effects followed by headache, respiratory, and dental studies. Neonates in need of medical services are shown to have the least effect to music which may be related to their developmental stage neurologically and musically.

Table 2

Meta-Analysis Results: Generalizations from the Research Literature About the Use of Music in Medical Treatment

---

Sex	Women (ES=.90, n=30) respond to music with greater effect than do men (ES=.57, *n*=14). These data were based on studies utilizing subjects of only 1 gender group.
Age	Children and adolescents (ES=.95, *n*=26) respond with marginally greater effect than do adults (ES=.93, *n*=159). Infants show the least response to music (ES=.48, *n*=34).
Pain	Music has greater effect when some pain is present (ES=.93, *n*=194) than when it is not a usual symptom of the diagnosis (ES=.81, *n*=22), though music seems to become less effective as the pain increases.
Type Dependent Measure	The least conservative measure of music's effect is patient self-report (ES=1.04, *n*=87) while systematic behavioral observation (ES=.83, *n*=50) and physiological measures (ES=.90, *n*=96) result in basically equivalent, conservative effect sizes. The most frequently utilized dependent variable is a physiological measure.
Diagnoses	Effects vary widely according to diagnosis. Music seems to be less effective when severe pain is a usual symptom or the diagnosis has serious implications. Effects are greatest for dental patients and those with chronic pain, i.e., migraine headaches. More minimal effects are reported for obstetrical, burn, coma and cancer patients with lowest effects being reported for neonates and for use of music in the emergency room for laceration repair.
Music	Live music presented by a trained music therapist (ES=1.13, *n*=16) has a much greater effect than does recorded music (ES=.86, *n*=217). Preferred music has the greatest effect (ES=1.40, *n*=30).
Dependent Measures	Effects vary greatly according to the specific dependent measure utilized. Greatest effects were reported for grasp strength of stroke patients, perceived effectiveness of the music, EMG, self-report of pain, relaxation, and anxiety reduction. Least effects were measured by days of hospitalization, peripheral finger temperature, ease of childbirth, time of recovery from anesthesia, formula intake of neonates and neonate apnea.

Table 3

Mean Music Effect Size by Patient Diagnosis/Treatment Area and Number of Variables Analyzed

Diagnosis/Area of Treatment	$\overline{ES}$	N
Podiatric Patients	3.28	1
Headache Patients	1.72	8
Respiratory Patients	1.46	3
Dental Patients	1.42	9
Chronic Pain Patients	1.26	14
Physical Rehabilitation Patients	1.17	4
Diabetes Patients	1.10	2
Cardiac Patients	1.05	23
Surgery Patients	.99	64
Obstetric Patients	.84	21
Abortion Patients	.84	2
Hypertension Patients	.83	1
Burn Patients	.82	8
Kidney Dialysis Patients	.71	4
Multi-Diagnosis Patients	.61	6
Coma Patients	.60	4
Cancer Patients	.57	18
Families of Patients	.45	5
Neonatal Patients	.40	32
Emergency Laceration Repair Patients	.05	4

N=233

Reported effects are related to sample size, with very small groups producing much greater effects (Table 4). This table also shows that most research in this area has occurred with groups of more than 10 subjects. Most studies have also used the more stringent experimental/control group designs, which have produced the smallest effect sizes (Table 5). These two tables demonstrate that the great majority of the reported effects of music in the medical literature are on the conservative side.

In the design of clinical procedures, it may be important to know how various physiological, self-report, and observed responses reflect the effects of music. Music in medicine research has widely used the three types of dependent measures with somewhat less reliance on behavioral observation than on physiological or self-report measures. Self-report data have produced the least conservative effects as expected (Table 2). Effect sizes appear to be differentiated more by specific dependent measure than by type of dependent measure with the greatest effects measured by grasp strength of stroke patients and the least effects measured by infant apnea (Table 6).

Table 4
Mean Music Effect Size by Sample Size

	≤ 10	11–30	31–60	61–100	>100
$\overline{ES}$	1.46	.85	.67	.72	1.05
N	34	85	74	21	19

N=233

Table 5
Mean Music Effect Size by Type of Design

	Experimental/Control	Subject as own Control	Posttest Only
$\overline{ES}$	.66	1.28	1.52
N	152	66	15

N=233

Summary

A comprehensive review of literature in music and medicine revealed that clinical research in this area has occurred primarily in the last 10 years and has included highly diverse diagnostic categories. A meta-analysis of the effects of music and combined techniques on patient responses during actual medical/dental treatment revealed an emphasis on conservative reporting of the effects of music, an overall average effect size (ES) of .88 for music versus nonmusic conditions (*n*=233 dependent variables from 92 studies), an average ES of 1.17 for the primary dependent variables of the 92 studies analyzed, and an average ES of 1.40 for those studies utilizing the patients' preferred music. In all of the studies analyzed, music conditions enhanced medical objectives on at least one dependent variable whether measured by physiological, psychological/self-report, or behavioral observation.

Table 6

Mean Music Effect Size by Dependent Measure and Number of Variables Analyzed

	$\overline{\text{ES}}$	*N*
Grasp	1.94	1
Effectiveness-SR	1.63	4
EMG	1.47	13
Pain-SR	1.29	37
Relaxation	1.16	3
Anxiety - BO	1.13	4
Anesthesia Choice	1.12	4
VO_2	1.12	1
Hemoglobulin	1.07	1
Respiration Rate	1.05	8
Amount of Analgesic Medication	1.03	10
Anxiety-SR	1.01	25
Pulse	.98	16
Pain-BO	.97	13
IntraCranial Pressure	.94	2
Mood/Attitude	.83	12
Apgar Score	.73	1
Blood Pressure	.71	16
Stress Hormones	.69	9
Crying	.61	6
Length of Labor	.57	2
Movement	.55	4
Cervical Dilation	.52	1
Emesis	.52	6
Family Responses	.50	1
GSR	.47	1
Autonomic Sensations	.47	1
Time Listening	.45	1
Music Choice	.44	1
Oxygen Saturation/Amount Oxygen	.44	12
Sleep	.42	1
Amount of Anesthesia	.36	2
Neonatal Weight	.35	4
Skin Color	.29	1
Length of Hospitalization	.25	3
Peripheral Temperature	.14	4
Ease of Birth	.10	1
Anesthesia Recovery Time	.07	2
Infant Formula Intake	−.59	1
Infant Apnea	−1.53	1

N=223

SR=Self-Report

BO=Behaviorally Observed

CLINICAL APPLICATIONS IN THE MEDICAL SETTING

As medical music therapy develops, it is expected that its methodology will begin to emulate the medical model, i.e., a priori treatment protocols dictated by specific diagnoses and proven options, predictable outcomes for a known frequency and duration of applications, and systematic documentation procedures to readily identify positive or negative health consequences. A meta-analysis synthesizes data from separate studies to provide some basis for generalization about the effects of music in medical treatment. In this section these formulated generalizations and collective research results have been organized into a medical music therapy model of applications and procedures. Emphasis has been placed on specificity, a priori determination of objectives, procedures consistent with research findings, and documentation of results. It should be noted that the magnitude of individual differences encountered in any therapeutic situation makes sole reliance on generalization questionable and ongoing documentation of specific, individual clinical effects is certainly desirable.

These clinical applications have been categorized according to the types of other medical or therapeutic techniques paired with the music activity. Each music therapy technique cited includes a description of the intended function of music, the possible therapeutic objectives, target populations with probable treatment duration, suggested means for clinically documenting results, and specific music therapy procedures.

The function of music to elicit pleasurable experiences and the capabilities of the professional music therapist to structure music activities for pleasure are assumed as an integral part of all music therapy procedures and are not specifically discussed in these techniques. Clinical applications are primarily given as individual treatment programs, since the majority of medical research has dealt with patients using music in an individualized format, and since medical treatments are so individualized as to seldom occur in groups. The uses of group music activities for therapeutic reasons have been summarized in the final section of this discussion. A brief discussion of music therapy to meet the special needs of children and infants and those in hospice care are also included.

Music Therapy Medical Techniques

Technique I. Music Listening and Anesthesia, Analgesia, and/or Suggestion

Music Function:
   To serve as an audioanalgesic, anxiolytic or sedative.

Therapeutic Objectives:
   · Reduction of pain, anxiety, or stress.
   · Enhancement of chemical anesthetic/analgesic in order to reduce amount of medication required, duration of use, and aversive side effects.
   · Reduction in length of hospitalization.

Population:

Surgical—Music used preoperatively to reduce anxiety; patients may require less medication to achieve desired anesthetized state in operating room (½ to 1 hour). Used in operating room, especially with local anesthesia, to reduce anxiety and mask operating room sounds (across several hours). Used postoperatively in the recovery room to promote wakefulness and to reduce discomfort from pain (½ to 1½ hours). Used in first 48 hours following surgery to reduce amount of analgesics required and the aversive effects of anesthesia (e.g., vomiting, headaches, restlessness, etc.).

Kidney dialysis—Music used to reduce discomfort and serve as a distraction during this frequent, long term, lengthy, uncomfortable (pain, nausea, restricted movement) procedure (2 to 3 times per week for 4½ to 5 hours across months or years).

Burn victims—Music used to reduce pain and anxiety in hydrotherapy, intravenous fluid therapy, skin grafts, etc. (daily for each medical procedure or as requested across weeks or months). Note: Research seems to indicate that with severe pain the combination of music and imagery is contraindicated. Each is effective alone, but benefits seem to be reduced when combined.

Neonates—Music used with premature or sick infants to promote weight gain, to reduce pain or stress, and to reduce length of hospitalization (½ hour twice per day for 5–6 weeks). Music has been slightly more beneficial than the mother's voice as an audio stimulus; however, for enhancement of infant/mother relationship, paired music with mother's voice might be most effective.

Office patients—Music used in conjunction with stressful office treatments such as dental procedures, abortions, podiatry treatments (across treatment duration).

Notes: Music listening has historically been used as an audioanalgesic in childbirth but now is usually paired with Lamaze exercises and is therefore included in Technique II. Research in music listening and suggestion to increase immune function is just beginning to appear and seems to hold promise for documented benefits.

Documentation:

Record one or more of the following measures:

Physiological: Blood pressure, pulse, amount of medication used, blood analysis of stress hormone levels.

Behaviorally Observed: Overt pain/anxiety responses, time in recovery room, length of hospitalization, number of anesthetic/analgesic side effects experienced.

Self-Report: Ratings of pain/anxiety, State-Trait Anxiety Scale (Spielberger, Gorsuch, & Lushene, 1970), pain/anxiety adjective selection.

Procedure:

· Use patient's preferred music and equipment with quality reproduction capabilities.
· Begin music prior to pain/fear-inducing stimuli.
· Use earphones when possible, with pillow speaker as an alternative.
· Verbally suggest that music will aid pain relief, comfort, anxiety, etc.
· Combine music with pleasant verbal associations such as focused thought, guided imagery, etc. If pain is severe, use music or imagery alone but not combined.

· Maintain pain-free association by not assisting medical staff with pain-inducing procedures, especially when working with children.
· Allow patient to control as much of the procedure as possible: volume, cassette manipulations, etc.
· Reinforce overt signs of relaxation, cooperation, and verbalizations free of pain or anxiety content.

Technique II. Music Listening/Participation and Exercise

Music Function:
To serve as a focus of attention and/or to structure exercise (tempo, repetition, duration, force, or fluidity).

Therapeutic Objectives:
· Reduction of pain from physical movement or muscle contractures.
· Increased joint motility.
· Increased motor abilities—duration, strength, coordination.
· Shortened labor in childbirth.
· Increased respiration ability: capacity, strength.

Population:
Childbirth—Music used during pregnancy to structure Lamaze exercises and practice focusing attention (1 hour session per week in 8th and 9th months plus daily practice of ½ hour). Used in labor and delivery to focus attention, structure breathing, and reduce pain perception (8–12 hours, average). Selected music used at birth to enhance joy in the event (length of selection). Music and prescribed exercises can be used after birth to reduce pain from contractions and help uterus return to normal size while rehabilitating abdominal muscles (½ hour per day across weeks).
Chronic pain—Music paired with appropriate exercises for involved muscles (½ hour to 1 hour per day across days or weeks).
Respiratory problems—Music used to structure deep breathing exercises or therapeutic coughing to relieve congestion (5 minutes several times each day across days). Music performance (singing, pianica, harmonica) used to structure breathing and enhance lung capacity (½ hour per day across days or weeks).
Patients requiring physical therapy regimen—Music used to structure physical therapy regimen as conducted or prescribed by professional physical therapist, such as stroke victims, burn patients, heart transplant patients, orthopedic patients, cerebral palsied persons, paralyzed persons (½ to 1 hour per day across days, weeks, or months).
Gait problems—Music paired with walking and gait training to increase duration and to shape gait length, width, and/or rhythm (½ to 1 hour per day across days or weeks).

Documentation:

Record one or more of the following:

Physiological: Amount of analgesic medication used, electromyographic (EMG) muscle capacity, exhalation strength (spirometer), degrees of movement in joints (goniometer).

Behaviorally Observed: Frequency and duration of exercises, pain-free verbalizations, length of labor in childbirth, overt pain responses, walking distance, gait length-width, and/or duration.

Self-Report: Ratings of improvement, ratings of pain, personal log of exercises completed.

Procedure:

· Evaluate patient's baseline capacity for exercise in terms of speed, duration, repetitions, etc.

· Select style of music which matches above traits and also desired kind of motor movement (i.e., disco music for forceful movements, waltz music for fluid movements).

· Model appropriate movements and teach patient to match them to music.

· Change music in successive approximations as patient progresses. In this category, patient's music preference is important but is secondary to the music's matching properties with desired exercise.

· Teach focusing (if exercise routine requires it) by pointing out musical elements for which the patient might listen.

· Reinforce exercising (see Example 1), pain-free verbalizations, matching the exercise to the music, focusing attentiveness, and overt signs of patient's motivation to succeed or progress (see Example 2).

Example 1.

*Pinpoint:	8-year-old male in traction with broken leg beginning to develop bed sores from limited movement; refusal to cooperate in using traction pull to increase movement.
Record:	Patient asked to use traction pull and he refused, covering his face with sheet and replying, "I'm tired."
Consequate:	Therapist played and sang song, then made music contingent upon use of traction pull.
Evaluate:	By third session, patient used traction pull 100% of requests at 90° angle to prone position. Verbal and motor responses to music increased.

Jama King, RMT (1982)

---

*Format according to Madsen, C. H., Jr., & Madsen, C. K. (1981).

Example 2.

Pinpoint:	Female in mid-60s with Parkinson's disease and rigidity on left side due to recent stroke. Patient nonresponsive during physical therapy and to visitors.
Record:	No response to recorded instrumental music, live singing with guitar, or placement of music instruments in right hand. Family interview revealed patient formerly played the piano.
Consequate:	First Session: Presentation of patient's favorite recording (Poulenc's Piano Concerto for Two Pianos) prior to physical therapy. Patient immediately opened eyes and reached for recorder with right hand and began answering yes/no questions.
	Subsequent Sessions: Piano music played for 1 minute prior to physical therapy to arouse patient, who was then told that music would be contingent upon open eyes and attempts at physical movement.
Evaluate:	Awareness responses (opened eyes and physical movement) increased to 2–3 minute intervals throughout physical therapy sessions after 1 month. Verbal responses also increased. Patient discharged to long-term care facility.

Dawn Ferrell, RMT (1984)

Technique III. Music Listening/Participation and Counseling

Music Function:
    To initiate and enhance therapist/patient/family relationships

Therapeutic Objectives:
- Reduction of distress/trauma/fear related to terminal or serious illness or injury to self or significant others.
- Acceptance of death, permanent disabilities, scarring. Enhancement of effective interpersonal interactions in times of distress.
- Management of illness and personal affairs, i.e., selection of treatment options and making personal or family decisions.

Population:
    Patients or families in distress, including those with traumatic injuries or illness, permanent disabilities or disfiguration, terminal prognosis; hospitalized children; organ transplant patients, etc. Music used to initiate and maintain counseling interaction (½ hour per day across days or weeks).

Documentation:

Record one or more of the following:

Physiological: Amount of analgesic or sedative medication used, blood pressure, pulse, stress hormone levels.

Behaviorally Observed: Verbalizations free of distress or fear, actions implementing decisions, overt signs of distress/fear, family interaction patterns.

Self-Report: Ratings of attitudes such as satisfaction/contentment, diary of feelings, attitude scales.

Procedure:

· Use live music listening or participation to offer opportunities for pleasure, reminiscence, verbalization, closeness, etc. Use music content for initiating discussion (see Example 3). Therapist's presence and warmth are usually crucial, so earphones or patient listening to music alone are usually contraindicated.

· If specific patient problem is not evident, identify source of distress by listening carefully or by watching patient reactions.

· Help patient identify decisions that can or must be made, all possible options, consequences of each option, preferred option, and actions to implement selected option (see Example 4).

· Serve as advocate for the patient or family who has made a firm decision about course of treatment by making supportive statements and giving assistance with medical hierarchy.

· Teach effective interpersonal relationship abilities, i.e., positivism, avoidance of guilt for self or imposition of guilt on others, openness in stating feelings, avoidance of blame.

· Assist terminally ill persons who wish to get closure on some aspect of their life, such as selection of music for their funeral, recording a song to leave for a loved one, etc.

· Assist permanently disabled persons to identify and develop assets and abilities, perhaps in an area of musical endeavor.

· Reinforce reality-based (acceptance) verbalizations and those free of blame, bitterness, guilt, regrets, etc. Also reinforce verbalizations about the present rather than the past.

· When patient is uncommunicative, provide music and leave. Continue offering opportunities for communication in later visits.

Example 3.

Pinpoint:	15-year-old male with terminal abdominal cancer and paralysis in lower extremities referred for counseling due to depression and failure to cooperate with therapists, including homebound instructional program.
Record:	In initial interview, patient moody and withdrawn, noncommunicative until guitar presented. Immediate interest displayed.
Consequate:	Patient given guitar lessons to increase interest, motivate cooperation, reduce loneliness.
	First Day: Patient learned two chords and sang several songs. Asked how much guitar cost.

Third Day: Patient loaned guitar and folder of songs for use in hospital, and music therapist recommended that he play when his legs hurt and concentrate on the music. Patient too sick from chemotherapy to play, but listened to therapist play and sing.

Two Weeks: Patient's eye contact and verbalization increased, great motivation to learn more about guitar and singing demonstrated. Patient reinforced for plans to do more school work.

Three Weeks: Guitar lessons continued. Patient also revealed fear and tension over shots for nausea from chemotherapy. Given relaxation techniques and recorded music to listen to prior to shots. Patient discharged.

Five Weeks: Music therapist and social worker visited patient's home to continue guitar lessons. Patient reported excitement over guitar and interest in school work via homebound instruction. Music therapist talked with family about guitar as Christmas present.

Eight Weeks: Patient readmitted, guitar lessons continued. Patient played Christmas concert for medical staff and pediatric ward and was excited by their reaction. Received guitar for Christmas.

Next Six Months: Patient periodically readmitted for chemotherapy. Guitar lessons continued at home and hospital. University music therapy students covered holiday and vacation periods so that patient had music therapy on regular basis.

Nine Months: Patient constantly in hospital, too ill for schoolwork or playing guitar. Music therapist visited daily and played and sang for him.

Thirteen Months: Patient in ICU, semi-comatose, continued receiving music therapy visits and concerts from therapists and students.

Fourteen Months: Patient died. Last music therapy concert occurred the day before his death.

Sue Sanderson, RMT, (1984)

Example 4.

Pinpoint:	21-year-old male, paraplegic as result of trauma, in need of counseling for depression and decisions about long-term care.
Record:	Patient was asked in initial interview to describe one good thing that had happened to him that day. Response took 5 minutes to formulate, with frequent interruption of eye contact, use of vague comments, and switching of topics.
Consequate:	Pop/rock music added to weight training during physical therapy using some of patient's own tapes from home. Relaxation routines to music after physical therapy sessions and followed by discussion each day of "good things" and "bad things" happening and option for decisions about

long-term care. Patient reinforced for positive, motivated verbalizations and for decisions communicated to music therapist.

Evaluate: Patient chose plan for long-term care and became very motivated in physical therapy. Patient able to verbalize "good things" that happened to him each day. Patient discharged to long-term care facility.

Dawn Ferrell, RMT (1984)

Technique IV. Music Listening/Participation and Developmental or Educational Objectives

Music Function:
    To reinforce or structure learning.

Therapeutic Objectives:
    · Increased academic learning.

Population:
    Hospitalized children (birth to 18 years) and their families—Music used as reinforcement for attentiveness to educational tasks, as reinforcement for learning, and as a structure to provide academic information. Music activities used with family members to teach parents the importance of helping children maintain developmental milestones and avoid regression (½ hour per day across days).

Documentation:
    Record one or more of the following:
    Physiological: N/A.
    Behaviorally Observed: Number of academic tasks completed, correctness of academic work, time spent on task, amount of information learned, incidence of independent self-care (i.e., feeding self, toileting independently, walking instead of being carried, etc.), positive verbalization.
    Self-Report: Log or checklist of independent self-care tasks performed daily.

Procedure:
    · Use child's preferred music activities to reinforce or structure desired developmental maturity (see Example 5).
    · If music is to be a reinforcer, tell child ahead of time the criteria for participation. At music time, determine if educational or developmental criteria were met and provide music contingently.
    · If music is to structure academic content, determine the teacher's specific education objectives for child and materials being used, and develop music activities accordingly.
    · Leave activities or music "assignments" with the child that will structure independence and increase positive interactions with others in his environment.

   · Invite parents to participate in a music activity with child. Tell them ahead of time that you will be cuing them to reinforce the child for independence and cooperation. Discuss with parents the age-appropriate developmental milestones which they might reinforce during the hospital stay.

   · Reinforce children for on-task behavior, learning, assignments completed, independent self-care.

   · Reinforce families for positive interactions and for allowing children to be independent.

Example 5.

Pinpoint:	7-year-old male admitted for asthma and reported as crying all day following several hypodermics.
Record:	Patient hysterical when therapist entered room.
Consequate:	Therapist played guitar and sang one song. Patient became quieter. Music continued and patient reinforced for interest and positive responses.
Evaluate:	Patient began to strum guitar and sing along with therapist. Music therapy session terminated after 30 minutes.

Lawson Miller, music therapy student (1984)

Technique V. Music Listening and Stimulation

Music Function:
    To stimulate auditorily and increase awareness of other forms of stimuli.

Therapeutic Objectives:
   · Increased overt responses to stimuli (auditory, sensory, olfactory, and visual).
   · Reduced depression/anxiety due to sensory deprivation in aesthetically sterile environments.

Population:
    Comatose or brain damaged patients/stroke victims/premature neonates—Music used to elicit physiological and overt responses which are then increased through reinforcement (½ hour per day across days, weeks, or months).

OR

    Patients in sterile environments (e.g., burn victims, organ transplant patients and those with contagious diseases) or long term hospitalization—Music used to reduce depression or anxiety due to deprivation and to increase patient awareness and pleasure (½ hour 3 times per week, across weeks or months).

Documentation:

    Record one or more of the following:

        Physiological: Vasoconstriction (plethysmograph), respiration rate, pulse, blood pressure.

        Behaviorally Observed: Overt gross or fine motor responses such as sucking, eyeblinks, head movement, mouth movements; auditory responses; pleasure responses, such as smiling; positive verbalizations.

        Self-Report: Ratings of depression/anxiety.

Procedure:

    For elicitation of response:

- Use patient's preferred music, which might be ascertained through family interviews. With infants, lullabies are traditional and have proven somewhat effective.
- Use pillow speaker so that music source may be moved in space for maximum stimulation.
- Combine music with pleasurable multistimulation activities which include physical stroking, moving visual stimuli, pleasurable olfactory stimuli, and other auditory stimuli such as patient's name and family voices. Vibrotactile stimulation and musical electroacupuncture have also proven beneficial
- Watch for and identify overt responses. If no overt responses occur, use physiological measures to determine any response to selected stimuli.
- When response begins to occur, discontinue noncontingent stimulation. Give selected stimulus, wait until patient emits response, then reinforce immediately with other multistimulation activities.
- Pair eliciting stimulus with verbal command so that patient will begin to respond to the human voice.
- If patient's response is apparent through physiological measures, begin moving the patient's body in an overt response timed to coincide with the physiologic event.
- Continue with these procedures and lengthen chain of events to which patient will respond (see Example 6).

    For reducing deprivation:

- Use patient's preferred music.
- Combine music with age-appropriate multistimulation activities, such as looking at slides or pictures to music, reminiscing about memories related to smells (e.g., flowers, vanilla flavoring, lemons, etc.), touching a variety of surfaces (e.g., velvet, sandpaper, or fur). Use a variety of puppets and toys with children. If sterile conditions prohibit use of real materials such as these, use guided imagery techniques with music to imagine multisensory events.
- Reinforce pleasure responses and responses to commands.

Example 6.

Pinpoint: 13-year-old male automobile accident victim appeared comatose and failed to respond to stimuli following prefrontal lobotomy.

Record: Patient responded inconsistently with upper extremity movement to variety of music stimuli after 5 to 10 second delay.

Consequate: Patient presented with variety of music stimuli paired with verbal commands and all responses of any type noted and reinforced by verbal approval and stroking. As patient began to respond consistently, music and commands varied and visual stimuli were added. Progress documented. (See Table 7.)

Evaluate: Patient discharged after 4½ months with vastly improved ability to respond, including statement to music therapist that "music makes me happy."

Table 7

Progress of Patient With Prefrontal Lobotomy

	Fine Motor	Expressive Language	Respiratory	Cognitive	Gross Motor	Social/ Emotional
Aug. 5					Moved arms, feet, mouth, & eyes on command	
Aug. 12					Turned head in direction of stimuli	
Aug. 28				Chose songs by shaking/ nodding head		
Sept. 9	Used left hand to squeeze electronic instrument				Used left hand to manipulate bells, wave goodbye	Smiled
Sept. 30				Identified specific objects from a group by looking at them		

Table 7
Continued

	Fine Motor	Expressive Language	Respiratory	Cognitive	Gross Motor	Social/ Emotional
Oct. 7	Pointed to objects during singing games			Pointed to "named" objects in singing game		
Oct. 14		Talked in sentences to communicate	Talked in sentences. Sang along on words to songs	While singing required cues for words at beginning of phrases		
Oct. 21			Produced tones on harmonica (exhaling & inhaling)		Brought stick to face when attempting to strike drum	
Oct. 28			Sang up to 2 phrases	Sang up to 2 phrases independently	Right hand trembled involuntarily	
Nov. 4	Used left hand to hold pick, depress button on Omnichord				Used left hand to play instruments	
Nov. 12	Used left fingers to play piano	Read short, simple words			Used left hand to play drum	Asked to sing with group of other patients
Nov. 18		Said "Music makes me happy!"	Whistled melodies	Correctly named songs during "Name That Tune"		Said "Music makes me happy!"

Technique VI. Music and Biofeedback

Music Function:
   To serve as reinforcer or structure for physiological responses.

Therapeutic Objectives:
   · Increased awareness, self-control, and monitoring of physiological state.

Population:
> Epilepsy—Music used to reduce frequency of seizures by induced relaxation as reaction to stress or prior to fatigue (total of 5–6 hours across days or weeks).
>
> Coronary—Music used to lower blood pressure, heart rate, tension responses (total of 5–6 hours across days or weeks).
>
> Habituated tension response—Music used to lower blood pressure, lower stress hormone levels, and to relax muscle tension (total of 5–6 hours across days or weeks).
>
> Migraine headaches—Music used to reduce frequency through relaxation responses to stress rather than tension responses (total of 5–6 hours across days or weeks).
>
> Poor circulation—Music used to increase blood flow to extremities through temperature measurement (total of 5–6 hours across days or weeks).

Documentation:
> Record one or more of the following:
>
> > Physiological: Blood pressure, pulse, vasoconstriction, stress hormone levels, EEG waves, EMG muscle tension, temperature, seizure frequency, migraine frequency, etc.
> >
> > Behaviorally Observed: Overt signs of relaxation, verbalizations free of content about stress.
> >
> > Self-Report: Log of relaxation practice and incidence of physiological problem, ratings of improvement.

Procedure:
- Use patient's preferred music.
- Use headphones if possible.
- Pair music with selected biofeedback procedures for specific physiological problem. Noncontingent background music may be used to enhance patient's ability to relax or contingent music may be used as reinforcement for patient maintaining desired physiological response.
- Transfer ability to relax from the biofeedback clinic to other locations through the use of procedures that can be paired with music in any setting (home, work, car, etc.).
- Reinforce relaxation, desired physiologic state, and positive verbalizations about improvement.

Technique VII. Music and Group Activities

Music Function:
> To structure pleasurable and positive interpersonal interactions.

Therapeutic Objectives:
- Reduction of depression/anxiety due to isolation.
- Increased pleasure and feelings of well-being

Population:

Any patients capable of joining a group and desiring to do so, especially children and persons with long-term hospitalization—Music used for pleasure, group interaction and to reduce stress of hospitalization (1 hour twice per week, ongoing).

Documentation:

Record one or more of the following:

Physiological: Pulse (self-monitored).

Behaviorally Observed: Pleasure responses, such as smiling or laughing; positive verbalizations free of "illness" content; time spent in group and out of hospital room.

Self-Report: Ratings of pleasure or feelings of well-being.

Procedure:

· Use variety of age appropriate activities that maximize time in music. Match types of activities to areas in which they are conducted, (i.e., quieter activities in areas for the seriously ill.)

· Identify meeting space for group which is deemed by staff as being compatible with medical routine, i.e., not disruptive.

· Combine focused listening and participation activities to reduce fatigue.

· Ensure that individuals are familiar with others' names to personalize the interaction.

· Perform live music for audience pleasure.

· Invite patients, visitors, staff, volunteers, etc., to participate.

· Feature medical personnel and staff in music activities.

· Use relaxation/guided imagery to music techniques to reduce discomfort and prepare patients for rest. Suggest patients try similar techniques at night when falling asleep.

· Use drawing to music or song improvisation, composition, or discussion to promote expression of feelings.

· Reinforce pleasure responses, "non-sick" verbalizations, music participation, spontaneous contributions to musical activities, and musical talent of participants.

Pediatric Music Therapy Objectives

Research has demonstrated that pediatric music therapy is a specialty area which benefits both neonatal and older pediatric patients. Neonatal benefits of music therapy include sedation, weight gain, and shorter hospital stays (Caine, 1991; Chapman, 1975), respiration rate (Ammon, 1968) and oxygen saturation levels (Collins & Kuck, 1991; Standley & Moore, 1993). Music seems to function in this setting to mask aversive auditory stimuli thereby reducing stress, to provide stimulation in a stimulus deprived environment, to promote bonding with parents and/or to facilitate developmental milestones.

Music therapy with children accomplishes both medical and psychosocial goals: anxiety and pain reduction (Aldridge, 1993); cooperation during painful procedures (Chetta, 1981; Micci, 1984; Pfaff et al., 1989; Rasco, 1992); sedation (Marley, 1984; McDonnell, 1984; Rudenberg & Royka, 1989); increased immune response (Lane, 1991); tension release and relaxation; provision of opportunities to exercise control of an aversive environment; expression of feelings; nurturing, normalization and improvement of the quality of life; development of trust; improvement in parent/child relationships; promotion of self-esteem, and celebration of the healthy/positive aspects of the child's life (Standley & Hanser, 1994); acceptance of friends' death; dealing with medical crises; and dealing with isolation (Brodsky, 1989). Family members are regularly integrated into music therapy activities to assist children in bonding with parents during times of medical crisis. By participating actively in music therapy, family members are also empowered at a time when they may feel that they lack control.

For children with terminal illnesses, music therapists assist patients to cope with pain and anxiety while assisting the patient and their family to deal with this painful transition. Music is especially beneficial in creating an environment for warm, intimate sharing of this most personal experience (Fagen, 1982). Live music performance for sedation and song composition based on personal patient experiences are particularly powerful at this time (Bailey, 1984).

Music Therapy Objectives in Hospice Care

Though little research has been done with music and the terminally ill patient, Gilbert proposed music therapy applications in 1977. Susan Munro (1984) developed a hospice-based music therapy program and provided a definitive description of the clinical process to assist the dying patient. Curtis (1986) studied the effects of music listening for hospice patients and found diverse results in self-report data depending upon the individual's perception of each descriptor (physical comfort vs. relaxation vs. pain relief vs. contentment). These results indicate a need for careful consideration in the selection of words to describe the benefits of music during the complex and critical latter stages of an illness.

Music therapists providing hospice care have described clinical case studies indicating profound impact on patients' lives (Brown, 1992a, 1992b; Lochner & Stevenson, 1988; Ridgeway, 1983; Wylie & Blom, 1986). Others have applied these music therapy counseling techniques to assisting the bereavement of the survivors (Bright, 1986; Wexler, 1989). Hospice care music therapists have concluded that the benefits of music counseling include: enhanced pain relief; increased sense of control over one's life, treatment and death; perceived celebration of life through reminiscence, the composition of a musical legacy, and/or imagery; and increased ability to express feelings and communicate with loved ones about the experience of death and dying.

PROGRAM DEVELOPMENT IN THE MEDICAL SETTING

A variety of program components could be developed from the techniques and patient groups previously cited in the research literature. The specific ones included by any music therapist in a single program are determined by the priorities of the therapist, the priorities of the facility in which the program is located, and the music therapy program's funding base. The following section discusses issues and procedures deemed important to medical music therapy program development, and provides examples of clinical forms for program documentation.

Funding

Funding a music therapy position in a comprehensive medical setting is possible in several ways: (1) as a staff position comparable to a medical social worker, (2) as a consultant with hospital privileges comparable to a physician or psychologist but not status as a hospital employee, or (3) as a combination of the first two with status as a hospital employee but payment of services charged directly to the patient as with a consultant. Each of these possibilities has implications for program development.

If the music therapist is in a position comparable to a medical social worker, the salary is paid by the medical facility and costs are recovered by an overhead charge added to the per diem room rate charged to all patients. A staff music therapist could then function throughout the facility providing direct and indirect patient services.

Direct services could involve physicians' prescribed treatment (music therapy counseling with a terminally ill person), staff referred treatment (music therapy interaction with crying child), and/or patient request service (music therapy group for pleasure and relaxation). Indirect services could include designing, implementing, and monitoring nonprescriptive music listening programs which might be staffed by volunteers or aides in areas such as the kidney dialysis clinic, obstetrics, pre-op, recovery, neonate nursery, or patient and family waiting areas. Other services might involve organization of a volunteer corps to assist in acquiring, preparing, and distributing music tapes or in entertaining; staff development training in the appropriate use of music activities to promote "wellness"; development of an internship program to increase services; etc.

The advantage of this funding procedure would be a more comprehensive program involving both direct and indirect client services which could serve a large number and variety of patients at relatively low cost to the facility. The disadvantage would be the facility's resistance to initially increasing costs by adding a staff position.

Since implementation of the Diagnostic Related Group (DRG) procedure for Medicare reimbursement, hospitals have great incentive to control costs and increase profits by discharging patients prior to the allotted time limit per their diagnosis and as soon as possible after their need for skilled nursing care (as opposed to custodial care) has ended. Many hospitals now place great emphasis on providing services on outpatient status. The prospective music therapy hospital employee might justify a position by citing the music therapy research results previously discussed that report shorter hospital stays and fewer side effects or complications, with little or no additional costs to the facility.

If the music therapist functions as a hospital consultant, the program would probably develop into a smaller, more individualized, direct service design than the one previously discussed. In this system, the music therapy service would have to be requested by the physician and approved by the patient; this system would entail a major public relations effort in the community to educate and motivate physicians to refer patients. The client would be billed directly; therefore, the client must also be educated to feel a need for such treatment.

It is apparent that developing a public relations/advertising base to promote a specific medical music therapy treatment could be a costly, time consuming, and extended process. It would also be more difficult to bill individuals for the type of indirect services previously discussed, and these might never become cost effective. The music therapist developing a medical private practice might therefore expect high start-up costs sustained over an extended period of time with little return on the investment while providing free "volunteer" or "demonstration" services to educate the public, and spending many hours in recruiting or promoting referrals. The advantage of a consultant funding base is that it would probably be the most attractive to the facility administration since it requires little or no financial commitment from them.

Some hospitals employ staff and recover costs through direct patient billing for a specific service as with rehabilitation therapists (physical therapy, speech therapy, occupational therapy, respiratory therapy, etc.). This procedure is advantageous to the hospital because it is compatible with the third party payment requirements, and the volume of patient need can cover the personnel, office, and equipment costs. The patients accept a billed item resulting from a direct service they perceive to be necessary and at a reasonable hourly rate (much of which is paid by insurance). The cost of these services, like other medical services deemed appropriate by third party payment guidelines, is budgetarily identified and can be tracked so that profit margin or loss is readily apparent. The disadvantages of this funding base for music therapy program development are that indirect service costs are not usually recoverable under any circumstances, and direct music therapy services may not be covered under third party payment guidelines (Medicare, Blue Cross, etc.). The process of including music therapy in such eligibility guidelines has some of the same problems as the establishment of a private practice.

Music therapists wishing to develop medical programs might consider these issues and pursue the funding base best suited for the type of program or service delivery desired. Justification of music therapy treatment to meet patient needs more effectively than other established therapies will be crucial to success, as will perseverance. Such justification can definitely come from documented results with specific diagnoses and a priori, specified objectives.

Medical Objectives

Patients in general hospital settings are extremely diverse in age, medical diagnosis, and treatment. These extremes range in urgency from patients who are terminally ill to others hospitalized for a "rest" or to women giving birth who are considered to be participating in a "wellness" event instead of being sick. Patients also differ in length of stay, prognosis, response to illness, etc. Medicine is, therefore, extremely individualized in diagnosis and treatment with ongoing documentation of effect often determining course of treatment. Music therapy in a medical setting must comply with the expectations and requirements inherent in the medical model. Music therapy patient objectives should be specific, and should be relevant to medical diagnosis, course of treatment, and discharge timeline; benefits should be described in medical terms, not musical terms (see therapeutic objectives previously cited).

Consent

Therapists must be sensitive to those procedures which require physician, patient, and/or family consent. As each program component is implemented, the need for consent could be determined and, if necessary, initiated in advance of problems or questions.

Scheduling

Music programs must be incorporated into the hospital schedule without jeopardizing crucial medical routines. It is important that medical staff consider music therapy as important and perceive it as a benefit rather than a disruption. The volume of free field music stimuli must be controlled to the satisfaction of staff and other patients on the floor. Music therapy should occur in areas of the facility that are agreed upon by staff, patients, and families as being facilitative, not disruptive.

Referral

The strength of a music therapy program is increased by a viable, active referral system that matches patient needs to available services. Medical staff can be trained to refer patients to music therapy for specific medical reasons. As each program component is implemented, medical staff need to be informed of the type of patient problem appropriate for referral.

Keeping paperwork to a minimum helps maximize patient contact time. Conversely, some program forms are desirable for documentation, education, and justification. A referral form serves the primary function of notifying the music therapist of specific patients in need of specific services. It should also provide enough information about the various program components to educate medical staff, patients, or families completing the form about the intended therapeutic objectives and eligibility for inclusion. It is recommended that references to music (e.g., preference, musical interests, music study, etc.) not be included in such a form since this tends to miseducate by circulating the misconception that music therapy is for those who have prior music study or musical talent. A referral form should require only information that is crucial to an initial interview, and should be constructed for quick completion, or it will not be used by busy staff. Figure 1 shows a general hospital form developed by King (1984), with notation of important issues included. This form does not list programs in those areas where referral would not be needed since music could be available to all participants as common practice or as required, e.g., kidney dialysis, obstetrics, surgery, biofeedback, etc.

Referrals do not necessarily lead to the provision of a music therapy service due to time constraints or program priorities. All referrals should be acknowledged immediately and the referring party given a specific reason for treatment inclusion or denial. Lack of feedback would possibly "teach" medical staff that referrals are unimportant or ineffective.

Assessment

The music therapist usually assesses the patient in the initial stages to determine specific objectives and to develop a treatment plan. Assessment procedures should identify both problem areas and patient assets for treatment participation and prognosis. Forms for overall assessment should be constructed for efficient use, applicable to short-term and long-term treatment programs, and preserved as documentation of the patient's condition prior to music therapy treatment. Figure 2 provides an example of an assessment form developed for use following the initial patient interview.

Music Therapy Referral Form

Patient's
Name:_____Name:_____

Date
of Birth:_____Physician:_____   Person to give
Room:_____Admission Date:_____Diagnosis:_____   permission fo
Expected Date of Discharge:_____   MT if necessary
Concurrent Therapies: ___ST ___PT ___OT ___Respiratory
___Dialysis ___Radiation ____Other_____

Determines   Patient Information: (Check Yes or No)
whether MT   Is the patient mobile?   Yes   No   Yes/No
must occur in   If so, via ambulation? _____   format faster
patient's room   via wheelchair? _____   than open ended
which usually   via stretcher? _____   questions
precludes group   Is the patient receiving any type of medication?   Yes   No
involvement   If so, does this medication impair mental alertness?
                                  Explain_____
                                  Are the medications being administered via IV   Yes   No
                                  therapy?
                                Does the patient have any physical disabilities?   Yes   No
                                  If so, explain_____

Teaches medical   Is this the patient's first hospitalization?   Yes   No
staff reasons   Is the patient having difficulty adjusting to the
for MT referral   hospital environment?   Yes   No
                                Does the patient seem withdrawn or hyperactive since
                                  hospitalization?   Yes   No
                                Is the patient experiencing difficulty in dealing with
                                  disability or illness?   Yes   No
                                Since hospitalization, does the patient cry excessively
                                  or display any other overt, inappropriate behavior? Yes   No
                                Objectives and Recommended Services (Check all that apply):
                                _____Hospital Orientation (for new patients)
                                _____Anxiety Reduction (for preop patients and families and seriously
Teaches medical   ill)
staff about   _____Patient/Family Counseling (for terminally ill, traumatically
what MT   injured, seriously ill)
accomplishes   _____Music and Movement (in conjunction with Physical Therapy
                                        and/or Occupational Therapy)
                                _____Large Group Activity (for socialization, rehabilitation and
                                        pleasure. Open to all who wish to attend.)
                                _____Music for Developmental Training/Education
                                _____Stimulation (for comatose patients, neonates, long term
                                        admissions, patients in sterile environments)
                                _____Pain Reduction
                                Referred by:_____Phone:_____   Identifies
                                                                                                    person to
                                Developed by Jama King, RMT (1984)   contact for
                                Modified by Standley   further
                                                                                                    information

Figure 1
Music Therapy referral form.

Music Therapy Initial Assessment Form

Name:_____Date:_____

Sex:_____Date of Birth:_____Room No._____

Medical Problems/Diagnosis:_____

Other Disabilities:_____

Current Therapies:___ ST___ OT___ PT___Respiratory ___ Dialysis___ Radiation

Interview Results (Rate those that apply):

	Poor						Excellent				Comment
Sensory Awareness	1	2	3	4	5	6	7	8	9	10	_____
Affect	1	2	3	4	5	6	7	8	9	10	_____
Verbalization	1	2	3	4	5	6	7	8	9	10	_____
Self Concept	1	2	3	4	5	6	7	8	9	10	_____
Attention Span	1	2	3	4	5	6	7	8	9	10	_____
Eye Contact	1	2	3	4	5	6	7	8	9	10	_____
Social/Behavior Skills	1	2	3	4	5	6	7	8	9	10	_____
Coping Skills	1	2	3	4	5	6	7	8	9	10	_____
Pain Management	1	2	3	4	5	6	7	8	9	10	_____
Stress/Anxiety Management	1	2	3	4	5	6	7	8	9	10	_____
Acceptance of Medical Problem	1	2	3	4	5	6	7	8	9	10	_____
Gross Motor Skills	1	2	3	4	5	6	7	8	9	10	_____
Fine Motor Skills	1	2	3	4	5	6	7	8	9	10	_____

Other Patient Assets:_____
Objectives:_____
Recommended Programs:_____

Frequency and Duration of Therapy:_____

Figure 2
Music therapy initial assessment form

Once a specific therapeutic objective (or pinpoint) is identified, recording of baseline status begins. This may be considered a second level of patient assessment and is specific to the measurement of desired treatment outcome.

Treatment Documentation

All medical practitioners need to be concerned about liability because of this society's propensity for litigation. Medical insurance, skill in one's profession, and meticulous records are important considerations.

Treatment procedures and effects of music therapy in a medical setting should be regularly documented and recorded in each patient's medical record. The research has shown that music therapy's effects can be verified through physiological, self-report, or behaviorally observed measures.

Medical staff members usually record a variety of physiological measures several times per day in patient charts, and selected charts might be retrieved for inclusion in music therapy records. Some physiological measures such as pulse rate can be effectively taken by the music therapist and recorded directly.

Self-report data can be collected from oral interviews or through completion of written forms or diaries. Figure 3 represents an example of the self-report procedure used by Curtis (1982) with terminally ill cancer patients. Note that the words across the bottom of each scale delineate degree while also demarcating the line into 20 equal spaces for ease in scoring. Similar procedures could be used with adjectives describing any emotion, attitude, or health concept.

Reliability of behavioral observations is facilitated by simplification of observation forms into discrete categories with minimal recording requirements. One might use duration, event, or frequency recording procedures according to the specified objective. Figures 4 through 7 are examples of recording forms developed especially for medical music therapy techniques. Users of such forms (or observers) might be the music therapist, other medical staff, patient's relatives, or volunteers.

The Trippett Objective Music Relaxation Inventory has been used effectively in music therapy obstetrical programs by Codding (1982) and Winokur (1984), and is usually completed by spouses of women in labor (see Figure 4). The Dialysis Rating Form was developed by Schuster (1985) to evaluate the effect of music listening during kidney dialysis; it was designed for nurses to complete at the time that mandatory blood pressure readings were accomplished (see Figure 5).

Chetta (1981) developed several forms to evaluate preoperative anxiety in pediatric patients. The Observed Behavior Time Sampling (Figure 6) form is an example of interval recording of behavior across an entire music interaction. The predominant behavior categories list is an example of event recording at specified times of stress, specifically before and after the initial sedative by hypodermic (see Figure 7).

In documenting benefits, the therapist should be able to compare effects before and after music or under music/no music conditions. Chapman (1975) and Caine (1991) found that premature neonates listening to music in their incubators achieved weight criteria and were discharged an average of 5 days to 1 week sooner than those with no music. Chapman calculated that this resulted in an average cost savings of $4,800 per "music" infant, a definitely effective way of justifying the cost of a music therapy program.

Baseline status or control conditions might be retrieved from prior records such as the assessment form or the medical record so that treatment could be implemented immediately. If these are not possible, then the music therapist must evaluate premusic conditions in other ways. King (1984) documented music therapy effects on the disruptive, bizarre behavior of a 9-year-old child who had been subjected to a high voltage of electricity in the past and had recently developed unusual behavior patterns. In each session, King contrasted 5-minute intervals of baseline (patient interacting with nurse and other patients) with 5-minute intervals of verbal then music interaction with the music therapist. Results showed that the child progressed across intervals and across sessions on subsequent days and that there was no delay in implementing treatment (see Figure 8).

Directions

Put a mark on the line at the point which best describes how you feel right now.

1. No
   pain relief
           A little Moderate A lot

2. No physical
   comfort
           A little Moderate A lot

3. No
   relaxation
           A little Moderate A lot

4. No
   contentment
           A little Moderate A lot

Complete
pain relief

Complete
physical
comfort

Complete
relaxation

Complete
contentment

Figure 3
Curtis self-recording form

THE TRIPPET OBJECTIVE MUSCLE RELAXATION INVENTORY

(Father's Assessment of Tension Observed in the Mother During <u>Active Labor</u>)

BODY AREA	LEAST RELAXED 1	2	3	4	MOST RELAXED 5	SCORE Ent. 4 6 8cm.
Use of Forehead:	Not able to move forehead very much; muscles tight	Some gesturing with forehead, but expression fixed	Able only to frown or raise forehead[a]	Able to frown, raise forehead somewhat naturally	Able to raise forehead, to frown, or both[a] expressively	___
Use of Eyes:	Unable to change expression of eyes; fixed look	Eyes unnaturally wide or clenched shut; some change of expression	Able to open eyes wide or shut tight but not both; some change of eye expression	Can generally open eyes wide or shut them naturally; change in eye expression	Eyes calm, expressive, open and shut them with ease	___
Typical Facial Expression:	Has an extremely fixed facial expression; (grimace)[a]	Has a moderately strained expression	Has a slightly fixed expression (frown or smile)[a]	Has a moderately relaxed expression	Has a relaxed expression on her face[a]	___
Use of Mouth and Jaw:	Teeth appear clenched; jaw fixed	Teeth together with a little apparent relaxation of the jaw	Mouth closed or slightly open with some relaxation of the jaw	Mouth slightly open with approx. 1 cm. between teeth as felt on outside of cheek	Mouth open, jaw natural and relaxed	___
Use of Head and Neck:	Turns head from side to side with minimal range of motion and great difficulty[a]	Head moves from side to side with partial range of motion[a]	Head moves from side to side and up and down with moderate range of motion	Head turns from side to side and up and down with circular motion as if head and neck are moderately relaxed	Head turns freely in all directions with ease	___

c ___ E ___

Developed by Susan Trippet, R.N. Obstetrics
Indianapolis, Indiana

Modified by Peggy A. Codding, RMT

[a]from Plutchik, R., Wasserman,
M., and Mayer, M. "Muscle Tension
Rating Scale" (1975)

Figure 4
The Trippet objective muscle relaxation inventory

THE TRIPPET OBJECTIVE MUSCLE RELAXATION INVENTORY

BODY AREA	LEAST RELAXED 1	2	3	4	MOST RELAXED 5	SCORE Ent. 4 6 8 cm.
Neck and Shoulders:	Muscles in neck and shoulders tense with minimal range of motion	Muscles at front and sides of neck and/or muscles between shoulder blades tense	Muscles at front and sides of neck and/or shoulder blades somewhat relaxed	Neck and shoulder muscles moderately relaxed	All muscles relaxed	___ ___ ___
Chest:	Is unable to take a deep breath between contractions	Breathes deeply with effort, cannot exhale fully	Can breathe with little effort, but does not exhale fully with ease	Breathes deeply, inhales and exhales as if moderately relaxed	Breathes deeply, inhales and exhales naturally, is relaxed	___ ___ ___
Arms:	Tense: no swing from body	Little relaxation: (15 degree swing from body)	Some relaxation: (25 degree swing from body)	Moderate relaxation: (45 degree swing from body)	Arm muscles relaxed: (45 degree swing from body and muscles "loose")	___ ___ ___
Legs:	Tense: Mother puts legs to floor with care to sit	Little relaxation: mother carefully puts legs ¼ way to floor to sit then lets legs fall	Some relaxation: mother puts legs ¼ way to floor to sit then lets legs fall	Moderate relaxation: mother puts legs ¾ way to floor to sit then lets legs fall	Muscles relaxed mother lets legs drop to the floor naturally as she moves from lying to sitting position	___ ___ ___

Date _____

Time of Hospital Admittance _____ (AM) (PM)

Length of Active Labor _____

Dilation of Cervix at Hospital Admittance _____ centimeters

Hospital _____

This child is the _____ (1st 2nd 3rd 4th 5th) delivered by my wife.

Figure 4
Continued

Please rate _____ in the following

categories. (Circle one for each.)

Nurse's Signature _____

Date _____

	Extremely calm, relaxed, compliant	Occasionally hesitant to follow directions	Occasional complaints but cooperated	Very anxious, frequent complaints	Extremely anxious—complained anxious constantly—complained constantly—complained spite attention of de- nurses, appeared of agitated
1. Emotional adjustment prior to onset of treatment	1	2	3	4	5
2. Behavior at onset of treatment	1	2	3	4	5
3. Behavior after one hour of treatment	1	2	3	4	5
4. Behavior after two hours of treatment	1	2	3	4	5
5. Behavior after three hours of treatment	1	2	3	4	5
6. Behavior upon completion of treatment	1	2	3	4	5
7. General interaction with nursing staff	1	2	3	4	5
8. Overall level of anxiety	1	2	3	4	5

Figure 5
Schuster dialysis rating form

Patient Number _____

+ −	N M R	+ −	N M R	+ −	N M R	+ −	N M R
+ −	N M R	+ −	N M R	+ −	N M R	+ −	N M R
+ −	N M R	+ −	N M R	+ −	N M R	+ −	N M R
+ −	N M R	+ −	N M R	+ −	N M R	+ −	N M R
+ −	N M R	+ −	N M R	+ −	N M R	+ −	N M R
+ −	N M R	+ −	N M R	+ −	N M R	+ −	N M R
+ −	N M R	+ −	N M R	+ −	N M R	+ −	N M R
+ −	N M R	+ −	N M R	+ −	N M R	+ −	N M R
+ −	N M R	+ −	N M R	+ −	N M R	+ −	N M R
+ −	N M R	+ −	N M R	+ −	N M R	+ −	N M R
+ −	N M R	+ −	N M R	+ −	N M R	+ −	N M R

FIGURE 6.
Chetta observed behavior time-sampling form.

OPERATIONAL DEFINITIONS FOR OBSERVED BEHAVIOR TIME-SAMPLING FORM

+ = Patient exhibits no evidence of anxiety. He readily follows directions, is cooperative, his speech is calm, his movements are appropriate and there is no sign of resistance.

- = Patient exhibits evidence of anxiety. He hesitates or refuses to follow directions, cries, fights, or resists in some way.

N = Noise indicating anxiety, e.g., nervous chatter, repetitive questions, crying, screaming, etc.

M = Body movements indicating anxiety, e.g., tapping fingers, distorting face, resisting, refusing to follow directions, pulling away from nurse, flinching, fighting, etc.

R = Patient is resistant to the point that he must be restrained. Number of people restraining him should be indicated. Parent should not be counted if he is only holding patient's hand but should be counted if he is helping restrain patient.

N, M, and R should be indicated only in the - category.

For the interval during which the injection is given, circle the entire block after is had been appropriately marked.

Mark all appropriate symbols per interval but do not mark any symbol more than once per interval.

Scoring: For each ten-second interval, a cumulative score will be computed according to the following formula:

+ = +4

- = 0

-N = -1

-M = -1

-R = -1 (or 1 or 2 persons restraining)
    -2 (for 3 persons restraining)

Figure 6
Continued

Observer _____

Patient Number _____

Date _____

	Before nurse enters	After nurse enters, before shot	During shot	After shot, before nurse leaves	After nurse leaves
Sleeping	A	B	C	D	E
No continuous sounds	A	B	C	D	E
Calm Speech	A	B	C	D	E
Nervous speech	A	B	C	D	E
Smiling	A	B	C	D	E
Singing	A	B	C	D	E
Whining	A	B	C	D	E
Crying	A	B	C	D	E
Screaming	A	B	C	D	E
No continuous body movement	A	B	C	D	E
Purposeless or restless movement	A	B	C	D	E
Withdrawing body (flinch)	A	B	C	D	E
Striking or pushing away	A	B	C	D	E
Thrashing arms or legs	A	B	C	D	E
Facial Distortion	A	B	C	D	E

Figure 7
Chetta predominant behavior categories list

OPERATIONAL DEFINITIONS FOR PREDOMINANT BEHAVIOR CATEGORIES LIST

Observer:
The following is an overall assessment of predominant behaviors during the observation period. It is to be completed immediately after the observation period and is to be used to summarize the patient's overall behavior.

Category	Operational Definition
Sleeping	Patient's eyes are closed, body appears relaxed, his is roused only when spoken to, etc.
No continuous sounds	Patient is generally quiet throughout observation period. He does not converse continually with people in room. Short responses to questions, etc., are allowed in this category. Singing with therapist is not be considered in this category.
Calm speech	Patient is conversing appropriately with someone in room; he is asking pertinent questions or is discussing topics other than his upcoming surgery or injection.
Nervous speech	Patient is jabbering, talking to himself, asking repeated questions, etc., which would indicate a general restlessness.
Smiling	Patient readily smiles during eye contact or verbal/motor interaction with someone in room.
Singing	Patient engages in the music activities either by humming, singing, clapping hands, etc.
Whining	Patient utters continuous groans or moans that would not yet be considered actual crying. Tears would probably not be evident.
Crying	Patient's groans are to the point that tears are present.
Screaming	Patient indicates intense pain or distress through very loud crying and/or shouting.
No continuous body movement	Patient is generally still throughout observation period and does not evidence repetitive nervous movements.
Purposeless or restless movement	Patient evidences repetitive movement such as turning back and forth in bed, tapping his fingers, wiggling his feet, etc., which would indicate general nervousness.
Withdrawing body or limb	Patient moves body or limb either before or during a procedure--flinch.
Striking or pushing away	Patient actively resists procedure by hitting or pushing another person.
Thrashing arms and legs	Patient throws arms and legs back and forth and therefore must be forcefully restrained.
Facial Distortion	Patient changes facial gesture in response stimuli, e.g., eyes widening when he sees syringe, frown or squint, etc.

Scoring: One point will be given for each incidence of "anxious" behavior:

nervous speech	screaming	striking or pushing away
whining	purposeless or restless movement	thrashing arms or legs
crying	withdrawing body (flinch)	facial distortion

Figure 7
Continued

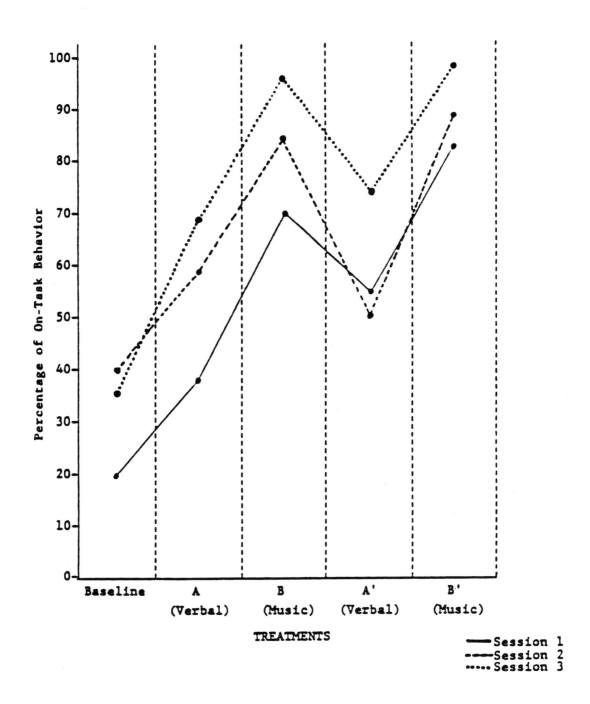

Figure 8
Client's percentage of on-task behavior

Preferred Music

Much of the benefit of music therapy depends upon determining the patient's music preference. The medical music therapist must develop an efficient means for determining such preference. With patients not experiencing distress, an interview about music likes and dislikes may be an effective way of initiating nonthreatening contact. If the patient is unable to respond, family interviews might reveal the patient's history of musical taste. To meet individual needs in this setting, the music therapist obviously needs to maintain a large tape library of all types of musical selections.

Equipment and Space

The music therapist in the hospital setting must be highly mobile and must often take music to the patient's location. In the general hospital there may be no music therapy activity room, only a therapist's office. Basic equipment would consist of portable accompanying instruments such as guitar, autoharp, electronic keyboard; rolling carts for transporting supplies; rhythm instruments; a large supply of small, good quality tape recorders with small, lightweight earphones and pillow speakers; instruments or supplies which can be made relatively sterile and left in sterile environments; and puppets, toys, and supplies for children such as crayons and paper, etc.

Volunteers

It is difficult for one music therapist or a small staff to provide a therapy with universal appeal such as music to all those who might desire it. A well-trained corps of volunteers could greatly expand patient services. Volunteers might coordinate a music library service throughout the facility, providing tape recorders and tapes as desired. They might also record special requests or programs of music for individual clients. Volunteer musicians might perform regularly in group music therapy activities or in visiting wards. Records could be kept of volunteer/patient contact hours and activities for administratively documenting the impact of this aspect of the music therapy program.

Research

Prior discussion has shown that documentation of therapeutic effect would by necessity be an integral part of a hospital music therapy program. With such documentation, evaluation of overall results would be possible. The music therapist in the medical setting would have a unique opportunity to provide a clinical service in a format consistent with research techniques. The field will be greatly enhanced by increased research publication in this area.

References

Aldridge, K. (1993). The use of music to relieve pre-operational anxiety in children attending day surgery. *The Australian Journal of Music Therapy, 4,* 19–35.

Ammon, K. (1968). The effects of music on children in respiratory distress. *American Nurses' Association Clinical Sessions,* 127–133.

Armatas, C. (1964) *A study of the effect of music on postoperative patients in the recovery room.* Unpublished master's thesis, The University of Kansas.

Atterbury, R. (1974). Auditory pre-sedation for oral surgery patients. *Audioanalgesia, 38*(6), 12–14.

Bailey, L. M. (1983). The effects of live music versus tape-recorded music on hospitalized cancer patients. *Music Therapy, 3*(1), 17–28.

Bailey, L. (1984). The use of songs in music therapy with cancer patients and their families. *Music Therapy, 4,* 5–17.

Bailey, L. (1986). Music therapy in pain management. *Journal of Pain and Symptom Management, 1*(1), 25–28.

Barker, L. (1991). The use of music and relaxation techniques to reduce pain of burn patients during daily debridement. In C.D. Maranto (Ed.), *Applications of music in medicine* (pp. 163–178). Washington, DC: National Association for Music Therapy, Inc.

Bason, P., & Celler, B. G. (1972). Control of the heart rate by external stimuli. *Nature, 238,* 279–280.

Beck, S. (1991). The therapeutic use of music for cancer-related pain. *Oncology Nursing Forum, 18*(8), 1327–1336.

Behrens, G. A. (1982). *The use of music activities to improve the capacity, inhalation, and exhalation capabilities of handicapped children's respiration.* Unpublished master's thesis, Kent State University.

Bob, S. R. (1962). Audioanalgesia in podiatric practice, a preliminary study. *Journal of American Podiatry Association, 52,* 503–504.

Bolwerk, C. A. (1990). Effects of relaxing music on state anxiety in myocardial infarction patients. *Critical Care Nursing, 13*(2), 63–72.

Bonny, H. L. (1983). Music listening for intensive coronary care units: A pilot project. *Music Therapy, 3*(1), 4–16.

Boyle, M., & Greer, R. (1983). Operant procedures and the comatose patient. *Journal of Applied Behavioral Analysis, 16*(1), 3–12.

Bright, R. (1986). *Grieving: A handbook for those who care.* St. Louis, MO: MMB Music, Inc.

Brodsky, W. (1989). Music therapy as an intervention for children with cancer in isolation rooms. *Music Therapy, 8,* 17–34.

Brook, E. (1984). *Soothing music during the active phase of labor: Physiologic effect on mother and infant.* Unpublished master's thesis, University of Florida.

Brown, J. (1992a). When words fail, music speaks. *American Journal of Hospice and Palliative Care, 9*(2), 13–16.

Brown, J. (1992b). Music dying. *American Journal of Hospice and Palliative Care, 9*(4), 17–20.

Budzynski, T., Stoyva, J., & Adler, C. (1970). Feedback-induced muscle relaxation: Application to tension headache. *Journal of Behavior Therapy and Experimental Psychiatry, 1,* 205–211.

Burt, R. K., & Korn, G. W. (1964). Audioanalgesia in obstetrics: White noise analgesia during labor. *American Journal of Obstetrics and Gynecology, 88,* 361–366.

Caine, J. (1991). The effects of music on the selected stress behaviors, weight, caloric and formula intake, and length of hospital stay of premature and low birth weight neonates in a newborn intensive care unit. *Journal of Music Therapy, 28*(4), 180–192.

Caire, J., & Erickson, S. (1986). Reducing distress in pediatric patients undergoing cardiac catheterization. *Children's Health Care, 14*(3), 146–152.

Camp, W., Martin, R., & Chapman, L. (1962). Pain threshold and discrimination of pain intensity during brief exposure to intense noise. *Noise, 135,* 788–789.

Carlin, S., Ward, W., Gershon, A., & Ingraham, R. (1962). Sound stimulation and its effect on dental sensation threshold. *Science, 138,* 1258–1259.

Chapman, J. S. (1975). *The relation between auditory stimulation of short gestation infants and their gross motor limb activity.* Unpublished doctoral dissertation, New York University.

Chalmers, I., Enkin, M., & Keirse, M. (1989). *Effective care in pregnancy and childbirth.* Oxford: Oxford Medical Publications.

Cherry, H., & Pallin, I. (1948). Music as a supplement in nitrous oxide oxygen anesthesia. *Anesthesiology, 9,* 391–399.

Chetta, H. D. (1981). The effect of music and desensitization on pre-operative anxiety in children. *Journal of Music Therapy, 18,* 74–87.

Christenberry, E. (1979). The use of music therapy with burn patients. *Journal of Music Therapy, 16,* 138–148.

Clark, M. E., McCorkle, R. R., & Williams, S. B. (1981). Music therapy-assisted labor and delivery. *Journal of Music Therapy, 18,* 88–109.

Clinton, P. K. (1984). *Music as a nursing intervention for children during painful procedures.* Unpublished Master's thesis, The University of Iowa.

Codding, P. A. (1982). *An exploration of the uses of music in the birthing process.* Unpublished master's thesis, The Florida State University.

Cofrancesco, E. (1985). The effect of music therapy on hand grasp strength and functional task performance in stroke patients. *Journal of Music Therapy, 22*(3), 125–149.

Cohen, A. (1984). *The development and implementation of a pediatric music therapy program in a short-term medical facility.* Unpublished Master's thesis, New York University.

Colgrove, T. (1991). *The effects of music versus guided imagery and progressive muscle relaxation versus guided imagery and progressive muscle relaxation with music on the pulse rate and peripheral finger temperature of hemodialysis patients undergoing treatment.* Unpublished master's thesis, The Florida State University.

Collins, S., & Kuck, K. (1991). Music therapy in the neonatal intensive care unit. *Neonatal Network, 9*(6), 23–26.

Cook, J. (1982). *The use of music to reduce anxiety in oncology patients exposed to the altered sensory environment of betaron radiation.* Unpublished master's thesis, The University of Texas.

Corah, N., Gale, E., Pace, L., & Seyrek, S. (1981). Relaxation and musical programming as means of reducing psychological stress during dental procedures. *Journal of the American Dental Association, 103,* 232–234.

Crago, B. (1980). *Reducing the stress of hospitalization for open heart surgery.* Unpublished dissertation, University of Massachusetts.

Curtis, S. L. (1986). The effect of music on pain relief and relaxation of the terminally ill. *Journal of Music Therapy, 23*(1), 10–24.

Davila, J. M., & Menendez, J. M. (1986). Relaxing effects of music in dentistry for mentally handicapped patients. *Special Care in Dentistry, 6*(1), 18–21.

Davis, C. (1992). The effects of music and basic relaxation instruction on pain and anxiety of women undergoing in-office gynecological procedures. *Journal of Music Therapy, 29*(4), 202–216.

Davis-Rollans, C., & Cunningham, S. (1987). Physiologic responses of coronary care patients to selected music. *Heart & Lung, 16*(4), 370–378.

Durham, L., & Collins, M. (1986). The effect of music as a conditioning aid in prepared childbirth education. *Journal of Obstetrical, Gynecological, and Neonatal Nursing, 15*(3), 268–270.

Eagle, C. T., Jr. (1976). *Music Therapy Index, Vol. 1.* Lawrence, KS: NAMT, Inc.

Eagle, C. T., Jr. (1978). *Music Therapy Index, Vol. 2.* Lawrence, KS: NAMT, Inc.

Eagle, C. T., Jr., & Minter, J. J. (1984). *Music Psychology Index, Vol. 3.* Phoenix, AZ: Orynx Press.

Ellis, D., & Brighouse, G. (1952). Effects of music on respiration and heart rate. *American Journal of Psychology, 65,* 39–47.

Epstein, L., Hersen, M., & Hemphill, D. (1974). Music feedback in the treatment of tension headache: An experimental case study. *Journal of Behavior Therapy and Experimental Psychiatry, 5,* 59–63.

Fagen, T. (1982). Music therapy in the treatment of anxiety and fear in terminal pediatric patients. *Music Therapy, 2,* 13–23.

Falb, M. (1982). *The use of operant procedures to condition vasoconstriction in profoundly mentally retarded (PMR) infants.* Unpublished master's thesis, The Florida State University.

Ferrell, D. (1984). *Music therapy case studies of patients in a regional medical center.* Unpublished research manuscript, The Florida State University.

Foutz, C. (1970). Routine audio-nitrous oxide analgesia simplified. *Arizona Dental Journal, 16,* 15–16.

Fowler-Kerry, S., & Lander, J. (1987). Management of injection pain in children. *Pain, 30,* 169–175.

Frank, J. (1985). The effects of music therapy and guided visual imagery on chemotherapy induced nausea and vomiting. *Oncology Nursing Forum, 12*(5), 47–52.

Froelich, M. (1984). A comparison of the effect of music therapy and medical play therapy on the verbalization behavior of pediatric patients. *Journal of Music Therapy, 21,* 2–15.

Gardner, W. J., & Licklider, J. C. (1959). Auditory analgesia in dental operation. *Journal of American Dental Association, 59,* 1144–1150.

Gardner, W., Licklider, J., & Weisz, A. (1960). Suppression of pain by sound. *Science, 132,* 32–33.

Getsie, R., Langer, P., & Glass, G. (1985). Meta-analysis of the effects of type and combination of feedback on children's discrimination learning. *Review of Educational Research, 55*(1), 9–22.

Gettel, M. (1985). *The effect of music on anxiety in children undergoing cardiac catheterization.* Unpublished master's thesis, Hahnemann University.

Gfeller, K., Logan, H., & Walker, J. (1988). The effect of auditory distraction and suggestion on tolerance for dental restorations in adolescents and young adults. *Journal of Music Therapy, 27*(1), 13–23.

Gilbert, J. (1977). Music therapy perspectives on death and dying. *Journal of Music Therapy, 14,* 165–171.

Glass, G., McGaw, B., & Smith, M. (1984). *Meta-analysis in social research.* Beverly Hills, CA: Sage Publications.

Godley, C. (1987). The use of music therapy in pain clinics. *Music Therapy Perspectives, 4,* 24–28.

Goloff, M. S. (1981). The responses of hospitalized medical patients to music therapy. *Music Therapy, 1*(1), 51–56.

Goroszeniuk, T., & Morgan, B. (1984). Music during epidural caesarean section. *The Practitioner, 228,* 441–443.

Grundy, A. (1989). *The effects of music and the Somatron on the physiological and speech responses of head injured and comatose subjects.* Unpublished master's thesis, The Florida State University.

Guzzetta, C. (1989). Effects of relaxation and music therapy on patients in a coronary care unit with presumptive acute myocardial infarction. *Heart and Lung, 18,* 609–616.

Hanser, S. (1985). Music therapy and stress reduction research. *Journal of Music Therapy, 22,* 193–206.

Hanser, S. B., Larson, S. C., & O'Connell, A. S. (1983). The effect of music on relaxation of expectant mothers during labor. *Journal of Music Therapy, 20,* 50–58.

Heitz, L., Symreng, T., & Scamman, F. (1992). Effect of music therapy in the postanesthesia care unit: A nursing intervention. *Journal of Post Anesthesia Nursing, 7*(1), 22–31.

Hoffman, J. (1980). *Management of essential hypertension through relaxation training with sound.* Unpublished master's thesis, University of Kansas.

Howitt, J. (1967). An evaluation of audio-analgesia effects. *Journal of Dentistry for Children, 34,* 406–411.

Howitt, J. W. (1972). In this intensive care unit, the downbeat helps the heartbeats. *Modern Hospital, 118,* 91.

Hyde, I. (1924). Effects of music upon electrocardiograms and blood pressure. *Journal of Experimental Psychology, 7,* 213–224.

Jacobson, H. L. (1957). The effect of sedative music on the tensions, anxiety and pain experienced by mental patients during dental procedures. In E. T. Gaston (Ed.), *Music Therapy 1956: Book of Proceedings of the National Association for Music Therapy, Inc.* (pp. 231–234). Lawrence, KS: National Association for Music Therapy, Inc.

Jellison, J. (1975). The effect of music on autonomic stress responses and verbal reports. In C. K. Madsen, R. D. Greer, & C. H. Madsen, Jr. (Eds.), *Research in music behavior* (pp. 206–219). Teachers College Press, Columbia University.

Judd, E. (1982). *Music therapy on a kidney dialysis unit: A pilot study.* Unpublished master's thesis, Hahnemann University.

Kaempf, G., & Amodei, G. (1989). The effect of music on anxiety. *AORN Journal, 50*(1), 112–118.

Kamin, A., Kamin, H., Spintge, R., & Droh, R. (1982). Endocrine effect of anxiolytic music and psychological counseling before surgery. In R. Droh & R. Spintge (Ed.), *Angst, schmerz, musik in der anasthesie* (pp.163–166). Basel: Editiones Roche.

Kamps, M. (1992). *The effects of singing on the respiratory abilities of cystic fibrosis patients.* Unpublished research paper, The Florida State University.

Katz, V. (1971). Auditory stimulation and developmental behavior of the premature infant. *Nursing Research, 20,* 196–201.

King, J. (1982). *Music therapy results with pediatric patients.* Unpublished research manuscript, The Florida State University.

King, J. (1984). *Five case studies: The integrative use of music therapy with hospitalized children on a pediatric ward.* Unpublished research study, The Florida State University.

Kopp, M. (1991). Music's affect on stress-related responses during surgery. *The Kansas Nurse, 66*(7), 4–5.

Kozak, Y. (1968). Music therapy for orthopedic patients in a rehabilitative setting. In E.T. Gaston (Ed.), *Music in Therapy* (pp. 166–168). New York: The Macmillan Co.

Landreth, J., & Landreth, M. (1974). Effects of music on physiological response. *Journal of Research in Music Education, 22,* 4–12.

Lane, D. L. (1991). The effect of a single music therapy session on hospitalized children as measured by salivary Immunoglobulin A, speech pause time, and a patient opinion Likert scale. *Pediatric Research, 29*(4, part 2), 11A.

Larson, K., & Ayllon, T. (1990). The effects of contingent music and differential reinforcement on infantile colic. *Behavior Research Therapy, 28*(2), 119–125.

Lavine, R., Buchsbaum, M., & Poncy, M. (1976). Auditory analgesia: Somatosensory evoked response and subjective pain rating. *Psychophysiology, 13,* 140–148.

Levine-Gross, J., & Swartz, R. (1982). The effects of music therapy on anxiety in chronically ill patients. *Music Therapy, 2*(1), 43–52.

Liebman, S. S., & MacLaren, A. (1993). The effects of music and relaxation on third trimester anxiety in adolescent pregnancy. In F. J. Bejjani (Ed.), *Current research in arts medicine* (pp. 427–430). Chicago, IL: A Cappella Books.

Light, G., Love, D., Benson, D., & Morch, E. (1954). Music in surgery. *Current Researches in Anesthesia and Analgesia, 33,* 258–264.

Lindsay, K. (1981). The value of music for hospitalized infants. *Journal of the Association for the Care of Children in Hospitals, 9*(4), 104–107.

Lininger, L. (1987). *The effects of instrumental and vocal lullabies on the crying behavior of newborn infants.* Unpublished master's thesis, Southern Methodist University.

Livingood, A., Kiser, K., & Paige, N. (1984). *A study of families to determine the effect of sedate music on their state anxiety level while they await the out-come of surgery.* Unpublished study, Eastern Kentucky University.

Livingston, J. (1979). Music for the childbearing family. *JOGN Nursing, 8,* 363–367.

Lochner, C. W., & Stevenson, R. G. (1988). Music as a bridge to wholeness. *Death Studies, 12*(2), 173–180.

Locsin, R. (1981). The effect of music on the pain of selected post-operative patients. *Journal of Advanced Nursing, 6,* 19–25.

Long, L., & Johnson, J. (1978). Dental practice using music to aid relaxation and relieve pain. *Dental Survey, 54,* 35–38.

MacClelland, D. C. (1979). Music in the operating room. *AORN Journal, 29*(2), 252–260.

Madsen, C. H., Jr., & Madsen, C. K. (1981). *Teaching/discipline: A positive approach for educational development.* Boston, MA: Allyn & Bacon, Inc.

Malloy, G. (1979). The relationship between maternal and musical auditory stimulation and the developmental behavior of premature infants. *Birth Defects: Original Article Series, 15*(7), 81–98.

Mandle, C., Domar, A., Harrington, D., Leserman, J., Bozadjian, E., Friedman, R., & Benson, H. (1990). Relaxation response in femoral angiography. *Radiology, 174*(3), 737–739.

Mann, C. (1990). Meta-analysis in the breech. *Science, 249,* 476–480.

Marchette, L., Main, R., Redick, E., Bagg, A., & Leatherland, J. (1991). Pain reduction interventions during neonatal circumcision. *Nursing Research, 40*(4), 241–244.

Marley, L. (1984). The use of music with hospitalized infants and toddlers: A descriptive study. *Journal of Music Therapy, 21*(3), 126–132.

Marrero, D., Fremion, A., & Golden, M. (1988). Improving compliance with exercise in adolescents with insulin-dependent diabetes mellitus: Results of a self-motivated home exercise program. *Pediatrics, 81*(4), 519–525.

Martin, M. (1987). *The influence of combining preferred music with progressive relaxation and biofeedback techniques on frontalis muscle.* Unpublished master's thesis, Southern Methodist University.

Maslar, P. (1986). The effect of music on the reduction of pain: A review of the literature. *The Arts in Psychotherapy, 13,* 215–219.

McDonnell, L. (1984). Music therapy with trauma patients and their families on a pediatric service. *Music Therapy, 4,* 55–66.

McDowell, C. R. (1966). Obstetrical applications of audioanalgesia. *Hospital Topics, 44,* 102–104.

McElwain, J. (1993). The effect of Somatron and music on headache. In F. J. Bejjani (Ed.), *Current research in arts medicine* (pp. 437–439). Chicago, IL: A Cappella Books.

Melzack, R., Weisz, A., & Sprague, L. (1963). Stratagems for controlling pain: Contributions of auditory stimulation and suggestion. *Experimental Neurology, 8,* 239–247.

Menegazzi, J., Paris, P., Kersteen, C., Flynn, B., & Trautman, D. (1991). A randomized, controlled trial of the use of music during laceration repair. *Annals of Emergency Medicine, 20*(4), 348–350.

Metzler, R., & Berman, T. (1991). The effect of sedative music on the anxiety of bronchoscopy patients. In C. D. Maranto (Ed.), *Applications of music in medicine* (pp. 163–178). Washington, DC: National Association for Music Therapy, Inc.

Micci, N. (1984). The use of music therapy with pediatric patients undergoing cardiac catheterization. *The Arts in Psychotherapy, 11,* 261–266.

Miller, L. (1984). *Spontaneous music therapy sessions for hospitalized children*. Unpublished research paper, The Florida State University.

Miller, A., Hickman, L., & Lemasters, G. (1992). A distraction technique for control of burn pain. *The Journal of Burn Care and Rehabilitation, 13*(5), 576–580.

Monsey, H. L. (1960). Preliminary report of the clinical efficacy of audioanalgesia. *Journal of California State Dental Association, 36,* 432–437.

Moore, W., Browne, J., & Hill, I. (1964). Effect of white sound on pain threshold. *British Journal of Anaesthesia, 36,* 268–271.

Morosko, T., & Simmons, F. (1966). The effect of audioanalgesia on pain threshold and pain tolerance. *Journal of Dental Research, 45,* 1608–1617.

Moss, V. (1987). The effect of music on anxiety in the surgical patient. *Perioperative Nursing Quarterly, 3*(1), 9–16.

Mowatt, K. (1967). Background music during radiotherapy. *Medical Journal, Australia, 1,* 185–186.

Mullooly, V., Levin, R., & Feldman, H. (1988). Music for postoperative pain and anxiety. *The Journal of the New York State Nurses Association, 19*(2), 4–7.

Munro, S. (1984). *Music therapy in palliative/hospice care*. St. Louis, MO: MMB Music, Inc.

Ohlsen, J. (1967). Audioanalgesia in podiatry. *Journal of the American Podiatry Association, 57,* 153–156.

Owens, L. D. (1979). The effects of music on the weight loss, crying, and physical movement of newborns. *Journal of Music Therapy, 16,* 83–90.

Oyama, T., Hatano, K., Sato, Y., Kudo, M., Spintge, R., & Droh, R. (1983). Endocrine effect of anxiolytic music in dental patients. In R. Droh & R. Spintge (Eds.), *Angst, schmerz, musik in der anasthesie* (pp. 143–146). Basel: Editiones Roche.

Oyama, T., Sato, Y., Kudo, M., Spintge, R., & Droh, R. (1983). Effect of anxiolytic music on endocrine function in surgical patients. In R. Droh & R. Spintge (Eds.). *Angst, schmerz, musik in der anasthesie* (pp. 147–152). Basel: Editiones Roche.

Padfield, A. (1976). Letter: Music as sedation for local analgesia. *Anasthesia, 31,* 300–301.

Peretti, P., & Swenson, K. (1974). Effects of music on anxiety as determined by physiological skin responses. *Journal of Research in Music Education, 22,* 278–283.

Pfaff, V., Smith, K., & Gowan, D. (1989). The effects of music-assisted relaxation on the distress of pediatric cancer patients undergoing bone marrow aspirations. *Children's Health Care, 18*(4), 232–236.

Phillips, J. (1980). Music in the nursing of elderly persons in nursing homes. *Journal of Gerontological Nursing, 6*(1), 37–39.

Rasco, C. (1992). Using music therapy as distraction during lumbar punctures. *Journal of Pediatric Oncology Nursing, 9*(1), 33–34.

Rider, M. S. (1985). Entrainment mechanisms are involved in pain reduction, muscle relaxation, and music-mediated imagery. *Journal of Music Therapy, 22*(4), 183–192.

Rider, M., & Kibler, V. (1990). Treating arthritis and lupus patients with music-mediated imagery and group psychotherapy. *The Arts in Psychotherapy, 17,* 29–33.

Ridgeway, R. W. (1983). Another perspective: A story—and a question. *Music Therapy Perspectives, 1*(2), 2–3.

Roberts, C. (1986). *Music: A nursing intervention for increased intracranial pressure.* Unpublished master's thesis, Grand Valley State College.

Robinson, D. (1962). Music therapy in a general hospital. *Bulletin of the National Association for Music Therapy, 11*(3), 13–18.

Robson, J., & Davenport, H. (1962). The effects of white sound and music upon the superficial pain threshold. *Canadian Anaesthetists' Society Journal, 9,* 105–108.

Roter, M. (1957). *The use of music in medical reception rooms.* Unpublished master's thesis, University of Kansas.

Rudenberg, M. T., & Royka, A. M. (1989). Promoting psychosocial adjustment in pediatric burn patients through music therapy and child life therapy. *Music Therapy Perspectives, 7,* 40–43.

Sammons, L. (1984). The use of music by women in childbirth. *Journal of Nurse-Midwifery, 29*(4), 266–270.

Sanderson, S. (1984). *Music therapy with a terminally ill cancer patient.* Unpublished research manuscript, The Florida State University.

Sanderson, S. (1986). T*he effect of music on reducing preoperative anxiety and postoperative anxiety and pain in the recovery room.* Unpublished master's thesis, The Florida State University.

Scartelli, J. P. (1982). The effect of sedative music on electromyographic biofeedback assisted relaxation training of spastic cerebral palsied adults. *Journal of Music Therapy, 19,* 210–218.

Scartelli, J. (1984). The effect of EMG biofeedback and sedative music, EMG biofeedback only, and sedative music only on frontalis muscle relaxation ability. *Journal of Music Therapy, 21,* 67–78.

Schermer, R. (1960). Distraction analgesia using the stereogesic portable. *Military Medicine, 125,* 843–848.

Schieffelin, C. (1988). *A case study: Stevens-Johnson Syndrome.* Paper presented at the Annual Conference, Southeastern Conference of the National Association for Music Therapy, Inc., April, Tallahassee, Florida.

Schneider, F. (1982). *Assessment and evaluation of audio-analgesic effects on the pain experience of acutely burned children during dressing changes.* Unpublished doctoral dissertation, University of Cincinnati.

Schuster, B. L. (1985). The effect of music listening on blood pressure fluctuations in adult hemodialysis patients. *Journal of Music Therapy, 22,* 146–153.

Schwankovsky, L., & Guthrie, P. (1982). Music therapy for handicapped children: Other health impaired. NAMT Monograph Series. Washington, DC: National Association for Music Therapy.

Sedei, C. (1980). *The effectiveness of music therapy on specific statements verbalized by cancer patients.* Unpublished manuscript, Colorado State University.

Shapiro, A. G., & Cohen, H. (1983). Auxiliary pain relief during suction curettage. In R. Droh & R. Spintge (Eds.), *Angst, schmerz, musik in der anasthesia* (pp. 89–93). Basel: Editiones Roche.

Siegel, S. L. (1983). *The use of music as treatment in pain perception with post surgical patients in a pediatric hospital.* Unpublished master's thesis, The University of Miami.

Skille, O., Wigram, T., & Weeks, L. (1989). Vibroacoustic therapy: The therapeutic effect of low frequency sound on specific physical disorders and disabilities. *Journal of British Music Therapy, 3*(2), 6–10.

Slesnick, J. (1983). *Music in medicine: A critical review.* Unpublished master's thesis, Hahnemann University.

Snow, W., & Fields, B. (1950). Music as an adjunct in the training of children with cerebral palsy. *Occupational Therapy, 29,* 147–156.

Spielberger, C., Gorsuch, R., & Lushene, R. (1970). *State-trait anxiety inventory test manual.* Palo Alto: Consulting Psychologists Press, Inc.

Spintge, R. (1982). Psychophysiological surgery preparation with and without anxiolytic music. In R. Droh & R. Spintge (Eds.), *Angst, schmerz, music in der anasthesie* (pp. 77–88). Basel: Editiones Roche.

Spintge, R., & Droh, R. (1982). The pre-operative condition of 1910 patients exposed to anxiolytic music and Rohypnol (Flurazepam) before receiving an epidural anesthetic. In R. Droh & R. Spintge (Eds.), *Angst, scherz, music in der anasthesie* (pp. 193–196). Basel: Editiones Roche.

Standley, J. (1986). Music research in medical/dental treatment: Meta-analysis and clinical applications. *Journal of Music Therapy, 23*(2), 56–122.

Standley, J. (1991a). Long-term benefits of music intervention in the newborn intensive care unit: A pilot study. *Journal of the International Association of Music for the Handicapped, 6*(1), 12–23.

Standley, J. (1991b). The role of music in pacification/stimulation of premature infants with low birthweights. *Music Therapy Perspectives, 9,* 19–25.

Standley, J. (1992a). Clinical applications of music and chemotherapy: The effects on nausea and emesis. *Music Therapy Perspectives, 10*(1), 27–35.

Standley, J. (1992b). Meta-analysis of research in music and medical treatment: Effect size as a basis for comparison across multiple dependent and independent variables. In R. Spintge & R. Droh (Eds.), *MusicMedicine* (pp. 364–378). St. Louis, MO: MMB, Inc.

Standley, J., & Hanser, S. (1994). Music therapy research and applications in pediatric oncology treatment. *Journal of Pediatric Oncology Nursing,* Oct.

Standley, J., & Moore, R. (1993). *The effect of music vs. mother's voice on NBICU infants' oxygen saturation levels and frequency of bradycardia/apnea episodes.* Paper presented at Tenth National Symposium, Research in Music Behavior, Tuscaloosa, AL, April, 1993.

Staum, M. J. (1983). Music and rhythmic stimuli in the rehabilitation of gait disorders. *Journal of Music Therapy, 20,* 69–87.

Steelman, V. M. (1990). Intraoperative music therapy. *AORN Journal, 52*(5), 1026–1034.

Stein, A. (1991). Music to reduce anxiety during Cesarean births. In C.D. Maranto (Ed.), *Applications of music in medicine* (pp. 179–190). Washington, DC: National Association for Music Therapy, Inc.

Steinke, W. (1991). The use of music, relaxation, and imagery in the management of postsurgical pain for scoliosis. In C. D. Maranto (Ed.), *Applications of music in medicine* (pp. 141–162). Washington, DC: National Association for Music Therapy, Inc.

Tanioka, F., Takazawa, T., Kamata, S., Kudo, M., Matsuki, A., & Oyama, T. (1985). Hormonal effect of anxiolytic music in patients during surgical operations under epidural anaesthesia. In R. Spintge & R. Droh, (Eds.), *Music in medicine* (pp. 285–290). Basel: Editiones Roche.

Taylor, D. (1981). Music in general hospital treatment from 1900 to 1950. *Journal of Music Therapy, 18,* 62–73.

Tsao, C., Gordon, T., Maranto, C., Lerman, C., & Murasko, D. (1991). The effects of music and directed biological imagery on immune response (S-IgA). In C. D. Maranto (Ed.), *Applications of music in medicine* (pp. 85–121). Washington, DC: National Association for Music Therapy, Inc.

Updike, P. (1990). Music therapy results for ICU patients. *Dimensions of Critical Care Nursing, 9*(1), 39–45.

Updike, P. A., & Charles, D. M. (1987). Music Rx: Physiological and emotional responses to taped music programs of preoperative patients awaiting plastic surgery. *Annals of Plastic Surgery, 19*(1), 29–33.

Vincent, S., & Thompson, J. (1929). The effects of music upon the human blood pressure. *The Lancet, 1,* 534–537.

Wagner, M. (1975). Brainwaves and biofeedback: A brief history. *Journal of Music Therapy, 12,* 46–58.

Walther-Larsen, S., Diemar, V., & Valentin, N. (1988). Music during regional anesthesia: A reduced need of sedatives. *Regional Anesthesia, 13*(April–June), 69–71.

Weisbrod, R. (1969, Jan.). Audio analgesia revisited. *Anesthesia Progress,* 8–15.

Wexler, M. M. D. (1989). The use of song in grief therapy with Cibecue White Mountain Apaches. *Music Therapy Perspectives, 7,* 63–66.

White, J. (1992). Music therapy: An intervention to reduce anxiety in the myocardial infarction patient. *Clinical Nurse Specialist, 6*(2), 58–63.

Winokur, M. A. (1984). *The use of music as an audio-analgesia during childbirth.* Unpublished master's thesis, The Florida State University.

Wolfe, D. (1978). Pain rehabilitation and music therapy. *Journal of Music Therapy, 15*(4), 184–206.

Wolfe, D. (1980). The effect of automated interrupted music on head posturing of cerebral palsied individuals. *Journal of Music Therapy, 17,* 184–206.

Wylie, M., & Blom, R. (1986). Guided imagery and music with hospice patients. *Music Therapy Perspectives, 3,* 25–29.

Zimmerman, L., Pierson, M., & Marker, J. (1988). Effects of music on patient anxiety in coronary care units. *Heart & Lung, 17*(5), 560–566.

Zimmerman, L., Pozehl, B., Duncan, K., & Schmitz, R. (1989). Effects of music in patients who had chronic cancer pain. *Western Journal of Nursing Research, 11*(3), 298–309.

Zimny, G., & Weidenfeller, E. (1963). Effects of music upon GSR and heart rate. *American Journal of Psychology, 76,* 311–314.

MUSIC FOR PHYSICAL REHABILITATION: AN ANALYSIS OF THE LITERATURE FROM 1950–1993 AND APPLICATIONS FOR REHABILITATION SETTINGS

Myra J. Staum

Introduction

OVER the centuries, the influence of music on mind and body has been addressed by a myriad of people, from the ancient Greeks and the American Indians to current medical personnel. Partially out of the necessity for innovative procedures in military hospitals during the 1940s, music was successfully developed as a viable treatment method in clinics, hospitals and rehabilitation centers.

It has been suggested that man is a rhythmic being, that there is a strong relationship between auditory and motor systems, particularly between rhythm and human motion (Cross, McLellan, Vomberg, Monga, & Monga, 1984; Gaston, 1968; Giacobbe, 1972; Licht, 1946; Verdeau-Paillès, 1985). It is implied that human movement requires an orderliness, a temporal pattern, which, when not in synchrony with itself, results in aberrant motor patterns in breathing, gestures, speech, walking or functional daily activities, apparent even to the most naive observer. Moreover, it has been suggested that the temporal structure of rhythm is inherent in every being from heartbeats to brainwaves to minute biological processes.

> Even the motor, sensory, and reflex reactions to electrochemical stimuli are rhythmic, as are the peristaltic waves of the gastrointestinal tract, the microscopic movement of the villi in the intestine, and the ciliary action of the mucosa of the respiratory system. Many organs, such as the kidney and liver, cannot function for long without the presence of a rhythmic pulsation in the blood stream. (Giacobbe, 1972, p. 41)

It can be assumed then, that the use of music's rhythm " . . . to stimulate, accompany, and regulate physical movement is one of the most primitive functions of music for man" (Michel, 1976, p. 39). Gollnitz (1975) states that rhythm is a natural facilitator of harmonious movement. It is understandable, then, how the application of music, by its inherent rhythmic nature, could influence and regulate the perfectly timed nuances of human movement behavior when carefully applied in a therapeutic setting.

Such applications imply that rhythm, when accompanying rehabilitation, may interfere with or override poorly established motor patterns. When this rhythmic structure is further reinforced by one's own production, as in singing, playing instruments, or rhythmic chanting, there appears to be an inherent drive to synchronize the two activities. This forcing to precision is perhaps what is meant by music's ability to "activate the human rhythm" or "regulate movement" (Altshuler, 1960; Alvin, 1966; Cotton, 1965; Gilliland, 1957) and this apparent synchrony or "entrainment" has been verified experimentally in the past several years (Thaut, 1985; Thaut, Schleiffers, & Davis, 1991; Thaut, McIntosh, Prassas, & Rice, 1992a, 1992b).

Occasionally, music has been utilized as a distractor or audioanalgesic while an individual attempts a difficult or painful motion (Mason, 1978; Rudenberg, 1984). More often, however, music has rendered the physical movements and exercises less arduous (Fielding, 1954) and less monotonous (Bennis, 1969; Benton-Mednikoff, 1943; Bruner, 1952). Sometimes it appears to be the uniqueness of a music activity within rehabilitation that sustains the patient's interest (Fultz, 1949); sometimes the music is simply an additional motivation. This factor has resulted in a number of positive reports of increased enjoyment when music has accompanied physical rehabilitation (B. Cohen, 1993; Creasman, 1985; Cross et al., 1984; Dewson & Whiteley, 1987; Gilliland, 1956; Kearney & Fussey, 1991; Kelly, 1959; Olson, 1984; M. D. Palmer, 1977; Snow & Fields, 1950). Denenholz (1955) made a succinct observation about his work at a rehabilitation center for children: "There has been one strikingly universal reaction . . . the youngsters love music" (p. 131).

It is the purpose of this review and analysis to summarize pertinent findings concerning music in physical rehabilitation and to clarify some of the various procedures for applying rhythm, melody, and sound in general, to rehabilitate motor disabled individuals.

The tables illustrate some of the pertinent findings in the literature from 1950–1993. Entries were made only when the literature mentioned a specific component, therefore no extrapolations were made from the sources. For instance, in Table 1, if the article described the use of music with an elderly person, an inference was not made that the therapy occurred in a "nursing facility." A category was left blank if no clear statement was made. Also, if one article listed six different clinical settings in which music was applied, then all six were tallied individually. However, if six nursing homes were used in one study, the listing was tallied only once, under nursing homes. Thus, all tables reflect each discrete occurrence of the tabled components mentioned in the literature. Table 5 is an accumulation of all experimental studies completed from 1950–1993, based on accepted experimental design which produced data on the measurements indicated. Only experimental or behavioral designs specifically entailing rehabilitation were included in this table.

In order to complete a thorough investigation of the literature in this field, certain limitations were made regarding acceptable source materials. The search was restricted to books, articles, master's theses, doctoral dissertations, and published reports (with the exception of abstracts) written in English, relating to the use of music for actual physical rehabilitation of handicapped persons or improvement of psychomotor skills in motor deficient individuals. Actual rehabilitation was defined as any case studies, or experimental research of real, ongoing therapy with actual patients. Excluded were philosophical essays, reviews of literature, simulated studies, testing of normal individuals, normal motor responses to sound, developmental learning of motor or imitative skills, enhancement of self-help skills or motor work tasks, reduction of hyperactivity or stereotypes, and physical relaxation, unless the release of muscular tension was a prerequisite to rehabilitation. References listed as "Related," however, include the above areas as they pertain to this subject. Physical handicaps included in this review are all neuromuscular or skeletal disorders. Visual, hearing, and speech disorders were excluded. It is to be noted however, that a number of studies are now showing implications for positive applications of music in rehabilitation as determined by experimentation with normal subjects. Many of these are excellent studies and are listed in the "Related References."

All auditory stimuli, except clicks or tones used as aversive stimuli (as in tone avoidance feedback), were considered for this analysis, as were tone frequencies implemented as positive auditory cues, such as rising/falling frequencies occurring simultaneously with variations in muscular tension. This analysis also encompassed an extensive range of music activities, including passive/active listening, instrumental performance, singing, movement, and conducting. Since the goal of physical rehabilitation was the primary variable of interest, studies or reports emphasizing music with the physically handicapped for purposes of developing music skills, self-esteem, or encouraging productive social skills were not included unless they also encompassed a component of motor rehabilitation. In these cases, only the physical components were analyzed for this review. Additional benefits of music for the physically handicapped, which were reported in almost all the studies, were not analyzed, although they are mentioned briefly at the end of this manuscript and in Table 6.

The literature search was initiated by looking at two monographs, one on music and physical handicaps (Rudenberg, 1984) and another on music and other health impaired individuals (Schwankovsky & Guthrie, 1984). An article on music in medical settings (Standley, 1986), the music psychology indices, and all the bulletins, proceedings, and journals in music therapy were surveyed. Finally, the following indices were thoroughly examined: Nursing Studies Index, Cumulative Index to Nursing and Allied Health Literature; Cumulative Index Medicus; *Psychological Abstracts; Dissertation Abstracts* as well as MEDLINE and PsychINFO databases. All searches covered the period between 1950 and 1993.

Applications of Music

Settings

Music to enhance physical rehabilitation has been applied in a number of settings, including as an adjunct to physio- or hydrotherapy (Abel, 1955; Bright, 1972; G. Cohen, 1953; Gilliland, 1956; Graham & Beer, 1980; Heylmun, 1952; Miller, 1979; Proietto, 1977; Quinto, 1952). Table 1 lists settings and frequency in which music and physical therapy have occurred in the literature from 1950 to 1993. The most frequent locations have been various units or departments of the general medical hospital, followed closely by state hospitals or institutions and then public schools.

Throughout this entire review, it is clear that the majority of applications are case studies, testimonial reports of individual work, and observations of patients, all of which are hereafter referred to as case/reports. For those studies specifically mentioning a setting in the literature, 62% were case/reports while 38% were experimental clinical studies. The majority of case/reports occurred in general hospitals and state hospital/institutions, while the majority of experimental studies occurred in physical therapy centers and public schools. As a whole, there are 15 major settings in which music has been applied as a rehabilitative aid.

Table 2 is an alphabetical listing of the various disorders mentioned in the literature which benefited from musical intervention. Cerebral palsy, developmental disabilities with accompanying physical disorders, and paralyses are the most frequently cited. Arthritis, stroke, brain injury, general geriatric and general orthopedic areas, and poliomyelitis are second in frequency. The

Table 1
Frequency of Therapeutic Settings

Setting	Experimental Studies	Case/Reports	Total
General hospital (all regular & rehab. units; special clinics)	6	18	24
State hospital (psyc hosp; institutions; state schools)	7	13	20
Public schools (special ed classes; regular classes)	9	8	17
Comprehensive rehab. Center (+U. Rehab. center)	2	11	13
Nursing facility/retirement center	3	9	12
Physical therapy center (specialized P.T. schools, centers)	8	4	12
Hospital schools (special day schools)	3	2	5
Neurological institutes (+neuropsych. hosp.)	1	3	4
V.A. hospitals		3	3
U. movement lab/research clinic	2	1	3
Private home	2		2
Burn centers		1	1
Biofeedback labs	1		1
Independent pain clinics	1		1
Private music therapy clinic		1	1

frequency of poliomyelitis was due to the earlier literature in the 1950s, when post-polio rehabilitation was prevalent in this country.

The most consistent application of music in physical rehabilitation has been with cerebral palsied patients, for decreasing tremors, spasticity, and athetosis. In a review of the literature from the 1930s to the early 1960s, E. H. Schneider (1961) suggested that music had a beneficial effect upon the tension levels and hypersensitivity of cerebral palsied children. He and others agreed that music must be carefully balanced so as to provoke a rhythmic response closely approximating the physical control needs of the child while not exacerbating muscular tension by eliciting too much excitement (Alvin, 1961). With athetoid cerebral palsy, it was observed that by pairing auditory stimuli with athetoid movements, an increase in regular motions would be achieved initially, but later the athetoid motions would consistently exceed the sound in time (M. F. Palmer, 1953). It was very difficult, then, to regulate these movements on a consistent basis. In a similar study, the patient was able to control his rate of tremor with paired music stimuli. Subsequent cessation of the auditory stimuli produced remission of the tremor for a long period of time (Palmer & Zerbe, 1945). An interesting observation was made with spastic and athetoid cerebral palsied individuals: background stimulative music seemed to improve motor control with spastics yet was detrimental to athetoids. Sedative music, on the other hand, improved the motor control of athetoids but decreased that of spastic cerebral palsied individuals (E. H. Schneider, 1954, 1957a, 1957b). Although these studies were completed in the 1950s, there is to date a dearth of experimentally verified information with sufficient replication to determine how well generalized these applications are across patients. There appears, however, to be ongoing testimony regarding the stimulative force of rhythm to facilitate movement (Evaggelinou & Drowatzky, 1991; Olson, 1984; Thaut, 1985; Thaut, Schleiffers, & Davis, 1992; Weigl, 1963).

Some music procedures have required caution when applied to physical rehabilitation. Alvin (1965) inferred that percussive music could "upset the harmony" required in general motor coordination because its presence required too much precision. She suggested the implementation of a strong rhythmic melodic line instead. It was also suggested that elderly people might require an extremely firm rhythm superimposed over a slow tempo (Mason, 1978), and that when developing muscular control, one should utilize clear, simple rhythmic music uncomplicated by orchestration while closely matching the temporal structure of the movement task (Thaut, 1985). Others have observed that music activities requiring some mental concentration, such as listening to unfamiliar improvised music or simply humming along, actually facilitated therapy (Milligan, 1986: Reeves, 1952). Milligan (1986) also suggested that familiar music, for the same reason, was best applied when performing familiar physical motions.

Table 3 lists, in order of frequency, the rehabilitative purposes for which auditory stimuli were applied in clinical settings. There are 399 occurrences of specific areas mentioned, 83% of which are case/reports, and 17% derived from experimental investigation. The most frequently mentioned areas were coordination, stimulation, control, and reestablishment of neuromotor patterns, all of which are broad in scope. Functions least mentioned were improvement of muscle tone and endurance.

Neuromuscular Coordination

By far the most frequently cited function of music was in facilitating coordination in a number of physical disorders. The act of coordination results in the kind of smooth, harmonious motion

Table 2

Type and Frequency of Primary Patient Disability

Disability	Experimental Studies	Case/Reports	Total
Amputations (& prostheses)		6	6
Arthritis (stiff joints-general)	1	9	10
Asthma		1	1
Autism		1	1
Blindness (mobility; coordination)		3	3
Brain injury (general)	2	6	8
Burn		3	3
Bursitis (& tendonitis)	1		1
Cerebellar disorder	1		1
Cerebral palsy (spastic, athetoid, ataxic, tremor; spasms-general)	7	31	38
Chronic hospitalized	1	1	2
Congenital deformities		4	4
Coma	1		1
Developmental disabilities (mental handicaps; general motor dysfunction or delay)	3	16	19
Epilepsy		1	1
Fractures	1		1
Geriatrics (general)	1	8	9
Hemophilia		1	1
Hip dislocation	1		1
Huntington's Chorea		1	1

Table 2
Continued

Disability	Experimental Studies	Case/Reports	Total
Hypotonia		1	1
Learning disabilities (rhythmic coord. dysfunctions)	2	3	5
Microcephaly	1		1
Multiple sclerosis	1	5	6
Muscular dystrophy		5	5
Myasthenia gravis		1	1
Neurological disorders (general)		2	2
Orthopedically impaired (general)	2	11	13
Paralysis; paresis (hemi-; di-; quadri-; Duchenne; spinal injuries)	5	21	26
Parkinson's disease		5	5
Perthe's disease		1	1
Poliomyelitis		10	10
Psychiatric disorders	1	4	5
Physical therapy (general) (hydro-, physio-; muscular training)		3	3
Respiratory; pulmonary disorders	1	4	5
Scoliosis	1		1
Spina bifida	2	2	4
Stroke	4	6	10
Tension headache	1		1
Transverse myelitis	1		1
Tumors		1	1

Table 3
Frequency of Intended Function of Music and Rehabilitation

Function	Experimental Studies	Case/Reports	Total
Neuromuscular coordination (gross, fine)	6	71	77
Movement/Muscular stimulation (includes: stretching; exercise; vestibular stim.; proprioception; responsiveness to stimuli)	5	35	40
Muscular/Motor control (& control of tremors)	12	27	39
Reestablish neuromotor patterns (basic motor skills; rhythmic motion)	10	29	39
Muscular relaxation (tension release of rigid or spastic muscles)	6	30	36
Joint mobility/agility (& prevent stiffness)		31	31
Muscular & joint strength	5	26	31
Respiration (capacity; rate of)	2	24	26
Balance/Posture (& weight bearing)	2	24	26
Locomotion (& gait training)	6	15	21
Range of motion (& extension/flexion of limbs)	9	10	19
Muscle tone (& to counteract atrophy)	1	7	8
Muscular endurance (and reaction time)	1	4	5

one often witnesses in the display of ballet or in synchronized, well-timed athletic events. It is this ability to experience and express a range of energy dynamics, i.e., force, time, and space, that creates this effect (Bartenieff & Davis, 1965; Leventhal, 1977). Dyskinesia, on the other hand, is temporally inconsistent, lacking this ongoing, flowing motion. This is why even the most naive observer may be alerted to another individual's physical tensions by barely noticeable discontinuities of movement through space and time.

Although practically none of the 77 studies which mentioned improvement in neuromuscular coordination offered a rationale for this outcome, the majority of therapists almost intuitively had used movement exercises or dance activities to facilitate this skill (Bornell, 1984; Caplow-Lindner, Harpaz, & Samberg, 1979; Cotton, 1965; Doll, 1961; Eagle & Lathom, 1982; Fraser, 1961; Harbert, 1953, 1955, 1959; Harrison, Lecrone, Temerlin, & Trousdale, 1966; James, 1986; Kaslow, 1974; Nelson, Anderson, & Gonzales, 1984; Petersen, 1952; Smith, 1953; Taylor, 1950; Thaut, 1984; Weigl, 1954, 1955, 1963). Rhythm instruments accompanying singing also enhanced motor coordination, as did instrumental training or performance (Bruner, 1952; Denenholz, 1955; Dunton, 1969; Fenwick, 1975; Fisher, 1980; Gilliland, 1951, 1956, 1957; Gollnitz, 1975; Herron, 1970; Josepha, 1964, 1968; Kennard, 1983; Maxham, 1952; May, 1956; Myers, 1954; Pickett, 1978; Roan, 1952a, 1952b; Snow & Fields, 1950). Many of the other studies simply mentioned that improved muscular coordination was an additional benefit derived while working on other skills, or that the presence of rhythmic music facilitated coordinated movement (Bright, 1972; Drier, 1955; Fields, 1954; Kurz, 1962; Sheerenberger, 1953). Very few experimental studies emphasized the improvement of coordination as their major objective, but when they did, the data indicated nonsignificant improvement in two studies (Fisher, 1980; Harrison et al., 1966), and significant improvement in another (Jenkins, 1974).

It would seem that while considerable muscular coordination is a prerequisite for most performance aspects of music such as conducting, dancing, singing, or playing instruments, the use of music to accompany movement in motor dysfunctional persons provides the timing, melodic continuity, and qualitative features effective in coordinating movement patterns. In this respect it would seem erroneous from a physical rehabilitation point of view, simply to teach a folk dance to a group of elderly physically impaired individuals, or to have a cerebral palsied child play a xylophone without understanding the specific deficit areas present, all the requisites of the musical task, and precisely how the activities can contribute to achieving the objective of muscular coordination.

Muscular and Joint Strength

Strengthening joints and muscles requires resistance against other forces across time. Sometimes the resistance is against gravity, as in lifting the arm. Adding a weight such as a clarinet can offer even more resistance to effect greater long term benefits. Instrumental playing, in fact, has been cited frequently in the literature to facilitate strengthening of the bones and muscles (Burnett, 1983; Cofrancesco, 1985; Denenholz, 1959; Gilliland, 1951; Josepha, 1961, 1968; Rogers, 1968; Snow & Fields, 1950). One experimental study demonstrated that instrumental playing strengthened the hand grasp of stroke patients (Cofrancesco, 1985). Obviously, careful analysis of the type of instrument and degree of assistance desired is essential in utilizing instruments in this manner.

Other strength developing activities mentioned in the literature are conducting (Weigl, 1954), auditory feedback to strengthen lower extremity musculature (Baker, Hudson, & Wolf, 1979), and movement exercises with music (M. D. Palmer, 1977; Weigl, 1954). Dance movements can be used therapeutically as well, but one should exercise caution when using traditional dances. Choreographing to provide repetitive use of the muscles to be strengthened and monitoring for fatigue would encourage more directed and expedient results.

Muscular/Motor Control

Motor control encompasses factors of both coordination and strength and many reports attest to enormous success when music activities are used to develop neuromuscular control. For instance, children who initially were unable to control their limbs, were able to do so after engaging in a musically paired gymnastics program. In addition, they acquired enough manual control to play some instruments (Salomon, 1972). Patients recovering from polio were able to hold and control a harmonica and to control the arms, shoulders, fingers, and hand muscles after training on the piano (Denenholz, 1955; Rogers, 1968). Others reported that listening to music while performing simple motor tasks also helped control tremors (Palmer & Zerbe, 1945), spasticity (Amato, Hermsmeyer, & Kleinman, 1973; Lathom, 1961), athetosis (Lathom, 1961; M. F. Palmer, 1953), inadequate control of writing (Fraser, 1961), and various other disabilities (Burnett, 1983; B. Cohen 1993; Nordholm, 1954; Reeves, 1952; E. H. Schneider, 1954, 1956).

Experimental studies reporting increased motor control seem to suggest the variables possibly involved in this success. Most of these studies use augmented feedback, where small successive approximations are differentially reinforced toward improved neuromuscular control. Biofeedback technology utilized in these studies is continuous auditory feedback and visual feedback presented contingently when muscle tension falls below a preset threshold. These studies have involved reducing spastic muscles (Inman, 1976), improving ankle, wrist and hand control in an adult hemiparetic individual (Nafpliotis, 1976), and controlling head and neck muscles in severely handicapped children (Ball, McCrady, & Hart, 1975; Dewson & Whiteley, 1987; Walmsley, Chrichton, & Droog, 1981). One might speculate that while there is no magic in developing finger control after several weeks of piano instruction, it is possible that the aesthetic nature of the sound or the psychological perception of creating a musical product might motivate the individual to work longer and harder toward a desired end. Thus the feedback of the correct sound might function to reinforce successive approximations. Experimental studies in which music listening was played contingent on proper head/neck control also supports this thesis (Kearney & Fussey, 1991; Wolfe, 1980). Continued experimentation in this area also confirms the strength of auditory rhythm used in synchrony to facilitate muscular control in children with gross motor dysfunction (Thaut, 1985). If these assumptions are correct, then structured music, whether listening, playing, or moving in synchrony with the music, should be selected not only with the movement in mind but for the potentially reinforcing value to the individual.

Mobility/Agility

Mobility and agility are so important in the world of normal functioning that the fear of losing even the slightest degree of agility drives an entire society to various forms of exercise. Patients with severely impaired mobility in their joints and physical musculature must frequently endure prolonged and painful therapy to correct the problem. Several studies have mentioned the use of music to accompany physiotherapy for mobility (D. M. Allen, 1977; Boxberger & Cotter, 1968; Boxill, 1985; Caplow-Lindner et al., 1979; Denenholz, 1959; Josepha, 1964; Milligan, 1986; Rogers, 1968; Tanner & O'Briant, 1980). In paralytic disorders these exercises were used to keep the currently mobile side functioning; in most other cases they were used to work the potential in nonfunctioning parts of the body. Instruments to mobilize specific parts of the body were mentioned (Goward & Licht, 1957; Josepha, 1968), as were movement exercises accompanied by music. One might ascertain that the factor most responsible for improvement in mobility and agility through music is the process of motivated repetition. As in the areas of neuromuscular coordination and control, the presence of music in any form may simply provide an enjoyable and perhaps timed structure in which to practice the necessary movements.

Range of Motion

A number of disabilities involve joint range of motion. Stiffness or paralysis impair the ability of a joint to move through its entire normal range of movement. Since this area is closely related to mobility and agility, some of the literature overlaps.

Movement/dance exercises seem most likely to facilitate this area, although only two studies specifically mention the use of music and movement for increasing range of motion in arthritis, stroke, and Parkinson's patients (Caplow-Lindner et al., 1979; M. D. Palmer, 1977). One experimental study investigated music listening as an audioanalgesic and another, instrument training to improve upper extremity range of motion. Instrument training resulted in significant differences in range of motion for spastic/rigid upper extremities, compared with those who had no training (Jenkins, 1974). Patients in the audioanalgesic procedure gained 15–30% more shoulder motion than those in treatment without music (Echternach, 1966).

These two studies, while not representing a substantial amount of information, at least encourage the possible applications of music in this area. Certainly active rather than passive listening, where range of motion exercises are paired with the dynamic range of music, might be an interesting area to investigate. Instrumental training might also be a unique focus as instruments are adapted to meet the successive range needs of the patient, as in one case study where a piano composition required various crossover patterns to develop horizontal adduction of the shoulder (Josepha, 1964).

Range of motion, including flexion and extension of the wrist and dorsiflexion of the foot, has been monitored using augmented feedback with hemiparetic patients. Results demonstrated improvement (Basmajian, Kukulka, Narayan, & Takebe, 1975; Mroczek, 1976; Nafpliotis, 1976) and suggest another possible application for sound stimuli. While it is probably not the aesthetic value of single tone frequencies alone which contributes to this improvement, the fact that there is ongoing immediate feedback should not be taken lightly. It would seem not only a challenge but imperative in the area of music and rehabilitation to determine if music can provide both the aesthetic motivation to pursue physical rehabilitation and simultaneous, ongoing feedback as the patient improves.

Movement/Muscular Stimulation

Music to stimulate movement has been discussed frequently in the literature. While this is a broad area, it covers the gamut from stimulating exercise of large muscle groups to almost imperceptible movements in nonresponsive patients. Music has often been utilized for exercise where the rhythm and melody motivate patients to move (Berrol, 1989; Donahue, 1954; Garnet, 1977; Krout, 1987; Olson, 1984; Tanner & O'Briant, 1980; Van de Wall, 1946; Weigl, 1954, 1963; Wells, 1954). Weigl (1954) noticed much more cooperation when using rhythmic music with cerebral palsied children. Others have also noticed that by giving children the opportunity to play, listen to, or move with rhythmic music, motivated physical participation was increased (Brown-Wynkle, 1956; Browne & Winkelmayer, 1968; Eagle & Lathom, 1982; Erickson, 1973; Fields, 1954; Hall, 1957; Kennard & Gilbertson, 1979; Korson, 1959; Lapp, 1978; Lesak, 1952; Roan, 1952a; Snow & Fields, 1950). Highly rhythmic drum playing elicited muscular responses even from usually nonresponsive patients (Shatin, Kotter, & Douglas-Longmore, 1962). Several explanations of these results have been offered in the literature. One is that the changing tempi and rhythmic pulse "encourage" motion (Ford, 1984). Another is that rhythm offers motivation to start and stop activities (Lathom, 1980). Alvin (1961) emphasizes that link between rhythm and motion:

> Music possesses rhythm and duration which can be linked with motor control in time and space. The regular recurrence of the accent and the continuity of the melody may help the child to coordinate his movements, to make a more sustained effort and to stretch perhaps further than without music. (p. 257)

And in an explanation of why instrumental performance stimulates movement, Josepha (1964) suggested that:

> Instrumental performance is of value as a type of physical therapy in that it provides its own work incentive. The musical results, meager as they may be, serve as an immediate reward and, as such, tend to stimulate further and continued effort. Both this incentive and the rhythmic drive of the music help to make instrumental performance therapeutically effective, even with the severely handicapped. (p. 74)

It would be difficult to ignore the obvious as it related to any of us and our responsiveness to music. Indeed, music has the capacity to stimulate movement. How this powerful factor can be applied to successive degrees of improvement in movement dysfunctional individuals remains to be analyzed and monitored carefully over time.

Muscle Tone

The development of muscle tone is a result of strengthening muscle over time. Therefore the literature in this area is quite similar to that on utilizing music for increasing muscular strength. Only a few studies specifically mention development of muscle tone as a distinct category (Burnett, 1983; Caplow-Lindner et al., 1979; Eagle & Lathom, 1982; Phillips, 1980). These reports give no indication why or how music activities help, but they describe patients with differing neuromuscular needs engaging in movement, instrumental, and singing activities. It might be assumed, as with muscular strength, that the resistance manifested by playing certain instruments or repeating dance movements against gravity increases the probability of improved muscle tone in the bodily parts exercised.

Muscular Endurance

One obvious aspect of music is that people choose to listen to it, often for long periods of time. Whatever factors are inherent in that choice, it is inevitable that one can get "caught up" in the music and forget time. This is the premise on which most reports in the literature are based in regard to utilizing various music activities to increase muscular endurance and frequency of activity. One experimental study in this area demonstrates this phenomenon (Wolfe, 1978), but other studies on normal Ss indicate that background or paired music might exceed muscular fatigue points in physical rehabilitation when compared with the absence of music (Thaut et al., 1991). There are also general case descriptions of increasing patients' physical endurance with the aid of music (Denenholz, 1955, 1959; M. D. Palmer, 1977; Weisbrod, 1972).

Another related aspect of muscular endurance is reaction time. Studies concerning reaction time indicate only that reaction time to auditory stimuli is faster than that made to visual stimuli with spina bifida patients (Evaggelinou & Drowatzky, 1991). In this study the auditory stimulus was a buzzer, therefore no parallels can be made with the intrinsically motivating stimulus of music in regard to enhancing reaction time with other physical impairments.

Muscular Relaxation

One area in the literature that is addressed frequently is the use of music to relax muscles. Usually this entails physically passive music listening as opposed to singing or playing instruments, which can create additional muscular tensions. Relaxation periods are commonly preceded by energy-exerting activities such as movement/dance or exercise.

A few case/reports and experimental studies have used music listening to reduce tremors or muscle spasticity (Reeves, 1952; Scartelli, 1982; E. H. Schneider, 1954, 1957b). Scartelli (1982) reported that sedative instrumental background music with electromyographic feedback reduced the degree of muscular tension over twice as much as feedback alone. Studies of this nature may eventually clarify how motivating factors in music interact with the immediacy of feedback.

One study used feedback as "entrainment" (mood-shift stimulus) to measure muscular tension in patients with spinal cord injuries. Music which shifted from tension to relaxation was the most effective in reducing EMG levels (Rider, 1985). Regular augmented feedback with tones varying as muscular tension increased or decreased was also effective in reducing tension attributed to headaches (Budzynski, Stoyva, & Adler, 1970). Once again, feedback immediacy appeared to be a beneficial factor.

Some case/reports in the literature suggest that synchronization of music with movement can bring about muscular relaxation (Graham, 1959) while others simply mention the outcome of relaxation in various patient populations (Caplow-Lindner et al., 1979; Drier, 1955; Giacobbe, 1972; Josepha, 1961; Lesak, 1952; Toombs, Walker, & Bonny, 1965; Weigl, 1954). While a number of experimental studies report positive effects of music on relaxation, one should be wary of generalizing across types of music and types of disabilities without some consistent results in these areas. Even in the mid 50s, E. H. Schneider (1957a, 1957b) observed inverse effects in spastic and athetoid cerebral palsied individuals in response to stimulative and sedative music.

Because of these observed inconsistencies, it would seem that generalization in this area is not yet possible.

Balance/Posture

Balance and posture are prerequisite to locomotion and for most gross motor skills which involve motion away from the body's center of gravity. While dance activities would seem a natural means of improving balance and posture, instrumental training tends to be more effective at first because small balance changes can be effected by gradually changing the position of the instrument as the patient holds it. Instrumental activities have been utilized successfully for this purpose with a variety of physical impairments (Gollnitz, 1975; Pickett, 1978).

Reports on movement activities to improve balance and posture almost all mention rhythmic activities (E. P. Allen, 1955; Boxill, 1985; Bright, 1972; Kaslow, 1974), with two utilizing Dalcroze eurhythmics as a catalyst (Fraser, 1956; C. W. Schneider, 1961). It is likely that very slow choreographed motions to music which gradually and systematically shift balances while calling for stretches in different directions could be included in therapy for balance and posture.

Locomotion

The literature on music to improve locomotion, although related to that on mobility/agility and neuromuscular control, warrants a separate section. Paralysis, lower extremity amputations, stroke, arthritis, cerebral palsy, cerebellar disorder, muscular dystrophy, and transverse myelitis are some of the conditions that can cause difficulties in walking.

The precision offered by implementing either sung or instrumental background music with walking has successfully aided locomotion (Kennard, 1983) and encouraged properly controlled gait patterns (McIntosh, Thaut, Rice, & Prassas, 1993; Staum, 1983; Thaut, McIntosh, et al., 1992b). Rhythmic movement to music has extended from the initiation of small movements such as hand clapping and foot tapping to full ambulation with a number of disorders (Bright, 1972; Kozak, 1968; M. D. Palmer, 1977; Phillips, 1980). The flexibility of music allows for extended progressions of locomotor patterns that can be dynamically changed (strong and weak, even and uneven).

Augmented feedback has been implemented in gait training with stroke patients (Baker et al., 1979) and cerebral palsied children (Conrad & Bleck, 1980; Flodmark, 1986; Wooldridge, Leiper, & Ogston, 1976). Results of the first two experimental studies report overall improvement with spastic children and diplegic and hemiplegic youngsters, but less progress when spasticity and paralysis exist simultaneously.

Locomotion and gait training are readily adaptable to many kinds of music intervention. The difficulty, however, lies in the complexity inherent in almost any locomotive disability. Lower extremities are the gravitational base of movement; thus the rest of the body follows in either appropriate or dysfunctional action. Locomotive training through music therefore requires monitoring of several facets of the body for alignment and posture, as well as for controlled timing of steps. The choice of musical activity, then, must be such that it does not create additional tensions or imbalances. Ongoing research measuring EMG patterns on temporal variables relating to gait will pave the way toward determining musical selections most applicable to these patients.

Development of Neuromotor Patterns and Response

Some studies describe using music activities to elicit novel movements and to reestablish previously acquired patterns of mobility (Bixler, 1968; Bornell, 1984; Eagle & Lathom, 1982; Kennard, 1983; Larson, 1978; Lathom, 1980; Levitt, 1982; Schmais, 1977). Several experimental studies were completed in this area. Music was used contingently for eliciting motor responses in comatose patients with varied outcomes (Boyle & Greer, 1983), and also used as a reinforcer to develop functional motor behaviors (Holloway, 1980). In the latter study, contingent music listening and instrumental playing were superior in eliciting motor behaviors from severely handicapped children and adolescents than no reinforcement at all. Both these studies suggest that music functions as both a stimulus and reward for motor responsiveness.

When music was played in the background to accompany motor tasks, both significant and nonsignificant results were observed when the tasks were practiced with and without music (Karper, 1979; Karper & Gym, 1982). When music was applied as a paired auditory cue, positive gains were observed in one study (James, Weaver, Clemens, & Plaster, 1985), while no significant differences were observed in another (Creasman, 1985). In the Creasman study, while various speeds of music paired with play did not dramatically affect gross and fine motor skills, music was reported to be an enjoyable structure for the participants.

Much of the literature in this area appears to support the motivating, enjoyable reward factors of music. If developing new skills and new responses is an ongoing process, then it would seem that creating an enjoyable structure for this behavior to occur would be an ideal long term objective.

Respiration

Functional respiration involves sustained, timed inhalations and exhalations utilizing the musculature of the diaphragm and lungs. Disabilities of respiration influence the capacity, timing, and sustained nature of breath. These are the areas given the most attention in the literature concerning music intervention and respiratory disorders.

An experimental study by Ammon (1968) used music listening as a treatment procedure for young hospitalized children with acute respiratory distress. "Soothing" music (slow movement of a symphony) was played at their bedsides to decrease respiration. Respiratory rate was significantly improved, compared to that of patients who heard no music. Most of the other studies are case reports of singing (Bolger & Judson, 1984; Brim, 1951; Christenberry, 1979; Gilliland, 1957; Shapiro, 1969), instrumental playing (Herman, 1968; Herron, 1970; Lee, 1985; Pickett, 1978; Rogers, 1968), or movement (Caplow-Lindner et al., 1979).

It has been reported that singing requires approximately 90% of the vital capacity; thus it can serve not only to exercise the lungs but also to stimulate the cough reflex, for clearing out secretions from the airway resulting from long term pulmonary disorders (Bolger & Judson, 1984). Its success as a treatment modality in patients with respiratory difficulties is possibly due to its sustained nature and to its ability to stop, start, and successively time respiration.

Like singing, wind instruments utilize the respiratory muscles with an addition of a mouthpiece, reed, or other air passage. Wind resistance in blowing is forced respiration, which develops the lungs, intercostals, and abdominal muscles. Wind instrument playing is probably the most demanding in terms of controlled air capacity, air flow and pressure required. Teaching a person to control forced exhalation through wind instruments can directly influence the ability to inhale. One experimental study explored the ability to improve respiration through daily practice on a pianica with young handicapped children. There was a significant increase in the capacity and duration of respiration after five weeks of practice, compared with a no-contact control group (Behrens, 1982). While it is no more reasonable to assume that blowing into an instrument will facilitate respiration than to assume that conversing with a patient will facilitate respiration because speaking requires breathing, an assumption is made in this kind of study that the resistance of air flow in a blowing instrument exercises the muscles involved in respiration while increasing endurance and control.

Implementations and Adaptations

Implementations

It is the objective of music, when applied to physical rehabilitation, to increase efficient, synergistically appropriate uses of muscles as they relate to movement. Each muscle contraction in normal motion is rhythmically coordinated, contracting with appropriate strength at specified moments in time. If this complex interplay of muscle contractions and accompanying joint motions is within normal bounds, the entire process is performed automatically. If it is not, the individual may have to pay vigilant attention to the muscles or limbs in order to perform specific actions or to relearn these patterns in an individualized program of rehabilitation. Numerous methods must be utilized by the therapist to effect a specific type of neurophysiological change so that voluntary sensory awareness of these changes can be internalized by the patient. Such a process often requires long-term rehabilitation and careful structuring so that the therapeutic activities closely parallel that which is being practiced.

It would be important, then, with the complexity of neuromuscular and skeletal disorders for a therapist to carefully observe, operationally define the areas to be changed, then successively shape the desired outcome. For instance, it would be counterproductive to immediately implement oboe playing for strengthening an individual's oral musculature or for increasing lung capacity, because the mere act of holding the instrument might create additional muscular tensions in the upper extremities during the initial learning process. It might be more beneficial to pinpoint the area requiring rehabilitation and to work systematically through a successive sequence, monitoring progress periodically.

Two models are suggested which could facilitate the implementation of an organized treatment procedure. The first can be observed in Figure 1. It involves operationally and clearly defining objectives, recording the rate of or lack of occurrence, delineating specific consequences, and evaluating progress with consideration for contraindications due to specific disorders (Madsen, 1981). The example is completed for these purposes with data for a patient with severe respiratory difficulties.

The next model is a comprehensive task analysis, entailing the development and selection of appropriate activities by specifying the objectives to be taught, simplifying complex tasks into a hierarchical order, determining prerequisite skills for the activity, then ordering these steps from least to most difficult (Jellison, 1977). The model in Figure 2 is completed for these purposes with an example of a patient with muscle spasticity, inhibiting proper extension and flexion of the right elbow.

Pinpoint: Develop lung/vital capacity: Increase duration of sustained exhalation

Record: Yes___(currently in client's repertoire)

or

Behavior contraindicated because of specific handicap(s):

Hearing____Visual____Motor____Other____

(Revise pinpoint or delete as an objective)

Consequate: Sustained exhalation without breaks up to 1 minute for:

1) bubbles in water through straw 2) whistle 3) recorder 4) melodica
5) clarinet 6) oboe

Evaluate: Can do #1, #2, #3, #4, up to one minute. #5 creates too much tension in neck

Conditions under which behavior occurs:

____without prompt____with reinforcer evident

Yes ____with verbal prompt____with assistive device

____with physical prompt

__X__Task too difficult: Successively approximate by:

No For #5 & #6: Play/relax alternations 5 secs/5 secs:
Increase to 10/10, etc.

____Reinforcer or prompt inappropriate: Change by:

Model from Madsen (1981)

Figure 1
Model for task analysis and patient evaluation
Example: Respiration

These applications are simply examples for individual cases. As can be surmised from the varying disabilities reported in the literature and reflected in Table 2, it is erroneous to generalize musical applications across disorders or patient populations. The literature thus far is unable to demonstrate that such generalizations are feasible. Yet with systematic, clearly observed procedures, an effective and motivating process of music with physical rehabilitation is possible for the majority of patients.

Adaptations

There are a number of articles and books describing the use of mechanical adaptations of musical instruments, adapted processes of playing for performance by physically handicapped individuals, and sources analyzing the physical components necessary for playing commonly established instruments. In all cases, the literature contains some excellent suggestions for both adaptations and analyses of musical instruments (Brown-Wynkle, 1956; Chadwick & Clark, 1980; Clark & Chadwick, 1979; Denenholz, 1959; Dunn, 1982; Elliot, 1982; Erickson, 1973; Miller,

Skill Area: Increased movement of flexors/extenders of right arm

Prerequisite Skills: Ability to contract and release muscles at elbow joint

Terminal Objective: Increase flexion to 90°, extension to 0°

Secondary Objective: Increase flexion to 120°, extension to 0°

Measurement: Protractor, Goniometer, or other angle measure

Materials/Equipment: Drums placed in different positions in front of right arm and cymbal
                                     hung vertically near right ear or in back of right shoulder; mallet;
                                     piano for accompaniment

Procedures:
  a) Determine baseline degree of flexion and extension.
  b) Place mallet in hand of individual with palm turned up, and drums placed 5° past
     initial extension.
  c) Hand shape slow, controlled strikes of drum, then remove hand gradually until
     person is playing independently.
  d) When accurately sounding strikes are made for 20 trials with piano as
     accompaniment, change position of drum until extension demands approach 0°.
  e) Recheck degree of flexion, then position cymbal behind right ear or shoulder so that
     it is 5° past angle of comfortable flexion.
  f) Hand shape slow, controlled strikes of drum with upswing to cymbal, palm still up.
     Remove hand gradually until person is playing independently.
  g) Encourage stronger drum strikes with greater release into flexion.
  h) When accurately sounding strikes are made on the drum and cymbal for 20 trials with
     piano as accompaniment, change position of cymbal to approach 90°.
  i) When 90° flexion is achieved, increase to 120°.
  j) When 120° flexion is achieved, increase speed and duration of both flexion &
     extension on drum and cymbal.
  k) Transfer skill to nonmusical skill areas.

Model from Jellison (1977)

Figure 2
Model for task analysis and patient evaluation.
Example: Elbow flexion/extension

1979; Schoenberger & Braswell, 1971). It should be cautioned once again, that the complex process of playing an instrument is capable of creating other muscular tensions not immediately apparent. Furthermore, the act of playing while mobilizing or strengthening certain muscles or limbs may not be the most direct means of rehabilitating a specific disorder. If an adaptation encompasses the best of these areas, then it may provide an excellent structure for motivated use of the impaired body parts.

Summary and Discussion

This literature review of music and physical rehabilitation from 1950 to 1993 encompasses applications of singing, instrumental playing, movement/dance, listening, and conducting for the restoration of physical abilities in motor impaired individuals. Instrumental playing and movement exercises have been applied most often in clinical settings, while background and contingent listening have been the most frequently investigated areas in experimental studies, as can be observed in Table 4.

Table 4
Frequency and Type of Musical Applications

Type	Experimental Studies	Case/Reports	Total
Instrumental (solo; ensemble; instrument adaptations; instrum. exercises; special rhythm bands)	6	47	53
Movement/Dance (exercise & hand rhythms; general exercise; eurhythmics; gymnastics; rhythmic speech & movement.; movement in play)	4	44	48
Listening (passive; active-paired; contingent listening)	15	15	30
Singing (& action songs)	5	15	20
Tone/Sound (bio)feedback	8	5	13
Conducting		1	1

Singing activities for rehabilitation are generally focused on modifying the rate of respiration. Both the capacity for rhythmic inhalation and exhalation and the ability to develop and maintain an even resistance for prolonged periods of time can be improved by singing activities. For respiratory objectives, vocal content is of less importance than timing, accent, and phrase; when songs are used to stimulate movement, vocal material may be equally important.

The use of instrumental performance or practice is therapeutically directed according to the physical requirements of the instruments and the physical limitations of the individual, with necessary mechanical or procedural adaptations. Private lessons, ensemble groups, and individual group instrumental exercises are provided primarily for coordination, strength, and endurance. There appears to be inherent satisfaction, and thus motivation, in this participation: "Many a child will strive to attain rhythmic muscle movements while working with a band, but to get him to accomplish the same exercises without this stimulus is almost impossible" (Bruner, 1952, p. 3). Movement/dance activities are most commonly implemented in physical rehabilitation to stimulate movement, develop coordination and control, and to increase range of motion and general mobility. The success of this medium appears to be attributable to the parallel nature of selected exercises and final movement objectives and also in the ability of the " . . . auditory rhythmic input to change the functional status of the lower motor neuron pool, by bringing more motor units into action for a more focused and consistent muscular effort" (Thaut, McIntosh, et al., 1992a, p. 440). These applications are widely implemented among populations and age groups.

Both passive and active listening activities are reported in the literature primarily to stimulate movement or relax muscles, often as a form of augmented feedback. The potential range of listening applications to physical restoration is vast and depends on the various attentional demands of a given task.

It is surprising that conducting is mentioned only briefly in the literature, considering its possibilities for coordination, mobility, control of movement, and range of motion. The capacity for synchronizing music to upper extremity movement would provide an excellent means for practicing such exercises.

Reported and potential contributions of music for physical rehabilitation are due to the flexibility, immediacy, and motivation derived from this form of intervention. The flexibility lies in music's inherent features, which can be paired with various physical objectives. For instance, slow/fast tempi to movement speed, loud/soft dynamics to hard/soft efforts, and accented or sustained phrases and discrete beginnings/endings to assist in movement timing. Motor tasks, then, can be performed to these rhythmic and qualitative features to produce specific muscular patterns (Safranek, Koshland, & Raymond, 1982). In essence, music influences the precision of physical movement when it is adapted to the task at hand.

The aspects of immediacy and motivation are somewhat interrelated. When feedback for movement approximations is imminent, the immediate presence of music in time provides necessary and expedient information for continued progress. This feedback also provides the internal motivation derived from success. Motivation is further enhanced not only by therapeutic achievement but by the aesthetic enjoyment of the medium as well. It appears to "provide its own work incentive" (Josepha, 1964, p. 74). For this reason, the great majority of studies, both experimental and case/reports, have described longer periods of practice and unusual attentiveness, motivation, and enjoyment in the process of rehabilitation. If individuals attend, learn, and experience happy productivity in any setting, the process is considered a success. If an otherwise painful or arduous process can be structured into a pleasant and productive one, the potential benefit to the patient more than justifies the procedures.

Clinical Acceptance and Development

Clinical Acceptance

In 1955, a survey of 346 facilities was made to determine the status of music therapy and music education in facilities serving physically handicapped children. While many of those surveyed agreed that music could be used therapeutically, the majority utilized music only for enrichment and entertainment (Myers, 1955). Since then nonmusical applications have become increasingly more common during the past 43 years, and acceptance of music therapy for its nonmusical benefits continues to be integrated on a widespread clinical basis.

In order to develop acceptable therapeutic music intervention in clinical facilities, it is important to know to what degree music has been consistently substantiated in these settings. Table 5 is an analysis of experimental studies completed between 1950–1993 which utilized auditory stimuli for motor improvement with actual patients. It is noted that 19% of these studies were completed from 1950–1970, while 81% were completed since 1971. The interest in verifiable applications seems to be progressing more rapidly in these two decades. The overall use of music or auditory stimuli in the various clinical settings seems to be applied for movement stimulation; to elicit movement, or to facilitate movement through paired stimuli, and for neuromuscular feedback. Procedures for muscular relaxation and respiration are studied less frequently.

Total duration of therapeutic intervention is also an important variable as it relates to experimental treatment results. When the music intervention lasted less than 1 hour, results demonstrated more variability. Studies which reported procedures lasting for more than 25 hours demonstrated greater consistency in improvement. While many variables are inherent in interpreting quality of treatment time, it would seem that this would be an important area both to control and to compare with traditional intervention methods.

Additional benefits can be derived from music applied to rehabilitation. A list of such benefits appears in Table 6. The most frequently mentioned are aesthetic enjoyment and improved self-esteem. Others include cognitive or mental skills, social and emotional benefits, and physical outcomes such as improved circulation, overall relaxation, and pain reduction. While these are primarily testimonials and do not take the place of systematic research findings, self-reports of this kind are sufficiently frequent in the literature to presume that such benefits exist.

Clinical Development

Music therapy can be implemented in clinical facilities in a number of ways, depending on the funding resources of the institution. Therapists can be hired on an hourly purchase-of-service basis, where direct patient contact is paid for by the patient directly to the therapist or supporting institution. This procedure allows for facility administrators or professional personnel to evaluate

Table 5
Experimental Studies: Music and Rehabilitation

	Author	Year	Source	Rehab. Loc.	Treatmt. Time Hrs. Min.
(1)	E.H. Schneider	1957b	Book of Proceedings	outpatient clinic public school	
(2)	C.W. Schneider	1961	Book of Proceedings	state hospital	36.00
(3)	Lathom	1961	Association bulletin	rehab. foundation	00.15
(4)	Echternach	1966	Journal	phys. therapy lab	23–70.00
(5)	Harrison et al.	1966	Journal	state school	6.40
(6)	Ammon	1968	Report	general & pediatric hospital	3.00
(7)	Budzynski et al.	1970	Journal	biofeedback lab	4–12.00
(8)	Jenkins	1974	Masters thesis	state hospital	45.00
(9)	Ball et al.	1975	Journal	state hospital	6.00
(10)	Basmajian et al.	1975	Journal	univ. rehab. center; research center	10.00
(11)	Inman	1976	Doctoral dissert.	phys. handicapped center	
(12)	Mroczek	1976	Doctoral dissert.	general hosp; homes; phys. handicap inst.	
(13)	Larson	1978	Journal	school	4.50
(14)	Wolfe	1978	Journal	medical hospital	6.00
(15)	Karper	1979	Journal	public school	0.50
(16)	Conrad & Bleck	1980	Journal	home	90.00
(17)	Fisher	1980	Masters thesis	Special ed. classroom	21.00
(18)	Holloway	1980	Journal	State institution	5–10.00
(19)	Wolfe	1980	Journal	Educational, residential settings	6–8.00

Table 5
Continued

	Patient Diagnosis	Age	Male/Female	N	Groups	Design Type
(1)	Cerebral palsy	child/ adolesc	50/50	10	1	Repeated measures
(2)	Schizophrenia	adult	100/0	16	2	Exp/Con Pre-Post
(3)	Cerebral palsy	child/ adolesc	70/30	10	1	ABC
(4)	Chronic frozen shoulder; various etiologies	adult		32	2	Exp/Con
(5)	Mental retardation	child/ adolesc	0/100	40	4	3 Exp/Con
(6)	Acute respiratory distress	infant/ child	35/65	20	2	Exp/Con
(7)	Chronic tension headache	adult	20//80	5	1	AB
(8)	Upper extremity dysfunctions; mental retardation	adolesc/ adult	12/88	17	2	Exp/Con Pre-Post
(9)	Cerebral palsy; quadriplegia; other	child/ adolesc	50/50	2	1	ABAB
(10)	Stroke and foot paresis	adult	50/50	20	2	Exp/Con
(11)	Quadriplegia & other; spasticity	child/ adolesc/adult	50/50	6	1	ABA
(12)	Stroke; hemiparesis	adult	0/30	10	2	AB/BA
(13)	Learning disabilities	child	60/40	10	2	Exp/Con
(14)	Chronic hospitalized	adult	0/100	2	1	AB
(15)	EMR	child	100/0	71	3	2 Exp/Con Pre-Post
(16)	Equinus gait; CP; other	child		8	1	AB
(17)	Mental retardation (motor dysfunction)	adolesc		27	2	Exp/Con; Pre-Post
(18)	Cerebral palsy (spastic)	child/adolesc		8	1	Mltp Bsl; Chang crit
(19)	Cerebral palsy & other	child/ adolesc/adult	25/75	12	1	ABAC

Table 5
Continued

	Dependent Variables	How Measured	Independent Variables	Auditory Stimulus
(1)	Motor control (quality of tasks)	BO	Stim/Sed music/ No music	Movement stimulus/ muscle relaxant
(2)	1) Equilibrium 2) Reaction time	BO BO	Dalcroze eurhythmics training/ No training	Movement stimulus
(3)	Frequency of: 1) stationary bike riding 2) wall pulley	BO BO	Sed/Stim music/ No music	Movement stimulus
(4)	Range of motion	PO	Music & white noise	Audioanalgesia
(5)	Completion of neuromuscular tasks	BO	Sung music & exercise/ Exer/ Music/ Nothing	Feedback
(6)	Respiratory rate	PO	Slow music at bedside/ No music	For respiratory reduction
(7)	1) EMG levels: frontalis 2) Headache intensity	PO SR	Tone feedback/No feedback	Muscle relaxation feedback
(8)	1) Coordination 2) Range of motion	BO PO	Instrumental music training/ No training	Movement stimulus
(9)	Duration of correct head posture	PO	Contingent radio broadcast/ No sound	Feedback
(10)	Range of motion Foot strength	PO	Phys therapy/Pt + biofeedback	Movement stimulus
(11)	Muscle tension	PO	Biofeedback: tones+ clicks+lights	Feedback
(12)	1) EMG 2) Range of motion 3) Latency of movement	PO + BO	Biofeedback: dots + tone	Feedback
(13)	Standardized perceptual motor test	SC	Training with Motorvator (rhythmic sounds)/ No training	Paired movement stimulus
(14)	Exercise/Activity level	BO	Music w/exercise & discussions	Movement stimulus
(15)	Gross motor skills	BO	Background popular mus/ Classical mus/No mus	Movement stimulus
(16)	1) Pedographs 2) Range of motion 3) # secs; total # heel contacts	BO PO PO	Contingent auditory signal on foot	Feedback
(17)	Finger dexterity Range of motion	BO PO	Clarinet instruction/ No instruction	Movement stimulus
(18)	Frequency of functional motor performance	BO	Contingent music listening/ Instrument playing/No music	Contingent feedback/ Reinforcement
(19)	Incorrect head posturing	PO & BO	Interrupted music-silence/ Interrupted music-tone	Contingent feedback

Table 5
Continued

	Statistic Used	Reported Variable	*p*	Result
(1)	ANOVA	Quantity & quality ratings		*Stimulus improved spastics--hindered athetoids; sed mus improved athetoids--hindered spastics
(2)	Wilcoxan Mann Whitney	Reaction time	.02	*Improvement in RT with eurhythmics training
(3)	Sum; Means; SD	Graphic cumulation of motor performance		No differences; great variability
(4)	Individual gains	Degrees of ROM		Exp group improved in ROM, rate of regaining motion, length of time
(5)	*t*	Neuromuscular coordination	<.02 <.0 <.05	*mus + exerc vs exerc *mus + exerc vs mus *mus + exerc vs nothing
(6)	*t*	Change in respiratory rate	.005	*Decrease in respiratory rate with music
(7)	Sign test; Bsln vs avg	Intensity EMG microvolts	<.03 <.03	*Decrease in: Headache intensity; EMG levels
(8)	*t*	# of accurate strikes; Degree of angle	.05	*Strikes improved w/ music; Angle improved w/ music
(9)	Means	Minutes of correct head posture		Improvement w/ conting mus noncontingent music
(10)	Mean change	ROM degrees; Strength-kg		Exp group improved 2x con group
(11)	Mean rate	EMG voltage time integral		Biofeedback resulted in stimulus control of muscles
(12)	*t*	EMG microvolts; ROM; Latency		*EMG & ROM improvement
(13)	Sign test	Scores: Purdue Perceptual-Motor	.031	*gains on PPMS
(14)		Survey Frequency		Increase in exercise frequency
(15)	*F*	Rate of tossing ball		No signif diff; No treatment higher
(16)	Pre/Post %	Degrees of ROM; Duration of heel down; # of heels down		Improvement in: ROM; Heel durations; Heel contacts
(17)	Mann Whitney	ROM degrees; Finger dexterity scores	>.05 >.05	More ROM in exp group; Scores slightly higher in exp group
(18)	ANOVA	Behavior frequency means	<.05	*Higher in both music conditions vs no music
(19)	Means	Mercury switch: duration & frequency		Mus-silence & mus-tone improved head posture over bsln for majority

Table 5
Continued

	Author	Year	Source	Rehab. Loc.	Treatmt. Time Hrs. Min.
(20)	Walmsley et al.	1981	Journal	Hosp. school program	6.00
(21)	Behrens	1982	Masters thesis	Home	2.50
(22)	Karper & Gym	1982	Journal	Public school	0.40
(23)	Scartelli	1982	Journal	Cerebral palsy center	5.00
(24)	Burnett	1983	Doctoral dissert.	Center for children & families	48.00
(25)	Boyle & Greer	1983	Journal	Rehab. hospital; nursing facility	84.00
(26)	Staum	1983	Journal	Public school; nursing home; hosp.	15.00
(27)	Cofrancesco	1985	Journal	Rehab. hospital; nursing home	7.50
(28)	Creasman	1985	Masters thesis	Special ed. classroom	7.50
(29)	James et al.	1985	Journal	State hospital	6.00
(30)	Rider	1985	Journal	Spinal pain clinic	7.50
(31)	Thaut	1985	Journal	U. center for human performance	0.90
(32)	Flodmark	1986	Journal	School for physical handicaps	25.00
(33)	Olson	1984	Journal	Retirement home	7.50
(34)	Dewson & Whiteley	1987	Journal	State hospital	0.30
(35)	Evaggelinou & Drowatzky	1991	Journal	Public school	0.40
(36)	Kearney & Fussey	1991	Journal	Physical therapy clinic	22.00
(37)	Thaut et al.	1992a	Article in book	University research center/hospital	(5 individual stride cycles)

Table 5
Continued

	Patient Diagnosis	Age	Male/Female	N	Groups	Design Type
(20)	Cerebral palsy; mental retard; quadriplegia	child		5	1	Pre-Post
(21)	Down Syndrome dev. delayed	child		8	2	Exp/Con; Pre-Post
(22)	Learning disabled; motor disabilities	child		69	3	2 Exp/Con; Pre-Post
(23)	Cerebral palsy (spastic)	adult	50/50	6	2	Exp/Con; Pre-Post
(24)	CP; spina bifida & other	child	48/52	23	2	Exp/Con; Pre-Post
(25)	Comatose	adult	67/33	3	1	ABAB; Mltp Bsln
(26)	Gait disorders; varying etiology	child/ adolesc/adult	40/60	25	1	AB; Chang crit
(27)	Stroke	adult		3	1	Mltp Bsln; Pre-Post
(28)	Retardation; cerebral palsy; other	child	80/20	5	1	ABC
(29)	Severe/profound retardation	adult	42/58	24	2	Exp/Con
(30)	Spinal cord injury			23	1	Pre-Post; Repeat. meas.
(31)	Gross motor dysfunction	child	100/0	24	3	2 Exp/Con
(32)	Cerebral palsy: paralysis	child	29/71	7	1	ABABABA
(33)	Elderly (multiple physical and mental)	adult	10/90	10	1	O-XO-O
(34)	Microcephaly, quadriplegia, encephalopathy, scoliosis, cerebral atrophy, epilepsy, hypertonia, diplegia, hip dislocation	child/ adolesc.	20/80	6	1	Variable Bsln/
(35)	Spina bifida	child/adolesc	61/39	23	3	Repeated measures
(36)	Brain injury	adult	100/0	1	1	A-BC-B-BC-A
(37)	Stroke, cerebellar disorder, trans. myelitis	adult	37/63	8	1	OX

Table 5
Continued

	Dependent Variables	How Measured	Independent Variables	Auditory Stimulus
(20)	1) # head posture errors 2) Duration of errors	PO PO	Contingent/ No music	Feedback
(21)	1) Capacity forced respir 2) dB & duration of sound	PO+BO	Pianica practice/No practice	To increase respiration
(22)	Gross motor--ball tossing	BO	Practice: w/ music/ w/o music With music but test w/o music	Motivation
(23)	Relaxation of finger extensor muscle	PO	Sedative music + relaxation	Muscle relaxation feedback
(24)	Gross & fine motor	SC	Rhythmic training/No training	Mvmt stimulus
(25)	Finger, mouth, eye mvmt	BO	Contingent music/No music	Feedback
(26)	1) Arrhythmic steps 2) Step inconsistencies 3) Ratings of appearance	BO BO BO	Rhythmic music and pulse	Paired mvmt stimulus
(27)	1) Hand grasp strength 2) Finger agility	PO BO	Instrument training	Movement stimulus
(28)	1) Fine motor skills 2) Gross motor skills	BO BO	Movement play with varying speeds music/ Movement play alone	Motivation stimulus
(29)	Standardized motor develop test	SC	Music paired with vestib mvmt/No treatment	Paired movement stimulus
(30)	Muscle relaxation	PO	Repetitive music/Entrainmt music/ No mus + relax/ No mus + no relax	Muscle relaxant
(31)	Performance of motor sequence	PO	Aud rhythm/Rhythmic speech/Vis model only	Paired movement stimulus
(32)	Knee joint angle	BO+PO	Auditory signal on knee	Feedback
(33)	Extremity movement Body movement Rhythmic	BO	Listening to player piano rolls	Movement stimulus
(34)	Rate of head turning per minute	BO	Pictures, music, vibration/pictures & music/pictures alone/music alone/VP/MV/V alone and variable R schedules	Contingent music
(35)	Response latency	BO	Visual lights & auditory (buzzer) stimulation/V alone/ A alone Also ambulatory/assisted ambulatory/ nonambulatory	Movement stimulus
(36)	Time correct head posturing while walking	BO	Headband and music/ headband only/ tokens only	Contingent movement stimulus
(37)	EMG; stride; gait mechanics on walking	PO & BO	Recorded rhythmic music/ no music	Paired mvmt. stimulus

Table 5
Continued

	Statistic Used	Reported Variable	p	Result
(20)	Wilcoxan	Correct head angle	.063	Overall improvement in head orientation
(21)	ANOVA	% peak performance scores Av duration & dB of sound	<.01 <.05	*Increase in respiration by 5th week with pianica practice
(22)	F	Accuracy of toss	<.01	*Accuracy better without music
(23)	Mean % change	EMG microvolts		Mus + biofdbk: 65% decrease Biofdbk only: 33# decrease
(24)	ANOVA	Standardized motor tests	<.01	*Gains on mvmt & motor skills w/training
(25)	Individual means	Behavioral responses		Variability; increase for one pt; partial increase for one pt.
(26)	Seconds difference	Arrhythmia: # of R vs L footfalls		All Ss improved in rhythmic or consistent gait
(27)	Individual change	Hand grasp strength		All Ss improved, esp in R hand function
(28)	Means	Successful performance of fine/gross motor skills		No strong effects with or without music
(29)	t	Levels on Gesell Develop Eval	<.01	*Gain in motor skills for music group
(30)	ANOVA	EMG	<.0001	*EMG reduction; Entrainmt most effective
(31)	ANCOVA	Rhythmic accuracy	<.05	* Auditory rhythm and rhythmic speech aided temporal muscular control
(32)	% change	Feedback signals & errors responded better to aud feedback		71% of Ss improved; paralysis
(33)	Number of responses	Amount of activity		Increase in physical and rhythmic activity during music
(34)	Mean rate	Head turning responses		Systematically varying stimuli for reinforcement elicited higher response rates, but results were variable.
(35)	Tukey posthoc Mean standard deviations	Response time among Ss Response variability Auditory vs. visual stimuli	<.05 <.07	Ambulatory group was fastest Ambulatory group was less variable than others Auditory responses were faster than visual responses for all groups
(36)	Autocorrelation & linear regression ANOVA	% means and S.D. of correct head position Deviation between stride time	<.01 <.05	Contingent music increased correct head position External auditory rhythmic stimulation decreased stride deviations and improved gait rhythmicity
(37)	Mean SD for EMG duration	EMG changes of gastrocnemius muscle Kinematic analysis		Timing of EMG became more consistent; magnitude of EMG increased in most Ss

BO = Behaviorally observed
SR = Self-Report
PO = Physiologically observed
SC = Scores (Standardized Tests)
* = Statistical significance

Table 6
Ancillary Benefits of Music and Physical Rehabilitation

	Provide	Improve	Increase	Decrease
Physical		Circulation Sleep habits Elimination Digestion Relaxation		Hyperactivity Pain
Social/ Emotional	Success experience Sense of achievement Aesthetic enjoyment Emotional outlet	Communication Interpersonal relationships Socialization Personal insight	Self-confidence Self-esteem Independence Responsiveness Adaptability Cooperativeness Self-acceptance	Fears Anxiety Confusion
Cognitive/ Mental		Reality orientation Judgment	Memory Alertness	Boredom

these services after a period of time and recommend increased hours, eventually leading to a full time staff position.

Music therapists might also be hired as consultants to an institution or in an adjunct position with the physical therapy staff. As consultants, the therapists might evaluate specific patients and formulate procedures for the staff to implement during the weeks or months of patient care. As consultant or adjunct to the physical therapy staff, the music therapist might be hired to develop activities which eliminate the monotony of repetitive physical rehabilitation, or to implement procedures which exercise certain body parts while simultaneously focusing attention on the music. As consultants or adjuncts to an existing staff, payment would be on a fee basis predetermined by therapist and facility.

Currently almost all music therapists are paid according to the amount of time they spend with patients. These costs are sometimes recovered through insurance reimbursement; however, individual institutional guidelines or government legislation on this issue should be consulted. Obviously, well documented procedures and results would increase the probability of third party reimbursement by traditional medical insurance.

Whether the music therapist works in any of the positions described here or in private practice, a substantive referral system in the community would be beneficial. Such a system will never be implemented uniformly unless physicians are convinced of its importance through workshops, in-service, and successful local experience. While most of the currently documented procedures for music and rehabilitation are published in the music therapy journals, none of these journals are referenced in the main indices of the medical profession. Therefore, as can be observed in Table 7, hospital and rehabilitative staff are less likely to learn of the potential benefits of music therapy from the medical and nursing literature. Applications by nonmusic professionals where music is used primarily as audioanalgesia or augmented feedback may be their only exposure to the applications of music in rehabilitative settings. It is clearly up to music therapists initiating programs in these settings to be prepared to educate the staff not only regarding the content of this field but also of potential criteria for referring patients to music therapy. Treatment documentation and assessments of patient progress must then be accurate, specific, and, most importantly, communicated to those medical and administrative personnel involved in obtaining, maintaining, and funding music therapy services.

Table 7
Frequency of References Cited

Source	Experimental Studies	Case/ Reports	Total
Physical Therapy/Special Ed			
Physical Therapy	1	6	7
Books, Monographs (& articles in)		6	6
Crippled Child		3	3
Dissertations	3		3
Physiotherapy		3	3
American Journal of Mental Deficiency	1	1	2
Exceptional Children		2	2
Occupational Therapy & Rehabilitation		2	2
Physiotherapy Canada		2	2
Canadian Journal of Occupational Therapy		1	1
Cerebral Palsy Bulletin		1	1
Cerebral Palsy Review		1	1
International Journal of Rehab. Research	1		1
Journal of Rehabilitation		1	1
Journal of Speech Disorders		1	1
Mental Retardation		1	1
Rehabilitation Record		1	1
Research in Developmental Disabilities	1		1

Table 7
Continued

Source	Experimental Studies	Case/ Reports	Total
Music Therapy/Music Ed/Creative Arts			
Proceedings of the National Association Music Therapy	2	38	40
Books, Monographs (& articles in)	1	28	29
Journal of Music Therapy	11	9	20
Music Educators Journal		6	6
Master's Theses	4		4
British Journal of Music Therapy		3	3
Bulletin of the National Association for Music Therapy	1	1	2
Music Education for the Handicapped Bulletin		2	2
Music Therapy Perspectives		3	3
International Musician		1	1
Journal of the American Association for Music Therapy		1	1
Arts in Psychotherapy	1	1	
			112
Medical/Nursing			
Brain Injury	1		1
Developmental Medicine and Child Neurology	3	1	4
American Journal of Physical Medicine		2	2
Books, Monographs (& articles in)		2	2
Acta Paedopsychiatria		1	1
American Nurses' Association Clinical Sessions	1		1
Archives of Physical Medicine and Rehabilitation	1		1
Gerontologist		1	1
Hospital Management		1	1
Inter-Clinic Information Bulletin		1	1
International Journal of Orthodontics		1	1
Journal of Gerontological Nursing		1	1
New England Journal of Medicine		1	1
Continuing Care		1	1
			19
General Psychology/Motor Learning			
Perceptual & Motor Skills	3		3
Books, Monographs (& articles in)		2	2
Journal of Applied Behavioral Analysis	1		1
Journal of Behavioral Therapy and Experimental Psychiatry	1		1
			7

References

Abel, H. (1955). Music and recreation therapy. *Music Therapy 1954: Book of proceedings of the National Association for Music Therapy,* 181–186.

Allen, D. M. (1977). Music therapy with geriatric patients. *British Journal of Music Therapy, 8,* 2–6.

Allen, E. P. (1955). Let there be music . . . *Crippled Child, 33,* 11–15.

Altshuler, I. M. (1960). The value of music in geriatrics. *Music Therapy 1959: Book of proceedings of the National Association for Music Therapy,* 109–115.

Alvin, J. (1961). Music therapy and the cerebral palsied child. *Cerebral Palsy Bulletin, 3,* 255–262.

Alvin, J. (1965). *Music for the handicapped child.* London: Oxford University Press.

Alvin, J. (1966). *Music therapy.* New York: Humanities Press.

Amato, A., Hermsmeyer, C. A., & Kleinman, K. M. (1973). Use of electromyographic feedback to increase inhibitory control of spastic muscles. *Physical Therapy, 53,* 1063–1066.

Ammon, K. J. (1968). The effects of music on children in respiratory distress. *American Nurses' Association Clinical Sessions,* 127–133.

Baker, M. P., Hudson, J. E., & Wolf, S. L. (1979). A "feedback" cane to improve the hemiplegic patient's gait. *Physical Therapy, 59,* 170–171.

Ball, T. S., McCrady, R. E., & Hart, A. D. (1975). Automated reinforcement of head posture in two cerebral palsied retarded children. *Perceptual and Motor Skills, 40,* 619–622.

Bartenieff, I., & Davis M. A. (1965). *Effort-shape analysis of movement: The unity of expression and function.* New York: Albert Einstein College of Medicine, Yeshiva University.

Basmajian, J. V., Kukulka, B. S., Narayan, M. D., & Takebe, M. D. (1975). Biofeedback treatment of foot-drop after stroke compared with standard rehabilitation technique: Effects on voluntary control and strength. *Archives of Physical Medicine and Rehabilitation, 56,* 231–236.

Behrens, G. A. (1982). *The use of music activities to improve the capacity, inhalation, and exhalation capabilities of handicapped children's respiration.* Unpublished master's thesis, Kent State University, Kent, OH.

Bennis, J. A. (1969). The use of music as a therapy in the special education classroom. *Journal of Music Therapy, 6,* 15–18.

Benton-Mednikoff, P. (1943). Musical therapy used for post-operative and corrective work in orthopedics. *Occupational Therapy and Rehabilitation, 22,* 136–139.

Berrol, C. (1989). A view from Israel: Dance/Movement and the creative arts therapies in special education. *The Arts in Psychotherapy, 16*(2), 81–90.

Bixler, J. W. (1968). Music therapy practices for the child with cerebral palsy. In E. T. Gaston (Ed.), *Music in therapy* (pp. 143–151). New York: Macmillan.

Bolger, E. P., & Judson, M. A. (1984). The therapeutic value of singing. *New England Journal of Medicine, 311,* 1704.

Bornell, D. G. (1984). Movement is individuality: An interabilities approach using dance taps. *Music Therapy, 4,* 98–105.

Boxberger, R., & Cotter, V. W. (1968). The geriatric patient. In E. T. Gaston (Ed.), *Music in therapy* (pp. 271–280). New York: Macmillan.

Boxill, E. H. (1985). *Music therapy for the developmentally disabled*. Rockville, MD: Aspen Systems.

Boyle, M. E., & Greer, R. D. (1983). Operant procedures and the comatose patient. *Journal of Applied Behavioral Analysis, 16*, 3–12.

Bright, R. (1972). *Music in geriatric care*. New York: St. Martin's Press.

Brim, C. L. (1951). Music, vital capacity, and post-respirator patients. *Music Educators Journal, 37*, 18–19.

Brown-Wynkle, M. H. (1956). Devices as aids to rehabilitation through music therapy. *Music Therapy 1955: Book of proceedings of the National Association for Music Therapy*, 79–85.

Browne, H. E., & Winkelmayer, R. A. (1968). A structured music therapy program in geriatrics. In E. T. Gaston (Ed.), *Music in therapy* (pp. 285–289). New York: Macmillan.

Bruner, O. P. (1952). Music to aid the handicapped child. *Music Therapy 1951: Book of proceedings of the National Association for Music Therapy*, 3–6.

Budzynski, T., Stoyva, J., & Adler, C. (1970). Feedback-induced muscle relaxation: Application to tension headache. *Journal of Behavior Therapy and Experimental Psychiatry, 1*, 205–211.

Burnett, M. H. (1983). *The effect of rhythmic training on musical perception and motor skill development of preschool handicapped children, male and female*. Unpublished doctoral dissertation, U.S. International University, San Diego. (University Microfilms No. 8315094)

Caplow-Lindner, E., Harpaz, L., & Samberg, S. (1979). *Therapeutic dance/movement: Expressive activities for older adults*. New York: Human Sciences Press.

Chadwick, D. M., & Clark, C. A. (1980). Adapting music instruments for the physically handicapped. *Music Educators Journal, 67*, 56–59.

Christenberry, E. B. (1979). The use of music therapy with burn patients. *Journal of Music Therapy, 16*, 138–148.

Clark, C. A., & Chadwick, D. M. (1979). *Clinically adapted instruments for the multiply handicapped*. Westford, MA: Modulations.

Cofrancesco, E. M. (1985). The effect of music therapy on hand grasp strength and functional task performance in stroke patients. *Journal of Music Therapy, 22*, 129–145.

Cohen, B. (1993, June). The sound of music. *Continuing Care*, 16–18, 20–22.

Cohen, G. (1953). Coordination of music therapy with rehabilitation therapies. *Music Therapy 1952: Book of proceedings of the National Association for Music Therapy*, 70–73.

Conrad, L. & Bleck, E. E. (1980). Augmented auditory feedback in the treatment of equinus gait in children. *Developmental Medicine and Child Neurology, 22*, 713–718.

Cotton, E. (1965). The institute for movement therapy and school for "conductors," Budapest, Hungary. *Developmental Medicine and Child Neurology, 7*, 437–446.

Creasman, C. D. (1985). *The effect of music in BKR intensive play—A teaching method for profoundly mentally handicapped preschoolers*. Unpublished master's thesis, Florida State University, Tallahassee.

Cross, P., McLellan, M., Vomberg, E., Monga, M., & Monga, T. N. (1984). Observations on the use of music in rehabilitation of stroke patients. *Physiotherapy Canada, 36*, 197–201.

Denenholz, B. (1955). Music therapy with handicapped children at the Institute of Physical Medicine and Rehabilitation: A demonstration. *Music Therapy 1954: Book of proceedings of the National Association for Music Therapy*, 131–134.

Denenholz, B. (1959). Music as a tool of physical medicine. *Music Therapy 1958: Book of proceedings of the National Association for Music Therapy*, 67–84.

Dewson, M., & Whiteley, J. (1987). Sensory reinforcement of head turning with non ambulatory, profoundly mentally retarded persons. *Research in Developmental Disabilities, 8*(3), 413–426.

Doll, E. E. (1961). Therapeutic values of the rhythmic arts in the education of cerebral palsied and brain-injured children. *Music Therapy 1960: Book of proceedings of the National Association for Music Therapy*, 79–85.

Donahue, W. (1954). The challenge of growing older. *Music Therapy 1953: Book of proceedings of the National Association for Music Therapy*, 119–126.

Drier, J. C. (1955). Music therapy for exceptional children. *Music Therapy 1954: Book of proceedings of the National Association for Music Therapy*, 124–130.

Dunn, R. H. (1982). Selecting a musical wind instrument for a student with orofacial muscle problems. *International Journal of Orthodontics, 20*, 19–22.

Dunton, M. J. (1969). Handicapped children respond to music therapy. *International Musician, 67*, 8, 21.

Eagle, C. T., Jr., & Lathom, W. B. (1982). Music for the severely handicapped. *Music Educators Journal, 68*, 30–31.

Echternach, J. L. (1966). Audioanalgesia as an adjunct to mobilization of the chronic frozen shoulder. *Physical Therapy, 46*, 839–846.

Elliot, B. (1982). *Guide to the selection of musical instruments with respect to physical ability and disability*. St. Louis: Magnamusic-Baton.

Erickson, L. B. (1973). Keyboard fun for children with osteogenesis imperfecta and other physical limitations. *Inter-clinic Information Bulletin, 12*, 9–17.

Evaggelinou, C., & Drowatzky, J. (1991). Timing responses of children with spina bifida having varying ambulatory abilities. *Perceptual and Motor Skills, 73*(3), 919–928.

Fenwick, A. (1975). Music and the physically handicapped child. In *The nature and scope of music therapy with handicapped children*, (pp. 21–32). London: British Society for Music Therapy.

Fielding, B. B. (1954). Two approaches to the rehabilitation of the physically handicapped. *Exceptional Children, 20*, 336–341.

Fields, B. (1954). Music as an adjunct in the treatment of brain-damaged patients. *American Journal of Physical Medicine, 33*, 273–283.

Fisher, G. L. (1980). *The effect of instrumental music instruction on fine motor coordination and other variables of mentally retarded adolescents*. Unpublished master's thesis, Florida State University, Tallahassee.

Flodmark, A. (1986). Augmented auditory feedback as an aid in gait training of the cerebral-palsied child. *Developmental Medicine and Child Neurology, 28*, 147–155.

Ford, S. C. (1984). Music therapy for cerebral palsied children. *Music Therapy Perspectives, 1*(3), 8–13.

Fraser, L. W. (1956). Music therapy for the retarded child. *Music Therapy 1955: Book of proceedings of the National Association for Music Therapy*, 55–58.

Fraser, L. W. (1961). The use of music in teaching writing to the retarded child. *Music Therapy 1960: Book of proceedings of the National Association for Music Therapy*, 86–89.

Fultz, A. F. (1949). Music in occupational therapy and rehabilitation. In W. H. Soden (Ed.), *Rehabilitation of the handicapped* (pp. 334–344). New York: Ronald Press.

Garnet, E. D. (1977). A movement therapy for older people. In K. C. Mason (Ed.), *Dance therapy: Focus on Dance VII* (pp. 59–61). Washington, DC: American Alliance for Health, Physical Education, and Recreation.

Gaston, E. T. (Ed.). (1968). *Music in therapy*. New York: Macmillan.

Giacobbe, G. A. (1972). Rhythm builds order in brain-damaged children. *Music Educators Journal, 58*, 40–43.

Gilliland, E. G. (1951). Prescriptions set to music—musical instruments in orthopedic therapy. *Exceptional Children, 18*, 68–70.

Gilliland, E. G. (1956). Music therapy rehabilitation. *Hospital Management, 81*, 46–48, 98–99.

Gilliland, E. G. (1957). Music therapy. In H. A. Pattison (Ed.), *The handicapped and their rehabilitation* (pp. 628–649). Springfield, IL: Charles C. Thomas.

Gollnitz, G. (1975). Fundamentals of rhythmic-psychomotor music therapy. An objective-oriented therapy for children and adolescents with developmental disturbances. *Acta Paedopsychiatria, 41*, 130–134.

Goward, B., & Licht, S. (1957). Music for the hospitalized patient. In W. R. Dunton & S. Licht (Eds.), *Occupational therapy: Principles and practices* (pp. 127–141). Springfield, IL: Charles C. Thomas.

Graham, R. M. (1959). Procedures for conducting rhythmic activities on wards of chronic and regressed mental patients. *Music Therapy: Book of proceedings of the National Association for Music Therapy*, 157–161.

Graham, R. M., & Beer, A. S. (1980). *Teaching music to the exceptional child*. Englewood Cliffs, NJ: Prentice-Hall.

Hall, D. (1957). Music activity for the older patient. *Music Therapy 1956: Book of proceedings of the National Association for Music Therapy*, 115–118.

Harbert, W. K. (1953). Some results from specific techniques in the use of music with exceptional children. *Music Therapy 1952: Book of proceedings of the National Association for Music Therapy*, 147–161.

Harbert, W. K. (1955). Music education for exceptional children. In *Music in American education: Music education source book II* (pp. 263–271). Reston, VA: Music Educators National Conference.

Harbert, W. K. (1959). Music therapy clinic—A bridge from home to school. *Music Therapy 1958: Book of proceedings of the National Association for Music Therapy*, 112–115.

Harrison, W., Lecrone, H., Temerlin, M. K., & Trousdale, W. W. (1966). The effect of music and exercise upon the self-help skills of nonverbal retardates. *American Journal of Mental Deficiency, 71*, 279–282.

Herman, F. K. (1968). Music therapy for children hospitalized with muscular dystrophy. In E. T. Gaston (Ed.), *Music in therapy* (pp. 152–156). New York: Macmillan.

Herron, C. J. (1970). Some effects of instrumental music training on cerebral palsied children. *Journal of Music Therapy, 7*, 55–58.

Heylmun, J. W. (1952). Music to aid the handicapped child. *Music Therapy 1951: Book of proceedings of the National Association for Music Therapy*, 17–18.

Holloway, M. S. (1980). A comparison of passive and active music reinforcement to increase preacademic and motor skills in severly retarded children and adolescents. *Journal of Music Therapy, 17*, 58–69.

Inman, D. P. (1976). *Using biofeedback to establish stimulus control in spastic muscles.* Unpublished doctoral dissertation, University of Oregon, Eugene.

James, M. R. (1986). Neurophysiological treatment of cerebral palsy: A case study. *Music Therapy Perspectives, 3*, 5–8.

James, M. R., Weaver, A. L., Clemens, P. D., & Plaster, G. A. (1985). Influence of paired auditory and vestibular stimulation on levels of motor skill development in mentally retarded population. *Journal of Music Therapy, 22*, 22–34.

Jellison, J. A. (1977). Music instructional programs for the severly handicapped. In E. Sontag (Ed.), *Educational programing for the severely and profoundly handicapped* (pp. 250–259). Reston, VA: Council for Exceptional Children, Division of Mental Retardation.

Jenkins, M. A. (1974). *The use of rhythm instrument training to improve arm and hand function in physically handicapped mentally retarded adolescents and adults.* Unpublished master's thesis. California State University, Long Beach.

Josepha, Sister M. (1961). Music therapy with certain physically handicapped children. *Music Therapy 1960: Book of proceedings of the National Association for Music Therapy*, 90–96.

Josepha, Sister M. (1964). Therapeutic values of instrumental performance for severely handicapped children. *Journal of Music Therapy, 1*, 73–79.

Josepha, Sister M. (1968). Music therapy for the physically disabled. In E. T. Gaston (Ed.), *Music in therapy* (pp. 110–135). New York: Macmillan.

Karper, W. B. (1979). Effects of music on learning a motor skill by handicapped and non-handicapped boys. *Perceptual and Motor Skills, 49*, 734.

Karper, W. B., & Gym C. (1982). Effects of music on motor performance by learning disabled children in elementary school. *International Journal of Rehabilitation Research, 5*(1), 74–75.

Kaslow, F. W. (1974). Movement, music and art therapy techniques adapted for special education. In R. Hyatt & N. Rolnick (Eds.), *Teaching the mentally handicapped child* (pp. 233–248). New York: Behavioral Publications.

Kearney, S., & Fussey, I. (1991). The use of adapted leisure materials to reinforce correct head positioning in a brain-injured adult. *Brain Injury, 5*(3), 295–302.

Kelly, M. E. (1959). Music with the spastics. *Music in Education, 176.*

Kennard, D. (1983). A touch of music for physiotherapists. *Physiotherapy, 69*, 114–116.

Kennard, D., & Gilbertson, M. (1979). *Music to help disabled children to move* (2nd ed.). W. Yorkshire, England: Association of Paediatric Chartered Physiotherapists.

Korson, F. (1959). Canadian pilot study in music therapy with muscular dystrophy children. *Canadian Journal of Occupational Therapy, 26*, 45–49.

Kozak, Y. A. (1968). Music therapy for orthopedic patients in a rehabilitative setting. In E. T. Gaston (Ed.), *Music in therapy* (pp. 166–168). New York: Macmillan.

Krout, R. (1987). Music therapy with multihandicapped students: Individualizing treatment with a group setting. *Journal of Music Therapy, 24,* 2–13.

Kurz, C. E. (1962). Some considerations for music therapy with epileptic patients. *Music Therapy 1961: Book of proceedings of the National Association for Music Therapy,* 105–108.

Lapp, N. S. (1978). Music activities to aid perceptual-motor development in the perceptually underdeveloped. *Mental Retardation, 16,* 59–60.

Larson, B. A. (1978). Use of the Motorvator in improving gross-motor coordination, visual perception and IQ scores: A pilot study. *Journal of Music Therapy, 15,* 145–149.

Lathom, W. B. (1961). The use of music with cerebral palsied children during activities involving physical control. *Bulletin of the National Association for Music Therapy, 10,* 10–16.

Lathom, W. B. (1980). *The role of the music therapist in the education of severely and profoundly handicapped children and youth* (Grant. No. G007091336). Washington, DC: Bureau of Education for the Handicapped.

Lee, M. H. M. (1985). Music therapy for rehabilitation of the severely disabled: A model of excellence. *Music Education for the Handicapped Bulletin, 1,* 44–49.

Lesak, E. (1952). Rhythm and movement. *Music Therapy 1951: Book of proceedings of the National Association for Music Therapy,* 49–51.

Leventhal, M. B. (1977). Movement therapy with minimal brain dysfunction children. In K. C. Mason (Ed.), *Dance therapy: Focus on Dance VII,* (pp. 42–48). Washington, DC: American Alliance for Health, Physical Education, and Recreation.

Levitt, S. (1982). *Treatment of cerebral palsy and motor delay* (2nd ed.). Boston: Blackwell Scientific Publications.

Licht, S. H. (1946). *Music in medicine.* Boston: New England Conservatory of Music.

Madsen, C. K. (1981). *Music therapy: A behavioral guide for the mentally retarded.* Lawrence, KS: Meseraull Printing.

Mason, C. (1978). Musical activities with elderly patients. *Physiotherapy, 64,* 80–82.

Maxham, G. (1952). Demonstration rhythm techniques. *Music Therapy 1951: Book of proceedings of the National Association for Music Therapy,* 52–53.

May, E. (1956). Music for children with cerebral palsy. *American Journal of Physical Medicine, 35,* 320–323.

McIntosh, G., Thaut, M., Rice, R., & Prassas, S. (1993). Auditory rhythmic cueing in gait rehabilitation with stroke patients. *Canadian Journal of Neurological Sciences, 20*(4), 168.

Michel, D. E. (1976). *Music therapy: An introduction to therapy and special education through music.* Springfield, IL: Charles C. Thomas.

Miller, K. J. (1979). *Treatment with music: A manual for allied health professionals.* Kalamazoo, MI: Western Michigan University Printing Dept.

Milligan, E. (1986). Will you join in the dance? *Physiotherapy, 72,* 475–478.

Mroczek, N. S. (1976). *A treatise on psychology and voluntary motor behavior with an investigation of biofeedback effects on hemiplegias resultant from cerebrovascular accident.* Unpublished doctoral dissertation, University of Minnesota, St. Paul.

Myers, A. (1954). *Music as a therapeutic agent in the rehabilitation of physically handicapped children with special reference to cerebral palsy and a survey of music education and music therapy in facilities educating physically handicapped children.* Unpublished doctoral dissertation, Iowa State University, Ames. (University Microfilms No. 10232)

Myers, A. (1955). Music education and music therapy in facilities educating physically handicapped children. *Bulletin of the National Association for Music Therapy, 4,* 7–8.

Nafpliotis, H. (1976). Electromyographic feedback to improve ankle dorsiflexion, wrist extension, and hand grasp. *Physical Therapy, 56,* 821–825.

Nelson, D. L., Anderson, V. G., & Gonzales, A. D. (1984). Music activities as therapy for children with autism and other pervasive developmental disorders. *Journal of Music Therapy, 21,* 100–116.

Nordholm, H. (1954). Music for the cerebral palsied child. *Music Therapy 1953: Book of proceedings of the National Association for Music Therapy,* 91–94.

Olson, K. (1984). Player piano music as therapy for the elderly. *Journal of Music Therapy, 21*(1), 35–45.

Palmer, M. D. (1977). Music therapy in a comprehensive program of treatment and rehabilitation for the geriatric resident. *Journal of Music Therapy, 14,* 190–197.

Palmer, M. F. (1953). Musical stimuli in cerebral palsy, aphasia and similar conditions. *Music Therapy 1952: Book of proceedings of the National Association for Music Therapy,* 162–168.

Palmer, M. F., & Zerbe, L. E. (1945). Control of athetotic tremor by sound stimuli. *Journal of Speech Disorders, 10,* 303–319.

Petersen, E. D. (1952). Music to aid the mentally handicapped. *Music Therapy 1951: Book of proceedings of the National Association for Music Therapy,* 19–21.

Phillips, J. R. (1980). Music in the nursing of elderly persons in nursing homes. *Journal of Gerontological Nursing, 6,* 37–39.

Pickett, M. (1978). A one-day conference on music therapy for mental and physical handicaps. A report. *British Journal of Music Therapy, 9,* 13–17.

Proietto, D. (1977). Music in rehabilitation. *British Journal of Music Therapy, 8,* 2–7.

Quinto, L. (1952). Scope of the hospital music program and professional opportunities in Veterans Administration hospitals. *Music Therapy 1951: Book of proceedings of the National Association for Music Therapy,* 70–72.

Reeves, V. (1952). Music to aid the handicapped child. *Music Therapy 1951: Book of proceedings of the National Association for Music Therapy,* 10–15.

Rider, M. S. (1985). Entrainment mechanisms are involved in pain reduction, muscle relaxation, and music-mediated imagery. *Journal of Music Therapy, 22,* 183–192.

Roan, M. Z. (1952a). Music can help the crippled child. *Crippled Child, 29,* 10–11, 28–29.

Roan, M. Z. (1952b). Music to aid the handicapped child. *Music Therapy 1951: Book of proceedings of the National Association for Music Therapy,* 26–33.

Rogers, L. (1968). Music therapy in a state hospital for crippled children. In E. T. Gaston (Ed.), *Music in therapy* (pp. 156–159). New York: Macmillan.

Rudenberg, M. T. (1984). Music therapy for orthopedically handicapped children. In W. B. Lathom & C. T. Eagle, Jr. (Eds.), *Music therapy for handicapped children: Project music monograph series* (pp. 37–116). Lawrence, KS: Meseraull Printing.

Safranek, M. G., Koshland, G. F., & Raymond, G. (1982). Effect of auditory rhythm on muscle activity. *Physical Therapy, 62,* 161–168.

Salomon, E. J. (1972). Music and gymnastics for toddlers. *Rehabilitation Record, 13*, 37.

Scartelli, J. P. (1982). The effect of sedative music on electromyographic biofeedback assisted relaxation training of spastic cerebral palsied adults. *Journal of Music Therapy, 19*, 210–218.

Schmais, C. (1977). Dance therapy in perspective. In K. C. Mason (Ed.), *Dance therapy: Focus on Dance VII* (pp. 7–12). Washington, DC: American Alliance for Health, Physical Education, and Recreation.

Schneider, C. W. (1961). The effects of Dalcroze eurhythmics upon the motor processes of schizophrenics. *Music Therapy 1960: Book of proceedings of the National Association for Music Therapy*, 132–140.

Schneider, E. H. (1954). The use of music with the brain damaged child. *Music Therapy 1953: Book of proceedings of the National Association for Music Therapy*, 95–98.

Schneider, E. H. (1956). Music therapy research for physically handicapped. *Music Therapy 1955: Book of proceedings of the National Association for Music Therapy*, 183–188.

Schneider, E. H. (1957a). New concepts in the uses of music with cerebral palsied children. *Music Therapy 1956: Book of proceedings of the National Association for Music Therapy*, 153–155.

Schneider, E. H. (1957b). Relationships between musical experiences and certain aspects of cerebral palsied children's performance on selected tasks. *Music Therapy 1956: Book of proceedings of the National Association for Music Therapy*, 250–277.

Schneider, E. H. (1961). Music for the cerebral palsied child. *Music Therapy 1960: Book of proceedings of the National Association for Music Therapy*, 97–100.

Schneider, E. H. (1968). Music therapy for the cerebral palsied. In E. T. Gaston (Ed.), *Music in therapy* (pp. 136–151). New York: Macmillan.

Schoenberger, L., & Braswell, C. (1971). Music therapy in rehabilitation. *Journal of Rehabilitation, 37*, 30–31.

Schwankovsky, L. M., & Guthrie, P.T. (1984). Music therapy for other health impaired children. In W. B. Lathom & C. T. Eagle, Jr. (Eds.), *Music therapy for handicapped children: Project music monograph series*, (pp. 119–173). Lawrence, KS: Meseraull Printing.

Shapiro, A. (1969). A pilot program in music therapy with residents of a home for the aged. *Gerontologist, 9*, 128–133.

Shatin, L., Kotter, W. L., & Douglas-Longmore, G. (1962). Music therapy for schizophrenics. *Music Therapy 1961: Book of proceedings of the National Association for Music Therapy*, 99–104.

Sheerenberger, R. (1953). Description of a music program at a residential school for the mentally handicapped. *American Journal of Mental Deficiency, 57*, 573–579.

Smith, O. S. (1953). Music methods and materials for the mentally retarded. *Music Therapy 1952: Book of proceedings of the National Association for Music Therapy*, 139–144.

Snow, W. B., & Fields, B. (1950). Music as an adjunct in the training of children with cerebral palsy. *Occupational Therapy and Rehabilitation, 29*, 147–156.

Standley, J. M. (1986). Music research in medical/dental treatment: Meta-analysis and clinical applications. *Journal of Music Therapy, 23*, 56–122.

Staum, M. J. (1983). Music and rhythmic stimuli in the rehabilitation of gait disorders. *Journal of Music Therapy, 20*, 69–87.

Tanner, D. R., & O'Briant, R. M. (1980). Music can color a graying America. *Music Educators Journal, 67*, 28–30.

Taylor, E. J. (1950). Music as an adjunct to therapy. *Crippled Child, 28*, 8–10, 28–29.

Thaut, M. (1984). A music therapy treatment model for autistic children. *Music Therapy Perspectives, 1*(4), 7–13.

Thaut, M. (1985). The use of auditory rhythm and rhythmic speech to aid temporal muscular control in children with gross motor dysfunction. *Journal of Music Therapy, 22*(3), 108–128.

Thaut, M., McIntosh, G., Prassas, S., & Rice, R. (1992a). Effect of auditory rhythmic pacing on normal gait and gait in stroke, cerebellar disorder, and transverse myelitis. In M. Woollacott and F. Horak (Eds.), *Posture and Gait: Control Mechanisms* (Vol. 2, pp. 437–440). Eugene, OR: University of Oregon.

Thaut, M., McIntosh, G., Prassas, S., & Rice, R. (1992b). The effect of rhythmic auditory cuing on temporal stride and EMG patterns in normal gait. *Journal of Neurologic Rehabilitation, 6*, 185–190.

Thaut, M., Schleiffers, S., & Davis, W. (1991). Analysis of EMG activity in biceps and triceps muscle in an upper extremity gross motor task under the influence of auditory rhythm. *Journal of Music Therapy, 28*(2), 64–88.

Thaut, M., Schleiffers, S., & Davis, W. (1992). Changes in EMG patterns under the influence of auditory rhythm. In R. Spintge & R. Droh (Eds.), *MusicMedicine* (pp. 80–101). St. Louis: MMB Music, Inc. [Reprint of 1991 JMT article.]

Toombs, M. R., Walker, J., & Bonny, H. (1965). Dance therapy with retarded adolescents. *Journal of Music Therapy, 2*, 115–117.

Van de Wall, W. (1946). *Music in hospitals.* New York: Russell Sage Foundation.

Verdeau-Paillès, J. (1985). Music and the body. *Music Education for the Handicapped Bulletin, 1*, 8–21.

Walmsley, R. P., Chrichton, L., & Droog, D. (1981). Music as a feedback mechanism for teaching head control to severely handicapped children: A pilot study. *Developmental Medicine and Child Neurology, 23*, 739–746.

Weigl, V. (1954). Music as an adjunctive therapy in the training of children with cerebral palsy. *Cerebral Palsy Review, 15*, 9–10.

Weigl, V. (1955). Functional music with cerebral palsied children. *Music Therapy 1954; Book of proceedings of the National Association for Music Therapy*, 135–143.

Weigl, V. (1963). The rhythmic approach in music therapy. *Music Therapy 1962: Book of proceedings of the National Association for Music Therapy*, 71–80.

Weisbrod, J. A. (1972). Shaping a body image through movement therapy. *Music Educators Journal, 58*, 66–69.

Wells, A. M. (1954). Rhythm activities on wards of senile patients. *Music Therapy 1953: Book of proceedings of the National Association for Music Therapy*, 127–132.

Wolfe, D. E. (1978). Pain rehabilitation and music therapy. *Journal of Music Therapy, 15*, 162–178.

Wolfe, D. E. (1980). The effect of automated interrupted music on head posturing of cerebral palsied individuals. *Journal of Music Therapy, 17*, 184–206.

Wooldridge, C. P., Leiper, C., & Ogston, D. G. (1976). Biofeedback training of knee joint position of the cerebral palsied child. *Physiotherapy Canada, 28*, 138–143.

Related References

Anshel, M. H., & Marisi, D. Q. (1978). Effect of music and rhythm on physical performance. *Research Quarterly, 49*, 109–113.

Bailey, C. (1975). Curriculum guidelines for teaching profound and severely retarded students (I.Q. under 40), including those with physical handicaps. *American Association for the Education of the Severely/Profoundly Handicapped Review, 1*, 1–17.

Beisman, G. L. (1967). Effect of rhythmic accompaniment upon learning of fundamental motor skills. *Research Quarterly, 38*, 172–176.

Bond, M. H. (1959). Rhythmic perception and gross motor performance. *Research Quarterly, 30*, 259–265.

Boswell, B., & Vidret, M. (1993). Rhythmic movement and music for adolescents with severe and profound disabilities. *Music Therapy Perspectives, 11*(1), 37–41.

Boyle, C. M. (1954). Dalcroze eurhythmics and the spastic. *Spastics' Quarterly, 3*, 5–8.

Brackbill, Y., Adams, G., Crowell, D. H., & Gray, M. L. (1966). Arousal level in neonates and preschool children under continuous auditory stimulation. *Journal of Experimental Child Psychology, 4*, 178–188.

Brown, J., Sherrill, C., & Gench, B. (1981). Effects of an integrated physical education/music program in changing early childhood perceptual-motor performance. *Perceptual and Motor Skills, 53*(1),151–154.

Burch, M., Clegg, J., & Bailey, J. (1987). Automated contingent reinforcement of correct posture. *Research in Developmental Disabilities, 8*(1), 151–154.

Canner, N. (1968). *And a time to dance*. Boston: Beacon Press.

Central Council for the Disabled (Disabled Living Activities Group). (1971). *Music and the physically handicapped: An enquiry*. London: Author.

Couper, J. L. (1981). Dance therapy: Effects on motor performance of children with learning disabilities. *Physical Therapy, 61*, 23–26.

Crane, L. M. (1955). *The role of music in the interests and activities of 95 former polio patients*. Unpublished master's thesis, University of Texas, Austin.

Cratty, B. J. (1969). *Motor activity and the education of retardates*. Philadelphia: Lea & Ferbiger.

Dainow, E. (1977). Physical effects and motor responses to music. *Journal of Research in Music Education, 25*, 211–221.

Davis, R. (1990). A model for the integration of music therapy within preschool classrooms for children with physical disabilities or language delays. *Music Therapy Perspectives, 8*, 82–84.

Davis, R. C. (1948). Motor effects of strong auditory stimuli. *Journal of Experimental Psychology, 38*, 257–275.

Delmas-Marsalet, P. (1971). Music and the physically handicapped. *British Hospital Journal and Social Service Review, 81*, 258–259.

Dillon, E. K. (1952). A study of the use of music as an aid in teaching swimming. *Research Quarterly, 23*, 1–8.

Ditson, R. (1961). A study of the effects of moderate background music on the behavior of cerebral palsied children. *Bulletin of the National Association for Music Therapy, 10*, 6.

Dorney, L., Goh, E., & Lee, C. (1992). The impact of music and imagery on physical performance and arousal: Studies of coordination and endurance. *Journal of Sport Behavior, 15*(1), 21–33.

Douglass, D. (1975). *Rhymes and rhythms*. Phoenix: O'Sullivan Wooside.

Elrod, J. M. (1972). *The effects of perceptual-motor training and music on perceptual-motor development and behavior of educable mentally retarded children*. Unpublished doctoral dissertation, Louisiana State University and Agricultural and Mechanical College, Baton Rouge. (University Microfilms No. 72–28338)

Evans, J. R. (1986). Dysrhythmia and disorders of learning and behavior. In J. R. Evans & M. Clynes (Eds.), *Rhythm in psychological, linguistic and musical processes* (pp. 249–274). Springfield, IL: Charles C. Thomas.

Field, T. M., Dempsey, J. R., Hatch, G. T., & Clifton, R. K. (1979). Cardiac and behavioral responses to repeated tactile and auditory stimulation by preterm and term neonates. *Developmental Psychology, 15*, 406–416.

Fitzpatrick, F. K. (1959). The use of rhythm in training severely subnormal patients. *American Journal of Mental Deficiency, 63*, 981–987.

Foss, J., Ison, J., Torre, J., & Wansack, S. (1989). The acoustic startle response and disruption of aiming: I. Effect of stimulus repetition, intensity, and intensity changes. *Human Factors, 31*(3), 307–318.

Gilbert, J. P. (1983). A comparison of the motor skills of nonhandicapped and learning disabled children. *Journal of Research in Music Education, 31*, 147–155.

Glassman, L. (1991). Music therapy and bibliotherapy in the rehabilitation of traumatic brain injury: A case study. *The Arts in Psychotherapy, 18*(2), 149–156.

Grove, D. N., Dalke, B. A., Fredericks, H. D., & Crowley, R. F. (1975). Establishing appropriate head positioning with mentally and physically handicapped children. *Behavioral Engineering, 3*, 53–59.

Groves, W. C. (1969). Rhythmic training and its relationship to the synchronization of motor-rhythmic responses. *Journal of Research in Music Education, 17*, 408–415.

Harrison, D., & Pauly, R. (1990). Manual dexterity, strength, fatigue, and preservation: An initial test of asymmetry in cerebral activation. *Perceptual and Motor Skills, 70*, 739–744.

Hecox, B., Levine, E., & Scott, D. (1975). A report on the use of dance in physical rehabilitation. *Rehabilitation Literature, 36*, 11–15.

Hecox, B., Levine, E., & Scott, D. (1976). Dance in physical rehabilitation. *Physical Therapy, 56*, 919–923.

Hibben, J. (1984). Movement as musical expression in a music therapy setting. *Music Therapy, 4*(1), 91–97.

Hibben, J., & Scheer, R. (1982). Music and movement for special needs children. *Teaching Exceptional Children, 14*(5), 171–176.

Jorgenson, H. (1974). The use of a contingent music activity to modify behaviors which interfere with learning. *Journal of Music Therapy, 11*, 41–46.

Kaernbach, C. (1992). On the consistency of tapping to repeated noise. *Journal of the Acoustical Society of America, 92*(2), 788–793.

Kukulka, C. G., & Basmajian, J. V. (1975). Assessment of an audio-visual feedback device used in motor training. *American Journal of Physical Medicine, 54*, 194–208.

Lucia, C. (1987). Toward developing a model of music therapy intervention in the rehabilitation of head trauma patients. *Music Therapy Perspectives, 4*, 34–39.

Madsen, C. K., & Wolfe, D. E. (1979). The effect of interrupted music and incompatible responses on bodily movement and music attentiveness. *Journal of Music Therapy, 16*, 17–30.

Marley, L. S. (1984). The use of music with hospitalized infants and toddlers: A descriptive study. *Journal of Music Therapy, 21*, 126–132.

Molander, B., & Backman, L. (1990). Age differences in the effects of background noise on motor and memory performance in a precision sport. *Experimental Aging Research, 16*(2), 55–60.

Neiman, Z. (1989). Teaching specific motor skills for conducting to young music students. *Perceptual and Motor Skills, 68*, 847–858.

Owens, L. D. (1979). The effects of music on the weight loss, crying, and physical movement of newborns. *Journal of Music Therapy, 16*, 83–90.

Probst, W. (1985). Instrumental lessons with handicapped children and youth. *Bulletin of the Council for Research in Music Education, 85*, 166–174.

Robins, F., & Robins, J. (1968). *Educational rhythmics for mentally and physically handicapped children*. New York: Association Press.

Ross, D. M., Ross, S. A., & Kuchenbecker, S. L. (1973). Rhythm training for educable mentally retarded children. *Mental Retardation, 11*, 20–23.

Rossignol, S., & Jones, G. M. (1976). Audiospinal influence in man studied by the H-reflex and its possible role on rhythmic movements synchronized to sound. *Electroencephalography and Clinical Neurophysiology, 41*, 83–92.

Scartelli, J. P. (1984). The effect of EMG biofeedback and sedative music, EMG biofeedback only, and sedative music only on frontalis muscle relaxation ability. *Journal of Music Therapy, 21*, 67–78.

Sears, W. W. (1958). The effect of music on muscle tonus. *Music Therapy 1957: Book of proceedings of the National Association for Music Therapy*, 199–205.

Sears, W. W. (1959). *A study of some effects of music upon muscle tension as evidenced by electromyographic recordings*. Unpublished doctoral dissertation, University of Kansas, Lawrence.

Sidnell, R. (1986). Motor learning in music education. *Psychomusicology, 6*(1–2). 7–18.

Sims, W. (1998). Movement responses of pre-school children, primary grade children, and pre-service classroom teachers to characteristics of musical phrases. *Psychology of Music, 16*(2), 110–127.

Singer, R. N. (1980). *Motor learning and human performance*. New York: Macmillan.

Slosarska, M. (1986). Non-specific physiological changes of depressed patients as manifested by reactions to simple stimuli. *International Journal of Psychosomatics, 33*(3), 17–20.

Sorkin, R., Wightman, F., Kistler, D., & Elvers, G. (1989). An exploratory study of the use of movement-correlated cues in an auditory head-up display. *Human Factors, 31*(2), 161–166.

Stack, D., Muir, D., Sherriff, F., & Roman, J. (1989). Development of infant reaching in the dark to luminous objects and 'invisible sounds'. *Perception, 18*(1), 69–82.

Starkes, J., Deakin, J., Lindley, S., & Crisp, F. (1987). Motor versus verbal recall of ballet sequences by young expert dancers. *Journal of Sport Psychology, 9*, 222–230.

Staum, M. J. (1981). An analysis of movement in therapy. *Journal of Music Therapy, 28*, 7–24.

Staum, M. J. (1992). The role of music therapy in physical rehabilitation. In R. Spintge & R. Droh (Eds.), *MusicMedicine* (pp. 267–270). St. Louis: MMB Music, Inc.

Stratford, B., & Ching, E. (1989). Responses to music and movement in the development of children with Down's syndrome. *Journal of Mental Deficiency Research, 33*, 13–24.

Sutton, K. (1984). The development and implementation of a music therapy physiological measures test. *Journal of Music Therapy, 21*(4), 160–169.

Tarkka, I., Treede, R-D., & Bromm, B. (1992). Sensory and movement-related cortical potentials in nociceptive and auditory reaction time tasks. *Acta-Neurologica Scandinavica, 86*, 359–364.

Tarquinio, N., Zelazo, P., & Weill, M. (1990). Recovery of neonatal head turning to decreased sound pressure level. *Developmental Psychology, 26*(5), 752–758.

Thaut, M. (1988). Rhythmic intervention techniques in music therapy with gross motor dysfunctions. *The Arts in Psychotherapy, 15*(2), 127–137.

Thaut, M. (1990). Physiological and motor responses to music stimuli. In R. F. Unkefer (Ed.), *Music therapy in the treatment of adults with mental disorders* (pp. 33–49). New York: Schirmer Books.

Thompson, M. F. (1952). Scope of the hospital music program and professional opportunities in the northeastern states. *Music Therapy 1951: Book of proceedings of the National Association for Music Therapy*, 87–110.

Wolfe, D. E. (1982). The effect of interrupted and continuous music on body movement and task performance of third grade students. *Journal of Music Therapy, 19*, 74–85.

GROUP MUSIC THERAPY IN
ACUTE MENTAL HEALTH CARE: MEETING THE
DEMANDS OF EFFECTIVENESS AND EFFICIENCY

David E. Wolfe

IT has been estimated that 39 million citizens are presently unable to afford health care in the United States. This discouraging statistic would seem to be a result of the costs associated with the delivery of physical and mental health care that have increased much more dramatically than other consumer prices during more recent decades, making it impossible for many Americans to pay for these services directly or indirectly through the purchase of insurance premiums. Due to the ever-increasing costs of providing health care and the lack of affordable coverage for so many persons, national debate over health care reform continues today unabated. Currently there are legislative efforts at both the national and state levels of government to provide affordable access to health care. Some proposals, if passed, would guarantee health services to every American regardless of age, illness, social status, or ability to pay. These efforts of providing health benefits to all citizens would significantly increase the demand for health care. The advent of such a universal delivery system(s) would necessitate that it be carefully managed, since a limit on total spending for both private and public health care would most likely be instituted in order to keep health care costs in line with economic growth. These efforts at cost containment may place health care providers, music therapists included, in a position of competing for the opportunity to treat clients in the most cost-effective way (Clark & Ficken, 1988; Dziwak & Gfeller, 1988).

Trends in the delivery of mental health services during the past four decades have reflected a move toward community-based care with increasing use of general hospital psychiatric units, private psychiatric hospitals, and community mental health centers to provide both inpatient and outpatient treatment (Thompson, Bass, & Witkin, 1982). Today there are more acute admissions to these facilities with a corresponding decrease in hospital stay. This trend has been given impetus not only by an increase in the number of less seriously mentally ill patients who require shorter periods of treatment, but also by private and public health care providers that include time constraints on reimbursement claims for psychiatric care. Experts also estimate that 22% of the population, at any given time, is in need of mental health services, and with the population itself increasing, a continual trend toward short-term care would seem inevitable to keep up with the burgeoning need.

Because of ever-increasing demand and economic constraints in paying for health care delivery, including mental health provisions, renewed attention is being focused on services that are not only effective but also efficient. In acute psychiatric care, group compared to individual treatment, would seem to comply with these current health care concerns. Short-term groups provide treatment "in numbers" and can be more economical, yet often times more beneficial therapeutically, than other traditional treatment methods. Therefore the primary purpose of this chapter will be to delineate a particular form of group therapy, i.e., group music therapy, and provide a model of this unique service that meets the concerns for time-constrained and yet effective treatment. In accomplishing this objective, it will be necessary to identify the kinds of services rendered and to describe some of the groups that may be designed and conducted by a music therapist working within short-term psychiatric rehabilitation. It should be emphasized that the groups outlined below do not represent a comprehensive menu of all possible groups that may be conducted in music therapy. Instead, they are presented as examples of how these groups may be arranged and structured to assist music therapists in complying with the current trends in mental health delivery.

Group Treatment and Music Therapy

Clinical practice with short-term, acute care groups places less emphasis on traditional intra-psychic concepts of illness and more on an *interactional* paradigm. Christman (1967) states that therapists today are thinking, talking, and treating largely in social system terms, i.e., terms of learning, communication, social role, and small group theory. This is certainly true for music therapists conducting groups in which clients are helped to explore problems and to develop functional, relevant skills which can assist them in daily living (Bryant, 1987; Jellison, 1983; Robbins, 1966; Rubin, 1975).

Most acute care groups share some common characteristics. First of all, membership in these groups is brief, often diverse with respect to individual levels of functioning, and usually includes 6–9 members. Even with diversity, however, higher functioning patients may serve as appropriate models of effective interpersonal behavior for lower functioning group members. Patients are usually referred to these particular groups by attending physicians or recommended for referral by a multidisciplinary treatment team. Regular attendance is expected with sessions usually conducted on a daily basis, since an average inpatient hospital stay may only involve two to four weeks of care. Intensive, time-limited treatment is not only feasible but required in acute psychiatric treatment.

Most therapists would agree that the ultimate goal of short-term treatment is to facilitate the patient's return to the community through assisting the person with learning skills for coping with the society in which he/she must live. Other goals linked to group therapy may include helping members to recognize their own maladaptive behavior and to avert situations which may support them, and to realize that their problems are not unique. Group therapists also encourage members to give as well as receive support from others within the group (Maves & Schultz, 1985; Maxmen, 1973). Still other group goals include promoting success through presentation of tasks, reducing anxiety, solving of problems, giving of practical advice and exploring community resources (Yalom, 1983).

Therapists of short-term acute care groups use therapeutic techniques that initiate, facilitate, and encourage communication, as they support, reinforce and consensually validate the normal aspects of a patient's behavior (Maves & Schultz, 1985). Music therapists are well versed in using these techniques, and employ *content* and *affective* verbal responses necessary in helping group members to clarify and understand interpersonal interactions, and to identify the feelings associated with patients' verbalizations. The effective uses of *influencing, advice giving* and *questioning* responses, as well as the importance of non-verbal attending behavior (eye contact, postural positions, gestural and facial expressions, appropriate vocal quality) are all part of a therapeutic regimen used by music therapists in conducting short-term groups (Alpaugh & Haney, 1978; Carkhuff, 1969; Danish, D'Augelli, & Hauer, 1980; Egan, 1975; Gerrard, Boniface, & Love, 1980; Hanser, 1984; Morgenstern, 1982; Okun, 1976; Plack, 1980; Wheeler, 1983). Effective group leaders also employ supportive and reinforcing statements that are brief, simple, and clearly understood; these statements are directed toward observable behavior and toward discussion of current issues relevant to group members. Many of the verbal techniques used within acute care groups are similar regardless of the professional person(s) or discipline(s) that may use them. However, an examination of the specific services and kinds of treatment groups unique to music therapy would seem important.

Scope of Music Therapy Services

Therapeutic activity disciplines are currently being asked by various accrediting agencies to describe the scope or range of services provided to various clients, and to clearly delineate their major divisions of treatment (Lang & Mattson, 1985). Each is now being required to develop treatment services tailored to specific client problems. Based on current literature, as well as prevalent clinical practices in group music therapy, major *service components* (I), and major *divisions of treatment* (II) in short-term psychiatric care are illustrated in Figure 1. Service components of (a) assessment, (b) treatment/skills training, (c) monitoring/evaluation, and (d) discharge planning are common to music therapists involved in group work. Assessing the client in relationship to divisions of treatment, teaching of functional skills necessary for dealing with the demands of daily living, monitoring and evaluating client progress in various areas of treatment, and preparing the client for a return to the community are crucial to effective music therapy clinical group practice. The areas of assessment, monitoring/evaluation, and discharge planning will be briefly examined below, while skills training (the major divisions of group music therapy treatment) will receive a more extensive discussion in a succeeding section.

Assessment[1]

Assessment, the initial step involved in treatment planning, refers to the collection and processing of selected data that enables the identification of behavioral problems, as well as behavioral strengths of the patient (Galasso, 1987). This process is often necessary to securing reimbursement for services provided to the patient and for meeting accreditation requirements.

---

[1]The term *assessment* is used throughout this article when making reference to tests or examinations given at the time of hospital admission, or *prior to treatment* (and typically used as pre-post measures in intervention), while *monitoring/evaluation,* also a form of assessment, is used when referring to tests or observation procedures employed to determine client progress *during* or *throughout* treatment.

GROUP MUSIC THERAPY

I. Service Components

Assessment
Treatment/Skills Training
Monitoring/Evaluation
Discharge Planning

II. Division of Treatment

Relaxation/Anxiety Management Skills	Verbal/Interaction Skills	Leisure/Community Skills

III. Patient Problems

Relaxation/Anxiety Management Skills	Verbal/Interaction Skills	Leisure/Community Skills
Inability to relax Inability to concentrate Inability to deal with stressful situations	Inability to express self adequately Unable to express emotions appropriately	Unable to use leisure time Social isolation Unable to have fun Unable to try new experiences

IV. Treatment Goals

Relaxation/Anxiety Management Skills	Verbal/Interaction Skills	Leisure/Community Skills
Know process of progressive relaxation Select appropriate music for relaxation Recognize stressful situations	Increase self-expression Improve ability to express anger	Provide successful experience Increase self-esteem Increase motivation

Figure 1
Outline of group music therapy

Physical, emotional, intellectual, and social aspects of the patient are initially assessed utilizing subjective information obtained from the verbal reports of the patient's family members and/or significant others, as well as objective data obtained through systematic observation and examination of the patient. Most often these initial tests are conducted by the admitting physician, social worker, nurse practitioner, and/or psychologist, and include such information as the patient's social and medical history, physical and neurological examinations, laboratory and x-ray exams, a mental status test, and other psychological testings (Rowe, 1984).

Since a patient may have been seen by a psychiatrist prior to hospitalization, much of the assessment information may have already been completed and will appear in the patient's medical record at the time of admission. It may not be necessary for the music therapist to always be involved with conducting initial assessment procedures. This would only seem to be a "duplication of service" and an unnecessary expense. When information pertaining to diagnosis and the presenting problems of the patient has already been identified prior to hospitalization, the treatment team, including the music therapist, can focus immediately on determining a treatment plan for the patient, since time is of utmost importance in short-term care. Or additionally, when the presenting problem is related to one of the areas of music therapy treatment (e.g., relaxation/anxiety management, verbal/interaction, leisure/community skills), the music therapist can assess (after the client has been referred to music therapy) the functioning level of the patient as it relates to one or more of these particular areas (see Figure 2).

Figure 3 provides an example of a music therapy relaxation/stress management assessment. This initial music therapy assessment can provide important baseline data relevant to the commencement of treatment, and can also provide material valuable in constructing an individualized treatment plan. Assessment instruments can include those that are constructed by the music therapist (like the one in Figure 3), or other standardized tests: State-Trait Anxiety Inventory (Spielberger, Gorsuch, & Lushene, 1968), Fear Survey Schedule (Wolpe & Lang, 1964), Life Experiences Survey (Sarason, Johnson, & Siegel, 1978), and behavioral observations (Hanser, Larson, & O'Connell, 1983) which examine sources of anxiety and stress; the Simulated Social Interaction Test (Curran, 1982), Profile of Mood States (McNair, Lorr, & Droppelman, 1971), Beck Depression Inventory (Beck, Rush, Shaw, & Emery, 1979), Social Interaction Self-Statement Test (Glass, Merluzzi, Biever, & Larsen, 1982) which relate to social interaction skills; and the Music/Activity Therapy Intake Assessment (Braswell, Brooks, Decuir, Humphrey, Jacobs, & Sutton, 1983), Life Skills Assessment (Farkas, 1980), Reinforcement Survey Schedule (Cautela & Kastenbaum, 1967), Pleasant Events Schedule (MacPhillamy & Lewinsohn, 1971), and the Time Sample Behavior Checklist (Paul & Lentz, 1977), which examine leisure/community skills, and the Self-monitoring Scale (James, 1986).

The primary intent of assessment at the time of admission is to establish a diagnosis and to assist in the process of *problem identification.* Describing the presenting problem in behavioral terms can assist in delineating what the patient is actually doing that is maladaptive and is a prerequisite to establishing treatment goals and objectives. Galasso (1987) states that diagnosis alone cannot be considered a problem statement because a diagnosis represents a group of behaviors within which each individual patient may show considerable behavioral variations. She further illustrates that a patient, for example, with a diagnosis of undifferentiated schizophrenia may be withdrawn and isolative, while another may exhibit pacing and appear agitated. Still others may have hallucinations yet no delusions and vice versa.

REFERRAL FORM
MUSIC THERAPY SERVICES

Patient Name_____ Date of Birth_____

Physician_____ Room #_____

Admission Date_____ Expected Date of Discharge_____

Diagnosis_____

Precautions_____
_____
****
Presenting Problem(s):_____
_____
_____
_____
_____
_____
****
RECOMMENDED SERVICES (Check all that apply)

ASSESSMENT

_____ Relaxation/Stress Management
_____ Verbal/Interaction
_____ Leisure/Community

TREATMENT

_____ Relaxation/Stress Management Skills
_____ Self-Expression/Verbal Interaction Skills
_____ Leisure/Community
_____ Discharge Planning

****
Additional Comments:_____
_____
_____
_____

Referred by_____ Phone_____
Date_____

Figure 2
Referral form: Music therapy services

MUSIC THERAPY SERVICES
RELAXATION/STRESS MANAGEMENT ASSESSMENT

Date:_____
Name:_____ Age:_____ Sex:_____

PLEASE ANSWER THESE QUESTIONS AS COMPLETELY AS POSSIBLE. If additional space for comments is needed, please use the back of this form.

Music Preference

1. What types of music do you enjoy *listening* to? (please circle all that apply)

Rock and Roll	Pop	Classical	New Age	Religious
Bluegrass	Country	Jazz	Blues	Choral
Gospel		Alternative		Ethnic
Other_____				None

2. List three of your favorite musical groups and/or songs:
_____

3. What types of music do you find *relaxing*? (please circle all that apply)

Rock and Roll	Pop	Classical	New Age	Religious
Bluegrass	Country	Jazz	Blues	Choral
Gospel		Alternative		Ethnic
Other_____				None

Music Interests

4. What instrument(s) have you played? (please check all that apply)

   None_____
   Guitar_____   Piano_____
   Woodwind instrument (clarinet, flute, oboe, bassoon)_____
   Brass (trumpet, trombone, tuba)_____
   Percussion_____   Drums_____
   Orchestral strings (violin, viola, bass, cello)_____
   Electric (guitar, bass, keyboard)_____
   Other_____

5. Which of the above instruments do you find relaxing to play?

_____

Stressful Situations

6. Occasionally, people experience anxiety. In your case, what kinds of situations cause you to feel anxious? (list three, if possible)

(a)_____(b)_____(c)_____

7. What causes this anxiety?

_____

_____

8. How frequently do these anxiety-producing situations occur? (please circle)

      once/week   2-3/week   4-5/week   more than 5 per week

9. How do you relieve anxiety in these particular situations?

_____

_____

10. Occasionally, people feel angry. What kinds of situations make you feel angry? (list three, if possible) (a)_____

(b)_____(c)_____

11. What causes this anger?

_____

_____

12. How frequently do these anger-producing situations occur? (please circle)

      once/week   2-3/week   4-5/week   more than 5 per week

13. How do you relieve anger in these particular situations?

_____

_____

Coping Mechanisms

18. People deal with stress in many different ways. Place a check beside each of the following items that you use to cope with stress:

elevil____	television____	xanex____	others_____
smoking____	alcohol____	exercise____	_____
codeine____	meditation____	eating____	
physical work____	music____	valium____	

19. What musical activities help you relieve stress? (please circle)

Dancing	Listening to music	Attending concerts
Composing music	Playing instruments	Other_____

Sleeping Routine

20. How many hours a night do you usually sleep? _____

21. Has your sleep pattern changed recently? Yes_____ No_____
    How?_____

22. How rested do you feel after sleeping? (please check)
    Completely rested_____   Somewhat rested_____
    A little rested_____   Not at all rested_____

23. How often do you nap during the day? (please circle)
    once/day   2-3/day   4-5/day   more than 5 per day

Previous Therapy Experience

24. Have you attended Music Therapy sessions before? Yes_____ No_____
    When?_____
    What was the purpose of these sessions?_____
    In your opinion, was this purpose (circle one) (a) completely accomplished,
    (b) somewhat accomplished, (c) not at all accomplished

25. Have you attended stress management and/or relaxation seminars or groups before?
    No_____ Yes_____   When?_____
    Did you learn (circle one) (a) a great deal, (b) some things, (c) very little

26. Who in your life would be willing to support you in relaxation efforts when you are
    not attending therapy sessions? (circle all that apply) (a) spouse, (b) significant other,
    (c) friend, (d) relative, (e) other_____, (f) no one

Opinions

27. What do you think you will accomplish by attending Music Therapy
    sessions?_____

28. What do you want to accomplish from attending Music Therapy
    sessions?_____

29. Are you willing to commit yourself to attending (5) sessions a week in the pursuit of
    goals and objectives set by yourself and the music therapist?   Yes_____ No_____

This assessment form was adapted from one developed by Deans, C., Harkvoort, L., Macfarlane, C., Stewart-Cline, M., Toppozada, M. (1994).

Figure 3
Music Therapy Relaxation/Stress Management Assessment

Developing a problem statement requires the diagnosis to be broken down into specific behavioral components that can then be treated. Problem statements may resemble those stated below:

- The patient exhibits hallucinations as evidenced by talking and laughing to himself when alone.
- The patient is socially isolated as evidenced by seldom going out of the house, frequently watching television, and rarely talking to anyone.

Once the presenting problem(s) has been identified, the treatment team, as well as individual therapeutic disciplines, is prepared to formulate treatment goals and objectives. At this time the music therapist arranges a *pregroup interview* with the client. During this individual meeting, the therapist not only explores with the client his/her past musical interests and current music preferences, concerns and expectations, but also engages the client in verbalizing problems and assists the patient in defining them in terms of overt behaviors. The purposes and procedures employed in group music therapy are explained, and individual treatment objectives delineated. A behavioral contract (see Figure 4) is then presented to the client. The written document specifies what the client can expect from the therapist and what the therapist expects from the client during the course of treatment. The contract is agreed upon by both parties or can be renegotiated by mutual agreement (Rose, 1977).

Monitoring/Evaluation

Music therapists routinely collect, graph, and analyze data related to stated behavioral objectives (Gregory, 1977; Madsen, 1980; Wolfe, 1987). Through precise behavioral definitions, observation and recording procedures, and the use of visual graphic representations of the data, music therapists are able to determine when a treatment program is working or when it is ineffective, thereby necessitating a revision in treatment. Rate, duration, latency, accuracy and/or task analysis data are familiar to music therapists in group practice, and behavioral research designs can be employed when necessary to determine if the planned intervention is actually responsible for patient progress.

Sessions may be conducted by co-therapists, one primarily responsible for conducting the music therapy group, while the other therapist records and compiles individual and/or group data as necessary. Since observing and measuring, that is, assigning numerical values to the frequency, intensity, duration, or appropriateness of clients' behavior can consume considerable amounts of time on the part of the therapist, the use of self-monitoring procedures in music therapy can be easily taught, and can give the clients the responsibility for the gathering of data (see Figure 5). Through self-monitoring, the client becomes responsible for describing behavior (e.g., in a diary), rating it with scales concerned with the relative importance of the problem, and making the behavior amenable to counting (Rose, 1977). Other purposes of self-recording can be to assist in establishing a baseline, to serve as a therapeutic technique (behavior may improve as a result of merely being counted), and to aid in collecting information that can be used in a self-management program (Armstrong & Frith, 1984). When necessary, the co-therapist or other group members can serve as reliability observers to check on the accuracy of the collected data. Monitoring can provide each client and the group as a whole with ongoing feedback on successes and failures of treatment.

GROUP MUSIC THERAPY
TREATMENT CONTRACT

I. **As a music therapy group member, I agree to:**

A. Attend all sessions and arrive for each one on time (10:00 a.m.).
B. Participate in group activities and actively work on my individual treatment objective(s) as outline with the music therapist.
C. Show evidence of assignment completion when requested.
D. Assist in data collection when it relates to my particular treatment objective(s).
E. Allow data accumulated during the group to be used for research and/or educational purposes, with protection of confidentiality assured; and to allow the music therapist to contact me in the future, by mail or phone, for follow-up.

II. **As the music therapist, I agree to:**

A. Begin and end each session on time.
B. Help the client clarify his/her problems in such a way that something can be done about them.
C. Help the client to identify personal and other resources, and make use of them in dealing with problems.
D. Provide the client with procedures that offer the best chance of an effective and efficient resolution of the problem(s).
E. Respect confidentiality of client's communication.
F. Provide support and incentives for meeting conditions as outlined above.

_____   _____
(Client)   (Date)

_____   _____
(Music Therapist)   (Date)

(Adapted from Treatment Contract form by Rose, 1977)

Figure 4
Group music therapy treatment contract

GROUP MUSIC THERAPY VERBALIZATION ANALYSIS
SELF-MONITORING FORM

Your Name_____   # of Group Members_____

Date_____   Time of Session_____

DIRECTIONS: Place a tally mark (/) within the appropriate box each time you contribute to the group discussion.

M.T. Activity	Observation Interval	Positives*	Negatives**
	First 15 Minutes of Session		
	Second 15 Minutes of Session		
	Third 15 Minutes of Session		
	Fourth 15 Minutes of Session		

Your Comments/Observations:_____

_____

_____

  *Positives are comments defined as specified solutions to specific problems.
**Negatives are comments defined as the statement of problems with no defined solutions.

(Adapted from Interaction Analysis form by Madsen & Madsen, 1983)

Figure 5
Group music therapy self-monitoring form

Discharge Planning

In an effort to prepare the patient for the transition from the supportive hospital milieu to the less structured environment of home and community, the music therapist integrates within the group sessions procedures that will assist in helping the patient to transfer material learned in the group to actual activities of daily living which occur within the community. This is often accomplished by giving the client(s) homework assignments that are carried out during the evening hours and/or on weekends away from the hospital, with family members and/or significant others.

Formal "exit interviews" are scheduled and conducted in which the music therapist and the individual client meet, review and discuss treatment progress, and delineate specific programs and activities that the patient should carry out upon return to home/work environments. It is important that the music therapist be knowledgeable of music-related community resources (e.g., music stores, concert series, civic and/or religious-related choruses and bands, music instructors, etc.) to enable her to provide the client with specific names and telephone numbers of contact persons responsible for these kinds of community music activities. Once the therapist has made a referral to one or more of these resources, the therapist is then able to "follow-up," i.e., make a phone call(s) to the contact person(s) to determine when and/or if the client made a connection with the appropriate community resource. At this final interview, the music therapist may also want to request that the client complete an evaluation of the music therapy services that he/she has received (see Figure 6). This "satisfaction survey" can provide the music therapist with valuable feedback concerning services rendered, and can assist the therapist in providing sessions that are meaningful to the client (Heaney, 1992; Thaut, 1989).

Skills Training—Divisions of Treatment

The major divisions of treatment germane to music therapy in acute care programs may be comprised of structured groups relating to (a) relaxation/anxiety management skills, (b) verbal/interaction skills, and (c) leisure/community skills. As noted in the illustration (see Figure 1), each treatment division or skills training area is associated with particular kinds of *patient problems* (III). For example, relaxation training may be best suited to those individuals who may be described as anxious or unable to deal with stressful situations.

> [As previously stated, patients should be referred to music therapy on the basis of specific behavioral needs as they relate to the unique areas of music therapy treatment, not necessarily on the basis of "global" diagnosis.]

Along with the divisions of treatment and associated behavioral problems, a sampling of *treatment goals* is also listed (IV). Goals are statements of treatment outcomes that describe what the patient will know and/or be able to do at the time of discharge, and that represent a "standard" for judging the termination of treatment. In establishing goals, therapists usually think in terms of what a patient will be able to say, do, or look like upon discharge from the hospital (Galasso, 1987).

MUSIC THERAPY SERVICES
CLIENT SATISFACTION SURVEY

Date_____

Name of Your Music Therapist_____

Music Therapy Service(s) You Attended:

_____

_____

DIRECTIONS: Please rate the following items by selecting the corresponding number from one of the five choices listed below. Do not hesitate to use number 5 if you feel unable to make a fair judgment or if the item does not apply to your particular music therapy situation.

(1) Excellent   **(4) Unsatisfactory**
(2) Good   **(5) Unable to judge or does not**
(3) Fair   **apply**

_____ 1. Therapist's punctuality in beginning and ending sessions.

_____ 2. Therapist's ability to understand and clarify group members' problems.

_____ 3. Degree that stated goals were achieved through appropriate music activities.

_____ 4. Degree that homework assignments were appropriate.

_____ 5. Therapist's ability to identify feelings expressed by group members.

_____ 6. Therapist's ability to assist in identifying community resources that were appropriate for the group.

_____ 7. Therapist's ability to sequence sessions in a meaningful, interrelated manner.

_____ 8. Therapist's ability to deal with differences of opinion.

_____ 9. Your feelings toward recommending music therapy services to others.

_____ 10. Therapist's preparedness for each session.

_____ 11. Therapist's ability to explain session procedures/activities in an understandable manner.

_____ 12. Your perception of the benefit you received from group music therapy.

_____ 13. Therapist's ability to motivate and provide encouragement to group members for achieving goal(s).

_____

Please provide any additional comments concerning music therapy services:

_____

_____

_____

Figure 6
Client Satisfaction Survey

Once patient problems, treatment divisions, and general goals of therapy have been defined, it becomes relatively easy to then delineate objectives for each skills training area. Short-term objectives are more specific (Wheeler & Fox, 1972); represent expected treatment outcomes that will be demonstrated by the patients at various times during treatment, (e.g., at the end of the first week); are prerequisites to achieving treatment goals. Specifically stated objectives (both group and individual) assist the therapist in determining the progress of the clients and provide criteria for judging behavioral improvement. The obtainment of group treatment goals should correlate with the achievement of individual treatment goals.

The following paragraphs will review the literature related to each major treatment division, will present typical *group goals and objectives*[2] that a music therapist may prepare in structuring a series of treatment sessions, and then will give examples of *individual treatment plans* with accompanying goals and objectives, data collection procedures, interventions, and illustrated results. It should be remembered that the selection of group goals and sequencing of group treatment objectives for each skills area remain arbitrary at this point in time in the practice of music therapy. Further research can only begin to clarify the appropriate selection and sequencing of these sessions. These particular group goals and objectives represent only a sample of possible sequencing of treatment. The reader is referred to Plack (1980), Schulberg (1986), and Wolfe, Burns, Stoll, and Wichmann (1975) for listings of music therapy procedures and activities employed in group practice that may be arranged and conducted to meet specifically stated treatment goals and objectives.

Relaxation/Anxiety Management Skills

Hanser (1985) provides an excellent review of literature related to music therapy and stress reduction research, while Sandrock and James (1989) provide a comprehensive listing of assessment protocols used in music-assisted relaxation training. Numerous studies are cited to support the use of music within instrumental and palliative coping models of anxiety reduction. In clinical practice, music is most frequently paired with progressive muscle relaxation, autogenic procedures, guided imagery and/or biofeedback to induce relaxation (Curtis, 1986; Peach, 1984; Rider, 1985; Rider, Floyd, & Kirkpatrick, 1985; Schuster, 1985), and has been successfully employed to facilitate the production of mental imagery (Bonny, 1975; Bonny & Savary, 1973; Hanser, 1990; Quittner, 1980). Studies conducted by Clark, McCorkle, and Williams (1981) and Hanser, Larson, and O'Connell (1983), have emphasized the importance of music to: (a) prompt rhythmic breathing, (b) prompt pleasant associations conducive to relaxation, and (c) assist in focusing concentration on the music and away from other environmental sounds. Other variables which have been examined experimentally, relate to the kinds of music used for relaxation (Biller, Olson, & Breen, 1974; Borling, 1981; Logan & Roberts, 1984; Rohner & Miller, 1980; Scartelli, 1984; Taylor, 1973), and to the degree of preference for the music. Stratton and Zalanowski (1984) have found a significant correlation between liking for a particular musical selection and the degree of relaxation. Results from other studies suggest a sequenced presentation of

---

[2]All three case studies are excerpted from an unpublished manuscript, *Behavioral Music Therapy With Adult Psychiatric Clients,* by Celene A. Dembroski (1977), The Florida State University.

relaxation procedures and music in clinical practice (Bonny, 1975; Kovach, 1985; Saperston, 1989; Scartelli & Borling, 1986).

Group Goals and Objectives

WEEK ONE

> *Goal:* Group members will become familiar with procedures of progressive relaxation training.

Objectives: Given group music therapy sessions dealing with relaxation, group members will:
- a) know the muscle groups used in relaxation training and be able to identify them with 100% accuracy.
- b) discriminate feelings of tension and relaxation of differing muscle groups.
- c) contribute at least one comment concerning the value of music in association with tensing and relaxing muscle groups.
- d) identify and log situations that create anxiety and bring to group music therapy for discussion.

WEEK TWO

> *Goal:* Group members will become familiar with the use of guided imagery in relaxation and with the value of using music to facilitate it.

Objectives: Given group music therapy sessions, group members will:
- a) participate in a guided imagery "trip" and contribute two comments during group discussion concerning the experience.
- b) create their own imagery script in the form of a written product.
- c) select from a "music relaxation menu" three possible selections which could be used after discharge to enhance relaxation.
- d) continue to log stressful situations and will bring examples to sessions for discussion.

WEEK THREE

> *Goal:* Group members will become familiar with procedures combined with music for relaxation.

Objectives: Given group music therapy sessions, group members will:
- a) know autogenic self-statements and be able to list them when asked by the music therapist.
- b) (with use of portable cassette tape player and headphones) use individually selected relaxation music and autogenic procedures to induce relaxation twice daily and will record times in relaxation log.
- c) continue to record stressful situations and will bring log to sessions.
- d) write discharge plan on use of music and relaxation to be implemented at home or work.

Individual Treatment Plan: Relaxation/Anxiety Management Group

Client A: Presenting Problem

A is 32 years old and has the diagnosis of schizophrenic reaction, in good remission at this time. Medications currently being taken are Cogetin, Nadine and Prolixin. Client feels extremely fearful and lonely. She will not stay in the home or complete her chores when by herself. Since work does not get done, she feels stupid and cowardly.

Treatment Goal:

By the end of treatment, the client will feel calm and controlled.

Treatment Objective:

By the end of group music therapy sessions, the client will experience no more than one fearful episode per day, and the intensity of fearful episodes will be 4 or less on a scale from 1–10.

Recording Procedures:

Single event recording was employed with each number on the State Trait Anxiety Inventory (see Figure 7) being equivalent to that amount of anxiety units; e.g., 4 (representing Very Much So) would be equivalent to 4 units of anxiety. Client completed this test every day at 11 :30 a.m. Client was also instructed in recording data and kept a notebook in which she logged the day, time, and intensity of each fearful episode. The intensity of fearful episodes was measured by a rating scale ranging from 1 (indicated Little Anxiety) to 10 (indicating Extreme Anxiety). Each increment on the rating scale was equivalent to its number; e.g., a 5 was equivalent to 5 anxiety units. Each episode experienced was recorded as one unit.

Intervention:

Client experienced a relaxation exercise paired with music during music therapy sessions. This exercise was developed by the therapist and consisted of deep breathing, color and imagery, and harp music in the background. Client selected initial scenes that were used, with therapist creating the imagery to fit scenes. Behavioral design used was reversal: ABCBABAB.

Results and Discussion:

The frequency mean was 1.5 with an intensity mean of 4.8 for the phases of baseline (Condition A). The frequency mean was –.6 with an intensity mean of 3.8 for the treatment phases (Condition B) (see Figure 8). Scores from the State Trait Anxiety Test showed a mean of 25.8 for the phases of baseline and a mean of 18.1 for the treatment phases (see Figure 9). Results indicate that a relaxation exercise paired with music was effective in reducing the frequency and intensity of fearful episodes. Treatment program should be extended in order to give client time to learn exercise naturally through repetition, then should be included in her daily living pattern as a self-maintenance procedure (much like brushing teeth) and especially when experiencing a fearful episode.

STATE-TRAIT ANXIETY INVENTORY
A-STATE FORM

Developed by C.D. Spielberger, R.L. Gorsuch and R. Lushene

NAME_____ DATE_____

DIRECTIONS:

A number of statements which people have used to describe themselves are given below. Read each statement and then circle the appropriate number to the right of the statement to indicate how you **FEEL** right now; that is **AT THIS MOMENT**. There is no right or wrong answers. Do no spend too much time on any one statement but give the answer which seems to describe your present feelings best.

1 - Not at all　　　　**3 - Moderately so**
2 - Somewhat　　　　**4 - Very much so**

I feel calm	1	2	3	4
I feel secure	1	2	3	4
I am tense	1	2	3	4
. . .	1	2	3	4
. . .	1	2	3	4
. . .	1	2	3	4
. . .	1	2	3	4
. . .	1	2	3	4
. . .	1	2	3	4
. . .	1	2	3	4
. . .	1	2	3	4
. . .	1	2	3	4
. . .	1	2	3	4
. . .	1	2	3	4
. . .	1	2	3	4
. . .	1	2	3	4
. . .	1	2	3	4
I feel pleasant	1	2	3	4
I feel nervous and restless	1	2	3	4
I feel satisfied with myself	1	2	3	4

Figure 7
Client A: State-Trait Anxiety Inventory

THE EFFECTIVENESS OF A RELAXATION EXERCISE PAIRED WITH MUSIC ON FREQUENCY AND INTENSITY OF FEARFUL EPISODES

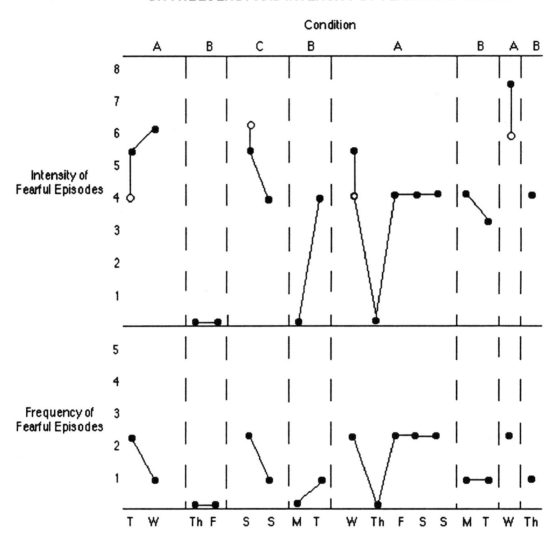

Figure 8
Client A: Music and relaxation exercise — graphed data

STATE TRAIT ANXIETY INVENTORY

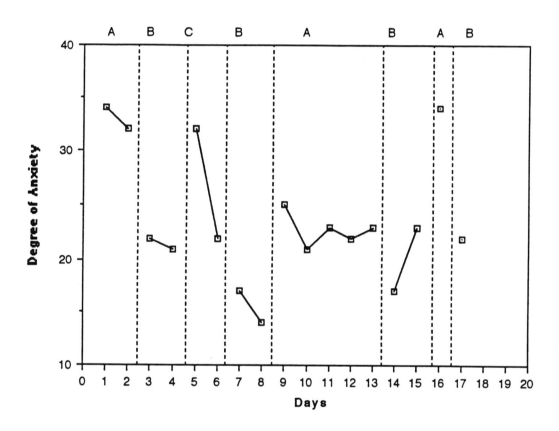

Figure 9
Client A: State Trait Anxiety Inventory —
graphed data

Verbal/Interaction Skills

The practice of using music to encourage group discussion is common in short-term acute settings. Music is used to "set the occasion" for discussion and can function to create a more stress-free environment in which productive group interactions can be maintained. Sears (1968) has stated that music evokes extra-musical ideas and associations, as well as feelings and emotions, and can serve as a springboard for discussion about present or past concerns. Patients are able to verbalize and project their own problems into the discussion more easily by using the lyrics of a song as the object of verbalization (Butler, 1966; Cyrus, 1966; James, 1988; Thaut, 1987). Others state that using music to stimulate group discussion is an effective format for the expression of feelings—a means for verbalizing emotions and ideas that may be threatening to express otherwise (Barker & Brunk, 1991; Behrens, 1988; Castellano, 1969; Ficken, 1976; Gilbert, 1977; Goldberg, 1989; Henderson, 1983; Moreno, 1980). Once discussion has been generated, the music therapist can guide interactions and provide support and feedback to individual group members concerning decisions related to present and future behavior.

Musical recordings are selected by the therapist prior to the session in order to prompt interaction on various issues, or are selected by individual group members as necessitated by a particular group activity (Plack, 1980; Schulberg, 1986; Wolfe et al., 1975). Common themes of discussion (reflected in lyrics of most popular music) can center around concerns of love, loyalty, fellowship, unity, a course of action, or a particular subject of special interest to the group (Maultsby, 1977; Schiff & Frances, 1974). When structured by the group activity, patients often select favorite music with lyrics relevant to solving personal problems in everyday life. Many popular selections are particularly helpful in demonstrating and promoting integration and positive effects—in finding useful resolutions to difficult situations (Douglass & Wagner, 1965; James & Freed, 1989; Schiff & Frances, 1974; Stith, 1965). The "standards" of popular music seem easily remembered, and many people are comfortable in commenting upon them. Selected musical recordings can convey to the group a sense of empathy that conflicts are universal (Boenheim, 1968). Group members can be assisted in recognizing that the same piece of music can elicit different effects in different group members, and that a particular situation or event can be viewed from many varying perspectives (Gaston, 1966).

Presently there are some experimental studies which support the use of music to increase verbalization. Changes in the verbalizing of complaints and non-complaints with psychiatric, as well as pain rehabilitation patients were reported in studies by Cook and Freethy (1973), Williams and Dorow (1983), and Wolfe (1978). Music therapy activities also were shown to facilitate an increase in verbalizations of pediatric patients (Froehlich, 1984), and were used to increase positive self-statements and verbal interactions in adolescent treatment (Kivland, 1986; Madsen & Madsen, 1968). Self-disclosure statements of cancer patients were increased through music therapy (Sedei, 1980), and Goloff (1981) found that adult patients demonstrated elevated mood and comfort perceptions during music therapy sessions. Finally, Levine-Gross and Swartz (1982) compared group music therapy sessions with group psychotherapy sessions; results indicated patients showed significantly less perceived anxiety following group music therapy procedures.

Group Goals and Objectives

WEEK ONE

> *Goal:* Group members will verbally express themselves within the group.

Objectives: Given group music therapy sessions dealing with verbal/interaction skills, group members will:

a) complete a self-knowledge questionnaire and will choose a song that describes to the group something about themselves.

b) listen to various kinds of music and will express a preference for particular one(s).

c) list five positive attributes they possess and then will select music that may describe one.

d) choose musical selection(s) that expresses a particular feeling or mood and verbalize at least two "feeling" statements about the selections during group discussion.

WEEK TWO

> *Goal:* Group members will listen and respond to other group members' comments.

Objectives: Given group music therapy sessions, group members will:

a) listen to various musical selections and will discuss the lyrics (meanings) of each one by expressing at least one spontaneous remark to another member's comments.

b) listen to musical recordings selected by group members and will rate each one on a scale from 1 to 5 ("strong dislike" to "love it"); then will participate in group discussion by expressing at least two spontaneous remarks concerning other members' ratings.

c) make a list of activities that one can do when depressed, and then will select a song describing one of the listed items; then contribute at least three suggestions or comments to other members regarding appropriate activities.

d) select a musical recording which describes experiences that occurred at home during past weekend, and will contribute at least three constructive remarks in support of other members' comments.

WEEK THREE

> *Goal:* Group members will express differences of opinion during discussions.

Objectives: Given group music therapy sessions, group members will:

a) compile a list of all types of music, listen to examples and express differences, similarities, and opinions of preferences for at least three of the selected styles.

b) listen to musical selections and following each one, will write down all the adjectives which could be used to describe the piece; express at least four opinions concerning similarities and differences in descriptors.

c) listen to musical selections that convey issues related to self-confidence, friendship, personal responsibility, loyalty, trust, etc.; group members will express at least three personal opinions regarding selections, two of which will contain "feeling" statements.

Individual Treatment Plan: Verbal/Interaction Group

Client M: Presenting Problem

M is 56 years old and has been hospitalized on several occasions with the diagnosis of alcohol/drug addiction and depressive neurosis. Medications currently being taken are Thorazine, Artane and Dalmene. Client lives in the past, worrying about how she let her daughter down. She is experiencing a high degree of self-guilt and regret.

Treatment Goal:

By the end of the treatment program, the client's verbalizations will focus on the present.

Treatment Objective:

During group music therapy sessions, at least 90% of client's verbalizations will refer to present attitudes, feelings, or behavior.

Recording Procedures:

Single event recording was employed. During group music therapy sessions, client recorded data on the frequency of verbalizations concerning the past. During group music therapy sessions and half-hour client's socializations after lunch, therapist recorded data on number of verbalizations per each observation period and on frequency of those concerning the past.

Intervention:

During each music therapy session, the client was permitted only statements which referred to current feelings, attitudes, or behaviors. Whenever she referred to a past feeling or wrong-doing or deficiencies, therapist and/or group peers told her to stop and asked her to make a comment on what was going on in the group at that moment. Each time client made a statement about the present, therapist provided verbal and/or physical reinforcement. Behavioral design used was partial reversal: ABCDC.

Condition A:

Client was requested to make statements only concerning the present. During the music therapy session, therapist recorded unobtrusively the number of client's verbalizations and the frequency of those concerning the past.

Condition B:

Client was instructed in self-observation recording. Client recorded on paper each statement she made concerning the past during the music therapy session. Therapist recorded data on paper in front of client, the number of client's verbalizations and the frequency of those concerning the past during the music therapy session. Data were recorded unobtrusively during the half-hour after-lunch socialization.

Condition C:

No music therapy session. Therapist unobtrusively recorded number of client's verbalizations and frequency of those concerning the past during the half-hour after-lunch socialization.

Condition D:

D1: Stimulus fading during music therapy session. Client recorded *on paper* each statement that she made concerning the past during the music therapy session. Therapist recorded unobtrusively the number of client's verbalizations and frequency of those concerning the past during the music therapy session and half-hour after-lunch socialization.

D2: Client recorded *mentally* the number of statements that she made concerning the past during the music therapy session. Therapist recorded unobtrusively the number of client's verbalizations and frequency of those concerning the past made during the music therapy session and half-hour after-lunch socialization.

D3: Client was requested not to record data. Therapist recorded unobtrusively the number of client's verbalizations and frequency of those concerning the past made during the music therapy session and half-hour after-lunch socialization.

Condition C:

Same as Condition C above.

Results and Discussion:

Baseline (Condition A) on client's present-oriented verbalizations was 0% to 20% during music therapy sessions (see Figure 10). When client began recording data (Condition B), present-oriented verbalizations had increased to 90% or above and remained throughout treatment. At that time client's present-oriented verbalizations ranged from 30% to 75% in after-lunch socializations. During Condition C (no music therapy session), client's present-oriented verbalizations increased to 80% in after-lunch socialization. During fading phase (Condition D) clients present-oriented statements ranged from 70% to 95% in half-hour after-lunch socialization. Upon returning to Condition C (no music therapy session), present-oriented statements increased to 95%–100% during after-lunch socializations. The results indicate that self-recording is not only a valuable part of a treatment program, but is also a successful method of changing behavior independent of other techniques.

Leisure/Community Skills

Braswell et al. (1983) have stated that "psychiatric patients often are rehospitalized for social role failures rather than for overt psychiatric symptoms, and that post-hospital adjustment depends more on employment than upon psychiatric treatment." (pp. 90–91). Certainly one's

THE EFFECTIVENESS OF SELF-RECORDING AND STIMULUS FADING ON TRANSFER OF THE BEHAVIOR ARTICULATING PRESENT ORIENTED STATEMENTS

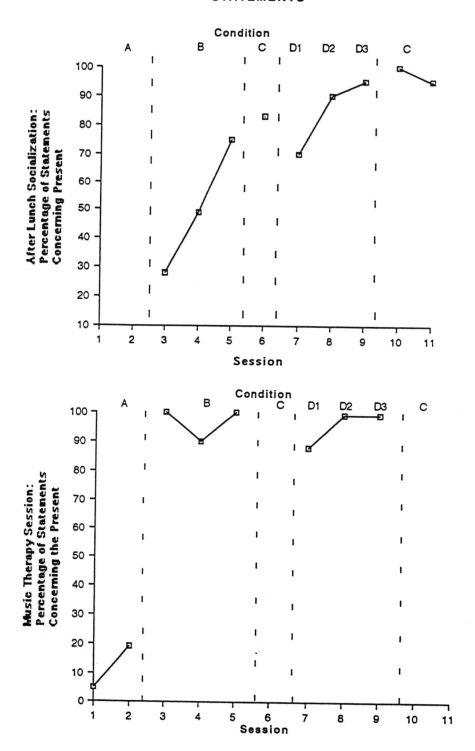

Figure 10
Client M: Self-recording of present oriented statements —
graphed data

ability to structure activities within leisure time that are fulfilling and productive is also an important social role which may equally contribute to post-hospital adjustment.

It is claimed that Americans spend more than one-third of their waking hours in the pursuit of leisure. Yet many seem unable to structure that time toward greater personal happiness (Madsen, 1977). This contemporary social dilemma is reflected not only in leisure counseling services contained within numerous health care programs, but also within corporations that establish leisure counseling services for harried executives and pre-retirement planning seminars for senior employees.

The development of new or rejuvenation of previously developed music-related leisure skills is a division of treatment well integrated in music therapy practice. Numerous studies have shown that self-concept can be changed through participation in structured music-related activities (Johnson, 1981; Michel & Martin, 1970; Rubin, 1973). Cassity (1976) found that through participation in group guitar lessons, group members gained in measures of peer acceptance and group cohesiveness. Research in the treatment of depression has demonstrated that reinforcing achievement of assigned tasks decreases the behaviors associated with depression (Rosenthal & Meyer, 1971). And Sears (1968) aptly said that structuring musical experiences so that group members receive satisfaction necessary for them to seek out more of such experiences lend themselves to the maintenance of better adjustment within his or her environment. Getting group members actively involved in "doing" or participating in music itself can contribute to feeling a part of the group, and can assist in one's personal and social rehabilitation (Bellamy & Willard, 1993; Clemetson, 1968; Crigler, 1966; Nebe, 1971; Van Stone, 1973).

With an emphasis on short-term acute care, a trend toward returning the patient to the community is evident. A major thrust of treatment, then, becomes one of enabling the patient to adapt to and function within the community (Braswell, 1967; Gaston, 1968; Stevens, 1967; Wolfgram, 1978). To function satisfactorily in the community, individual needs may include not only work-related skills, but also the ability to communicate effectively with others, to deal with stresses both at work and at home, and to deal effectively with one's leisure hours.

Berkowitz, Lurie, Chwast, Siegle, and Wachspress (1965) reported that many former patients do not become involved in social activities because they often lack the skills necessary to do so. It would appear that community resources must be identified that may assist in the patient's home and community adaptation, and patients must be assisted in making full use of the available community resources (Glick, 1966). The task for the music therapist, then, must be to give direction and training in skills that will enable the patient to function adequately within the home, work, and community environments.

Group Goals and Objectives

WEEK ONE

Goal: Group members will be introduced to various leisure-time musical instruments, will know the value of leisure in one's life, and will gain some basic instruction on at least one instrument.

Objectives: Given group music therapy sessions dealing with leisure and community skills, group members will:
a) identify main parts of a guitar correctly for two consecutive sessions.

b) demonstrate correct posture for holding and strumming a guitar for two consecutive sessions.

c) correctly identify string lines and fret lines on a guitar staff, and transfer the locations to the guitar two out of two trials for two consecutive sessions.

d) strum A, E, D, G chords with correct fingerings for three consecutive trials for two consecutive sessions.

e) play simple two and three chord songs on the guitar using correct chords for two consecutive sessions.

WEEK TWO

Goal: Group members will become acquainted with various community music resources and will demonstrate knowledge of behavior associated with concert attendance.

Objectives: Given group music therapy sessions dealing with leisure and community skills, group members will:

a) make a list of addresses and phone numbers of at least six organizations providing musical concerts within the community.

b) identify two sources for the purchasing/ordering of concert tickets and will locate two sources of transportation to the concerts.

c) contribute at least one comment concerning appropriate dress for an outdoor concert, rock or folk concert, classical performance at concert hall, etc.

d) attend one concert during evening hours or on weekend; bring concert program notes to group session.

WEEK THREE

Goal: Group members will become familiar with various kinds of music, and will learn how to operate and where to purchase recordings and audio equipment.

Objectives: Given group music therapy sessions dealing with leisure and community skills, group members will:

a) list five major kinds of musical styles and will designate a personal preference for at least one style listed.

b) list addresses of music stores which sell tapes/recordings of various music styles.

c) demonstrate ability to operate cassette recorder and/or stereo equipment.

d) make list of musical organizations (community chorus, band, orchestra), contact person(s), phone numbers, and audition requirements.

Individual Treatment Plan: Leisure/Community Group

(Note: The following is an example of the collection of group data as compared to the previous examples of individual data.)

Clients: Presenting Problem

Clients as a whole lacked experience with enjoyable leisure activities as well as exposure to different styles of music.

Treatment Goal:

Group members will become aware of leisure activities related to music.

Treatment Objective:

By the end of the group music therapy sessions, clients will be able to cite five places or ways in which they could listen to music, will increase individual listening time, will identify at least five different styles of music, five different uses of music, five different moods music can evoke, and five different groups/singers.

Recording Procedures:

Single event recording was employed, with each correct item on pretest and posttest being one unit (See Music Awareness Test).

Intervention:

Examples from three different kinds of music were explored each week involving the different styles, uses, moods evoked and various groups/singers from each kind of music presented. The sessions were didactic in nature with discovery and/or thought provoking questions; e.g., therapist would ask when a particular style of music would not be used. Emphasis was placed on the immediate experience and participation level of the client. During the sessions, therapist provided positive verbal and non-verbal reinforcement to clients who responded correctly to information seeking questions, and/or who displayed non-verbal involvement in music listening. Design used was pretest-posttest. A 25-item Music Awareness Test (see Figure 11) was administered at the beginning and end of each session. Tests were the same for each session and included items on styles, moods, and uses, as well as names of groups and singers. In addition, a pretest-posttest was administered at the beginning and end of the treatment program itself. This test focused on listening habits and music involvement.

Results and Discussion:

Scores from pretest for session one had a mean of 8 increasing to 12 for pretest for session two and 18 for session three (see Figure 12). This indicates that clients were retaining the new information. The greatest increase in information was in session one with a 50% increase. Group awareness increased 33½% from pretest for session one to posttest for session three. Since the group mean was 24 for the posttest of session three (ceiling on test was 25), and since individual listening time for each client increased a range of 30 to 60 minutes (see Figure 13), it can be concluded that the treatment program was successful. Perhaps the greatest flaw in the treatment design was not including observations of clients' participation during the music sessions themselves.

MUSIC THERAPY SERVICES
MUSIC AWARENESS TEST

Name_____

Date_____

Time_____

1) Name five (5) different styles of music

       1._____   4._____

       2._____   5._____

       3._____

2) Name five (5) different uses of music

       1._____   4._____

       2._____   5._____

       3._____

3) Name five (5) moods that music can make you feel

       1._____   4._____

       2._____   5._____

       3._____

4) Name five (5) different groups and/or singers

       1._____   4._____

       2._____   5._____

       3._____

5. Name five (5) different places or ways you can listen to music

       1._____   4._____

       2._____   5._____

       3._____

Figure 11

Clients: Music Awareness Test

THE EFFECTIVENESS OF MUSIC LISTENING SESSIONS ON MUSIC AWARENESS

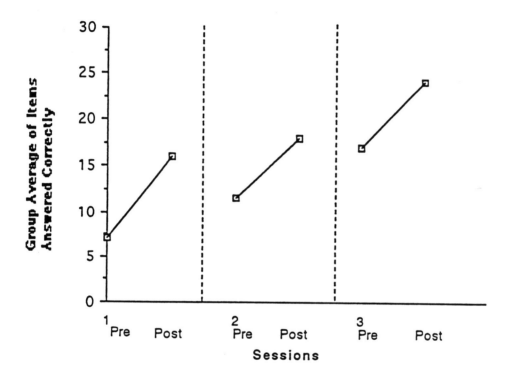

Figure 12
Clients: Group Data —
music listening and music awareness

**THE EFFECTIVENESS OF MUSIC LISTENING SESSIONS ON AMOUNT OF
LISTENING IN NATURAL ENVIRONMENT**

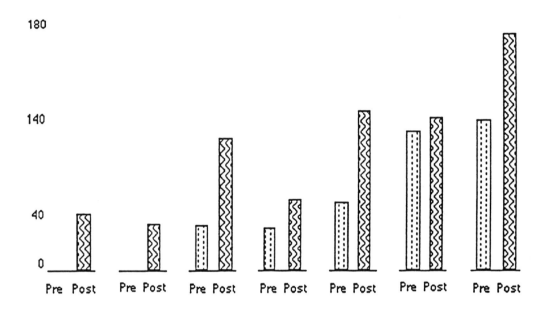

Figure 13

Clients: Group data — amount of listening in natural environment

Summary

Current music therapy practice in short-term, acute psychiatric care is directed toward group treatment with music therapists providing services related to (a) assessment, (b) treatment/skills training, (c) monitoring/evaluation, and (d) discharge planning. Major divisions of treatment in group music therapy may consist of the development of *relaxation/anxiety management skills, verbal/interaction skills,* and *leisure/community skills* that have been designed to meet specific client problems. Through standard assessments provided by other professional disciplines and those undertaken by the music therapist as they relate to various treatment groups, the identification of patient problems can be accomplished and can assist the treatment team in referring the patient to a particular music therapy treatment division(s). Once patient problems and appropriate treatment have been identified, the music therapist is prepared to collaborate with the client to establish treatment goals and objectives (pregroup interview) related to developing functional, relevant skills for daily living within the community. Additionally, therapists are responsible for developing a short-term treatment curriculum (composed of terminal goals and objectives) related to each treatment division. Specifically stated goals and objectives (both group and individual) assist the music therapist in determining the progress of clients, and provide criteria for judging behavioral improvement and for coordinating discharge planning. Assessing the client in relationship to a division(s) of treatment, teaching functional skills necessary for dealing with the demands of daily living, monitoring and evaluating client progress, and preparing the client for a return to the community are all essential to an effective music therapy group practice.

Based on the literature reviewed in this chapter, it is evident that an increasing number of research studies have demonstrated the therapeutic benefits of group music therapy. Since these particular procedures can be applied on a group basis and can be conducted in a time-limited manner, it can reasonably be assumed that incorporating these particular services within mental health programs, can be financially responsible. Cost per treatment can be significantly reduced compared to other more traditional psychotherapy procedures.

The efficient and effective operation of group music therapy requires the professional music therapist to be familiar with current literature related to specific areas of music therapy treatment, and to be able to transfer and integrate that current knowledge into daily clinical practice. A commitment to and perseverance in updating clinical skills and knowledge are important attributes in distinguishing one as a "professional." In addition, issues related to the selection and sequencing of appropriate group goals and objectives, to the adoption of applicable assessment instruments, to the selection of monitoring procedures which can easily be used by therapists and/or clients, to the determination of specific music therapy groups for specific client problems, and to the cost effectiveness of group music therapy will all require longitudinal data collection. Only through the concerted research efforts of both music therapy *educators and clinicians* can successful outcomes of group music therapy services be documented and the issues in question be addressed. Systematic implementation of research variables that have been shown to contribute to group practice should aid in developing more sophisticated and effective therapeutic procedures, making music therapy services an integral part of contemporary short-term psychiatric care.

References

Alpaugh, P., & Haney, M. (1978). *Counseling* the *older adult: A training manual for paraprofessionals and beginning counselors.* Lexington, MA: Lexington Books.

Armstrong, S. W., & Frith, G. H. (1984). *Practical self-monitoring for classroom use.* Springfield, IL: Charles C. Thomas.

Barker, V. L., & Brunk, B. (1991). The role of a creative arts group in the treatment of clients with traumatic brain injury. *Music Therapy Perspectives, 9,* 26–31.

Beck, A. T., Rush, A. G., Shaw, G. F., & Emery, G. (1979). *Cognitive therapy of depression.* New York: Guilford Press.

Behrens, G. A. (1988). An objective approach to the expression of feelings. *Music Therapy Perspectives, 5,* 16–22.

Bellamy, M. A., & Willard, P. B. (1993). Music therapy: An integral component of the oncology experience. *International Journal of the Arts in Medicine, 2*(1), 14–19.

Berkowitz, L., Lurie, A., Chwast, J., Siegle, N., & Wachspress, M. (1965). Community center resocialization of former psychiatric patients. *Mental Hygiene, 49,* 266.

Biller, J. D., Olson, P. J., & Breen, T. (1974). The effect of "happy" versus "sad" music and participation on anxiety. *Journal of Music Therapy, 11,* 68–73.

Boenheim, C. (1968). The position of music and art therapy in contemporary psychotherapy. *Journal of Music Therapy, 5,* 85–87.

Bonny, H. L. (1975). Music and consciousness. *Journal of Music Therapy, 12,* 121–135.

Bonny, H. L., & Savary, L. M. (1973). *Music and your mind: Listening with a new consciousness.* New York: Harper & Row.

Borling, J. E. (1981). The effects of sedative music on alpha rhythms and focused attention in high-creative and low-creative subjects. *Journal of Music Therapy, 18, 101–108.*

Braswell, C. (1967). Changing concepts in treatment. *Journal of Music Therapy, 4,* 63–66.

Braswell, C., Brooks, D. M., Decuir, A., Humphrey, T., Jacobs, K. W., & Sutton, K. (1983). Development and implementation of a music/activity therapy intake assessment for psychiatric patients. Part 1: Initial standardization procedures on data from university students. *Journal* of *Music Therapy, 20,* 88–100.

Bryant, D. R. (1987). A cognitive approach to therapy through music. *Journal of Music Therapy. 24* (1), 27–34.

Butler, B. (1966). Music group psychotherapy. *Journal of Music Therapy, 3,* 53–56.

Carkhuff, R. (1969). *Helping and human relations: A primer for lay and professional helpers: Vol. 2 practice and research.* New York: Holt, Rinehart & Winston.

Cassity, M. D. (1976). The influence of a music therapy activity upon peer acceptance, group cohesiveness, and interpersonal relationships of adult psychiatric patients. *Journal of Music Therapy, 13,* 66–76.

Castellano, J. (1969). Music composition in a music therapy program. *Journal of Music Therapy, 6,* 12–14.

Cautela, J., & Kastenbaum, R. A. (1967). A reinforcement survey schedule for use in therapy training and research. *Psychological Reports, 20,* 1115–1130.

Christman, C. (1967). Family group therapy: Implications for music therapy. *Journal of Music Therapy, 4,* 100–105.

Clark, M. E., & Ficken, C. T. (1988). Music therapy in the new health care environment. *Music Therapy Perspectives, 5,* 88–109.

Clark, M. E., McCorkle, R. R., & Williams, S. B. (1981). Music therapy-assisted labor and delivery. *Journal of Music Therapy, 5,* 6–10.

Clemetson, B. (1968). The development and process of a music appreciation group. *Journal of Music Therapy, 5,* 6-10.

Cook, M., & Freethy, M. (1973). The use of music as a positive reinforcer to eliminate complaining behavior. *Journal of Music Therapy, 10,* 213–216.

Crigler, C. (1966). The role of the music therapist in the therapeutic community. *Journal of Music Therapy, 3,* 19–21.

Curran, J. P. (1982). The Simulated Social Interaction Test. In J. P. Curran & P. M. Monti (Eds.), *Social skills training.* New York: Guilford Press.

Curtis, S. L. (1986). The effect of music on pain relief and relaxation of the terminally ill. *Journal of Music Therapy, 23,* 10–24.

Cyrus, A. E., Jr. (1966). Music for receptive release. *Journal of Music Therapy, 3,* 65–68.

Danish, S. J., D'Augelli, A. R., & Hauer, A. L. (1980). *Helping skills: A basic training program.* New York: Human Sciences Press.

Deans, C., Harkvoort, L., Macfarlane, C., Stewart-Cline, M., & Toppozada, M. (1994). *Music therapy relaxation/stress management assessment.* Stockton, CA: University of the Pacific Conservatory of Music.

Dembroski, C. A. (1977). *Behavioral music therapy with adult psychiatric clients.* Unpublished master's thesis, The Florida State University, Tallahassee.

Douglass, D. R., & Wagner, M. K. (1965). A program for the activity therapist in group psychotherapy. *Journal of Music Therapy, 2,* 56–60.

Dziwak, J., & Gfeller, K. (1988). Cost-effectiveness and music therapy practice. *Music Therapy Perspectives, 5,* 28–32.

Egan, E. (1975). *The skilled helper: A model for systematic helping and interpersonal relating.* Monterey, CA: Brooks/Cole Publishing.

Farkas, M. (1980). *The effects of training psychiatric staff in human relations and programming skills: Developing a rehabilitation model for chronic patients during deinstitutionalization.* Unpublished doctoral dissertation, Boston University.

Ficken, T. (1976). The use of songwriting in a psychiatric setting. *Journal of Music Therapy, 13,* 163–172.

Froehlich, M. R. (1984). A comparison of the effect of music therapy and medical play therapy on the verbalization behavior of pediatric patients. *Journal of Music Therapy, 21,* 2–15.

Galasso, D. (1987). Guidelines for developing multidisciplinary treatment plans. *Hospital and Community Psychiatry, 38,* 394–397.

Gaston, E. T. (1966). Sound and symbol. *Journal of Music Therapy, 3,* 90–92.

Gaston, E. T. (1968). Man and music. In E. T. Gaston (Ed.), *Music in therapy.* New York: MacMillan.

Gerrard, B. A., Boniface, W. J., & Love, B. H. (1980). *Interpersonal skills for health professionals.* Reston, VA: Reston.

Gilbert, J. P. (1977). Music therapy perspectives on death and dying. *Journal of Music Therapy, 14*, 165–171.

Glass, C. R., Merluzzi, T. V., Biever, J. L., & Larsen, K. H. (1982). Cognitive assessment of social anxiety: Development and validation of a self-statement questionnaire. *Cognitive Therapy and Research, 6*, 37–55.

Glick, L. G. (1966). Music as therapy in community agencies. *Journal* of *Music Therapy, 3*, 120–125.

Goldberg, F. S. (1989). Music psychotherapy in acute psychiatric inpatient and private practice settings. *Music Therapy Perspectives, 6*, 40–43.

Goloff, M. S. (1981). The responses of hospitalized medical patients to music therapy. *Music Therapy, 1*, 51–56.

Gregory, D. (1977). *Observation classifications: A manual for skill development.* Tallahassee: The Florida State University.

Hanser, S. B. (1984). Music group psychotherapy: An evaluation model. *Music Therapy Perspectives, 1*(4), 14–16.

Hanser, S. B. (1985). Music therapy and stress reduction research. *Journal of Music Therapy, 22*, 193–206.

Hanser, S. B. (1990). A music therapy strategy for depressed older adults in the community. *Journal of Applied Gerontology, 9*(3), 283–298.

Hanser, S. B., Larson, S. C., & O'Connell, A. S. (1983). The effect of music on relaxation of expectant mothers during labor. *Journal of Music Therapy, 20*, 50–58.

Heaney, C. J. (1992). Evaluation of music therapy and other treatment modalities by adult psychiatric-inpatients. *Journal of Music Therapy, 29*(2), 70–86.

Henderson, S. M. (1983). Effects of a music therapy program upon awareness of mood in music, group cohesion, and self-esteem among hospitalized adolescent patients. *Journal of Music Therapy, 20*, 14–20.

James, M. R. (1986). Verbal reinforcement and self-monitoring inclinations. *Journal of Music Therapy, 23*(4), 182–193.

James, M. R. (1988). Music therapy values clarification: A positive influence on perceived locus of control. *Journal of Music Therapy, 25*(4), 206–215.

James, M. R., & Freed, B. S. (1989). A sequential model for developing group cohesion in music therapy. *Music Therapy Perspectives, 7*, 28–34.

Jellison, J. A. (1983). Functional value as criterion for selection and prioritization of nonmusic and music educational objectives in music therapy. *Music Therapy Perspectives, 1*(2), 17–22.

Johnson, E. R. (1981). The role of objective and concrete feedback in self-concept treatment of juvenile delinquents in music therapy. *Journal of Music Therapy, 18*, 137–147.

Kivland, M. J. (1986). The use of music to increase self-esteem in a conduct disordered adolescent. *Journal of Music Therapy, 23*, 25–29.

Kovach, A. M. (1985). Shamanism and guided imagery and music: A comparison. *Journal of Music Therapy, 22*, 154–165.

Lang, E., & Mattson, M. (1985). The multidisciplinary treatment plan: A format for enhancing activity therapy department involvement. *Hospital and Community Psychiatry, 36*, 62–68.

Levine-Gross, J., & Swartz R. (1982). The effects of music therapy on anxiety in chronically ill patients. *Music Therapy, 2,* 43–52.

Logan, T. G., & Roberts, A. R. (1984). The effects of different types of relaxation music on tension level. *Journal of Music Therapy, 21,* 177–183.

MacPhillamy, D. J., & Lewinsohn, P. M. (1971). *Pleasant events schedule.* Portland: University of Oregon.

Madsen, C. K. (1977). *Modifying life's time.* Tallahassee: The Florida State University.

Madsen, C. K. (1980). *Behavior modification and music therapy: A guide to working with the mentally retarded.* Washington, DC: National Association for Music Therapy.

Madsen, C. K., & Madsen, C. H., Jr. (1968). Music as a behavior modification technique with a juvenile delinquent. *Journal of Music Therapy, 5,* 72–76.

Madsen, C. K., & Madsen, C.H., Jr. (1983). *Teaching/discipline: A positive approach for educational development.* Raleigh, NC: Contemporary Publishing.

Maultsby, M. C. (1977). Combining music therapy and rational behavior therapy. *Journal of Music Therapy, 14,* 89–97.

Maves, P. A., & Schulz, J. W. (1985). Inpatient group treatment on short-term acute care units. *Hospital and Community Psychiatry, 36,* 69–72.

Maxmen, J. S. (1973). Group therapy as viewed by hospitalized patients. *Archives of General Psychiatry, 28,* 404–408.

McNair, D. M., Lorr, M., & Droppelman, L. F. (1971). *Profile of mood state manual.* San Diego: Educational and Industrial Testing Services.

Michel, D. E., and Martin, D. (1970). Music and self-esteem research with disadvantaged problem boys in an elementary school. *Journal of Music Therapy, 7,* 124–128.

Moreno, J. J. (1980). Musical psychodrama: A new direction in music therapy. *Journal of Music Therapy, 17,* 34–42.

Morgenstern, A. M. (1982). Group therapy: A timely strategy for music therapists. *Music Therapy Perspectives, 1*(1), 16–20.

Nebe, H. J. (1971). Music therapy—Its function in supporting the rehabilitation of the handicapped. *Journal of Music Therapy, 8,* 3–11.

Okun, B. F. (1976). *Effective helping: Interviewing and counseling techniques.* North Scituate, MA: Duxbury.

Paul, G. L., & Lentz, R. J. (1977). *Psychosocial treatment of mental patients.* Cambridge, MA: Harvard University.

Peach, S. C. (1984). Some implications for the clinical use of music facilitated imagery. *Journal of Music Therapy, 21,* 27–34.

Plack, T. (1980). *The creative use of music in group therapy.* Springfield, IL: Charles C. Thomas.

Quittner, A. L. (1980). *The facilitative effects of music on visual imagery: A multiple measures approach.* Unpublished masters thesis, The Florida State University.

Rider, M. S. (1985). Entrainment mechanisms are involved in pain reduction, muscle relaxation, and music-mediated imagery. *Journal of Music Therapy, 22,* 183–192.

Rider, M. S., Floyd, J. W., & Kirkpatrick, J. (1985). The effect of music, imagery, and relaxation on adrenal corticosteroids and the re-entrainment of circadian rhythms. *Journal of Music Therapy, 22,* 46–58.

Robbins, L. L. (1966). Opening address—sixteenth annual conference. *Journal of Music Therapy, 3,* 1–7.

Rohner, S. J., & Miller, R. (1980). Degrees of familiar and affective music and their effects on *stale* anxiety. *Journal of Music Therapy, 17,* 2–17.

Rose, S. D. *(1977). Group therapy: A behavioral approach.* Englewood Cliffs, NJ: Prentice-Hall.

Rosenthal, T. L., & Meyer, V. *(1971).* Case report: Behavioral treatment of clinical abulia. *Conditioned Reflex, 6,* 22–29.

Rowe, C. J. (1984). *An outline of psychiatry.* Dubuque, IA: William C. Brown.

Rubin, B. (1973). Music therapy in an outreach station of the Milwaukee County Mental Health Center. *Journal of Music Therapy, 10,* 201–204.

Rubin, B. (1975). Music therapy in a community mental health program. *Journal of Music Therapy, 12,* 59–66.

Sandrock, D., & James, M. R. (1989). Assessment instruments for music-assisted relaxation training. *Music Therapy Perspectives, 7,* 44–50.

Saperston, B. M. (1989). Music-based individualized relaxation training (MBIRT): A stress-reduction approach for the behaviorally disturbed mentally retarded. *Music Therapy Perspectives, 6,* 26–33.

Sarason, I. G., Johnson, J. H., & Siegel, J. M. (1978). Assessing the impact of life changes: Development of the Life Experiences Survey. *Journal of Consulting and Clinical Psychology, 46,* 932–946.

Scartelli, J. (1984). The effect of EMG biofeedback and sedative music, EMG biofeedback only, and sedative music only on frontalis muscle relaxation ability. *Journal of Music Therapy, 21,* 67–78.

Scartelli, J. P., & Borling, J. E. (1986). The effects of sequenced versus simultaneous EMG biofeedback and sedative music on frontalis relaxation training. *Journal of Music Therapy, 23,* 157–165.

Schiff, M., & Frances, A. (1974). Popular music: A training catalyst. *Journal of Music Therapy, 11,* 33–40.

Schulberg, C. (1986). *The music therapy sourcebook: A collection of activities categorized and analyzed.* New York: Human Sciences Press.

Schuster, B. L. (1985). The effect of music listening on blood pressure fluctuations in adult hemodialysis patients. *Journal of Music Therapy, 22,* 146–153.

Sears, W. W. (1968). Processes in music therapy. In E. T. Gaston (Ed.), *Music in therapy.* New York: MacMillan.

Sedei, C. A. (1980). *The effectiveness of music therapy on specific statements verbalized by cancer patients.* Unpublished manuscript, Colorado State University.

Spielberger, C. D., Gorsuch, R. L., & Lushene, R. E. (1968). *Manual for the State-Trait Anxiety Inventory.* Palo Alto, CA: Consulting Psychologists Press.

Stevens, E. (1967). Changing approaches in treatment. *Journal of Music Therapy, 4,* 67–68.

Stith, G. K. (1965). Functions of a music therapist in a day treatment center. *Journal of Music Therapy, 2,* 121–123.

Stratton, V. N., & Zalanowski, A. H. (1984). The relationship between music, degree of liking, and self-reported relaxation. *Journal of Music Therapy, 21,* 184–192.

Taylor, D. B. (1973). Subject responses to precategorized stimulative and sedative music. *Journal of Music Therapy, 10,* 86–94.

Thaut, M. H. (1987). A new challenge for music therapy: The correctional setting. *Music Therapy Perspectives, 4,* 44–50.

Thaut, M. H. (1989). The influence of music therapy interventions on self-rated changes in relaxation, affect, and thought in psychiatric prisoner-patients. *Journal of Music Therapy, 26*(3), 155–166.

Thompson, J. W., Bass, R. D., & Witkin, M. A. (1982). Fifty years of psychiatric services: 1940–1990. *Hospital and Community Psychiatry 33,* 711–717.

Van Stone, W. W. (1973). Peer groups and drug rehabilitation. *Journal of Music Therapy, 10,* 7–12.

Wheeler, A. H., & Fox, W. L (1972). *A guide to writing instructional objectives.* Lawrence, KS: H & H Enterprises.

Wheeler, B. L. (1983). A psychotherapeutic classification of music therapy practices: A continuum of procedures. *Music Therapy Perspectives, 1*(2) 8–12.

Williams, G., & Dorow, L. G. (1983). Changes in complaints and non-complaints of a chronically depressed psychiatric patient as a function of an interrupted music/verbal feedback package. *Journal of Music Therapy, 20,* 143–155.

Wolfe, D. E. (1978). Pain rehabilitation and music therapy. *Journal of Music Therapy, 15,* 162–178.

Wolfe, D. E. (1987). Computer-based decision-making: Contemporary tasks for practicum students and professionals providing music therapy services for the handicapped. In K. Bruscia & C. Maranto (Eds.), *Readings in music therapy education and supervision.* Philadelphia: Temple University.

Wolfe, D. E., Burns, S., Stoll, M., & Wichmann, K. (1975). *Analysis of music therapy group procedures.* Minneapolis: Golden Valley Health Center.

Wolfgram, B. J. (1978). Music therapy for retarded adults with psychotic overlay: A day treatment approach. *Journal of Music Therapy, 15,* 199–207.

Wolpe, S., & Lang, P. T. (1964). A Fear Survey Schedule for use in behavior therapy. *Behavior Research and Therapy, 2,* 27.

Yalom, I. D., (1983). *Inpatient group psychotherapy.* New York: Basic Books.

MUSIC THERAPY AS A PART OF OLDER PEOPLE'S LIVES

Carol A. Prickett

THE recent growth in professional literature relating music therapy services to the needs of the elderly is a reflection of a broad and growing societal interest in all things pertaining to aging and the aged. Not so long ago, attempts to provide an overview of the music therapy geriatric literature uncovered an inadequate number of well-documented studies (Darrough & Boswell, 1992; Gibbons, 1988; Prickett, 1988; D. S. Smith, 1990). However, as of this writing, a decidedly different trend appears to be developing. In the relatively few years since the first edition of this book was published, the number of data-based articles in print has tripled, and countless more are underway. Furthermore, certain areas of focus have begun to emerge, so that it is no longer wishful thinking to state that a body of literature about older people's relationship to music is beginning to evolve, at long last.

The fact that the U.S. population's median age is moving upward, and that this will have profound implications for all foreseeable decades, has caught the attention of the general public and health care policy makers, as well as those who work directly with older people. Professional journals dealing with aging are proliferating, and established journals often devote special issues to general and specific concerns of the elderly and of caregivers. Media reports alert the public to new information about both healthy aging and problems of the aged, but exaggerations and distortions of medical and sociological findings are quite common. Conferences and guest speaker's lectures about such subjects as Alzheimer's dementia, even when highly technical in content, attract large audiences, including caregivers who are eager for guidance in helping those for whom they are responsible.

In 1991, the Senate Special Committee on Aging held a hearing during which many speakers pointed out the relevance of music therapy services for people over the age of 55 (Special Committee on Aging, United States Senate, 1991). Testimony from professional music therapists, from well-known members of the psychology and psychiatry communities, and from recipients of music services or their family members consistently supported the inclusion of music therapy in the list of services to be provided for the elderly. Subsequently, the reauthorization of the Older Americans Act included music therapy as a cited service which is appropriate for the aged.

Nevertheless, while it is good news to music therapists that interest in older people is increasing, the current published literature is obviously only a beginning step in documenting music therapy's effectiveness as treatment or in devising definitive clinical applications. This chapter focuses on the data-based conclusions about music therapy for the elderly which have appeared in refereed journals during the past two decades; as stated earlier, the number has increased, but at this point, all findings must be considered as preliminary foundations, rather than the "final word" in any respect. Only through expansion and replication will more definite conclusions be drawn. In contrast, a representative sample of experiential articles which contained no data are surveyed here, too; they all appeared in reputable professional literature and typify a large group of publications being read by professionals which describe clinical experiences and advocate music therapy.

The Research Population: Maximum Diversity

It is no secret that stereotypes about older people are widespread. Societal expectations vary from benign (the kindly old gentleman or the sweet, comforting grandma) to malignant (the mean old man, the doddering old fool, or the witch-like old hag), and they appear in literature, drama, and syntax when concerns of older people are discussed. Cohen and Krushwitz (1990) surveyed at least 300 pieces of sheet music published between 1830 and the 1950s whose lyrics somehow related to aging. They found that negative themes such as poverty, loneliness, and physical decline were predominant across time, although the theme of long marriages appeared in a positive light. Of course, personal attitudes toward older people are tempered by specific experiences with particular personalities. Societal and personal attitudes may come into play in the design and interpretation of research. To avoid biased comprehension, it may prove helpful to recall that, at bottom, the only factor common to the population designated "older," "aged," "elderly," "senior," or "geriatric" is that its members have lived past an arbitrary chronological age; this arbitrary age may range from 55 years old upward. Music therapists are acutely aware that diversity occurs in all populations, but nowhere is this more true than with older people. Physical health, mental capabilities, economic status, ethnic group, accessibility to family or close friends, and gender have been demonstrated to interact with chronological age in defining the various challenges aging people face. Additionally, the elusive factor of attitude appears to markedly enhance or detract from the perceived quality of all people's lives, not the least, the elderly.

Designing Clinical Treatment Based on Research

Music therapy professionals are accountable for providing efficient, beneficial treatment. As the formal discipline of music therapy has matured, a concerted effort has been made to verify treatment procedures by (1) collecting objective data, (2) examining them according to the principles of scientific method, and (3) reformulating practice when advancing knowledge demands.

It follows that clinical music therapists always face a dilemma when formulating treatment plans. On the one hand, if they wait until sufficient valid, empirical data on all aspects of a disability or music response are available before attempting to design a therapy session, they may well reach retirement age before even one client can be served. On the other hand, promulgating the efficacy of music therapy in general, or of specific music therapy techniques, in the absence of any substantiation other than intuition or tradition borders on professional recklessness.

It is possible that in no area of music therapy service is this dilemma more profound than in the treatment of older clients. The physical and mental health professions as a whole do not have a lengthy history of attention to the special problems of the aged. Advances in medicine and nutrition which are extending lifespans are mandating rapid development of knowledge and techniques to meet the needs of an increasingly large portion of the population. Although the focus and objectivity of the new journals begun since the mid-1970s is diverse, to say the least, the dearth of older published material which can withstand contemporary professional scrutiny is a serious consideration in selecting and evaluating appropriate music therapy procedures to meet older client's needs. For example, the oldest data-based articles included in this review were published in 1977; of the very few published writings appearing prior to that time in which data on older people were collected, documentation was inadequate for inclusion here. Experiential literature has been fairly consistent since about that same time.

This compilation of the published literature (since the mid-1970s) examining music therapy knowledge about and procedures for older clients is two-pronged. The empirical data will be summarized first. Documentation of theoretical and experiential treatment rationales will follow.

Data-Based Literature

Age-Related Physical and Memory Considerations, Apart From Dementia

Brain damage which could affect musical processing may occur at any age, and is of particular concern in the elderly. In two studies (Grossman, Shapiro, & Gardner, 1981; Shapiro, Grossman, & Gardner, 1981), the effects of localized brain damage on musical processing and strategies were investigated. One study (Shapiro et al., 1981) examined 28 patients, ranging in age from 35 to 65 years, and 5 control subjects. The authors concluded that "musical processing skills do not break down in an across-the-board fashion" (Shapiro et al., 1981, p. 167) after damage occurs. Instead, pitch, rhythm, and phrasing accuracy varied with the site of the damage. All right brain damaged groups, and particularly those with anterior lesions, showed greater difficulty in detecting pitch errors. A second investigation (Grossman et al., 1981) involved asking 26 lateralized brain damage patients, all between the ages of 35 and 65 and almost all stroke victims, to identify whether two musical phrases were from the same highly familiar song or not. Some pairs of phrases occurred close to each other in the song of origin, some occurred farther apart in the song of origin, and some were not from the same tune at all. For this latter group, some items' phrases were presented in contrasting moods. Results indicated that patients with either Broca's aphasia or right anterior lesion exhibited greater difficulty in making same/different song decisions, while their responses to mood changes point to a difference in musical processing strategy. It was concluded that strategies for processing musical input vary with the problem to be overcome. In both studies, the variable of handedness was controlled.

Later work by Prior, Kinsella, and Giese (1990) concluded that, at this point, the laterality for processing of specific musical tasks cannot be firmly stated. Two studies were combined so that 28 left cerebrovascular accident patients, 28 right cerebrovascular accident patients, and 28 control subjects could be compared. The age range for the subjects was 48–78 years old. All were tested to see if they could detect changes in rhythm or pitch in familiar and unfamiliar tunes, to see if they could sing a well-known song and three original melodies, and to see if they could imitate rhythm patterns by tapping their fingers. Patients who had left cerebrovascular accidents were poorer at detecting rhythmic variations and at singing new tunes. Control subjects were superior to all patients in singing a known song and in imitating a rhythm.

In a case study of a 73-year-old lawyer who was also an experienced musician, researchers explored the effects on musical memory of an ischemic stroke associated with a single intracerebral lesion in the left hemisphere (Hofman, Klein, & Arlazoroff, 1993). The patient, an accomplished violinist, imitated how instruments were played, but could not name them or any of their parts. He played a simple scale on the violin, but could not name the instrument components. He could not recognize previously known melodies and could not copy musical notation. Since the man's jargon amusia paralleled losses in his nonmusic language, the researchers theorized (and "theorized" is the operative word here) that language and music may share a common hemisphere.

In the area of perception and recall, Borod and Goodglass (1980) studied 102 right-handed males with no serious bilateral hearing loss. The volunteers fell almost equally into age groups of 24–39 years, 40–49 years, 50–59 years, 60–69 years, and 70–79 years. Asked to recall dichotically presented digit sequences and the initial phrases of nursery tunes, a significant difference associated with age was reported. As age increased, the number of correctly recalled responses decreased. At the outset, based on published literature, the investigators anticipated that there would be a decline in accuracy of recall for digits presented to the left ear and an increasing left ear advantage for melodies, both as functions of age. The results did not substantiate these hypotheses, but rather they demonstrated a more uniform decline in cerebral activity.

Bartlett and Snelus (1980) compared the recall for popular songs of 32 middle-aged (37–57 years old) and 32 elderly (60–76 years old) people. They concluded that long-term memory for songs exists, that recall of lyrics is better when prompted by a melodic cue than when given only a title cue, and that temporal placement of the decade of the song's popularity was more accurate for familiar tunes than unfamiliar tunes, even if lyrics for the former could not be remembered. Along these same lines, Maylor (1991) studied 37 middle-aged (55–64.3 years old) and 32 older (65.4–83.8 years old) listener's responses to theme tunes from past and recent television programs, with respect to how frequently the shows had been watched. Neither group performed well in identifying themes or giving information about shows they had not watched. However, for frequently watched programs, older responders recognized fewer theme tunes and gave less information about the shows than did younger ones. Age was a better predictor of the ability to recall than were measures of current cognitive capability. D. S. Smith (1991) concluded that, in a cued recall task of song lyrics from the 1940s and 50s, tempo, duration per word and the total number of words which could be recalled were more closely associated, at least for older adults, with lyric recall than with the familiarity of the song.

The findings of Bingea, Raffin, Aune, Baye, and Shea (1982) are of importance to music therapists, even though music was not investigated. Assessment of 151 nursing home residents, 54–95 years old ($M = 80.6$), revealed that 70% of the ears tested showed a hearing impairment classified as either moderate-to-severe or severe-to-profound. Even though 17 of those assessed (i.e., 8.8%) owned hearing aids, only 3 wore them to the testing site. Retrieving a total of 13 of the aids for examination, the researchers found them all to be malfunctioning in some way.

The relationship between the pervasiveness of presbycusis, problems with hearing aids, and music therapy practice may be more complex than is at first apparent. Riegler (1980b) tested 28 nursing home residents aged 63–90 ($M = 78.7$). Subjects expressed a preference for music listening levels to be "soft." D. S. Smith (1988) attempted to assess whether older listeners preferred listening to music recorded at a normal listening level or at a level enhanced by 15 dB. The results were inconclusive; the listeners may have had no preferences or may not have understood how to express their preferences in that particular testing situation. To gain more accurate information, D. S. Smith (1989) studied the loudness levels at differing frequencies selected by 180 people comprising six equal-sized groups ranging from 18 to 90 years old; these people were not residents of any institution. Loudness levels for each frequency band (110, 330, 1000, and 3000 kHz) were manipulated by subjects via a graphic equalizer until the preferred level for each band was reached. Older adults preferred lower intensity levels when listening to music than younger adults. Older adults did *not* increase loudness levels in the bands where their hearing capabilities were weakest. Based on these studies, a music therapist who assumes that music played for older clients should automatically be played at a louder than normal level may be in error.

Greenwald and Salzberg (1979) determined the vocal range of 30 geriatric nursing home residents, 65–90 years of age (*M* = 83). The average range was 13 semitones, considerably less than the range of young adults. The mean for the highest pitch which could be sung was the A above middle C, while the mean for the lowest singable pitch was G# below middle C. For 75% of these subjects, the functional vocal range stretched from A# below middle C to the G above it. It was concluded that songs should be transposed to fit within this pitch range.

Aptitude and Preference, Apart From Dementia

Aside from the physical limitations associated with normal or problematic aging, other factors have been examined in an attempt to gain information on which music therapy treatment decisions could be based. Early in the 1980s, ERIC, *Reader's Guide, Psychological Abstracts, Dissertation Abstracts International,* Music Therapy Index, Psychology of Music Index, Index Medicus, and the *Journal of Research in Music Education* contained no research into the musical capabilities of older people. Gibbons' pioneer study in this area was published in 1982 (a). One hundred nineteen non-institutionalized participants (mostly female Caucasians), 65 years old or older, completed the tasks of the Music Aptitude Profile (Gordon, 1965). It was concluded that there is no slippage in musical ability concomitant with aging. Further investigations by the same researcher (Gibbons, 1983a, 1983b) again dealt with elderly clients, most of whom were Caucasian females; however, these subjects lived in residential care facilities. Analysis of scores on the Primary Measures of Music Audiation test (Gordon, 1979) for 151 people once more led to the conclusion that aptitude does not diminish with age and also revealed that factors such as musical background and general morale are poor predictors of older clients' performance on this measure (Gibbons, 1983b). For 180 persons tested with the Tonal and Rhythm subtests of the PMMA, discrimination of small interval changes, duration changes, and complex rhythms proved difficult. Short-term memory lapses may have been responsible for poorer discrimination in unfamiliar music than in familiar music (Gibbons, 1983a). A later study by the same researcher, in which 70 elderly care home residents were given the PMMA Rhythm subtest, allowed comparison with the 1983 findings (Clair, 1991). Even though auditory discriminations of rhythmic changes may be occurring, residents' ability to imitate all but simple patterns was limited.

Following another line of research questioning, Gibbons (1982b) found that of 152 non-institutionalized elderly people, 84% wished to develop better musical skills. Specifically, 52% of the singers and 90% of the instrumentalists would have liked the chance to sing or play better.

Elsewhere, Gilbert and Beal (1982) surveyed the music activity preferences of 279 people over the age of 55 from a wide variety of living situations in the Midwest. Five favorite music activities were identified, the most liked of which were listening to popular music from earlier times and singing church hymns. Similarly, the five least liked music activities were named, most notably, performing musical solos and participating in barbershop quartets. Living setting and community size appeared to be associated with the preferences expressed, probably reflecting the access certain groups had to different activities or the general mobility level of older people who live in particular settings. For example, persons living independently rated activities involving movement considerably higher than did those in retirement homes or nursing homes.

Lathom, Petersen, and Havlicek (1982) investigated the relationship between the musical style preference of 104 persons (over the age of 55 years) and several other factors. Each subject gave information concerning age, religious preference, sex, marital status, health, education, previous musical experience, and residence category, then chose their favorite 20-second excerpt from each of 28 recorded pairs, representing folk, big band jazz, musical shows, music of the Twenties, opera, patriotic, religious and symphonic music. Half of the examples were vocal and half were instrumental. Patriotic and jazz music were the most preferred overall. Only those with the most education liked symphonies or opera; conversely, these people gave low ratings to the music of the Twenties, the same music which was rated very highly by those with ninth-grade educations.

A frequently cited study which has served as the basis for the selection of music in numerous research and experiential projects was published by Gibbons in 1977. She examined the popular music preferences of older people and found that while there was not a decided preference for stimulative or sedative music, the tendency was strong to select stimulative songs. Furthermore, when choices were analyzed by age group (e.g., 65–75. 75–85, 85–95), there was a significant preference for the songs which had been popular when respondents had been between 20 and 30 years old. Jonas (1991) interviewed 63 nursing home residents and administered a listening preference test. Each resident heard 16 selections, 4 from each genre of art music, country music, popular music of today and traditional jazz. Selections were rated for preference on a 5-point scale. Country music was preferred the most; traditional jazz, art music, and current popular music followed. It was noted that two of the country songs and two of the highly preferred jazz selections were from the 1930s and 40s, lending support to Gibbons' earlier conclusions.

Another investigation into this area studied the reactions of 20 healthy, non-institutionalized people in each of four age groups (20–30 years, 40–50 years, 60–70 years, and 80–86 years) (Tolhurst, Hollien, & Leeper, 1984). The music for the stimulus tapes was intuitively selected, based on six criteria, with one instrumental 20-second example per genre (i.e., soft rock, country/western, easy listening, and classical). Listeners rated each selection on a 5-point scale, as well as indicating their first and second preferences. It was concluded that young listeners' preferences differ from older listeners, who tended to choose easy listening and classical music.

An extensive investigation by Moore, Staum, and Brotons (1992) included a total of 514 people, ranging in ages from 60–110 years old. The subjects were recruited from a variety of situations, including supervised living/nursing home and highly active community service groups in different areas of the United States. In three investigations, aspects of preference for song repertoire, vocal range, tempo, and accompanying instrument were studied. Results indicated that patriotic, popular, and religious songs were preferred over folk songs, that average vocal ranges for women were from F3 to C5, that men's vocal ranges were nearly an octave lower, that slower tempos were preferred, and that live and recorded chordal accompaniments were preferred over a recorded melodic line or a synthesized accompaniment. This latter finding occurred despite the fact that for the live accompaniments, the performers minimized eye contact or other personal interaction and played in a very basic, unembellished style. It appears that even when musical accompanying skills or therapeutic encouragement are lacking, a live accompaniment is preferred to a recorded one.

Treatment Procedures, Apart From Dementia

Research dealing with establishing the efficacy of music therapy treatment procedures has explored many avenues, but, as of this writing, the surface has only been scratched. Smith and Lipe (1991) surveyed 176 trained music therapists, who had been identified as working with older patients, to gain information about who these therapists were, how they assessed their patients, and what treatment goals were most and least common in their work. The majority of respondents were themselves under 40 years old. Assessment systems were idiosyncratic to the institutions where they were working. The three most common music therapy treatment goals were (1) development of socialization skills, (2) sensory stimulation, and (3) maintaining cognitive skills; the two goals chosen with the least frequency were addressing problem behaviors and spiritual affirmation.

D. S. Smith (1990) reviewed gerontological literature in an attempt to discover the treatments, including nonmusic treatments, which are used with older people, the amount of documentation which verifies these treatments as effective, and the implications this information would have for music therapists. Behavioral interventions could be substantiated as being effective, especially with problems such as disorientation, declining interest in social activity, and sleeping problems. On the other hand, reality orientation and reminiscence, the other two treatment procedures with enough documentation to allow them to be evaluated, could not at this time be substantiated due to a wide variety of operational definitions, underlying assumptions, and use within clinical settings. Smith concluded that a great deal of work remains to be done.

The potential contributions of music activities to the lives of healthy older people have received less attention than have clinical applications for the institutionalized. Darrough and Boswell (1992) summarized some findings and theories which have appeared in publications read by professional musicians, although not all the information given was data-based. A study exploring the relationship between choral singing and successful aging compared 49 singers in a retirement community chorus with 49 retirement community residents who did not join the group (Wise, Hartmann, & Fisher, 1992). No differences were found between the two groups on demographic or general activity profiles, but their musical profiles differed. The singers had sung throughout their lives and had music in their homes prior to moving to the retirement community. The researchers concluded that this information supports the premise that continuity is a contributor to successful aging.

Questionnaires answered by 60 of 72 licensed nursing homes in St. Louis revealed that most held some sort of singing or listening session at least once per month, that these sessions were usually led by untrained persons, and that overall resident participation was rather low (Hylton, 1983). Clair (1990) asked the nursing supervisor and the activity director of six elderly care homes to rate the need for behavioral supervision of a total of 70 residents, ranging in age from

59 to 99 years old. Dementia patients were not included in the assessments. The raters felt that residents who were newer to the institution needed more supervision during activities than did those who had been there longer. Also, active participation activities, as opposed to passive, were indicated as requiring less supervision. After comparing the raters' predictions with patients' actual participation, Clair recommended that beginning music therapists not be put off by staff predictions that patients will not join in, but rather to trust that music will elicit active participation.

Specially designed questionnaires were used by VanderArk, Newman, and Bell (1983) to compare gains from pre- to postmusic therapy treatment in areas considered to indicate quality of life issues (i.e., self-concept, life satisfaction, socialization, music attitude, and self-concept in music). Twenty residents (*M* age=78) of one nursing home received two 45-minute music sessions per week for five weeks. Their responses were compared to those of 23 residents (*M* age = 82) of a similar home who received no music therapy. Significant improvement in gain scores was shown in the areas of life satisfaction, music attitude, and self-concept in music, although the researchers interpreted the latter finding cautiously, since there had been a significant difference between the two groups on this measure at the start of the study.

As for music modalities, Olson (1984) investigated the change in 11 clients' cognitive, affective, and behavioral reactions to taped player piano music. These clients were between 71 and 99 years old (*M* = 83.3) and lived in a Midwestern retirement home. Player piano music had been extremely popular when members of this group were in their teens and twenties. Trained observers reported that rhythm attempts, extremity movement, body movement, and smiles increased notably while music was playing, compared to observations just prior to and just following treatment. Reminiscent comments constituted 40% of the verbal responses. Short-term recollections were uncommon. Patients reported they liked hearing taped player piano music. There was no comparison to any other musical medium.

As D. S. Smith's 1990 review of general gerontology literature revealed, reminiscence is a popular theme for therapeutic interventions, even though consistent techniques have yet to be established and verified as effective. When Wylie (1990) compared the effects of four different types of materials on the number of reminiscent statements made by 60 nursing home residents (71–90 years old), the results were mixed. The materials used were antique objects, general questions, historical summaries, and therapist-selected old songs. The patients were divided into four groups and each group was presented with one, not all, of the stimulus materials. The residents who were asked general questions or given historical summaries made decidedly more reminiscent statements. However, the researcher reported uncertainty whether the structure of the tasks may have influenced the outcome of the study.

Reality Orientation, the other frequently used but as yet unstandardized technique noted by D. S. Smith (1990), has been linked with music therapy by several investigators. Riegler (1980a) compared pre- and posttest answers on questionnaires of four older patients who received a music-based Reality Orientation program with the answers of four similar persons who received standard RO treatment during the same period. The mean age for all patients was 79.6 years. Those receiving music-based treatment demonstrated significant improvement over their peers. In a later study (Wolfe, 1983), 22 regressed geriatric nursing home patients (*M* = 81.9 years) were equally divided to form a treatment and a control group. For 16 weeks, the treatment group received two 30-minute group sensory training sessions per week. Activities included experience with sound/music and other sensory stimulation. Control subjects, who received no treatment, maintained baseline levels on three assessment measures, while the treated patients exhibited significant improvement.

In a later investigation by Bumanis and Yoder (1987), 15 elderly patients who showed mild to severe confusion, orientation, and memory loss participated in traditional music and dance-based Reality Orientation sessions. Everyone notably improved on social and emotional variables, although, as might be expected, patients with severe organic brain syndrome showed the least amount of improvement. The small number of subjects tested may account for the improvements' not being statistically significant. Isenberg-Grzeda (1978) concluded that Reality Orientation needs to move beyond its usual concrete here-and-now focus to use music to incorporate reminiscence. She stated that these techniques, in combination, can assist a patient in seeing the continuous identity which he or she has retained across time.

One use of behavioral music therapy techniques was documented by Williams and Dorow (1983). A 79-year-old man with a long history of depression showed characteristic behaviors such as a lack of cooperation with staff, resistance to interaction, and numerous complaints about physical problems. The therapists used an ABABCA treatment rotation to compare the number of complaints and noncomplaints in a variety of treatment combinations. These treatment combinations incorporated such things as verbal sympathy for complaints, reprimands for complaints, praise for noncomplaints, and interrupted music listening following complaints. Interrupted music was associated with the fewest complaining statements.

Depression in older people has been the focus of three other studies. Hanser (1989) based the treatment in four case studies on a cognitive/behavioral theory. Four standard self-report scales were administered pre- and post-treatment, as well as at the four-week treatment midpoint. Music therapy strategies included instrumental music instruction, structured music experiences, and music-stimulated imagery for stress reduction. Each patient showed decided improvement. In another study by the same researcher, eight music listening techniques were combined with known relaxation methods (Hanser, 1990). Four music therapy recipients, ages 65 through 74, received eight weeks of music therapy treatment in their homes. Post-treatment gain scores on four psychological measures of depression increased after eight weeks of treatment. Redinbaugh (1988) worked with a 91-year-old depressed woman to establish, through music, a communication system between the patient and the therapist. When this communication system was in place, the woman's willingness to participate in social activities increased and a network of supportive people developed for her.

An attempt to reduce abusive behavior directed toward staff was reported by Meddaugh (1986). Four women plus five men (*M* age = 75) who regularly engaged in spitting, hitting, and scratching at staff members were involved in a nine-week "exercise to music" group. Originally, staff members predicted that no one would attend; also, it was noted that the group members had difficulty following directions without becoming abusive. At the end of nine weeks, attendance had been better than expected, and the group members showed an improvement in their ability to follow directions. However, no evaluation of the effect of the music exercise treatment was made; it was felt that the treatment was not in effect long enough to warrant statistical evaluation.

Cofrancesco (1985) observed changes in three geriatric (50–75 years old) stroke patients' hand grasp strength and task performance as a result of three weeks of music therapy treatment, five 30-minute sessions per week. A multiple baseline design was used. Sessions consisted of playing selected musical instruments in ways which coincided with individual physical therapy goals; relaxation training at the end of each session was accompanied by background music chosen by the patient. Improvement in functioning of both hands was shown and was particularly marked in the right hand.

Arrhythmic walking speeds of 9 children and 16 older adults (52–87 years) were the target of a behavioral treatment devised and tested by Staum (1983). While listening to tape recorded marches with consistent tempos, patients practiced matching their steps to the strong beats of the music. Since tapes had been prepared at eight different metronomic speeds, the appropriate pace could be selected for each person. A changing criterion design was used. At the end of three weeks of treatment, all patients showed improvement in rhythm or consistency of gait over baseline.

Alzheimer's Dementia

Prior to the late 1980s most documentations of clinical situations for the institutionalized elderly described a largely undifferentiated dementia population. Toward the decade's end, however, a great deal of public and professional information began to appear concerning Alzheimer's type dementia, a disorder first described early in the century. Sometimes called Alzheimer's disease or dementia (AD), dementia of the Alzheimer's type (DAT), or senile dementia of the Alzheimer's type (SDAT), as of this writing, definitive diagnostic tests have yet to be developed. Currently, diagnosis of a living patient is based on signs of dementia (e.g., confusion, impaired long- and short-term memory, personality aberrations, agitation when unable to answer verbal questions), indications that the dementia is progressive, and the ruling out of other possible causes of the disturbed behavior (American Psychiatric Association, 1994). Post-mortem diagnosis, the only conclusive evidence at this point, discloses neurofibrillary tangles and neuritic plaques throughout the cerebral cortex and especially concentrated in the hippocampus (deGroot & Chusid, 1988).

For the music therapy researcher interested in AD, the enigma of a definitive diagnosis is only part of the challenge of designing and carrying out a study. Despite reports that there are numerous AD patients in the U.S., it is not at all a simple matter to locate a large group of people who are similar enough in capacity or background, not to mention residing close enough together to make a study feasible, so that traditional statistical analysis of data is possible. Early stage AD patients usually reside in their homes, relatively geographically and logistically isolated from other AD patients. Many AD patients remain in their homes until they die, in which case they rarely receive therapeutic services. For those who relocate into special care facilities, the reason for relocation may be that the dementia has become quite advanced. While life may continue for quite some time after institutionalization, patients in latter stages of AD sleep most hours of the day and may not be accessible for research studies. Most of the studies in the following review of the data-based literature involved relatively few subjects, compared to standard social science research protocols. Widely cited conclusions may have been based on observations of one or two patients. Although a pattern of information may be deduced, it is suggested that readers keep this consideration firmly in mind.

Informal observations by clinical workers and family members that music therapy might have a unique function for AD patients have been abundant. Word of mouth, association newsletters, and testimonials such as those presented at the senate hearing (Special Committee on Aging,

United States Senate, 1991) have set the stage for the rapid development of research into the particular relationship of music therapy to AD patients' treatment. A 1987 survey of 27 facilities with special units for AD patients found that two-thirds (i.e., 18) reported that music-related activities were the second most frequent type of activities employed (Weiner, 1987). No information was given concerning the musical or therapeutic training of the persons leading these activities, however.

Physiological investigations which attempt to trace musical reactions in AD patients are few and preliminary. Researchers who administered musical stimuli to several AD patients during a brain imaging procedure raised questions about the mental processing of language and of music (Walton, Frisina, Swartz, Hantz, & Crummer, 1988). These investigators later postulated that Event Related Potentials (ERPs), measures of voltage changes on the scalp elicited by sensory events, could document internal cognitive events which characterize AD patients (Swartz, Hantz, Crummer, Walton, & Frisina, 1989); their article presents four individual graphs of reactions to timbre, intervals and meter. Although the number of people assessed is not entirely clear, and appears to be fewer than four, the authors propose the P3 aspect of the ERPs as a possible way to study music cognition. A larger study by three from this group of authors assessed 12 healthy and 6 SDAT subjects' P3 responses to an "oddball" paradigm adapted from music. Predictable musical stimuli were interlaced with unexpected stimuli (i.e., oddballs) and voltage changes thought to be indicative of psychological phenomena were recorded. In many respects, the SDAT patients' reactions paralleled those of the healthy people. The authors concluded that SDAT patients can attend to and discriminate differences in musical stimuli (Swartz, Crummer, & Frisina, 1992).

Documentation of AD patients' differing responses during music and nonmusic periods has been the focus of most of the clinical research in this area. Norberg, Melin, and Asplund (1986) laid the groundwork for a number of later studies with their observations of two people in the final stages of the disease. In 16 sessions conducted over 12 consecutive days, they compared the effects of music, touch, and the presentation of familiar objects through direct observation of mouth movements and eyeblinks, analysis of videotapes for the same behaviors, pulse, and respiration rate. The music was Norwegian (as were the patients) and was chosen from suggestions made by the patients' families; religious songs, ballads, and old folkdance melodies were heard through headphones. The two patients displayed differing behavioral reactions to the music, but in both cases, the music was the only stimulus which elicited reaction.

Clair and Bernstein (1990a) assessed three men, ranging in age from 56–72, who had been diagnosed with AD. The final 11 weeks of a 15-month music therapy treatment program were the primary focus of observations. Music therapy sessions consisted of a greeting song, singing, playing a chosen rhythm instrument, attempting to imitate rhythms given by the therapists, and a closing song. Data were collected for communication, watching others, singing, interaction with the instrument, and sitting in their chairs. The patients' deterioration across the 15 months, and especially during the 11 weeks in question, was substantial, but participation in the music activities remained constant or improved slightly. For example, the men sat in their chairs for the entire half hour session without physical restraint and interacted with other group members, although no such interaction was noted at any other time during the week.

In a later study, six advanced AD patients, men aged 62–73, were asked to participate in a total of 14 music therapy sessions; 4 of the sessions were designated as pilot and 10 served as the actual experimental tests (Clair & Bernstein, 1990b). Comparisons were made of vibrotactile responses (i.e., responses to touching a drum as it was struck), nonvibrotactile responses, and singing. Five of the six never sang, and for all, including the one who initially sang, responses to vibrotactile stimuli were stronger than to nonvibrotactile ones. Following up on the viability of vibrotactile stimulation as the basis for music therapy treatment, these researchers compared the responses of six DAT patients with those of three patients whose dementia had been diagnosed as alcohol related (Clair & Bernstein, 1993). These nine men required total care and supervision for their own safety. When their reactions to the vibrotactile stimulus of a Somatron® bed, to an auditory musical stimulus presented through a tape recorder, and to silence were compared, the results were inconclusive. Although they were given a method for choosing between the stimuli, they did not attempt to make any changes from whatever stimulus was initially presented.

Cognitive function is one of the primary interests for music therapists working with AD patients. G. H. Smith (1986) studied 12 female AD patients, aged 71–92 years, who lived in a nursing home. Six 30-minute sessions were divided equally between three treatment methods: musically cued reminiscence, verbally cued reminiscence, and music alone (i.e., no discussion). The music for two conditions and the verbal cues for the third were selected to be representative of the music of the patients' lifespans. Pre- and post-session scores on the Mini Mental State Examination, a common dependent measure in AD studies, were used for analysis. Language subsection scores were increased following musically cued and verbally cued reminiscence, but neither orientation subscores, attention subscores, nor total scores were increased under these conditions; in fact, the questioning appeared to produce anxiety in the patients. However, the music sessions, where discussion was avoided, significantly increased total scores without raising anxiety.

Prickett and Moore (1991) explored the ability of 10 AD patients (ages 69–87) to recall songs or spoken material which they were presumed to have known their entire lives and to recall a song or short verbal piece which were new to them. Each patient attended three 20-minute sessions about two days apart. Sessions were videotaped and the percentage of words which could be recalled, person by person, were determined. The patients recalled the words to songs decidedly better than spoken material or verbal information such as the therapists' names. Recall of long-familiar songs was far better than recall of a new song, but even when the new song's words could not be remembered, patients tried to sing, hum, or keep time to the music while the therapists sang.

A reversal behavioral design was used by Olderog-Millard and Smith (1989) to investigate differences in the behavior of 10 AD patients (71–98 years old) during alternating discussion and singing sessions held twice a week across five weeks. Patients were assessed by observers using a behavioral checklist. The behaviors of sitting in a chair and of walking with others were significantly higher during music sessions, as was vocal/verbal participation. The incidence of patients' walking with others after the music sessions also significantly increased.

Two case studies investigated the preserved musical memory or skill of musicians who developed AD. In one report, an 81-year-old woman's ability to play piano, to sight read, and to identify well-known songs and serious compositions was judged against the same skills of four pianists who were not impaired (Beatty, Zavadil, Bailly, Rixen, Zavadil, Farnham, & Fisher, 1988). Although she demonstrated many problems related to AD in everyday life and testing, her piano playing was comparable to unimpaired pianists of a similar age or background; she could sight read a little but was easily distracted; but she could not verbally identify the songs. The researchers concluded that the procedural memory necessary to play a known piece was fairly well preserved, but her declarative, semantic memory was impaired. The subject of the second case study was an 82-year-old man who was a musicologist and who had worked as a music editor for 40 years (Crystal, Grober, & Masur, 1989). He could play piano compositions which he had learned prior to the onset of AD from memory, but could not identify the titles or composers of the pieces. Again, procedural memory was not severely harmed, but declarative memory had been lost.

In a large study of the passive influence of music, Lord and Garner (1993) worked with 60 AD patients in the 72–103 age range. After the group was divided into three treatment groups (14 men and 6 women per group), patients received six sessions per week over a six month period. One group's treatment consisted of having big band music from the 1920s and 30s playing during the daily recreation period; the second group was given puzzle exercises; the third group drew and painted. The researchers used a pre-treatment questionnaire of their own devising which was administered orally and individually; daily observations totaled 36. After the six months of treatment concluded, the questionnaire was given again. The patients who had heard big band music were significantly more alert, happier, and better able to recall their past personal history than the other subjects. The observers noted that the AD patients who received music showed an enjoyment and enthusiasm for their daily sessions which was absent in the other two groups.

Pollack and Namazi (1992) studied the effects of a more active treatment format. Eight AD patients, ages 67–85, received six individual 20-minute sessions over a period of two weeks. Each person's music treatment was designed around his or her preferred music response and adjusted to the appropriate cognitive and motor difficulty level. Patients were evaluated before and after each session for direct verbal (talking, vocalizing), direct nonverbal (gesturing, smiling, touching, singing, humming, etc.), and indirect (sitting, standing, walking with others) behaviors. Following music sessions, there was a 24% increase in social behaviors and a 14% decrease in self-directed behaviors.

A different music therapy treatment format for AD patients was explored by Newman and Ward (1992). During five weeks of structured music therapy sessions, presented twice per day, children were included in one of each day's sessions. Videotaped observations revealed that there was significantly more touching and extension of the patients' hands when the children were in the room; in contrast, patients kept their hands folded more when the children were absent.

The agitation and aggression which is often present in AD patients' interpersonal behavior is of great concern to treatment personnel and family members. Several investigators have designed studies to see whether music or music therapy could help contain this problem. Bright (1986) queried 111 nurses and caregivers, none of whom worked at a facility where a music therapist was employed, about which aspects of working with AD patients were the most stressful. Questions also concerned if or how they used music with patients. The most frequent music oriented interaction was to select music the patient liked on his or her radio. Playing recordings or singing while walking a patient down the hall rarely occurred. Bright concluded that many of the stressful patient behaviors could be reduced if trained music therapists were available at the facilities.

Two observational reports document the apparent need for music therapy services for agitated AD patients. Cohen-Mansfield, Marx, and Werner (1992) spent three months observing

24 agitated and severely cognitively impaired patients, ranging in age from 62–93 years. The focus of their observations was the way patients were spending their time each day and how this use of time related to their agitation. For almost two-thirds of the observation (63%), the patients were not involved in any activity. Structured activities such as music therapy or socializing with visitors occupied very little time, even though analysis clearly showed that there were fewer agitated behaviors when structured activities or socialization were occurring. This confirmed the conclusion from earlier observations (Cohen-Mansfield, Werner, & Marx, 1989).

Perhaps the most extensive data-based documentation of agitated AD patients' reactions to one-to-one music therapy sessions is a study by Groene (1993). Thirty patients, all with a history of wandering (not remaining seated), were divided into two groups. One group's seven individual therapy sessions consisted of five music sessions featuring live music and two sessions where the therapist read aloud. For the other group, five individual reading sessions and two music sessions were presented. All sessions were 15 minutes long and were videotaped for later behavioral analysis. For both groups, the time these wandering patients remained seated or near the treatment area was substantially greater during music presentations than during reading. As the study progressed, the time seated or proximal during music sessions tended to increase. Based on these data, a strong recommendation for an active, stimulative, multisensory therapy such as live music therapy sessions was made by the author.

Summary

To locate data-based studies devoted to the uses of music therapy with the aged, the literature (since 1977) in music therapy, music education, psychology, recreation therapy, hospice, gerontology, psychomusicology, and neurology was searched; the PsychLIT CD-ROM and ERIC were also covered. A total of 63 data-based studies (excluding Bingea et al., which does not include musical tasks per se) were found. They fall into four categories: age-related physical considerations, aptitude and preference, treatment procedures, and Alzheimer's dementia.

The decision to set 1977 as the earliest publication date for consideration excluded a few writings from older music therapy literature. However, the gap of almost a decade between the last articles in the 1960s and the first ones in the 1970s; the changes in research style, observation techniques, and general knowledge about aging; and the fact that 90% of the studies were published in 1980 or later made comparing a few works across several decades questionable.

The relative scarcity of solid data on which treatment decisions for older clients can be based reflects several factors. First, although aging is hardly a new phenomenon, professional attention to the special psychological and health adjustments of later life has only recently gained ground. Second, "the aged" are as disparate as individuals in any other population. In some of the investigations cited above, the subjects were healthy, productive, mobile people. In other studies, the patients were severely disabled mentally and/or physically. Third, from the wording of the papers, it appears that most of the researchers were not employees of the center where the work was conducted. Hylton's work and the large number of non-music therapists conducting studies indicate that music therapy services are greatly appreciated by clients, but trained music therapists are rarely employed full time in senior citizen facilities.

Nevertheless, the need for more and better controlled empirical information is critical. For our literature to be able to support our claims that music therapy is beneficial for older patients, basic research precautions must be taken:

1. having more than one person administer treatment or evaluation, so that the music therapy treatment effect can be separated from the effect of an individual therapist's personality;

2. comparing music therapy treatment to contact control, instead of comparisons to no-contact control subjects or no control at all;

3. increasing the use of behavioral designs, such as multiple baseline, which are ideal when there are a small number of people to be studied or when there is a desire to provide, over time, all subjects with music therapy treatment;

4. comparing different music activities or presentation modalities to other music activities or modalities, rather than to the absence of music;

5. increasing the use of more objective dependent measures (e.g., videotape, timers, trained observers, or decreases in necessary medication) and decreasing sole reliance on nonstandardized measures.

Documentation of Clinical Practice: Theoretical and Experiential Literature

In the absence of empirical data, on what can clinical music therapists rely for guidance in formulating treatment for older clients? Discussing a similar accountability problem in a related profession, Wilson (1984) proposed that a therapist can fall back on models which do not violate either the existing data or the theoretical constructs which have proved valuable over time. If this premise is accepted and if the music therapy processes postulated by Sears (1968) can be said to serve as theoretical bases for music therapy treatment, the articles cited below fill some of the accountability gaps encountered when presenting music therapy as an effective treatment method for the particular problems of older clients.

A number of detailed reports of music and music therapy programs for older people have been published. Some of these contributions come from trained professionals (music therapists and those in related fields) whose scholarly diligence and up-to-date knowledge is praiseworthy. It is worth noting, however, that approximately one third of the articles/studies devoted to the uses of music therapy with the aged which have been published in the United Stated since the mid-1970s have been written by persons whose stated credentials contain no references to formal music therapy training, registration, certification, or any professional tie except interest or job title.

Geriatric nursing journals and textbooks, in particular, contain a number of authoritative-sounding articles and chapters about the uses and effects of music therapy (Bell, 1987; Glynn, 1986; Hennessey, 1976, 1984; Karr, 1985; Kartman, 1977, 1980, 1984, 1990; McCloskey, 1985; McMurray, 1989; Moore, 1978; Moses, 1985; Needler & Baer, 1982; Phillips, 1980). The quality of these pieces varies widely, but for naive readers, they are appealing in their simplicity. Therefore, caution is advisable, since the small amount of music therapy literature which is cited is rarely current. Furthermore, techniques mentioned in writings of several decades past which have never been verified in peer-reviewed journals (e.g., the Iso principle) are described as if they were universally accepted among professionals. That such a large portion of the literature available to health professionals was not written by trained music therapists, does not reflect current music therapy knowledge, and tends to overstate what is actually known of music's uses is an indication of the need for gathering and disseminating a greater amount of empirical information.

The articles which follow are representative of those which conform closely to the traditional practices and theories of music therapy. They also meet the criterion described by Wilson (1984) in that they do not violate either the existing data or the theoretical constructs which have proved valuable over time.

Background

Watts (1980), writing in the *Journal of Music Therapy,* describes two theories of aging which have adherents in the field of gerontology. The "Disengagement Theory" divides into two segments to describe a process of voluntary and necessary withdrawal from life by aging people. The aspect of societal disengagement explains how and why mainstream society and aging people increasingly go their separate ways. Individual disengagement refers to the self-limitation of activity and the increasing preoccupation with personal concerns sometimes demonstrated by the aged. In contrast, the "Activity Theory" states that the maintenance of middle-age activity levels as long as possible is ideal. Watt contends that music therapists are eclectic in their approaches to serving older people.

A review of some of the theories of death and dying which developed throughout the mental and physical health professions during the 1970s was prepared by Gilbert (1977). The ways in which music therapy could fit into the needs described in several prominent models (e.g., life review, religious expression, or expression of feelings to loved ones) were outlined.

Clinical Practices

Several rationales for music therapy's inclusion among the services for older people provide an overview for this section. Lipe (1987) made the case that there must be a distinction between diversional music activities and music therapy. Palmer (1989) developed three scenarios for music therapy services (well elderly, day care patients, extended care patients) and outlined how the training of music therapists should prepare them for this work. An article by Lynch (1987) emphasized the relationship between music and medicine, with emphasis on using music for relaxation.

Taking a different tack, Weissman (1983) decided not to develop a treatment program, but rather a model for planning treatment. Although the complete set of behavioral objectives was not included in the published article, examples demonstrate the specificity of the work. Of interest is the two-step method used for selecting appropriate treatment goals and behavioral objectives; they were garnered from the literature and then validated by experts from at least eight related fields. Goals addressed by the model were sensory, perceptual-motor, cognitive, physical fitness, self-image, and social. In Weissman's model, the basis for any individualized music activity program is rooted in the following steps: (1) determine purpose; (2) design individualized music activity program; (3) plan for implementation; (4) implement, observe, and record observations; and (5) evaluate feedback and re-determine program. Music activities were not specified, since the creativity of the therapist in using the model to meet the unique needs of the client is the reason such a model would be devised in the first place.

Palmer (1977) instituted a wide variety of music experiences and activities to promote and retain high level functioning (mental and physical) of a different group of nursing home patients. In a later report (Palmer, 1983), additional specific examples of the relationship between traditional music therapy activities and therapeutic goals are given; the nursing home where these activities took place served 380 residents.

Gibbons (1984) described the development of a program serving approximately 20 non-institutionalized older adults; these people could advance their music skills through individual instruction and/or a large group experience. In another example, the music therapy program in a geriatric day hospital offered activities addressing mobility, analgesia, reminiscence, communication, and coming to grips with memories (Randall, 1991).

Patients diagnosed with Alzheimer's disease have received attention in recent publications. S. Smith (1990) recommended singing, playing instruments, completing lyrics to familiar songs, exercising to music, and relaxing to music. Christie (1992) not only worked with individuals and small groups of AD patients, but added a 12-member bell ringing group once a week. Lipe (1991) described working with an individual patient, including a description of how the treatment objectives and strategies evolved. Shively and Henkin (1986) combined music therapy with dance/movement therapy; a month-long theme was the focus for each session. McCarthy (1992) zeroed in on stress management strategies, including music for relaxation, to help caregivers cope.

The combination of music and exercise is one common use of music with older people; LaRocque and Campagna (1983) gave a detailed description of an exercise routine which has been successfully used by patients aged 61–90. A program combining music, drawing, writing, and discussion to help depressed, anxious, or withdrawn older people was developed by Rosling and Kitchen (1992).

Colligan (1987) described the uses of music therapy in hospice care. An article by Bright (1981) described the use of music to help people work through grief reactions.

Older mentally retarded persons may need special assistance in expanding socialization and communication skills. Segal (1990) combined music, art, and creative movement to address these treatment goals.

Summer (1981) adapted the Guided Imagery and Music (GIM) technique developed by Bonny to the particular needs of nursing home residents.

Finally, the needs of healthy, active older adults for recognition and attention were addressed through the structure of a talent show (Glassman, 1983).

Conclusions

The body of data-based literature dedicated to music therapy's usefulness for older people has grown impressively in the last decade. Nevertheless, much remains to be done. To date, the careful documentation procedures which dominate the research literature in some areas of treatment (e.g., mental retardation) appear to have generated fewer similar studies in music therapy for geriatric clients. Published verification of treatment pervasiveness or effectiveness represents only a tiny portion of the literature and there appears to have been little overlap, replication, or follow-up. At a time of increasing accountability to clients, accrediting agencies, and third-party reimbursers, there remains an urgent need to increase and improve the data-based information concerning the indications, contraindications, and efficacy of music therapy for the fastest growing segment of the population.

References

American Psychiatric Association. (1994). *Diagnostic and statistical manual of mental disorders* (4th ed. revised). Washington, DC: Author.

Bartlett, J. C., & Snelus, P. (1980). Lifespan memory for popular songs. *American Journal of Psychology, 93,* 551–560.

Beatty, W. W., Zavadil, K. D., Bailly, R. C., Rixen, G. J., Zavadil, L. E., Farnham, N., & Fisher, L. (1988). Preserved musical skill in a severely demented patient. *International Journal of Clinical Neuropsychology, 10,* 158–164.

Bell, J. C. (1987). Music and the elderly. *Educational Gerontology, 13,* 147–155.

Bingea, R .L., Raffin, M. J. M., Aune, K., Baye, L., & Shea S. L. (1982). Incidence of hearing loss among geriatric nursing-home residents. *Journal of Auditory Research, 22,* 275–283.

Borod, J. C., & Goodglass, H. (1980). Lateralization of linguistic and melodic processing with age. *Neuropsychologia, 18,* 79–83.

Bright, R. (1981). Music and the management of grief reactions. In I. M. Burnside (Ed.), *Nursing and the aged* (pp. 137–142). New York: McGraw Hill.

Bright, R. (1986). The use of music therapy and activities with demented patients who are deemed "difficult to manage." *Clinical Gerontologist, 6,* 131–144.

Bumanis, A., & Yoder, J. W. (1987). Music and dance: Tools for reality orientation. *Activities, Adaptation and Aging, 10,* 23–35.

Christie, M. E. (1992). Music therapy applications in a skilled and intermediate care nursing home facility: A clinical study. *Activities, Adaptation and Aging, 16,* 69–87.

Clair, A. A. (1990). The need for supervision to manage behavior in the elderly care home resident and the implications for music therapy practice. *Music Therapy Perspectives, 8,* 72–75.

Clair, A. A. (1991). Rhythmic responses in the elderly and their implications for music programming. *Journal of the International Association of Music for the Handicapped, 6,* 3–11.

Clair, A. A., & Bernstein, B. (1990a). A preliminary study of music therapy programming for severely regressed persons with Alzheimer's type dementia. *Journal of Applied Gerontology, 9,* 299–311.

Clair, A. A., & Bernstein, B. (1990b). A comparison of singing, vibrotactile and nonvibrotactile instrumental playing responses in severely regressed persons with dementia of the Alzheimer's type. *Journal of Music Therapy, 27,* 119–125.

Clair, A. A., & Bernstein, B. (1993). The preference for vibrotactile versus auditory stimuli in severely regressed persons with dementia of the Alzheimer's type compared to those with dementia due to alcohol abuse. *Music Therapy Perspectives, 11,* 24–27.

Cofrancesco, E. M. (1985). The effect of music therapy on hand grasp strength and functional task performance in stroke patients. *Journal of Music Therapy, 23,* 129–145.

Cohen, E. S., & Krushwitz, A. L. (1990). Old age in America represented in nineteenth and twentieth century popular sheet music. *Gerontologist, 30,* 345–354.

Cohen-Mansfield, J., Marx, M. S., & Werner, P. (1992). Observational data on time use and behavior problems in the nursing home. *Journal of Applied Gerontology, 11,* 111–121.

Cohen-Mansfield, J., Werner, P., & Marx, M. S. (1989). An observational study of agitation in agitated nursing home residents. *International Psychogeriatrics, 1,* 153–165.

Colligan, K. G. (1987). Music therapy and hospice care. *Activities, Adaptation and Aging, 10,* 103–122.

Crystal, H. A., Grober, E., & Masur, D. (1989). Preservation of musical memory in Alzheimer's disease. *Journal of Neurology, Neurosurgery, and Psychiatry, 52,* 1415–1416.

Darrough, G. P., & Boswell, J. (1992). Older adult participants in music: A review of related literature. *Bulletin of the Council for Research in Music Education, 111,* 25–34.

deGroot, J., & Chusid, J. G. (1988). *Correlative neuroanatomy* (20th ed.) Norwalk, CT: Appleton and Lange.

Gibbons, A. C. (1977). Popular music preferences of elderly people. *Journal of Music Therapy, 14,* 180–189.

Gibbons, A. C. (1982a). Music aptitude profile scores in a non-institutionalized elderly population. *Journal of Research in Music Education, 30,* 23–29.

Gibbons, A. C. (1982b). Musical skill level self-evaluation in non-institutionalized elderly. *Activities, Adaptation, and Aging, 3,* 61–67.

Gibbons, A. C. (1983a). Item analysis of the *Primary Measures of Music Audiation* in elderly care home residents. *Journal of Music Therapy, 20,* 201–210.

Gibbons, A. C. (1983b). *Primary Measures of Music Audiation* scores in an institutionalized elderly population. *Journal of Music Therapy, 20,* 21–29.

Gibbons, A. C. (1984). A program for non-institutionalized, mature adults: A description. *Activities, Adaptation and Aging, 6,* 71–81.

Gibbons, A. C. (1988). A review of literature for music development/education and music therapy with the elderly. *Music Therapy Perspectives, 5,* 33–40.

Gilbert, J. P. (1977). Music therapy perspectives on death and dying. *Journal of Music Therapy, 14,* 165–171.

Gilbert, J. P., & Beal, M. R. (1982). Preferences of elderly individuals for selected music education experiences. *Journal of Research in Music Education, 30,* 247–253.

Glassman, L. R. (1983). The talent show: Meeting the needs of the healthy elderly. *Music Therapy 3,* 82–93.

Glynn, N. J. (1986). The therapy of music. *Journal of Gerontological Nursing, 12,* 7–10.

Gordon, E. (1965). *Musical Aptitude Profile.* Boston: Houghton Mifflin Company.

Gordon, E. (1979). *Primary Measures of Music Audiation.* Chicago: G.I.A. Publications.

Greenwald, M. A., & Salzberg, R. S. (1979). Vocal range assessment of geriatric clients. *Journal of Music Therapy, 16,* 172–179.

Groene, R. W. (1993). Effectiveness of music therapy 1:1 intervention with individuals having senile dementia of the Alzheimer's type. *Journal of Music Therapy, 30,* 138–157.

Grossman, M., Shapiro, B. E., & Gardner, H. (1981). Dissociable musical processing strategies after localized brain damage. *Neuropsychologia, 19,* 425–433.

Hanser, S. B. (1989). Music therapy with depressed older adults. *Journal of the International Association of Music for the Handicapped, 4,* 16–27.

Hanser, S. B. (1990). A music therapy strategy for depressed older adults in the community. *Journal of Applied Gerontology, 9,* 283–298.

Hennessey, M. J. (1976). Music and group work with the aged. In I. M. Burnside (Ed.), *Nursing and the aged* (pp. 255–269). New York: McGraw Hill.

Hennessey, M. J. (1984). Music therapy. In I. Burnside (Ed.), *Working with the elderly: Group processes and techniques* (2nd ed., pp. 198–210). Monterey, CA: Wadsworth Health Sciences Division.

Hofman, S., Klein, C., & Arlazoroff, A. (1993). Common hemisphericity of language and music in a musician: A case report. *Journal of Communication Disorders, 26,* 73–82.

Hylton, J. (1983). Music programs for the institutionalized elderly in a midwestern metropolitan area. *Journal of Music Therapy, 20,* 211–223.

Isenberg-Grzeda, C. (1978). Music therapy: Its implications for the mentally impaired aged. *Journal of the Canadian Association for Music Therapy, 6,* 2–6.

Jonas, J. L. (1991). Preferences of elderly music listeners residing in nursing homes for art music, traditional jazz, popular music of today, and country music. *Journal of Music Therapy, 28,* 149–160.

Karr, K. (1985). How to care for, comfort, and commune at the emotional level. *Activities, Adaptation and Aging, 7,* 51–76.

Kartman, L. L. (1977). The use of music as program tool with regressed geriatric patients. *Journal of Gerontological Nursing, 3,* 38–42.

Kartman, L. L. (1980). The power of music with patients in a nursing home. *Activities, Adaptation and Aging, 1,* 9–17.

Kartman, L. L. (1984). Music hath charms. *Journal of Gerontological Nursing, 10,* 20–24.

Kartman, L. L. (1990). Fun and entertainment: One aspect of making meaningful music for the elderly. *Activities, Adaptation and Aging, 14,* 39–44.

LaRocque, P., & Campagna, P. D. (1983). Physical activity through rhythmic exercise for elderly persons living in a senior citizen residence. *Activities, Adaptation and Aging, 4,* 77–81.

Lathom, W. B., Petersen, M., & Havlicek, L. (1982). Musical preferences of older people attending nutrition sites. *Educational Gerontology, 8,* 155–165.

Lipe, A. W. (1987). A justification of music therapy in the nursing home setting. *Activities, Adaptation and Aging, 10,* 17–22.

Lipe, A. W. (1991). Using music therapy to enhance the quality of life in a client with Alzheimer's dementia: A case study. *Music Therapy Perspectives, 9,* 102–105.

Lord, T. R., & Garner, J. E. (1993). Effects of music on Alzheimer's patients. *Perceptual and Motor Skills, 76,* 451–455.

Lynch, L. (1987). Music therapy: Its historical relationships and value in programs for the long-term care setting. Special issue: "You bring out the music in me": Music in nursing homes. *Activities, Adaptation and Aging, 10,* 5–15.

Maylor, E. A. (1991). Recognizing and naming tunes: Memory impairment in the elderly. *Journal of Gerontology, 46,* 207–217.

McCloskey, L. J. (1985). Music and the frail elderly. *Activities, Adaptation and Aging, 7*, 73–75.

McCarthy, K. M. (1992). Information sharing: Stress management in the health care field: A pilot program for staff in a nursing home unit for patients with Alzheimer's disease. *Music Therapy Perspectives, 10*, 110–113.

McMurray, J. (1989). Creative arts with older people. Special issue: Creative arts with older people. *Activities, Adaptation and Aging, 14*, 138.

Meddaugh, D. I. (1986). Exercise to music for the abusive patient. *Clinical Gerontologist, 6*, 147–154.

Moore, E. C. (1978). Using music with the elderly: Group processes and techniques. In I. M. Burnside (Ed.), *Working with the elderly: Group processes and techniques* (pp. 426–438). Monterey, CA: Wadsworth Health Sciences Division.

Moore, R. S., Staum, M. J., & Brotons, M. (1992). Music preferences of the elderly: Repertoire, vocal ranges, tempos, and accompaniments for singing. *Journal of Music Therapy, 29*, 236–252.

Moses, J. (1985). Stroking the child in withdrawn and disoriented elders. *Transactional Analysis Journal, 15*, 152–158.

Needler, W., & Baer, M. A. (1982). Movement, music and remotivation with the regressed elderly. *Journal of Gerontological Nursing, 8*, 497–503.

Newman, S., & Ward, C. (1992). An observational study of intergenerational activities and behavior change in dementing elders at adult day care centers. *International Journal of Aging and Human Development, 36*, 321–333.

Norberg, A., Melin, E., & Asplund, K. (1986). Reactions to music, touch and object presentation in the final stage of dementia: An exploratory study. *International Journal of Nursing Studies, 23*, 315–323.

Olderog-Millard, K. A., & Smith, J. M. (1989). The influence of group singing therapy on the behavior of Alzheimer's disease patients. *Journal of Music Therapy, 26*, 58–70.

Olson, B. K. (1984). Player piano music as therapy for the elderly. *Journal of Music Therapy, 21*, 35–45.

Palmer, M. D. (1977). Music therapy in a comprehensive program of treatment and rehabilitation for the geriatric resident. *Journal of Music Therapy, 14*, 190–197.

Palmer, M. D. (1983). Music therapy in a comprehensive program of treatment and rehabilitation for the geriatric resident. *Activities, Adaptation and Aging, 3*, 53–59.

Palmer, M. D. (1989). Music therapy in gerontology: A review and a projection. *Music Therapy Perspectives, 6*, 52–56.

Phillips, J. R. (1980). Music in the nursing of elderly persons in nursing homes. *Journal of Gerontological Nursing, 6*, 37–39.

Pollack, N. J., & Namazi, K. H. (1992). The effect of music participation on the social behavior of Alzheimer's disease patients. *Journal of Music Therapy, 29*, 54–67.

Prickett, C. A. (1988). Music therapy for the aged. In C. E. Furman (Ed.), *Effectiveness of music therapy procedures: Documentation of research and clinical practice* (pp. 209–222). Silver Spring, MD: National Association for Music Therapy.

Prickett, C. A., & Moore, R. S. (1991). The use of music to aid memory of Alzheimer's patients. *Journal of Music Therapy, 28*, 101–110.

Prior, M., Kinsella, G., & Giese, J. (1990). Assessment of musical processing in brain-damaged patients: Implications for laterality of music. *Journal of Clinical and Experimental Neuropsychology, 12,* 301–312.

Randall, T. (1991, September 11). Music not only has charms to soothe, but also to aid elderly in coping with various disabilities. *JAMA, 266,* 1323–1324, 1329.

Redinbaugh, E. M. (1988). The use of music therapy in developing a communication system in a withdrawn, depressed older adult resident: A case study. *Music Therapy Perspectives, 5,* 82–85.

Riegler, J. (1980a). Comparison of a reality orientation program for geriatric patients with and without music. *Journal of Music Therapy, 17,* 26–33.

Riegler, J. (1980b). Most comfortable loudness level of geriatric patients as a function of Seashore loudness discrimination scores, detection threshold, age, sex, setting, and musical background. *Journal of Music Therapy, 17,* 214–222.

Rosling, L. K., & Kitchen, J. (1992). Music and drawing with institutionalized elderly. *Activities, Adaptation and Aging, 17,* 27–38.

Sears, W. W. (1968). Processes in music therapy. In E. T. Gaston (Ed.), *Music in therapy.* New York: Macmillan.

Segal, R. (1990). Helping older retarded persons expand their socialization skills through the use of expressive therapies. *Activities, Adaptation and Aging, 15,* 99–109.

Shapiro, B. E., Grossman, M., & Gardner, H. (1981). Selective musical processing deficits in brain damaged populations. *Neuropsychologia, 19,* 161–169.

Shively, C., & Henkin, L. (1986). Information sharing: Music and movement therapy with Alzheimer victims. *Music Therapy Perspectives, 3,* 56–58.

Smith, D. S. (1988). The effect of enhanced higher frequencies on the musical preference of older adults. *Journal of Music Therapy, 25,* 62–72.

Smith, D. S. (1989). Preferences for differentiated frequency loudness levels in older adult music listening. *Journal of Music Therapy, 26,* 18–29.

Smith, D. S. (1990). Therapeutic treatment effectiveness as documented in the gerontology literature: Implications for music therapy. *Music Therapy Perspectives, 8,* 36–40.

Smith, D. S. (1991). A comparison of group performance and song familiarity on cued recall tasks with older adults. *Journal of Music Therapy, 28,* 2–13.

Smith, D. S., & Lipe, A. W. (1991). Music therapy practices in gerontology. *Journal of Music Therapy, 28,* 193–210.

Smith, G. H. (1986). A comparison of the effects of three treatment interventions on cognitive functioning of Alzheimer's patients. *Music Therapy, 6A,* 41–56.

Smith, S. (1990). The unique power of music therapy benefits Alzheimer's patients. *Activities, Adaptation and Aging, 14,* 59–63.

Special Committee on Aging, United States Senate. (1991). *Forever young: Music and aging: Hearing before the Special Committee on Aging, United States Senate* (Serial No. 102–9). Washington, DC: U.S. Government Printing Office.

Staum, M. J. (1983). Music and rhythmic stimuli in the rehabilitation of gait disorders. *Journal of Music Therapy, 20,* 69–87.

Summer, L. (1981). Guided imagery and music with the elderly. *Music Therapy, 1,* 39–42.

Swartz, K. P., Crummer, G. C., & Frisina, R. D. (1992). P3 event-related potentials and performance of healthy older and Alzheimer's dementia subjects for music perception tasks. *Psychomusicology, 11,* 96–118.

Swartz, K. P., Hantz, E. C., Crummer, G. C., Walton, J. P., & Frisina, R. D. (1989). Does the melody linger on? Music cognition in Alzheimer's disease. *Seminars in Neurology, 9,* 152–158.

Tolhurst, G. C., Hollien, H., & Leeper, L. (1984). Listening preferences for music as a function of age. *Folia-Phoniatrica, 36,* 93–100.

VanderArk S., Newman, I., & Bell, S. (1983). The effects of music participation on quality of life of the elderly. *Music Therapy, 3,* 71–81.

Walton, J. P., Frisina, R. D., Swartz, K. P., Hantz, E., & Crummer, G. C. (1988). Neural basis for music cognition: Future directions and biomedical implications. *Psychomusicology, 7,* 127–138.

Watts, T. D. (1980). Theories of aging: The difference in orientations. *Journal of Music Therapy, 17,* 84–89.

Weiner, A. (1987). A nationwide survey of special units. In A. Kalicki (Ed.), *Confronting Alzheimer's* (pp. 80–108). Washington, DC: American Association of Homes for the Aging.

Weissman, J. A. (1983). Planning music activities to meet needs and treatment goals of aged individuals in long-term care facilities. *Music Therapy, 3,* 63–70.

Williams, G., & Dorow, L. G. (1983). Changes in complaints and non-complaints of a chronically depressed psychiatric patient as a function of an interrupted music/verbal feedback package. *Journal of Music Therapy, 20,* 143–155.

Wilson, G. T. (1984). Behavior therapy. In R. J. Corsini (Ed.), *Current psychotherapies,* (3rd ed., p. 241). Itasca, IL: F. E. Peacock.

Wise, G. W., Hartmann, D. J., & Fisher, J. (1992). Exploration of the relationship between choral singing and successful aging. *Psychological Reports, 70,* 1175–1183.

Wolfe, J. R. (1983). The use of music in a group sensory training program for regressed geriatric patients. *Activities, Adaptation and Aging, 4,* 49–61.

Wylie, M. E. (1990). A comparison of the effects of old familiar songs, antique objects, historical summaries, and general questions on the reminiscence of nursing home residents. *Journal of Music Therapy, 27,* 2–12.

A CONTENT ANALYSIS OF MUSIC RESEARCH WITH DISABLED CHILDREN AND YOUTH (1975–1993): APPLICATIONS IN SPECIAL EDUCATION

Judith A. Jellison

INTRODUCTION

PROFESSIONAL music organizations of long standing recognize the importance of documentation to the maturation of their disciplines. The skillful and sensitive use of well-established observation and documentation procedures provides music professionals with ongoing evidence as to the effectiveness of their programs and the progress of their students. For these reasons, knowledge and skill in evaluation are integral curricular areas for study and practice for both prospective and experienced educators and therapists. The commitment of music professionals to the evaluation process is evidenced not only in training and professional practice but also in the publication of systematic, scholarly music research reports.

In 1952 a proposal for the establishment of a music education research journal appeared in the *Music Educators Journal,* and by the spring of 1953 the first issue of the *Journal of Research in Music Education* was published by the Music Educators National Conference (MENC) (Warren, 1984). Currently, MENC also publishes *Update: Applications of Research in Music Education; Update* contains articles that emphasize the interpretation and application of research findings in music education and is a bridge between researchers and practitioners. Both *JRME* and *Update* are under the auspices of the MENC's Society for Research in Music Education (Society for Research in Music Education, 1993). The National Association for Music Therapy (NAMT), founded in 1950, gave evidence of a commitment to research in its first publication, *Music Therapy 1951.* A statement of the objectives for the Association listed as its first objective, "to encourage and report research projects" (National Association for Music Therapy, 1952). This objective is realized through the publication of original research in (1) the *Music Therapy Annual Books of Proceedings,* published from 1952 through 1963, (2) the *Journal of Music Therapy,* a quarterly publication begun in 1964, and (3) *Music Therapy Perspectives,* first published in 1982. Although music research was conducted long before the establishment of music research journals, the study of the effects of music on behavior advanced rapidly with the development of major research journals in the fields of music education and music therapy.

Published research related to music and individuals with disabilities was an important dimension of the first federal grant project conducted by NAMT (Lathom, 1982). This special in-service project resulted in the publication of a report specific to the role of music therapy and disabled children (Lathom, 1980), a research-based book for music therapy and individuals with retardation (Madsen, 1980), an annotated indexed bibliography, and several monographs written by clinicians and educators (Lathom & Eagle, 1982). The materials resulting from the special education and music project reference early original published research studies demonstrating the effectiveness of music in teaching habilitative and educational objectives to disabled children and youth.

Although the study of music and children with disabilities is not new, the status and funding of music therapy as a related service (Hughes & Grice, 1986) in The Education of All Handicapped Children Act (P.L. 94–142) of 1975 (in 1990 amended by P.L. 101–476 and renamed the Individuals with Disabilities Education Act), and the expanding roles of the music therapist and music educator in special education programs provided impetus for increased research literature on the topic. As research activity increases, the research review provides a perspective for making informed decisions concerning future procedures and priorities in evaluation and research.

For the most part, the contents of research reviews in the present collection are specific to various populations. Following standards for professional accountability as an organizational format (Furman, 1986), each article gives consideration to data/documentation that are currently in the literature for that population, the kinds of data/documentation that are needed, methods that are effective for each client/student population, and the kinds of documentation that routinely should be the responsibility of the music therapist. Conducting a music research review in special education, however, presents a somewhat different challenge. Before such a review can be initiated, it is first necessary to define the body of literature comprising music research in special education.

Defining Music Research in Special Education

Findings from well-controlled systematic music research studies describe effective instructional strategies, identify important cause-and-effect relationships, and describe the social, emotional, physical, and musical behaviors of adults and children. The dissemination of these important findings has contributed to the establishment of standard procedures in music therapy and music education, many which are generalizable across persons, places, and settings (Alley, 1982; Madsen, 1986). Many of these studies, most of which were conducted in settings other than regular school settings, will be included in the present review.

Although germaneness to a given issue or topic has been identified as an essential criterion for the inclusion of studies in a research review (Slavin, 1986), the traditional school or special education setting in the regular school cannot, at this time, be considered a criterion for operationally defining music research in special education, given that few such "school" studies were identified in an earlier review of music research for the period 1975–1986 (Jellison, 1988). For the present review, music research in special education is defined broadly as the study of music behaviors of disabled children and youth (ages birth through 21), including the study of the functional use of music to reach nonmusic learning outcomes.

As a body of music research in special education develops, the results and relevance of that research will depend largely on the philosophy, goals, and methodology that are applied to it. The examination of extant research and the development of programmatic and evaluative priorities for special education provide a starting point for the analysis of music research with disabled students. The purposes of the present examination are (1) to review original data-based articles pertinent to music and disabled children and youth, (2) to categorize, code, and summarize the research outcomes, and, (3) to outline recommendations that may be used to broaden educationally valid music research and evaluation procedures in special education.

METHOD

Researchers in the social sciences recognize that reviews of social science literature inevitably will involve judgment and that no set of procedural or statistical canons can make the review process immune to a reviewer's biases (Slavin, 1986). Given the limited number of studies conducted within the context of regular or special education settings and the subsequent development of the operational definition of music research in special education, procedures for analysis, categorization, and quantification were selected to reflect the principles of egalitarianism and normalization that are inherent to special education legislation of this decade and that are visible in special education literature and practice. For example, although the Individuals with Disabilities Education Act of 1990 (Individuals with Disabilities Education Act, 1991) still relies somewhat on a categorical approach to labeling children, language throughout the law and language in much of the special education literature focuses on the "person first" and then the disability (e.g., children with mental retardation, children with serious emotional disturbance). The principle of "person first" is, therefore, followed throughout the text and in the "label" category of this review.

Additionally, several categories have been developed primarily as a result of the emphasis on transition that is found in special education legislation and literature. Transition outcomes and related requirements for curricular decisions and instructional practice are seminal issues in special education literature and practice. Although issues of transition are not new, having been identified in the special education literature nearly twenty years ago (Brown, Nietupski, & Hamre-Nietupski, 1976) and incorporated into the practice of music therapy in the educational setting (Jellison, 1979, 1983), transition services are now legally requisite according to the Individuals with Disabilities Act (IDEA).

By law, statements of the needed transition services are to be included within the Individualized Education Program (IEP) no later than age 16 and, when appropriate, beginning at age 14 or younger (Individuals with Disabilities Education Act, 20 U. S. C. Sec, 1401[a][20], 1991). The IDEA makes clear that "transition services means a coordinated set of activities for a student, designed within an outcome-oriented process, which promotes movement from school to post-school activities, including post-secondary education, vocational training, integrated employment (including supported employment), continuing and adult education, adult services, independent living, or community participation" (Individuals with Disabilities Education Act, 20 U. S. C. Sec, 1401[a][17], 1991). Essentially, individuals involved with the child's education must anticipate the child's transition into three elements of life: work, residential living, and recreation/leisure time activities.

In a thorough description and analysis of the transition amendment, Turnbull (1993) states that the law's provisions for the specific means of instruction, the identification of functional daily living and vocational skills, and the emphasis on community-referenced, community-based, and community-delivered instruction "acknowledges the principles of generalization and durability (students learn best when they must actually use their skills), and it acknowledges that skill development should take place in the least restrictive, most normal settings" (p. 126). Categories for analysis that are related to transition in this review include (1) integration, (2) contact with nondisabled individuals, (3) collection of longitudinal data, (4) collection of generalization data, and (5) the type of behavior (music and/or nonmusic) observed. The importance of the student's successful transition to natural environments with nondisabled individuals is also reflected in this review by an additional summary and analysis of those music research studies that observed children and adolescents engaged in functional behaviors and/or activities in integrated or natural settings of the home, school, or community.

Criteria for Including Studies

Criteria for the inclusion of studies were as follows: (1) original empirical research published in refereed English language journals between 1975 through 1993, inclusive, (2) research that reports data and uses well-established descriptive or experimental research methodologies, (3) research that investigates variables or elements specific to music, music education, or music therapy, (4) research that includes children with disabilities who receive special education services, (5) research that includes children who may be "at risk" and/or who receive educational services through federal and/or state assistance (e.g., homeless, Headstart), and (6) research that investigates the attitudes and behaviors of nondisabled children and youth in relation to issues concerning their peers with disabilities.

The review began with literature published in 1975 in order to mark the enactment of the Education for All Handicapped Children Act (P.L. 94–142). The review includes all children with disabilities birth through 21 in order to reflect the subsequent amendments that expanded the age coverage of the 1975 legislation. A few studies were included when subject pools included several adults over 21. Studies that described children using terminology that may imply a disability (i.e., hyperactive, nonverbal, etc.) also were included. Studies of infants and children in hospital settings (including psychiatric settings) were excluded when descriptions of the children did not imply that the children received special education services.

Literature Search, Review and Analysis

On-line data-base searches included Education Resources Information Center (ERIC), and abstracts published by The American Psychological Association (PsychINFO). Individual hand searches also were conducted of the following journals: the *Bulletin of the Council for Research in Music Education, Contributions to Music Education, Journal of the International Association of Music for the Handicapped* (formerly *MEH Bulletin*), *Journal of Music Therapy, Journal of Research in Music Education, Music Therapy,* and *Music Therapy Perspectives.*

The comprehensive search for published data articles from 1975 through 1993 using criteria outlined in this paper identified a total of 122 studies. The studies were analyzed, categorized, and quantified on twelve main categories and several subcategories. The subcategories were coded for presentation in Table 1. The categories, subcategories, codes, and criteria for interpretation are presented below:

Disability; Nondisabled; Population Age Range

Disabilities are identified using language in the IDEA and are consistent with the label reported in the article; "low achievement" was included if subjects were labeled special education; children described "at risk" or "homeless" were included; "Yes" or "No" for the category "nondisabled" indicates whether or not nondisabled students were subjects in the study; the age range may exceed 21 if fewer than 5 adults were included as subjects, or if adult data were reported separately.

Integration/Special Education

"Verbal" (V) indicates that the context of the article includes language specific to special education topics or issues (i.e., IDEA, P.L. 94–142, inclusion, integration, mainstreaming, school and community transitions, IEP) found predominately in special education literature but that does not include observations of behavior in integrated settings; "Behavior" (B) indicates that the individual(s) was observed in integrated, regular school, home, and/or community settings. Studies coded (B) may or may not include verbalizations. "No" indicates that neither verbalizations nor behaviors as defined in this category were reported in the article.

Data Collection

"Episodic" (E) indicates that data were collected in one or a few observations (e.g., pretest/posttest). "Longitudinal" (L) indicates that there were more than five observations of the same behavior(s) over days or weeks. Data collection procedures are also described as "Individual" (I) if collected from one subject at a time or "Group" (G) if collected from several individuals simultaneously.

Generalization

Coded "Yes" or "No" to indicate whether or not the behavior was observed and data were collected in more than one setting or with persons, cues, reinforcers, or materials different from those during treatment.

Behavior(s) Observed

In most cases, specific descriptions of the dependent variable(s)—the behavior(s), or task performance(s) that was measured.

Function of Music

Broadly categorized as the structure of music for the acquisition of "Music" (M) outcomes (singing, playing instruments, movement, vocabulary, discrimination pitch, timbre, dynamics, tempo, etc.) or "Nonmusic" (NM) outcomes (academic, motor, social, verbal). The function of music to teach nonmusic skills is further described as (1) a stimulus cue/prompt to facilitate learning (includes background music), (2) a structure or activity to provide a desired learning outcome (includes assessment), and (3) a contingency (includes music withdrawal and distortion).

Research Mode; Size of N

"Descriptive" research (D) is defined as interrelationship studies (comparisons and/or correlational studies), descriptions of existing phenomena or situations, surveys, and studies that present detailed descriptions of the effects of strategies. "Experimental" research (E) is defined as research in which there was a clearly controlled manipulation of an independent variable to determine cause and effect relationships. Experimental research was further coded as "Group" (G) if it included the use of statistical designs and analysis of group performance or "Behavioral" (B) if continuous measurement was used within behavioral designs with groups or single subjects. In some cases the size of N may include adults. N is indicated separately for multiple studies reported in a single article.

Populations and/or Independent Variables; Dependent Variables

Variables listed are those either occurring in the title or context of the article. In some cases, terms were summarized or changed for clarity. The population was listed under the Independent Variable Category for descriptive research studies.

In addition, studies that were identified as observing and documenting behavior in integrated or natural school, home, or community environments (coded "B" under integration category) and that included nondisabled individuals (coded "Yes" under nondisabled) were analyzed further to identify documentation procedures and salient findings of the research. Summaries of the variables studied, documentation procedures, and research findings are presented in the Appendix.

RESULTS

Descriptions of 122 studies (1975–1993) using the categories, subcategories and codes outlined in this paper are presented in Table 1, Parts 1a, 1b, and 1c. The categories and subcategories presented in Table 1 are further summarized and presented in Tables 2, 3, and 4. The results section of this paper is organized into two parts as follows: Part 1 presents the frequency data for the categories as summarized in Tables 2, 3, and 4, and Part 2 presents salient features of research studies that observed disabled students in integrated and natural settings. (Summaries of research with disabled and nondisabled students in integrated and natural settings are presented in the Appendix.)

Part 1: Frequency Data for Categories
Frequency of Publication; Source; Categories of Disabled and Nondisabled

A total of 122 studies were identified for the years 1975–1993 with the majority of the articles published in *The Journal of Music Therapy*. Although the publication rate is rather low, the rate of publication has been consistent over time with approximately seven publications per year for the past 18 years.

Frequency data presented in Table 2 indicate that 85 (70%) of the articles were with disabled students only and 29 (24%) with disabled and nondisabled students. Eight studies were with students labeled homeless, at risk, or low achievers. Of the studies with disabled and nondisabled students, a large majority (24 studies) did not require interaction or contact between the groups.

Table 1 (Part a)

A Content Analysis of Research With Disabled Children and Youth (1975–1993)

Author	Year	Source	Disability Label or Description	ND Data	Age	Inclusion/ Special Ed.
Kostka	1993	MTP	Autism	No	9	B
Staum	1993	JMT	Homeless	Yes	5–14	No
Wolfe & Hom	1993	JMT	Headstart	Yes	5	No
Cassidy	1992	JMT	Speech or Language	Yes	3–6	V
Darrow	1992	JMT	Hearing	No	8–11	V
Rogers-Wallgren, French, & Ben-Ezra	1992	PMS	Mental Retardation	No	10–18	No
Cassidy & Sims	1991	JRME	Nondisabled	Yes	12–13 & adults	V
Darrow	1991	JMT	Hearing	No	6–10	No
Darrow & Cohen	1991	MTP	Hearing	No	11–12	V
Edenfield & Hughes	1991	MTP	Mental Retardation	No	13–23	No
Humpal	1991	JMT	Mental Retardation	Yes	3–5	B
Jellison & Flowers	1991	JRME	Special Education	Yes	3–14	V
Madsen, Capperella-Sheldon, & Johnson	1991	JIAMH	Special Education	Yes	2–5	No
McGivern, Berka, Languis, & Chapman	1991	JLD	Learning	Yes	7–12	No
Velasquez	1991	MTP	Mental Retardation	No	18	V
Darrow	1990	JMT	Hearing	No	9–11	V
Gfeller & Rath	1990	JIAMH	Mental Retardation	No	5–13	V
Hairston	1990	JMT	Mental Retardation Mental Retardation with Autism	No	mean = 9	No
Burleson, Center, & Reeves	1989	JMT	Emotional	No	5–9	No

Table 1 (Part a)
Continued

Author	Year	Source	Disability Label or Description	ND Data	Age	Inclusion/ Special Ed.
Eidson	1989	JMT	Emotional	No	11–16	V
Haines	1989	MT	Emotional	No	11–16	No
Hill, Brantner, & Spreat	1989	ETC	Mental Retardation	No	17	No
Hunter	1989	JMT	Mental Retardation	No	9–21	No
Madsen & Darrow	1989	JMT	Visual	No	9–20	No
Spitzer	1989	MTP	Mental Retardation Emotional Physical	No	9–17	V
Braswell , Decuir, Hoskins, Kvet, & Oubre	1988	PMS	Mental Retardation	Yes	6–35	No
Cohen	1988	JMT	Brain Injury	No	18	No
Dawson, Finley, Phillips, & Galpert	1988	JADD	Autism	Yes	8–19	No
Ford	1988	JMT	Hearing	No	6–12	No
Garwood	1988	JMT	Mental Retardation	No	21	No
Gunsberg	1988	JMT	Mental Retardation	Yes	3–5	B
Hoskins	1988	JMT	Mental Retardation with Language or Speech	No	2–5	No
Madsen, Smith, & Feeman	1988	JMT	Learning and/or Behavior	Yes	elem. & kndgtn.	B
Spencer	1988	JMT	Mental Retardation	No	16–40	No
Thaut	1988	JADD	Autism	Yes	6–24	No
Ayres	1987	JMT	Mental Retardation	No	6–11	V
Darrow	1987	JMT	Hearing	Yes	mean = 8	V
Dattilo & Mirenda	1987	JASH	Mental Retardation	No	10–12	V
Hughes, Robbins, Smith, & Kinkade	1987	JIAMH	Mental Retardation	No	12–22	V

Table 1 (Part a)
Continued

Author	Year	Source	Disability Label or Description	ND Data	Age	Inclusion/ Special Ed.
Jones, Mandler-Provin, Latkowski, & McMahon	1987	CFBT	Behavior	No	9–17	No
Krout	1987	JMT	Multi-Disabilities	No	12–16	V
Miller	1987	AJMD	Mental Retardation	No	6	No
Moore & Mathenius	1987	JMT	Mental Retardation and Multi-Disabilities	No	13–21	V
Staum	1987	JMT	Hearing	No	3–12	No
Thaut	1987	JADD	Autism	Yes	4–11	No
Cripe	1986	JMT	Learning	No	6–22	No
Darrow & Starmer	1986	JMT	Hearing	No	9–12	V
Gfeller	1986	MEH	Hearing	No	6–12	No
Grant & LeCroy	1986	JMT	Mental Retardation	No	6–18	No
Jones	1986	JMT	Mental Retardation	No	6–22	No
Krout	1986	MTP	Low Achievement	No	10–12	No
Thompson	1986	MEH	Mental Retardation	Yes	elementary	B
Allen & Bryant	1985	ARMR	Mental Retardation	No	10–11	No
Grant & Share	1985	JMT	Mental Retardation	No	7–20	No
Jellison	1985	JRME	Nondisabled	Yes	9–12	V
Thaut	1985	JMT	Physical	No	6–9	No
Darrow	1984	JMT	Hearing	Yes	9–16	No
Flowers	1984	JMT	Mental Retardation	Yes	8–13	No
Gregoire	1984	JMT	Mental Retardation	No	6–11	V
Jellison, Brooks, & Huck	1984	JRME	Mental Retardation	Yes	8–15	B
Maranto, Decuir, & Humphrey	1984	MT	Mental Retardation	No	12–22	No
Staum & Flowers	1984	MTP	Autism	No	9	B

Table 1 (Part a)
Continued

Author	Year	Source	Disability Label or Description	ND Data	Age	Inclusion/ Special Ed.
Steele	1984	MTP	Learning	No	7–11	B
Witt & Steele	1984	MTP	Multi-Disabilities	No	14 months	B
Atterbury	1983	JRME	Learning	Yes	7–8	V
Force	1983	JMT	Nondisabled	Yes	7	B
Gfeller	1983	JMT	Learning	Yes	9–11	No
Gibbons	1983	MT	Emotional	No	11–15	V
Gilbert	1983	JRME	Learning	Yes	5–9	V
Hair & Graham	1983	JMT	Mental Retardation	Yes	School age	No
Staum	1983	JMT	Physical	No	5–19	No
Stratford & Ching	1983	JMDR	Mental Retardation	Yes	4, 12–13	No
Wylie	1983	JMT	Mental Retardation	No	8–20	No
Bottari & Evans	1982	JSP	Learning	No	9–11	No
Bruscia	1982	MT	Mental Retardation with Autism	No	14	No
Bruscia & Levinson	1982	JVIB	Blindness	No	10–17	No
Dorow & Horton	1982	JMT	Mental Retardation	No	11–20	V
Harding & Ballard	1982	JMT	Physical	No	3–5	No
Merle-Fishman & Marcus	1982	MT	Emotional	Yes	7–10	No
Michel, Parker, Giokas, & Werner	1982	JMT	Low Achievement (several studies)	No	12–15	No
Soraci, Deckner, McDaniel, & Blanton	1982	JMT	Mental Retardation	No	5–10	No
Wolfe	1982	JMT	Behavior	Yes	9–10	No
Cassity	1981	JMT	Physical	No	9–13	No
Larson	1981	JMT	Emotional	Yes	11–15	No

Table 1 (Part a)
Continued

Author	Year	Source	Disability Label or Description	ND Data	Age	Inclusion/ Special Ed.
Shehan	1981	JMT	Learning	No	7–10	No
Walmsley, Crichton, & Droog	1981	DMCN	Physical	No	under 12	No
Windwer	1981	JRME	Behavior	No	5–8	No
Ford & Veltri-Ford	1980	MR	Mental Retardation	No	9–11	No
Holloway	1980	JMT	Mental Retardation	No	3–11	No
Humphrey	1980	JMT	Mental Retardation	No	15	No
Wolfe	1980	JMT	Physical	No	3–adult	No
Applebaum, Egel, Koegel, & Imhoff	1979	JADD	Autism	Yes	14–18	No
Darrow	1979	JMT	Hearing Impairment	Yes	12–13	No
Karper	1979	PRd	Delinquency with Mental Retardation	No	Adolescents	No
Murphy, Doughty, & Nunes	1979	MR	Mental Retardation	No	14–19	V
Myers	1979	JMT	Mental Retardation	No	7–11	No
Roskam	1979	JMT	Learning	No	6–9	No
Cassity	1978	JMT	Mental Retardation	No	10–13	No
Giacobbe & Graham	1978	JMT	Emotional	Yes	9–11	No
Greenwald	1978	JMT	Mental Retardation	No	7–22	No
Grossman	1978	JMT	Emotional	No	6–12	No
McCarty, McElfresh, Rice, & Wilson	1978	JMT	Emotional	No	3–14	B
Spudic & Somervill	1978	ETMR	Mental Retardation	No	11–18	No

Table 1 (Part a)
Continued

Author	Year	Source	Disability Label or Description	ND Data	Age	Inclusion/ Special Ed.
Larson	1977	JMT	Mental Retardation	Yes	7–8	No
Miller	1977	AJMD	Mental Retardation	No	9–14	No
Rider	1977	JMT	Mental Retardation	No	7–13	No
Steele (several (studies)	1977	JMT	Learning, Behavior	No	9–15	V
Bokor	1976	JMT	Mental Retardation Brain Injury	No	10–17	No
Dileo	1976	JMT	Mental Retardation	No	8–26	No
Dorow	1976	JMT	Mental Retardation	No	mean=20	No
Eisenstein	1976	JMT	Low Achievement	No	10–11	No
Lienhard	1976	JMT	Mental Retardation	No	10–23	No
Schmidt, Franklin, & Edwards	1976	PRts	Autism	No	7, 10	No
Wilson	1976	JMT	Emotional	No	5–7	No
Decuir	1975	JMT	Mental Retardation	No	8–11	No
Dileo	1975	JMT	Mental Retardation	No	13–19	No
Dorow	1975	JMT	Mental Retardation	No	9–15	No
Greene, Hoats, & Dibble	1975	PRd	Delinquency with Mental Retardation	No	adolescents	No
Korduba	1975	JMT	Deafness	Yes	8–12	No
Reid, Hill, Rawers, & Montegar	1975	JMT	Behavior	No	8	B
Steele	1975	JMT	Behavior	No	pre-teen, teen	V
Zenatti	1975	JRME	Mental Retardation	Yes	5–16	No

Note. Refer to References for identification of journal codes and complete citations.

Table 1 (Part b)

A Content Analysis of Research With Disabled Children and Youth (1975–1993)

Author	Data Collection	Generalization	Behavior(s) Observed	Function of Music	
Kostka (1993)	L/I	No	Arm flapping, and body swaying; participation	NM:	Structured Activity motor; social
				M:	General Participation
Staum (1993)	L/G	No	Problem solve by giving positive and logical responses to questions	NM:	Structured Activity social
Wolfe & Hom (1993)	L/I	No	Recall six functional telephone numbers	NM:	Structured Activity academic
Cassidy (1992)	E/I	No	Verbally identify music excerpts as fast/slow and loud/soft	M:	Discrimination
Darrow (1992)	E/I	No	Nonverbally identify when pitch changes	M:	Discrimination
Rogers-Wallgren et al. (1992)	L/I	No	Perform selected physical fitness tasks	NM:	Contingency motor
Cassidy & Sims (1991)	E/G	No	Complete pencil-paper evaluations of music performance	NM:	Structured Activity attitude assessment
				M:	Listening
Darrow (1991)	E/I/G	No	Order selected, time playing, signed preference	M:	Listening; Playing Instruments
Darrow & Cohen (1991)	E/L/I	No	Reproduce, by singing, given pitches and patterns	M:	Singing
Edenfield & Hughes (1991)	E/I	No	Sing pitches and songs	M:	Singing
Humpal (1991)	L/G	No	Partner selected; interaction	NM:	Structured Activity social
Jellison & Flowers (1991)	E/I	No	Talk to interviewer; sing favorite song; clap steady beat	M:	Verbalizing; Singing; Movement (clapping)
Madsen et al. (1991)	E/I	No	Move lever to indicate levels of happiness while listening to music	M:	Listening
McGivern et al. (1991)	E/I	No	Identify rhythm patterns as same/different	NM:	Structured Activity assessment reading
				M:	Discrimination

Table 1 (Part b)
Continued

Author	Data Collection	Generalization	Behavior(s) Observed	Function of Music	
Velasquez (1991)	E/I	No	Play piano exercises	M:	Playing Instrument
Darrow (1990)	E/I	No	Match (sing) pitches	M:	Singing
Gfeller & Rath (1990)	E/G	No	Participate at one of three levels in autoharp, singing, and rhythm activities;	NM: M:	Structured Activity social General Participation on-task
Hairston (1990)	E/G	No	Work, verbalizations, contact received, play, observe teacher	NM: M:	Structured Activity academic, social General Participation
Burleson et al. (1989)	E/I	No	Sort four colors of chips	NM:	Stimulus Cue/Prompt academic
Eidson (1989)	L/I	Yes	Perform individual target behaviors in therapy and classroom	NM:	Structured Activity social
Haines (1989)	E/G	No	Answer question on self-esteem inventory	NM:	Structure Activity social
Hill et al. (1989)	L/I	No	Increase minutes seated in classroom chair	NM: M:	Contingency social Listening
Hunter (1989)	E/I	No	Press correct number on computer keyboard to match rhythm and melodic examples	M:	Discrimination
Madsen & Darrow (1989)	E/I	No	Verbally identify paired tonal patterns as same/different	M:	Discrimination
Spitzer (1989)	L/I	No	Use personal computer, typing keyboard, and music keyboard; individual objectives	M:	Singing; Playing instrument
Braswell et al. (1988)	E/I/G	No	Pencil and paper response to recorded test items on rhythm and tonality	M:	Discrimination
Cohen (1988)	L/I	Yes	Speak sentences	NM:	Stimulus Cue/Prompt verbal

Table 1 (Part b)
Continued

Author	Data Collection	Generalization	Behavior(s) Observed	Function of Music	
Dawson et al. (1988)	E/I	No	Event-related potential; P3 amplitude	NM:	Structured Activity assessment auditory event-related potential
Ford (1988)	E/I	No	Verbally or nonverbally identify paired tones as same/different	M:	Discrimination
Garwood (1988)	L/I	Yes	Keep bed dry throughout sleeping hours	NM:	Contingency social
Gunsberg (1988)	L/G	No	Various modes of behavior involving materials, persons, activities	NM: M:	Structured Activity social General Participation
Hoskins (1988)	E/I	No	Speak and sing responses to test items; imitate rhythm, pitch, melody	NM: M:	Structured Activity verbal Singing
Madsen et al. (1988)	E/I/G	Yes	Help teach kindergarten student basic skills	NM:	Contingency academic; social
Spencer (1988)	L/I	No	Perform movement or instrumental playing tasks	M:	Movement; Playing Instruments
Thaut (1988)	E/I	No	Play a minimum of 16 tones on a xylophone	M:	Playing instrument
Ayres (1987)	E/L/I	No	Decrease time eating; oral functions during feeding/eating	NM: M:	Structured Activity social Listening
Darrow (1987)	E/I	No	Discriminate pairs of tones and pairs of rhythms as same or different	M:	Discrimination
Dattilo & Mirenda (1987)	E/I	No	Activate (press) switch to indicate music or nonmusic preference	M:	Listening
Hughes et al. (1987)	E/I	No	Sing favorite song and "Jingle Bells"	M:	Singing
Jones et al. (1987)	E/I	No	Rate reinforcer preference among music and nonmusic activities	M:	Verbalization

Table 1 (Part b)
Continued

Author	Data Collection	Generalization	Behavior(s) Observed	Function of Music	
Krout (1987)	L/I	No	Perform individual target behaviors	NM:	Structured Activity academic; social; verbal
Miller (1987)	E/I	No	Listen to recorded piano melodies and accurately perform on piano	M:	Playing Instruments
Moore & Mathenius (1987)	L/I	No	Identify tempi as fast/slow; play steady beat; dance in synchrony with music	M:	General Participation
Staum (1987)	E/L/I	Yes	Speak sentences with rhythmic and intonational accuracy	NM:	Stimulus Cue/Prompt/Prompt; Structured Activity verbal
Thaut (1987)	E/I	No	Press button to watch slides or listen to music	NM: M:	Structured Activity assessment reinforcers Listening
Cripe (1986)	E/I	Yes	Demonstrate appropriate verbal/motor behavior	NM:	Stimulus Cue/Prompt/Prompt social
Darrow & Starmer (1986)	E/I	No	Speak sentences, questions, and statements	NM:	Structured Activity verbal
Gfeller (1986)	E/L/I	No	Speak rhythmically Cue/Prompt/Prompt	NM:	Stimulus verbal
Grant & LeCroy (1986)	E/I	No	Imitate rhythm patterns on drum	M:	Playing Instruments
Jones (1986)	E/I	No	Respond to music test items	NM: M:	Structured Activity assessment cognition Discrimination
Krout (1986)	L/I/G	No	Write answers to questions	M:	Listening
Thompson (1986)	E/I/G	No	Participate in classroom activities	M:	General participation
Allen & Bryant (1985)	L/I	No	Targeted behaviors	NM:	Contingency social
Grant & Share (1985)	E/I	No	Sing scales; identify pitches as same/different	M:	Singing; Discrimination

Table 1 (Part b)
Continued

Author	Data Collection	Generalization	Behavior(s) Observed	Function of Music	
Jellison (1985)	E/G	No	Complete paper & pencil attitude survey	NM:	Structured Activity assessment attitude
Thaut (1985)	E/I	No	Step and clap to movement cycles	NM: M:	Stimulus Cue/Prompt motor Movement
Darrow (1984)	E/I	No	Speech test items Music rhythm test	NM: M:	Structured Activity assessment speech Discrimination
Flowers (1984)	E/I	No	Indicate preference, high/low; loud/soft; rhythmic/nonrhythmic	M:	Listening
Gregoire (1984)	E/I	No	Match numerals; verbal/motor relaxation	NM:	Stimulus Cue/Prompt academic; motor; verbal
Jellison et al. (1984)	E/L/G	Yes	Interact positively; complete pencil-paper attitude survey	NM:	Structured Activity/ Contingency social; attitudes
Maranto et al. (1984)	E/I	No	Listen to and verbally repeat digit sequences; imitate rhythm patterns on drum	NM: M:	Stimulus Cue/Prompt verbal (cognitive assmt) Playing Instruments
Staum & Flowers (1984)	L/I	Yes	Shop in grocery store	NM:	Contingency social
Steele (1984)	L/I/G	Yes	Varied: social/academic music behaviors	NM: M:	Structured Activity/ social; academic General Participation
Witt & Steele (1984)	L/I	Yes	Maintain eye contact, reach for objects, etc.	NM:	Structured Activity/ social; academic
Atterbury (1983)	E/I	No	Recognize rhythms same/different; clap rhythms	M:	Discrimination
Force (1983)	E/L/G	No	Identify rhythm inst; dynamic level test items; on-off task	M:	General Participation
Gfeller (1983)	E/I	No	Recall multiplication facts from flash cards	NM:	Stimulus Cue/Prompt academic

Table 1 (Part b)
Continued

Author	Data Collection	Generalization	Behavior(s) Observed	Function of Music	
Gibbons (1983)	L/I	No	Respond to music/motor test items; imitate rhythm patterns	M:	Playing Instruments
Gilbert (1983)	E/I	No	Play instruments for motor skills test items	NM: M:	Structured Activity motor assessment Playing instrument
Hair & Graham (1983)	E/I	No	Verbalize word to tell how music changed	M:	Verbal
Staum (1983)	E/L/I	No	Rhythmic and consistent walking	NM: M:	Stimulus Cue/Prompt motor Movement
Stratford & Ching (1983)	E/I	No	Tap 3 rhythms of varying complexity with stimulus	ML:	Rhythm
Wylie (1983)	E/I	No	Length and frequency of sung response	M:	Singing
Bottari & Evans (1982)	E/I	No	Recall of pertinent points included in telling of the story; multiple choice questions	NM:	Stimulus Cue/Prompt academic
Bruscia (1982)	L/I	Yes	Use nonecholalic verbal responses	NM:	Structured Activity verbal
Bruscia & Levinson (1982)	L/I	No	Notational figures read using the Optacon	M:	Discrimination (music reading)
Dorow & Horton (1982)	E/L/I	No	Motor activity/eye contact/ vocalizations	NM:	Stimulus Cue/Prompt motor; verbal
Harding & Ballard (1982)	E/I	No	Verbalizations/on task	NM:	Stimulus Cue/Prompt academic; social Contingency social
Merle-Fishman & Marcus (1982)	L/I	No	Chose instrument and play; interaction with	NM: M:	Structured Activity verbal inst. and vocalizations General Participation
Michel et al. (1982)	E/I	No	Recall vocabulary and definitions	NM:	Stimulus Cue/Prompt academic

Table 1 (Part b)
Continued

Author	Data Collection	Generalization	Behavior(s) Observed	Function of Music	
Soraci et al. (1982)	E/G	No	Frequency of movement/ vocalizations	NM:	Stimulus Cue/Prompt motor; verbal
Wolfe (1982)	E/I	No	Body movements/ letter marking	NM:	Stimulus Cue/Prompt motor; academic
Cassity (1981)	E/I	No	Peer ratings on sociometric questionnaire	NM:	Structured Activity social
Larson (1981)	E/G	No	Rhythm pattern discrim. same/different	M:	Rhythm Discrimination
Shehan (1981)	E/G	No	Short-term memory of verbal paired associates	NM:	Stimulus Cue/Prompt academic
Walmsley et al. (1981)	L/I	No	Head posture	NM:	Contingency motor
Windwer (1981)	E/G	No	Intensity of body movements	NM:	Stimulus Cue/Prompt motor
Ford & Veltri-Ford (1980)	L/I	No	Target problem behaviors	NM:	Contingency social
Holloway (1980)	E/I	No	Follow directions; skills (throw ball, pick up, etc.)	NM:	Contingency social; motor
Humphrey (1980)	E/G	No	Identify word pictures	NM:	Stimulus Cue/Prompt academic
Wolfe (1980)	E/I	No	Head posture	NM:	Contingency motor
Applebaum et al. (1979)	E/I	No	Imitate pitch, rhythm, length	M:	General Participation
Darrow (1979)	E/I	No	Reproduce beat - strike woodblock	M:	Playing Instruments
Karper (1979)	E/I	No	Physical education related motor skills	NM:	Stimulus Cue/Prompt motor
Murphy et al. (1979)	L/I	No	Head posture	NM:	Contingency motor
Myers (1979)	E/I	No	Verbal recall of paired associates	NM:	Stimulus Cue/Prompt academic

Table 1 (Part b)
Continued

Author	Data Collection	Generalization	Behavior(s) Observed	Function of Music	
Roskam (1979)	E/G	Yes	Recognition/spelling/ comprehension	NM:	Stimulus Cue/Prompt academic
Cassity (1978)	E/G	No	Written IQ/MA/behavior/ personality/popularity tests	NM:	Structured Activity social; academic
Giacobbe & Graham (1978)	E/I	No	Written preference/choice of descriptors of music	M:	Listening; Verbal
Greenwald (1978)	L/I	No	Self-stimulation	NM:	Contingency motor; verbal
Grossman (1978)	E/I	No	Tell stories	NM:	Structured Activity personality assessment
McCarty et al. (1978)	L/G	No	Out of bus seat/fighting	NM:	Contingency social
Spudic & Somervill (1978)	E/I	No	Arithmetic problems completed accurately;	NM:	Stimulus Cue/Prompt academic; social activity level
Larson (1977)	E/I	No	Match singing pitches to piano scales	M:	Singing
Miller (1977)	E/I/G	No	Arithmetic problems completed accurately; Duration of music listening	NM: M:	Contingency academic Listening
Rider (1977)	E/I	No	Verbal affirmation to questions regarding recognition of same area, volume, rhythm, tempo	NM: M:	Structured Activity cognitive assessment Discrimination
Steele (1977)	E/I/G	Yes	Appropriate verbal/motor behavior	NM:	Structured Activity; Contingency social
Bokor (1976)	E/I	No	Spoken/sung 2-word/note sequences	NM: M:	Stimulus Cue/Prompt academic Singing
Dileo (1976)	E/I	No	Match singing pitches to organ scales; Various test scores	M:	Singing
Dorow (1976)	L/G	Yes	Correct math problems; correct music test questions	NM: M:	Contingency academic General Participation

Table 1 (Part b)
Continued

Author	Data Collection	Generalization	Behavior(s) Observed	Function of Music	
Eisenstein (1976)	L/I	No	Match music name labels to symbols (rhythm, notes, etc.)	M:	Verbal
Lienhard (1976)	E/I	No	Same/different response to rhythm patterns; various test scores	M:	Discrimination
Schmidt et al. (1976)	L/I	No	Appropriate music related responses (clapping, verbal, singing, instruments, etc.)	M:	General Participation
Wilson (1976)	E/G	No	Inappropriate classroom behavior	NM:	Contingency social
Decuir (1975)	E/G	No	Enthusiasm of singing	M:	Singing
Dileo (1975)	L/G	No	Appropriate social, academic, music behaviors (i.e. learn words to songs)	NM: / M:	Structured Activity/ social, academic / Singing
Dorow (1975)	L/I	Yes	Simple imitative behavior	NM:	Contingency social
Greene et al. (1975)	L/G	No	Decrease in group noise level	NM:	Contingency social
Korduba (1975)	E/I	No	Duplicate rhythm patterns on snare drum	M:	Playing Instruments
Reid et al. (1975)	L/G	Yes	Appropriate walking in community settings; riding in the car	NM:	Contingency social
Steele (1975)	E/L/I/G	Yes	Targeted behaviors of students/music therapists	NM:	Structured Activity, Contingency social
Zenatti (1975)	E/I/G	No	Same/different response to tonal/atonal 4-note sequences	M:	Discrimination

Table 1 (Part c)
A Content Analysis of Research With Disabled Children and Youth (1975–1993)

Author	Research Mode	*N*	Populations and/or Independent Variables	Dependent Variables
Kostka (1993)	D	1	Regular Music Class Special Ed. Music Class	Appropriate Participation Motor Behavior
Staum (1993)	E/G	varied	Music and Nonmusic Counseling Sessions	Problem-Solving Skills
Wolfe & & Horn (1993)	E/G	23	Telephone Numbers Sung with Familiar or Unfamiliar Melodies or Spoken	Retention of Sequential Verbal Information
Cassidy (1992)	E/G	48	Verbal, Verbal with Visual, and Verbal with Gestural Methods; Com. Disabled and Nondisabled	Labeling of Music
Darrow (1992)	E/G	17	Auditory Skills and Auditory and Tactile Skills	Identification of Pitch Change
Rogers-Wallgren et al. (1992)	E/G	12	Verbal Praise and Verbal Praise Plus Music or Vibration	Independence in Physical Fitness
Cassidy & Sims (1991)	E/G	209	Knowledge of Special Education Labels of Choir Members	Evaluation of Choir Performance and Attitude
Darrow (1991)	D	34/21	Hearing Impaired	Preference for Timbre & Musical Instruments
Darrow & Cohen (1991)	D	2	Programmed Pitch Practice and Private Instruction	Vocal Reproduction Accuracy
Edenfield & Hughes (1991)	D	22	Choral Music Curriculum	Singing Ability
Humpal (1991)	D	27	Integrated Music Program	Social Interactions
Jellison & Flowers (1991)	D	228	Disabled and Nondisabled	Music Preferences, Experiences, & Skills
Madsen et al. (1991)	D	14	Disabled and Nondisabled	Music Responses
McGivern et al. (1991)	D	59	Reading Impairments Discrimination	Temporal Pattern
Velasquez (1991)	D	1	Piano Teaching Method	Piano Performance
Darrow (1990)	E/G	8	Frequency Adjustment	Vocal Reprod. Accuracy

Table 1 (Part c)
Continued

Author	Research Mode	*N*	Populations and/or Independent Variables	Dependent Variables
Gfeller & Rath (1990)	D	14	Music Education Curriculum	Music Skills and On-Task
Hairston (1990)	E/G	8	Art and Music Therapy	Developmental & Behavioral
Burleson et al. (1989)	E/B	4	Background Music	Task Performance
Eidson (1989)	E/B	25	Behavioral Music Therapy	Generalization of Interpersonal Skills to Classroom
Haines (1989)	E/G	19	Music Therapy	Self-Esteem
Hill et al. (1989)	E/B	1	Contingent Music	In-Seat Behavior
Hunter (1989)	D	45	Mental Retardation	Melodic and Rhythmic Discrimination Skills
Madsen & Darrow (1989)	D	32	Visually Impaired	Music Aptitude Sound Conceptualization
Spitzer (1989)	D	4	Computer Aided Instruction	Music Learning Music Therapy
Braswell et al. (1988)	D	322	Mental Retardation, Normal Disadvantaged and Normal	Musical Aptitude
Cohen (1988)	E/B	1	Superimposed Rhythm	Rate of Speech
Dawson et al. (1988)	E/G	34	Autism and Normal; P3 Amplitude of ERPs to Phonetic and Chord Stimuli; Recording Site	Language Ability Intellectual Ability
Ford (1988)	D	39	Deaf Students Attending Two Different Residential Schools - One School with Structured Musical Experiences	Ability to Discriminate Pitch
Garwood (1988)	E/B	1	Contingent Mus & Bell Pad	Enuresis
Gunsberg (1988)	D	12	Improvised Musical Play	Social Play
Hoskins (1988)	E/G	16	Music Activities and Improve Expressive Language; Sung and Spoken Responses	Increase Verbal Response

Table 1 (Part c)
Continued

Author	Research Mode	*N*	Populations and/or Independent Variables	Dependent Variables
Madsen et al. (1988)	E/G	48	Cross-Age Tutoring	Academic and Social Effects
Spencer (1988)	E/G	27	Instrumental and Movement Activities	Follow Directions
Thaut (1988)	E/G	22	Nondisabled Children, Children with Autism, and Adults with Severe Retardation	Improvised Melodies
Ayres (1987)	E/G	5	Music Stimulus	Therapeutic Feeding
Darrow (1987)	D	28	Hearing Impairment	Musical Aptitude
Dattilo & Mirenda (1987)	E/B	3	Paired Music and Nonmusic Leisure Activities	Leisure Preferences
Hughes et al. (1987)	E/G	58	Choral Curriculum	Singing Ability
Jones et al. (1987)	D	19	Child Psychiatric (Behavior Problems)	Reinforcer Preferences
Krout (1987)	D	6	Group Music Therapy	Individualized Objectives
Miller (1987)	D	1	Musical Savant	Accuracy of Tonal Structure
Moore & Mathenius (1987)	E/G	8	Modeling, Reinforcement, and Tempo	Imitative Rhythmic Responses
Staum (1987)	D	35	Music Notation	Speech Prosody
Thaut (1987)	E/G	15	Visual and Auditory Stimuli	Preference
Cripe (1986)	E/G	8	Music Listening	Activity Level
Darrow & Starmer (1986)	D	22	Vocal Training	Rate of Speech
Gfeller (1986)	D	9	Musical Speech Rhythm	Speech Rhythm
Grant & LeCroy (1986)	E/G	30	Sensory Mode Input	Rhythmic Perception Task Attention Span
Jones (1986)	D	20	Mentally Retarded	Cognitive Development
Krout (1986)	E/B	6	Group List Contingency	Music Listening Skill
Thompson (1986)	D	28	Mainstreamed Class behaviors	Learning activities

Table 1 (Part c)
Continued

Author	Research Mode	*N*	Populations and/or Independent Variables	Dependent Variables
Allen & Bryant (1985)	D	2	Mentally Retarded Contingent Music	Targeted Behavior/
Grant & Share (1985)	D	9	Pitch Stimulus	Pitch Discrimination Vocal Ranges
Jellison (1985)	D	136	Students with Disabilities	Attitude Toward Students with Disabilities
Thaut (1985)	E/G	24	Auditory Rhythm Rhythm Speech	Temporal Muscular Control
Darrow (1984)	D	62	Hearing Impaired and Nonhandicapped	Rhythmic Responsiveness Supraseg. Aspects of Speech
Flowers (1984)	D	20	Mentally Retarded and Nonhandicapped	Sound Perception
Gregoire (1984)	E/G	17	Prior Music Listening	Task Performance
Jellison et al. (1984)	E/G/B	126	Small Group Contingent Music	Interactions (Dis-Nondis) Attitude Toward Students with Disabilities
Maranto et al. (1984)	D	25	Digit Spans, Rhythm Spans, Diagnostic Factors	Comparisons (correlation) of Scores
Staum & Flowers (1984)	E/B	1	Music Lessons	Appropriate Shopping Skills
Steele (1984)	D	1,1,5	Behavioral Techniques	Academic/Social/Music Behaviors
Witt & Steele (1984)	D	1	Structured Music Experiences with Mother	Academic/Social/Music Behavior
Atterbury (1983)	D	40	Input/Mode; Learning Disabled and Nondisabled	Rhythm Pattern Perception and Performance
Force (1983)	D	32	Integrated Classroom	Music Learning of Nondisabled Students
Gfeller (1983)	E/G	60	Music/Verbal Teaching Modes	Recall of Multiplication Tables
Gibbons (1983)	D	24	Emotionally Dis/Levels of Need for Structure	Rhythm Responses
Gilbert (1983)	D	103	Learning Disabled and Nondisabled	Motor Music Skill

Table 1 (Part c)
Continued

Author	Research Mode	*N*	Populations and/or Independent Variables	Dependent Variables
Hair & Graham (1983)	D	51	Children with Retardation	Verbal Descriptors of Music Therapists
Staum (1983)	E/B	25	Rhythmic Auditory Stimuli	Rhythmic Gait
Stratford & Ching (1983)	D	30	Complexity of Rhythm Patterns	Rhythm Perception
Wylie (1983)	E/G	28	Timbre of Musical Accompaniment	Vocal Responses
Bottari & Evans (1982)	E/G	24	Song/Spoken Presentation	Verbal Retention
Bruscia (1982)	D	1	Music Therapy (Singing)	Treatment of Echolalia
Bruscia & Levinson (1982)	D	7	Blind using Optacon	Reading Speeds/Accuracy
Dorow & Horton (1982)	E/B	8	Proximity of Aud Stim. Spoken/Sung Stimuli	Activity Levels
Harding & Ballard (1982)	E/B	3	Mus Therapy Participation Preferred Activities	Spontaneous Speech
Merle-Fishman & Marcus (1982)	E/G	16	Emotional Disorder and Normal	Musical Behaviors and Preferences
Michel et al. (1982)	E/G	10–19	Dichotic Presentation of Music and Words	Recall of Vocabulary and Definitions
Soraci et al., (1982)	E/G	11	Speed of Music	Stereotypic Behaviors
Wolfe (1982)	E/G	84	Interrupted and Continuous Music	Bodily Movement Task Performance
Cassity (1981)	E/B	13	Socially Valued Skill (Piano Playing)	Peer Acceptance
Larson (1981)	E/G	66	Visual/Auditory Rhythm Patterns; Emotional Disorder and Nondisabled	Rhythm Pattern Recognition
Shehan (1981)	E/G	16	Mediation Strategies: Music/Verbal/Visual	Paired Associate Learning
Walmsley et al. (1981)	D	5	Music as a Reinforcer	Head Control
Windwer (1981)	E/G	13	Ascending Music (Key)	Motor Activity

Table 1 (Part c)
Continued

Author	Research Mode	*N*	Populations and/or Independent Variables	Dependent Variables
Ford & Veltri-Ford (1980)	E/B	2	Time-Out from Auditory (Music) Reinforcement	Problem Behaviors
Holloway (1980)	E/B	8	Contingent Music Lis. Playing Instruments	Preacademic and Motor Skills
Humphrey (1980)	D	30	Music Ear Training (Choir Participation)	Auditory Discrimination
Wolfe (1980)	E/B	12	Interrupted Music	Head Posturing
Applebaum et al. (1979)	D	6	Autism and Nondisabled	Imitation of Music Stimuli
Darrow (1979)	D	75	Hearing Impaired	Beat Reproduction
Karper (1979)	E/G	71	Background Music	Novel Motor Skill
Murphy et al. (1979)	E/B	6	Contingent Music Listening	Head Posturing
Myers (1979)	E/G	18	Story/Song/Listening Presentations	Retention of Paired Associates
Roskam (1979)	E/G	36	Music Therapy Program Reading Skill	Auditory Awareness
Cassity (1978)	D	27	Performing/Nonperforming Music Groups	Social Development
Giacobbe & Graham (1978)	D	40	Music Listening	Music Preference and Description
Greenwald (1978)	E/B	4	Distorted/Interrupted Music	Self-stimulatory Behavior
Grossman (1978)	E/G	6	Songs	Autobiographical Stories
McCarty et al. (1978)	E/B	56	Contingent Music Listening	Bus Behavior
Spudic & Somervill (1978)	E/G	36	Musical Stimulation (Background Music)	Activity Level
Larson (1977)	D	29	Mental Retardation Nondisabled	Singing Ranges/Vocalization Published Song Ranges
Miller (1977)	E/G/B	30	Contingent Music Listening Music Preference	Arithmetic Performance

Table 1 (Part c)
Continued

Author	Research Mode	*N*	Populations and/or Independent Variables	Dependent Variables
Rider (1977)	D	40	Developmentally Delayed Conservation Task Response	Visual/Auditory
Steele (1977)	E/B	1–30	Structured Music Therapy Sessions; Music Contingencies	Appropriate Behavior
Bokor (1976)	D	44	Verbal/Music Sequences	Imitated Responses
Dileo (1976)	D	133	Mental Retardation Responses, Singing Ranges	Social and Diagnostic Tests
Dorow (1976)	E/B	17	Conting. TV Mus Lessons	Math/Music Test Responses
Eisenstein (1976)	E/B	3	Behavioral Techniques	Identification of Music Symbol Names
Lienhard (1976)	D	54	Mental Retardation Perception Test Responses	Social/Diagnostic/Rhythm
Schmidt et al. (1976)	E/B	3	Structured Music Activities	Appropriate Responses
Wilson (1976)	D	6	Contingent Music Listening	Classroom Behavior
Decuir (1975)	E/G	16	Piano, Organ, Guitar Accompaniments	Vocal Responses
Dileo (1975)	D	16	Token Economy	Social and Music Behaviors
Dorow (1975)	E/B	3	Approval/Music/Food	Imitative Behavior
Green et al. (1975)	D	8	Music Distortion	Decrease Inappropriate Behavior
Korduba (1975)	D	30	Deaf and Nondisabled	Rhythm Duplication
Reid (1975)	E/B	1	Contingent Mus Listening	Social Skills
Steele (1975)	D	varied	Music Therapists' Techniques	Student Behavior
Zenatti (1975)	D	876	Mental Retardation and Nondisabled	Melodic Memory Skills

Table 2

Frequency of Occurrence of Disabled Children, Nondisabled Children, Types of Disabilities, and Special Education/Integration Categories in Music Research (1975–1993)

Category	Frequency
Total Number of Studies Reviewed	122
Age Range of Children and Youth: 14 months to 22 years	
Studies that Include Data from Disabled Only	85
Studies that Include Data from Nondisabled and Other (low achievement, Headstart, homeless)	8
Studies that Include Data from both Disabled and Nondisabled	29
Comparative (No Contact Between Groups)	24
Combined (Contact Between Groups)	5
Total	122
Types of Disabilities	
Mental Retardation (includes multi-disabilities only)	51
Mental Retardation and Autism	2
Mental Retardation and Delinquency	2
Mental Retardation and Language/Speech	1
Mental Retardation and Multi-Disabilities	1
Deafness/Hearing Impairment	11
Emotional Disturbance	11
Learning Disability	10
Autism	7
Physically Disability	7
Behavior Problem	7
Brain Injury (includes neurological impairment)	2
Blindness/Visual Impairment	2
Speech/Language	1
Special Education (no type specified)	2
Other (Headstart, homeless, low achievement)	5
Integration/Special Education	
Topic not included	84
Verbal discussion only	26
Verbal discussion and/or behavior observed in integrated or natural settings	12
Total	122

Note. Totals of types of disabilities do not equal total number of articles due to the occurrence of more than one disability in several studies.

Five studies (Gunsberg, 1988; Humpal, 1991; Jellison, Brooks, & Huck, 1984; Madsen, Smith, & Feeman, 1988; Thompson, 1986) collected data from both groups of children as they interacted with each other in an integrated setting. An analysis of these and other studies in integrated settings are presented in the Appendix and in Part 2 of the Results section.

When occurrences of disability types were counted, mental retardation occurred 51 times, 11 occurrences were identified for deafness or hearing impairments, 11 for emotional disturbance, and 10 for learning disabilities. All other types occurred fewer than 10 times across the 122 studies.

Of the 24 comparative studies, the majority of the studies focused on a comparison of music discrimination skills, music knowledge, and music performance. Variables included various aspects of rhythm discrimination and performance (Atterbury, 1983; Darrow, 1979, 1984; Korduba, 1975; Larson, 1981; McGivern, Berka, Languis, & Chapman, 1991; Stratford & Ching, 1983), motor skills required to play classroom instruments (Gilbert, 1983), improvisational skills (Thaut, 1988), discrimination of pitches, dynamics, and rhythms (Flowers, 1984), rhythm and tonality discriminations (Braswell, Decuir, Hoskins, Kvet, & Oubre, 1988), imitation of pitch and rhythm (Applebaum, Egel, Koegel, & Imhoff, 1979), melodic memory (Zenatti, 1975), recall of multiplication tables (Gfeller, 1983), brain responses to auditory stimuli (Dawson, Finley, Phillips, & Galpert, 1988), singing ranges (Larson, 1977), verbal descriptions of music (Hair & Graham, 1983), verbal identification of tempi and dynamics (Cassidy, 1992), verbalizations about music preferences and experiences, singing performance, and clapping a steady beat (Jellison & Flowers, 1991), music preferences (Giacobbe & Graham, 1978; Madsen, Capperella-Sheldon, & Johnson, 1991; Merle-Fishman & Marcus, 1982; Thaut, 1987), and musical aptitude (Braswell et al., 1988; Darrow, 1987). In the studies comparing music-related task performance, many similarities were found between the disabled and nondisabled groups, although these similarities were not always highlighted in the reports. Issues of similarities and differences in the music behaviors of disabled and nondisabled children are presented in the next section.

Disabled/Nondisabled Comparative Studies

The results of a review of comparative studies indicate sufficient evidence of similarities between disabled and nondisabled students on task performances and similar outcomes as a result of specific instructional techniques to warrant caution in defining disabled students as "special" in all dimensions of music behavior and learning. Some similarities exist even in early studies when disabled students were educated in facilities separate from their nondisabled peers. With some studies, it is difficult to determine whether differences that were found between groups were a result of the "disability" itself or the educational setting. The limited number of comparative studies specific to a particular population as well as inconsistencies in findings between the two groups of subjects within single studies suggest caution in the interpretation of the data.

Perhaps the most notable outcome of an interview study with disabled and nondisabled children (Jellison & Flowers, 1991) was the similarity of responses between the students regarding music preferences, experiences, and skills (singing and clapping a steady beat), although nondisabled students had a higher frequency and greater variety of verbal responses. In this same study, the disabled students attended regular schools and most had music classes, although not all were in inclusive music classrooms with their nondisabled peers.

In study of music preferences, Madsen et al. (1991) used a nonverbal device (Continuous Response Digital Interface) for disabled and nondisabled preschool children to indicate their musical responses (feelings) as they listened to music. When comparing graphs of the subjects' responses, both disabled and nondisabled students showed the ability to differentiate among the musical examples, and there were some disabled and nondisabled students who did not discriminate between the musical examples. Flowers (1984) noted similar preferences between students with retardation and nondisabled students for rhythmic/arrhythmic music examples although differences were found in preferences for dynamics for the examples. No significant differences were found between boys labeled emotionally disturbed and nondisabled boys for preference and descriptions of orchestral selections in a study by Giacobbe and Graham (1978).

Several studies were found that compared the rhythm discrimination and performance skills of disabled and nondisabled students. Atterbury (1983) found no significant differences between learning disabled and nondisabled students in rhythm perception, although differences were observed in rhythm performance tasks. In a study by Darrow (1984), students with hearing-impairments performed as well as or better than normal hearing subjects with regard to beat identification, tempo change, accent as a factor in meter discrimination, and rhythm pattern maintenance. Similarly, Korduba (1975) found no significant differences between groups of deaf and normal hearing children on the execution of a rhythm pattern duplication task, and, in a beat reproduction task, deaf students were significantly better than their normal hearing peers. Larson (1981) found no significant differences between adolescents labeled emotionally disturbed and nondisabled adolescents' performances on auditory, visual, or combined scores for rhythmic pattern recognition. McGivern et al. (1991) found that children with reading impairments in all age groups (Grades 1 through 3) exhibited a marked deficit in the ability to discriminate rhythm patterns as "same" or "different" on a Seashore Rhythm Test when compared to nondisabled peers, although no differences were found between groups on four additional standardized tests.

In a study comparing young children with communication disorders and those who had normal language and speech development in their ability to label music characteristics (loud, soft, fast, slow) when assigned to verbal, verbal/visual, or verbal/gesture groups, Cassidy (1992) found no significant differences between the groups and found that all children responded more accurately when words were combined with either visuals or gestures.

When students with learning disabilities played classroom instruments, their performance scores were slightly lower than nondisabled students' scores on most subtests involving motor movements required to play the instruments; however, they scored higher than their nondisabled peers on compound motor skills (i.e., accuracy in playing striking patterns that were varied in speed, eye-hand, or range of movement criteria) (Gilbert, 1983). When children with autism were asked to play improvised tone sequences on a xylophone, and those patterns were analyzed and compared to musical improvisations by nondisabled children and children with retardation, results showed that the highest individual score was achieved by a child with autism and that the scores overall (particularly for rhythm, restriction, and originality) almost reached the scores of the nondisabled children (Thaut, 1988). Although children with autism scored higher than children with retardation, they were more similar in terms of complexity and rule adherence (their patterns were rather short and repetitive). In a study of rhythmic and pitch imitation, Applebaum et al. (1979) found that three children with autism performed the same or better on the tasks than did their musically experienced, nondisabled, age-matched peers.

The use of background music, whether it was interrupted or continuous, functioned similarly for students labeled "hyperactive" and typical children, and no significant difference was observed in either the frequency of body movements or performance on a writing task by the two groups (Wolfe, 1982).

Results of studies by Gibbons (1983) and Braswell et al. (1988) suggest that even within a disability category (emotional disturbance, mental retardation) there are consequential variations in responses. Gibbons' study revealed no significant differences in motor coordination and tempo aptitude among three groups of children labeled "emotionally disturbed" who were grouped according to their "need for external structure." However, when all groups were asked to imitate rhythm patterns, differences were evident for those students having a "severe need for external structure" compared to the other two groups (Gibbons, 1983). In a study with children with labels of mild, moderate, severe, or profound levels of retardation and disadvantaged and advantaged children, age and level of retardation were factors found to influence students' scores on standardized music tests (Braswell et al., 1988).

Several authors attribute differences between disabled and nondisabled groups of children to variations in educational experiences as well as age. In an early study of four different age groups of children with retardation in institutional settings and nondisabled peers, Zenatti (1975) found that music memory was better for older children compared to younger children, regardless of whether the children had a disability or not. However, when the older disabled and nondisabled children were compared and younger disabled and nondisabled children were compared, differences between the older disabled and nondisabled children were greater than the differences between younger disabled and nondisabled children. Although performance on the music memory task improved for older children, the institutionalized older children with retardation dropped further behind their nondisabled peers with age. These data appear consistent with data from several studies indicating that, over time, the academic performance of students with retardation in segregated environments falls farther and farther behind their nondisabled peers and also farther behind their peers with retardation who have been integrated into regular educational environments (Madden & Slavin, 1983).

Several studies indicate that music skills such as rhythm perception and performance (Atterbury, 1983), motor skills for playing classroom instruments (Gilbert, 1983), and melodic memory (Zenatti, 1975) improve with age. As might be expected, there are often significant correlations between age and music task performance, and between age and various standard measures of intelligence and social development (Braswell et al., 1988; Dileo, 1976; Rider, 1977).

Children with and without disabilities also have been shown to respond similarly to the same teaching techniques and methodologies. Several examples include the addition of spoken syllables to tapped rhythms to improve rhythm duplication (Atterbury, 1983), the addition of gestures or visuals to words to teach music terminology (Cassidy, 1992), auditory prompts and cues to improve rhythm pattern perception (Larson, 1981), and the use of a musical presentation of multiplication facts in conjunction with extended rehearsal, modeling, and cueing to increase recall (Gfeller, 1983). A early study by Dorow (1976) with 17 institutionalized children replicated the design and methodology of a previous study with disadvantaged public school first-graders (Madsen, Moore, Dorow, & Womble, 1976) and illustrated the use of music subject matter as reinforcement for mathematics subject matter, with achievement gains in both academic areas.

Topics of Integration/Special Education

Regarding the topic of special education/integration, 84 (69%) of the 122 studies did not include verbalizations or subject behavior that could clearly be related to special education language or to the integration of disabled individuals into natural environments (see Table 2). Twenty-six studies (21%) used some special-education-related terminology throughout the reports, and only 12 (10%) of the studies included observations of disabled students in integrated or natural environments (see Appendix for summaries of studies in integrated or natural environments). The 12 studies identified as examples of research in integrated or natural settings include examples of behaviors in integrated school, home, and community settings. Although McCarty, McElfresh, Rice, and Wilson (1978) observed the inappropriate bus behaviors of students in a bus transporting students with disabilities only, this study was included in the "integrated settings" category and coded "B" since the observations as well as the treatment were conducted in a natural setting (i.e., the actual bus) and because the learning outcomes could be transferred easily to an "inclusive school bus" setting. The study by Witt and Steele (1984) is included since the report documents the important role of the parent in the development and implementation of a music therapy program for interacting with her infant daughter. With these exceptions, other studies in this category, coded "B," report data from integrated settings in the schools and community.

Research Methodology; Data Collection; Generalization

Methodology and data collection frequencies are found in Table 3. Results indicate that experimental and descriptive studies appear with approximately equal frequency (64 experimental articles and 58 descriptive articles). Within the experimental literature category, 38 studies used group designs, 24 studies used behavioral designs, and two studies used both group and behavioral designs.

Observation data collection procedures were more often episodic (78, or 64% of the studies) than longitudinal (35, or 29% of the studies), and data were most often collected by observing individuals in separate sessions rather than in groups. Several studies included both episodic and longitudinal data. Only 17 (14%) of the 122 studies reported data concerning subjects' generalization of the target behavior to different settings, personal interactions, or places; 105 (86%) of the studies did not include generalization procedures as part of the treatment/research design.

Function of Music; Nonmusic and Music Outcomes

Examination of the "behavior observed," the "function of music," and the "dependent variable" categories indicate that researchers have structured music to facilitate the acquisition of academic, social, motor, and verbal behaviors that may be similar to those taught in special education settings. Many music behaviors that occur in music education settings for nondisabled children are also a focus for research with disabled children, whether structured as the independent variable (music activity) or as the dependent variable (learning outcome). Table 4 shows that both nonmusic and music outcomes appear frequently in the music research literature with disabled children (occurrences of nonmusic outcomes = 87; occurrences of music outcomes = 75). It should be noted that the categories of music and nonmusic were not mutually exclusive

Table 3

Frequency of Occurrence of Research Modes, Data Collection Procedures, and Generalization Data Categories in Music Research (1975–1993)

Category	Frequency
Total Number of Studies Reviewed	122
Research Modes	
Descriptive Research Articles	58
Experimental Research Articles	64
Experimental; Group Design/Methodology	38
Experimental; Behavioral Design/Methodology	24
Group and Behavioral Designs/Methodology	2
Total	122
Data Collection Procedures	
Episodic	78
Individual	57
Group	14
Individual and Group	7
Longitudinal	35
Individual	25
Group	8
Individual and Group	2
Episodic and Longitudinal	9
Total	122
Generalization Data	
None	105
Generalization	17
Total	122

Table 4

Frequency of Occurrence of Functions of Music for Nonmusic and Music Outcome Categories in Music Research (1975–1993)

Category	Frequency
Total Number of Studies Reviewed	122
Occurrences of Nonmusic Outcomes	87
Function of Music for Nonmusic Outcomes:	
Stimulus Cue/Prompt Academic, Motor, Social, Verbal Behavior	29
Structured Activity Academic, Motor, Social, Verbal Behavior, & Assessment	34
Contingency Academic, Motor, Social, Verbal, Behavior	24
Occurrences of Music Outcomes	75
Discrimination	17
Singing	14
Listening	13
General Participation	12
Playing Instruments	11
Movement	4
Verbalizing	4

Note. Totals for music and nonmusic categories do not equal the total number of articles due to the occurrence of more than one outcome in several studies.

in all cases, and, based on the behavior observed (Table 1, Part b), some studies were categorized as both music and nonmusic. Studies were categorized as both music and nonmusic when separate music and nonmusic behaviors were observed in the same study (e.g., speaking and singing) or when a single behavior could be categorized as both music and nonmusic (participating in interactive music activities and social behaviors).

Nonmusic Outcomes

The effect of music on nonmusic behaviors has been documented with many different disabled populations and numerous examples are present in the literature to describe the various functions of music as a stimulus cue or prompt (29 occurrences), as an ongoing activity (34 occurrences), and as a contingency (24 occurrences). Due to the large number of studies, several examples across the years will serve to demonstrate the diversity of the research across populations and the different functions of music to bring about changes in academic, motor, social, and verbal behavior. Examples of the use of music for assessment purposes also will be presented.

Rhythm and rhythm activities were used frequently as cues or prompts to bring about changes in motor and verbal behavior. Rhythmic auditory stimuli resulted in improvements in the rhythmic walking gait of children with neuromuscular or skeletal disorders (Staum, 1983); rhythmic speech improved temporal muscular control in children with motor dysfunctions (Thaut, 1985); melody and rhythm were effective to reach the desired outcome of slower speech in an adolescent with right-brain injuries (Cohen, 1988); and experience with notating rhythm patterns, playing rhythm patterns, and rhythmic association with speech improved the rhythmic speech of students with hearing impairments (Gfeller, 1986).

When music was structured as a cue or prompt, accuracy of recall responses of multiplication tables with students with learning disabilities increased (Gfeller, 1983); music mediation strategies resulted in increased performance accuracy on paired associate learning tasks for students with learning disabilities (Shehan, 1981); and preschool children learned telephone numbers more quickly (Wolfe & Hom, 1993). Song stimuli and the placement of the sound source affected the activity levels of adolescents with severe retardation (Dorow & Horton, 1982).

When music is not only presented to "get a response going" but is structured as a ongoing music activity (e.g., listening to music, playing instruments, singing) music may be said to function as a structured activity—a unique prompt for learning. Several examples follow: a child with autism showed fewer inappropriate behaviors during music activities in his regular music education compared to his special education setting (Kostka, 1993); structured music activities designed for interaction increased partner selection and interactions between disabled and nondisabled children (Humpal, 1991); and preferred music activities as contingencies and the use of structured music activities resulted in increases in spontaneous speech of preschool children with physical disabilities (Harding & Ballard, 1982). Participation in group music therapy activities resulted in developmental gains in children with retardation (Hairston, 1990), increased performance on targeted behaviors of students labeled low achieving (Krout, 1987), increased auditory awareness and improved reading skills of students with learning disabilities (Roskam, 1979), and increased appropriate music and nonmusic behavior of children with autism (Schmidt, Franklin, & Edwards, 1976). When preschool children with retardation engaged in antiphonal singing with picture cards, expressive language skills were found to increase (Hoskins, 1988), and choir and music lessons functioned to increase appropriate social behavior of children with several types of disabilities (Steele, 1975).

Music activities have been structured to bring about changes in behaviors but have also served as a means to "formally" assess nonmusic behaviors and attitudes. For example, specific music activities were structured to assess reading skills (McGivern et al., 1991), cognitive skills (Rider, 1977), suprasegmental aspects of speech (Darrow, 1984), and motor music skills (Gilbert,

1983). In order to assess attitudes, nondisabled students watched a video of a choir of disabled children singing and then assessed the musical performance of the disabled students (Cassidy & Sims, 1991). In another study of attitudes, nondisabled children answered questions regarding interacting with children with disabilities during music activities in various music environments (Jellison, 1985).

Numerous articles document the effectiveness of music as a contingency for teaching nonmusic behaviors. Examples of contingent music listening include music listening to improve head posturing of physically handicapped children and youth (Murphy, Doughty, & Nunes, 1979; Walmsley, Crichton, & Droog, 1981; Wolfe, 1980), to increase in-seat behavior (Hill, Brantner, & Spreat, 1989), to decrease bedwetting (Garwood, 1988), to increase acceptance and positive interactions among disabled and nondisabled students (Jellison et al., 1984), to motivate and to maintain appropriate tutoring skills (Madsen et al., 1991), and to improve arithmetic skills (Miller, 1977). As early as 1977, Miller found that preferred music can be structured as a listening contingency without music preference being negatively affected; that is, students still enjoyed the music after it was used as a contingency.

Contingent music listening along with playing instruments increased the preacademic and motor skills of children and adolescents with severe mental retardation (Holloway, 1980), and the structuring of contingent televised music lessons for correct mathematics responses resulted in improvements in both music learning outcomes and math responses for children and adolescents with mental retardation (Dorow, 1976). In another study by Dorow (1975), music was classically conditioned as an effective new reinforcer that was then used to teach imitative behavior to severely disabled young adults who had previously responded only to food rewards.

Music Outcomes

Music behaviors observed ranged from simple imitative and perception tasks to more complex tasks such as music reading or playing an instrument. When the studies were categorized into broad curricular areas, 17 of the 75 occurrences of music outcomes were related to some aspect of music discrimination (pitch, rhythm, melody, etc.). Other music activities that occurred frequently were singing (14 occurrences), listening (13 occurrences), general participation (12 occurrences), and playing instruments (11 occurrences) (see Table 4). Few studies were concerned with movement to music or verbalizations about music as learning outcomes. As presented in an earlier section of this paper, the majority of the 24 comparative studies with disabled and nondisabled students were concerned with students' performances of music and music related tasks (pitch discrimination, rhythm performance, music experiences, music preferences, singing, etc.). The reader is referred to the section "Disabled/Nondisabled Comparative Studies" for examples and findings of music outcome studies.

Part 2: Research with Disabled and Nondisabled Students in Integrated and Natural Settings

Twelve studies were identified that speak directly to the transition of disabled students into integrated or natural environments. Environments in which these investigations were conducted include: school and school-related studies (Force, 1983; Gunsberg, 1988; Humpal, 1991; Jellison et al., 1984; Kostka, 1993; Madsen et al., 1988; McCarty et al., 1978; Thompson, 1986), home and school (Steele, 1984), home (Witt & Steele, 1984), and community (Reid, Hill, Rawers, & Montegar, 1975; Staum & Flowers, 1984). The studies were analyzed further to determine documentation procedures and to report salient findings from the research. Summaries of the 12 articles may be found in Appendix. The following sections present selected results of the analyses specific to documentation, parent and teacher involvement in data collection and selection of behaviors, the use of contingent music as a technique in integrated and natural settings, and research findings specific to the school setting. Considering the few studies in this category, examples are limited, and several studies appear frequently throughout the sections.

Documentation of Behavior in Integrated/Natural Settings

The versatility of behavioral observation as a data collection procedure is demonstrated in studies of students in integrated and natural settings. Academic, social, motor, verbal, and music behaviors have been observed in environments such as regular music classrooms and special education music classrooms, the school bus, play time, practicing a musical instrument at home, interactions with a parent, shopping in a community store, and riding in a car with family. Six of the 12 studies (Jellison et al., 1984 ; McCarty et al., 1978; Reid et al., 1975; Staum & Flowers, 1984; Steele, 1984; Witt & Steele, 1984) reported data over a period of several weeks, used behavioral designs, and presented either generalization data or data documenting the behavior during and following fading of the instructional strategy.

Parent/Teacher Involvement in Research with Disabled Children in Natural Environments

Considering the recent emphasis on early intervention services for infants aged 0–2, Witt and Steele (1984) provide a model demonstrating the effectiveness of a music therapy program with a 14-month-old child with multiple disabilities. Of particular significance is the involvement of the parent in the development and implementation of the music program. The infant learned to interact positively with her mother and learned appropriate play with toys during music therapy sessions and at home. Staum and Flowers (1984) and Reid et al. (1975) also involved parents in the selection of the behaviors to be taught and in the implementation of the program.

Teachers have also been involved in the selection of the behavior for change in the evaluation of the outcomes of the study. In a study by Steele (1984), music teachers and staff played important roles in data collection during the transition of students from music lessons in the "therapy" setting to participation in ensembles and music lessons in the regular school music setting. In other examples, teachers, administrators, and counselors were involved in evaluating and selecting students to participate in a tutoring study (Madsen et al., 1988); teachers and staff members evaluated the benefits of inclusive music therapy sessions and specific activities (Humpal, 1991); teachers were consulted in the selection of inappropriate classroom behaviors (Kostka, 1993); and teachers, administrators, and bus drivers were involved in the selection of bus riding as a targeted behavior for change (McCarty et al., 1978).

Contingent Music as a Technique to Facilitate Appropriate Behavior in Integrated Settings

Contingent music listening, used alone or in conjunction with other strategies, appeared in many of the studies designed to facilitate positive social behaviors in a variety of school, home, and community settings. Contingent music listening was structured effectively to increase appropriate car riding and appropriate social walking in community settings (Reid et al., 1975) and appropriate school bus behavior (McCarty et al., 1978). When small groups of severely disabled and nondisabled students were structured for interaction in the regular music classroom and music listening was contingent upon "cooperative behavior," positive social interactions increased among the disabled and nondisabled students (Jellison et al., 1984). Students with behavior and/or learning problems were motivated to volunteer to be tutors for kindergarten children when they knew that they could listen to their favorite music after each tutoring session and that they had the possibility of earning their favorite cassette tape (Madsen et al., 1988).

Contingent music lessons have also been used to teach skills that are important for disabled students' successful transition into integrated environments. When a child with autism received piano lessons contingent on appropriate social behavior while shopping in the community with an adult, appropriate behavior increased (Staum & Flowers, 1984). Music lessons (drum, trumpet) were also found to be effective contingencies for children to learn appropriate social skills in the home and school (Steele, 1984).

The flexibility of contingent music as a technique for behavior change in natural and integrated settings is demonstrated in studies that structure music listening sessions using individual tape recorders worn by therapists, recorders operated by remote control, and group listening stations commonly found in schools. Contingent music lessons were provided by either music therapists and/or music educators.

DISCUSSION

Frequency of Studies with Disabled Children and Youth; School-Related Studies

Findings of the present review indicate that the overall publication frequency of data articles related to music and children with disabilities is rather low considering the number of music and nonmusic journals that publish original research specific to children with disabilities. A need for research in the arts with disabled populations was expressed in the 1980s by special education, music education, and music therapy professionals (Appell, 1980; Madsen, 1980, 1985; Radocy, 1983) and this need continues, particularly as it applies to music with disabled children in school settings. In a review of music research in special education printed in the 1988 edition of this book, the topic of integration and special education language (including any reference to regular schools, special education, issues of integration, etc.) occurred in 17 (23%) of the 73 studies reviewed and in the present review, 38 (31%) of the 122 studies. The number of studies that discuss integration issues is increasing but is still strikingly low given that P.L. 94–142 was enacted in 1975 and that, currently, approximately 93% of all children with disabilities receive education services in regular public school settings (United States Department of Education, 1993). It is paramount that music research speak to the issues of inclusion and provide knowledge that will assist professionals in meeting attitudinal, instructional, and curricular challenges as they occur in inclusive settings with disabled children and youth.

Some authors suggest that an increase in research publication may result as measures are taken to encourage both undergraduate and graduate music majors to gain independent scholarship and research prowess (Madsen & Furman, 1984), as professionals gain more skill in transferring research findings to their own work situations (Madsen, 1986), and as researchers include statements of application and transfer within research reports (Hedden, 1979; Nicholas & Gilbert, 1980). Additionally, if music research with disabled children is to become socially relevant, future music educators, therapists, and researchers (1) must study the values inherent to special education legislation, (2) must become knowledgeable of conflicting issues regarding inclusion, (3) must become knowledgeable of well-documented and effective strategies to facilitate successful transition into regular classrooms and natural environments, and (4) must advocate for transition services for disabled children through their practice. Students and professionals alike must also participate in field experiences in settings that provide positive models-settings where parents and professionals have worked to provide safe, happy learning environments in which disabled and nondisabled children learn and play together.

Additionally, it is unlikely that meaningful music research will be conducted in integrated school and community settings without interactions and cooperation among parents and various professionals working with students with disabilities. Cooperative projects that extend across disciplines and "place-oriented" boundaries may begin to ameliorate the logistical problems inherent in designing programs for collecting, evaluating, and reporting data. Mutual concern among competent professionals working to improve the quality of life for individuals with disabilities and closer proximity of professionals from different disciplines should lead to increasing research and evaluation within ongoing music programs.

Documentation is an ongoing process for most music therapists, and assessment and evaluation procedures are integral components of the music therapy curriculum; however, much of the important information that is being collected to evaluate individualized longitudinal programs for students is apparently not being disseminated through the journals. The IEP has long been an effective instrument for use by both music therapists and music educators (Alley, 1979) and could well serve as an effective research tool. After determining functional music and nonmusic objectives for the student, parents and professionals alike could engage in collecting data in a number of settings in order to document the student's progress. A case study of a single child though the IEP is rarely mentioned in the research literature (perhaps evidence of the fact that few music therapists may be actively involved with other professionals on the IEP team and therefore may not be influential in determining objectives outside of the separate music therapy session).

As discussed previously, employment practices, in part, may account for the limited number of studies that are specific to disabled students in school settings and the limited number of studies that address issues relating to the transition and inclusion of students with disabilities into natural school, home, or community environments. In a profile of the membership of the National Association for Music Therapy, only 15% of employed music therapists worked in school settings (National Association for Music Therapy, 1994). The definition of school setting is unclear, but, assuming that most music therapists are employed in public schools (schools with regular and special education classes), most likely, their role is to travel among several schools, serving children with the most severe disabilities in separate classrooms. Meeting difficult schedules in several segregated settings and lack of administrative support for inclusion are factors that discourage collaboration among professionals. As the number of inclusive classrooms increases and as parents become more actively involved in transition planning for their children, so will collaboration among professionals increase. The music therapist working in public schools can play an important role in collaborative efforts to prepare children for successful integration into inclusive settings. Hopefully, published documentation of these successful efforts will follow.

Although studies in school settings are limited, this fact does not preclude the application of the many techniques examined throughout the literature that may be used effectively with diverse populations in various school settings.

Comparative Studies with Disabled and Nondisabled Students

When disabled and nondisabled students have been compared, findings show both similarities and differences between the groups-important information that suggests caution in deriving generalizations regarding students' music abilities based on labels. For the most part, there is general agreement in the research literature that the practice of labeling and separating children involves a host of problems. Problems exist with regard to assessment procedures and operational definitions of disability categories. Additionally, teacher expectations for labeled children are lower than expectations for nonlabeled children when the labels indicate deficiencies or disabilities (Foster, Yesseldyke, & Reese, 1975; Reynolds, Wang, & Walberg, 1986; Rolison & Medway, 1985). Music educators' attitudes regarding the importance of the music objectives and how pleasurable it would be for students to learn the objectives are significantly and negatively influenced by a label indicating severe disabilities (Jellison & Wolfe, 1987). However, in a recent study of social and music expectations for labeled and unlabeled students entering the music classroom, teachers expressed a greater willingness overall to teach both social and music behaviors to a student with retardation than to a nonlabeled student and less willingness overall to teach social behaviors, compared to music behaviors, to either student (Jellison & Duke, 1994).

Professionals and researchers in special education are moving away from labels to describe differences and are moving toward the study and development of strategies that facilitate positive attitudes and social interactions among teachers, nondisabled students, and disabled students in the regular classroom (Biklen, 1985; Stainback, Stainback, & Forest, 1989). Future comparative music studies may study labeling effects related to music behaviors and strategies that may function to deemphasize differences and biases that have negative outcomes for students with disabilities. It seems important to study the strengths of students with disabilities and similarities between students with disabilities and their nondisabled peers as students are brought together in a single learning environment.

Although teachers' attitudes and expectations are influenced by labels, early research shows that when the student's actual performance is seen to be unlike that suggested by the label, initial biases can be overcome (Reschly & Lamprecht, 1979). Evidence suggests that unfamiliarity with an examiner interferes with the performance of school-age students with disabilities but does not necessarily interfere with the performance of nondisabled students (Fuchs, Fuchs, Dailey, & Power, 1985; Fuchs, Fuchs, Power, & Dailey, 1985). These findings present important methodological considerations for future comparative studies. Although subjects' familiarity with the examiner was not a dimension for analysis in the present review, data collection procedures frequently were individual (one-to-one). If unfamiliarity constitutes a source of error in evaluation and research, it obviously becomes important that the person collecting data be a person with whom the disabled student is familiar. Implications are important not only for research procedures but for any assessment procedures with disabled children.

Music and Nonmusic Learning Outcomes

Although specific special education terminology and references to integration and IDEA were not frequently found in the context of the articles reviewed, many parallels with special education were evident, particularly in the structuring of music in conjunction with well-established teaching principles to reach music and nonmusic learning outcomes. The research clearly shows the effectiveness of music as a stimulus cue/prompt, as an ongoing activity, and as an effective contingency to bring about desired changes in behavior and the effective uses of evaluation and systematic observation systems to document these changes.

It is interesting to find that music behaviors were frequently identified as dependent variables (learning outcomes). When the professions of music education and music therapy were discussed by Forsythe and Jellison (1977) in response to the passage of P.L. 94–142, the objectives for the two professions were clearly defined as either music or nonmusic, respectively. It now appears that the objectives, at least for music research with children with disabilities, are as often music or music-related as nonmusic. Music activities occur frequently in natural, integrated settings, and music activities, alone or with a group, are appropriate, functional recreation/leisure time objectives for a student's transition plan and IEP. As students are included into regular music education classrooms and appropriate leisure and recreation programs in natural community and home environments, the acquisition of social and music learning outcomes will take on increased importance in music programs in special education. Important to this end will be increased communication among music therapists and music educators in the development of a transition plan and objectives for the IEP. The development of appropriate music and nonmusic objectives will increase the probability that meaningful educational programs are developed that concern not only the learning outcomes for the student with disabilities but also the attitudes and behaviors of nondisabled populations in music classrooms and community environments.

Research Mode/Data Collection/Research Variables

Many of the experimental and descriptive studies reviewed have identified important strategies for instruction and data collection that may be transferred across various disability areas. Data collection was most often episodic and was collected from individual subjects. Recognizing that basic group research is indispensable to any discipline and that researchers must select the most appropriate design to control for bias, this review has identified a need that is generally unfulfilled in the music research literature, viz., few studies have reported long term benefits of the research for individual students with disabilities that participated in the study.

The selection of beneficial learning outcomes (research variables) has become a major concern for researchers and data-based teachers in special education (Voeltz & Evans, 1983). The music research literature would be strengthened by studies documenting the acquisition of meaningful behaviors by students with disabilities and the ways in which music functioned to teach those behaviors over time, ultimately increasing the quality of the students' lives. Such studies would provide an important contribution not only to the subjects but also to professionals responsible for developing, implementing, and monitoring longitudinal programs for individuals with disabilities. The selection and prioritization of beneficial behaviors is important in the development of program objectives for the IEP and transition plan and may well be important for the selection of variables in music research as well. Suggestions for the selection of beneficial behaviors, whether as variables in music research or program objectives, are presented in the following section.

RECOMMENDATIONS

The results and relevance of this growing body of research will depend on the philosophy, aims, and methodology that are applied to it. Special education issues and the results of this review of music research variables, data collection procedures, and methodologies were considered in the development of two sets of recommendations. The first presents specific criteria for the selection of beneficial behaviors (research variables and program objectives) for students with disabilities and the second presents broader recommendations for consideration in developing, implementing, and reporting educationally valid music research and documentation procedures in special education.

Criteria for Selecting Beneficial Behaviors for Disabled Students in Music Research and Music Therapy/Education Programs

The selection and prioritization of functional educational objectives is an important topic in special education and, similarly, there are implications for programs in music education and music therapy (Jellison, 1983). Longitudinal documentation of superior programs and research study with a focus on behaviors that will result in maximally beneficial short- and long-term outcomes would greatly strengthen the body of music research with disabled students, and would more closely parallel current educational and research priorities in special education. The following criteria are suggested for consideration:

1. *Select Meaningful Behaviors for Independence.* Select functional behaviors that are meaningful now and that will also prepare the student to be maximally independent in environments outside of the school setting and in future environments as adults.

Independence will be gained as functional skills are acquired. Skills should be selected that are functional for the child's current situation, but importance must also be given to those skills that will ultimately improve the quality of the student's current life style and his/her life style as an adult. Evaluating the use of music as a prompt to teach a teenage student to read and count numbers from 1 to 10 may serve to verify the strategy; however, the same strategy could also be examined with more meaningful, more *functional* life skills such as learning home and emergency phone numbers. Learning to count from one to 10 may be important and should be taught at some time; however, in selecting the sequence, consideration should first be given to information that will be most useful and normalizing in the daily life of the student. What could be more normalizing than learning the phone numbers of significant friends and family in order to increase pleasurable social contact? In another example, it may be more beneficial for a student to learn about dynamics by actually singing or playing a classroom instrument more softly (or loudly) following teacher directions or environmental cues than to learn only the verbal labels for the dynamic symbols. Learning to follow a teacher's cues or instructions for dynamic changes may avoid social embarrassment for a child in natural and inclusive environments with nondisabled peers and adults (i.e., school classroom, church, recreational settings) and, therefore, may increase the pleasure of participation in music activities. A repertoire of functional skills is extremely important as are those skills that can be used throughout adult life for pleasure and enjoyment alone or with friends (e.g., purchasing tickets and attending concerts, taking a city bus to a public library and listening to records, learning to play an instrument for individual pleasure, learning how to make personal selections of music to change or enhance an emotion).

2. *Select Behaviors with Multiple Positive Effects.* Select behaviors that have positive collateral or multiple effects for the student or for significant persons in the student's environment.

The limitation of educational time and the severity of the impairment suggests that researchers and therapists/educators select and document changes in behaviors that may have multiple effects. For example, inappropriate social behavior during free or leisure time in a disabled adolescent's natural or group home may decrease as the student learns to be more independent and uses his/her free time engaged in pleasurable, chronologically age appropriate music activities (e.g., playing an instrument, selecting and playing CDs or tapes with friends). Likewise, students who learn to interact positively with disabled students in structured music settings may interact positively with them during leisure and play time. Examples of positive collateral or multiple effects may be seen as (1) the generalization of the newly learned behavior to other persons, places, settings, or materials, (2) the acquisition of a new behavior used as an instructional strategy for another objective (e.g., learning to play the piano while increasing positive statements about oneself in the process), or (3) positive attitude changes in peers, parents, or teachers. Several research studies that were reviewed for this paper cited positive learning outcomes as a result of the research in addition to behaviors identified as dependent measures; however, documentation was not always provided to verify the positive changes and multiple effects.

3. *Select Socially Valued Behaviors.* Select behaviors that will be valued by significant persons in the student's environment (i.e., valued by peers, parents, teachers, future employers).

Communication among professionals and parents is imperative in order to meet this criterion. Although IEP procedures for the selection of goals and objectives is well defined, few guidelines, if any, are offered for the development of individualized goals and a transition plan for each student, and there seems to be an underlying assumption that the individuals involved in the selection process will derive the most appropriate programmatic objectives for the student. The involvement of the music therapist and music educator on the IEP team becomes critical as parents, teachers, and education agency representatives participate in the development of transition goals and objectives at team meetings. If a student is to be placed in a regular music classroom, the behaviors valued by the music educator must be communicated and must be included in the student's program prior to or concurrent with placement in the regular classroom.

The success of disabled students in the regular classroom is often determined by the students' social skills and acceptance by peers (Brinker, 1985; Evans, Salisbury, Palombaro, Berryman, & Hollowood, 1992). Jellison and Duke (1994) found that teachers felt it more important for students (disabled and nondisabled) to have learned social behaviors (i.e., enter the room quietly, raise hand to talk, start and stop playing instruments when instructed) than to have learned music behaviors prior to becoming a member of the class.

Many behaviors valued by teachers and nondisabled students as well could be incorporated into research studies and documented as they occur in the daily routine of students in the classroom or therapy sessions. Most special educators now realize that the involvement of the parent/guardian and input from the classroom teacher are critical in the selection of educationally sound goals and objectives. Acquisition of behaviors valued by significant persons in the student's life will increase the probability that those behaviors will be reinforced and maintained by persons with whom he or she will often interact.

4. *Select Social Interaction Behaviors.* Select behaviors that will result in or involve appropriate and positive social interactions with nondisabled peers engaged in chronologically age-appropriate activities.

There are benefits for both nondisabled and disabled individuals engaged in positive interactions as they work and play in integrated settings. Music activities, in and of themselves, do not necessarily result in positive interactions between disabled and nondisabled students, but interactions will increase as opportunities are structured and positive consequences follow (Jellison et al., 1984). Although it is important that individuals learn music skills for quality leisure time alone (e.g., listening to favorite CDs or playing an instrument), the group nature of many music activities provides an excellent setting for structuring quality interactions among students with diverse abilities and disabilities. Opportunities for positive interactions with small groups of peers may be structured through participation in choral or band organizations, attending concerts with friends, dancing, sharing tapes and CDs with friends, sharing music knowledge and skills (tutoring), or small group experiences and projects in the general music classroom setting.

Recommendations for Developing, Implementing, and Reporting Educationally Valid Music Research with Children with Disabilities

Based on the results of this review, the following broad recommendations are presented:

1. Continue to identify effective instructional strategies and descriptions of cause and effect phenomena using appropriate experimental and descriptive research methodologies that are transferable across situations and students with varying abilities and disabilities.

2. Increase data-based research and data-based programs to include longitudinal studies that are designed to document the effectiveness of comprehensive music therapy/education programs in bringing about the successful transition of disabled students into natural and inclusive settings with nondisabled peers and adults.

3. Study the impact of inclusion on social/interpersonal relationships among students in music environments and the impact of inclusion on the acquisition of music knowledge and skill.

4. Study the impact of inclusion on the role of the music educator and music therapist.

5. Extend research to include the study of behaviors that are particularly meaningful for students serving as subject(s) and that will maximize their independence in natural home, school, and community environments.

6. Include parents, significant music professionals, other significant persons, and the disabled student, if possible, in the selection of music behaviors (dependent variables), implementation of the strategies (independent variables), and the collection of data.

7. Continue the study of music-related learning within curricular areas commonly found in the music education classroom (i.e., singing, playing instruments, movement, listening).

8. Include procedures to document the maintenance of behavior change and include generalization data of behaviors in natural and inclusive settings with nondisabled persons, different cues, materials, etc.

9. Examine issues in music research that parallel those identified as priority issues in the special education literature.

10. Report the outcomes of music research and the evaluation of music programs with disabled children using the language and terms commonly found in the special education literature and discuss implications for transition and inclusion.

11. Collect data for comparative studies from students in similar educational settings and provide implications for curricular and instructional practice.

12. Continue publication in music journals that are readily accessible to music professionals, undergraduate, and graduate students who will be or who are currently working with disabled children.

CONCLUSIONS

Educators and therapists actively engaged in the study of music as it improves quality of life are rightly proud of the knowledge that has been gained throughout the past two decades. As a result of a developing body of research literature, students with disabilities have benefited from music programs that have implemented stringently studied and well-established instructional techniques. These techniques, as well as the observation and evaluation procedures employed in programs and research, parallel those used in the field of special education.

Results of the review of 122 music research studies published between 1975 and 1993 provide sufficient evidence to support conclusions that music can be structured effectively as a stimulus cue/prompt, as a learning activity, and as a contingency to teach academic, social, motor, and language objectives to students with varying disabilities. Additionally, music outcomes (music preferences, music knowledge, and music skills) have been documented in numerous studies, and several of these studies provide encouraging information regarding similarities among children in their perception, performance, and responsiveness to music and music teaching. Only a few studies were found that focused on students in integrated or natural settings, and these studies may serve as models for future research designed to examine issues that concern direct services and the successful transition of students with disabilities into inclusive settings.

Parents, professionals, and advocates concerned with direct services for individuals with disabilities have watched dramatic changes occur as specialized instruction has moved from models based on the residential schools of Europe to instruction in the "least restrictive environment." The history of special education in the United States began in the early 19th century with the establishment of the first educational program for disabled children. Services at that time were clearly place oriented, in that training, curricula, and instruction decisions were greatly influenced by the parameters of the educational setting. The challenges of P.L. 94–142 in 1975 and the amendments that followed and led to The Individuals with Disabilities Education Act of 1993 (replacing P.L. 94–142) have forced new approaches-approaches that have identified the limitations of specialized places and have resulted in expanding the life space of individuals with disabilities.

Children with disabilities are now being moved among varied environments, encountering many people—disabled and nondisabled, friendly and unfriendly. The transitions and the factors that facilitate success and that ultimately improve quality of life can become important dimensions of music research. As music researchers and practitioners approach evaluation with questions that concern direct benefits for a single disabled child, issues of transition and inclusion will evolve, and communication among professionals and other individuals in the child's life will likely occur. New questions demanding innovative procedures can be examined on many levels without diminishing or compromising the quality and stringency of research and evaluation methodology.

This review has focused on the collection of information over the past 18 years that has enabled us to document various aspects of music in the lives of disabled children. A commitment to the dissemination of music research clearly exists. Results of the review indicate a solid research base that provides evidence of the functional use of music to teach habilitative and educational objectives. The challenge to expand our research base to answer new questions concerning music and quality of life issues is an exciting one which will, no doubt, be prominent within the next decade of music research in special education.

References

Allen, L. D., & Bryant, M. C. (1985). A multielement analysis of contingent versus contingent-interrupted music. *Applied Research in Mental Retardation, 6,* 87–97.

Alley, J. M. (1979). Music in the IEP: Therapy/education. *Journal of Music Therapy, 16,* 111–127.

Alley, J. M. (1982). Music therapy. In C. R. Reynolds & T. B. Gutkin (Eds.), *The handbook of school psychology* (pp. 667–678). New York: John Wiley & Sons.

Appell, M. J. (1980). Arts for the handicapped: A researchable item. *Journal of Music Therapy, 17,* 75–83.

Applebaum, E., Egel, A. L., Koegel, R. L., & Imhoff, B. (1979). Measuring musical abilities of autistic children. *Journal of Autism and Developmental Disorders, 9,* 279–285.

Atterbury, B. W. (1983). A comparison of rhythm pattern perception and performance in normal and learning-disabled readers, age seven and eight. *Journal of Research in Music Education, 31,* 259–270.

Ayres, B. R. (1987). The effects of a music stimulus environment versus regular cafeteria environment during therapeutic feeding. *Journal of Music Therapy, 24,* 14–26.

Biklen, D. (1985). *Achieving the complete school: Strategies for effective mainstreaming.* New York: Teachers College Press.

Bokor, C. (1976). A comparison of musical and verbal responses of mentally retarded children. *Journal of Music Therapy, 13,* 101–108.

Bottari, S. S., & Evans, J. R. (1982). Effects of musical context, type of vocal presentation, and time on the verbal retention abilities of visual-spatially oriented and verbally oriented learning disabled children. *The Journal of School Psychology, 20,* 329–338.

Braswell, C., Decuir, A., Hoskins, C., Kvet, E., & Oubre, G. (1988). Relation between musical aptitude and intelligence among mentally retarded, advantaged, and disadvantaged subjects. *Perceptual and Motor Skills, 67,* 359–364.

Brinker, R. P. (1985). Interactions between severely mentally retarded students and other students in integrated and segregated public school settings. *American Journal of Mental Deficiency, 89,* 587–594.

Brown, L., Nietupski, V., & Hamre-Nietupski, S. (1976). Criterion of ultimate functioning. In M. A. Thomas (Ed.), *Hey, don't forget about me!* Reston, VA: Council for Exceptional Children.

Bruscia, K. (1982). Music in the assessment and treatment of echolalia. *Music Therapy, 2,* 25–41.

Bruscia, K. E., & Levinson, S. (1982). Predictive factors in Optacon music-reading. *Journal of Visual Impairment & Blindness, 76,* 309–312.

Burleson, S. J., Center, D. B., & Reeves, H. (1989). The effect of background music on task performance in psychotic children. *Journal of Music Therapy, 26,* 198–205.

Cassidy, J. W. (1992). Communication disorders: Effect on children's ability to label music characteristics. *Journal of Music Therapy, 29,* 113–124.

Cassidy, J. W., & Sims, W. (1991). Effects of special education labels on peers' and adults' evaluations of a handicapped youth choir. *Journal of Research in Music Education, 39,* 23–34.

Cassity, M. D. (1978). Social development of TMRs involved in performing and nonperforming groups. *Journal of Music Therapy, 15,* 100–105.

Cassity, M. D. (1981). The influence of a socially valued skill on peer acceptance in a music therapy group. *Journal of Music Therapy, 18,* 148–154.

Cohen, N. S. (1988). The use of superimposed rhythm to decrease the rate of speech in a brain-damaged adolescent. *Journal of Music Therapy, 25,* 85–93.

Cripe, F. F. (1986). Rock music as therapy for children with attention deficit disorder: An exploratory study. *Journal of Music Therapy, 23,* 30–37.

Darrow, A. A. (1979). The beat reproduction response of subjects with normal and impaired hearing: An empirical comparison. *Journal of Music Therapy, 16,* 91–98.

Darrow, A. A. (1984). A comparison of rhythmic responsiveness in normal and hearing impaired children and an investigation of the relationship of rhythmic responsiveness to the suprasegmental aspects of speech perception. *Journal of Music Therapy, 22,* 48–66.

Darrow, A. A. (1987). An investigative study: The effect of hearing impairment on musical aptitude. *Journal of Music Therapy, 24,* 88–96.

Darrow, A. A. (1990). The effect of frequency adjustment on the vocal reproduction accuracy of hearing impaired children. *Journal of Music Therapy, 27,* 24–33.

Darrow, A. A. (1991). An assessment and comparison of hearing impaired children's preference for timbre and musical instruments. *Journal of Music Therapy, 28,* 48–59.

Darrow, A. A. (1992). The effect of vibrotactile stimuli via the Somatron on the identification of pitch change by hearing impaired children. *Journal of Music Therapy, 29,* 103–112.

Darrow, A. A., & Cohen, N. (1991). The effect of programmed pitch practice and private instruction on the vocal reproduction accuracy of children with hearing impairments: Two case studies. *Music Therapy Perspectives, 9,* 61–65.

Darrow, A. A., & Starmer, G. J. (1986). The effect of vocal training on the intonation and rate of hearing impaired children's speech: A pilot study. *Journal of Music Therapy, 23,* 194–201.

Dattilo, J., & Mirenda, P. (1987). An application of a leisure preference assessment protocol for persons with severe handicaps. *The Journal of the Association for Persons with Severe Handicaps, 12,* 306–311.

Dawson, G., Finley, C., Phillips, S., & Galpert, L. (1988). Reduced P3 amplitude of the event-related brain potential: Its relationship to language ability in autism. *Journal of Autism and Developmental Disorders, 18*, 493–504.

Decuir, A. A. (1975). Vocal responses of mentally retarded subjects to four musical instruments. *Journal of Music Therapy, 12*, 40–43.

Dileo, C. L. (1975). The use of a token economy program with mentally retarded persons in a music therapy setting. *Journal of Music Therapy, 12*, 155–160.

Dileo, C. L. (1976). The relationship of diagnostic and social factors to the singing ranges of institutionalized mentally retarded persons. *Journal of Music Therapy, 13*, 17–28.

Dorow, L. G. (1975). Conditioning music and approval as new reinforcers for imitative behavior with the severely retarded. *Journal of Music Therapy, 12*, 30–39.

Dorow, L. G. (1976). Televised music lessons as educational reinforcement for correct mathematical responses with the educable mentally retarded. *Journal of Music Therapy, 13*, 77–86.

Dorow, L. G., & Horton, J. J. (1982). Effect of the proximity of auditory stimuli and sung versus spoken stimuli on activity levels of severely/profoundly mentally retarded females. *Journal of Music Therapy, 19*, 114–124.

Edenfield, T. N., & Hughes, J. E. (1991). The relationship of a choral music curriculum to the development of singing ability in secondary students with Down Syndrome. *Music Therapy Perspectives, 9*, 52–55.

Eidson, C. E. (1989). The effect of behavioral music therapy on the generalization of interpersonal skills from sessions to the classroom by emotionally handicapped middle school students. *Journal of Music Therapy, 26*, 206–221.

Eisenstein, S. R. (1976). A successive approximation procedure for learning music symbol names. *Journal of Music Therapy, 13*, 173–179.

Evans, I. M., Salisbury, C. L., Palombaro, M. M., Berryman, J., & Hollowood, T. M. (1992). Peer interactions and social acceptance of elementary-age children with severe disabilities in an inclusive school. *The Journal of the Association for Persons with Severe Handicaps, 17*, 205–212.

Federal Register. (1977). Education of Handicapped Children. Implementation of Part B of the Education of the Handicapped Act, *42*(163), pp. 42474–42518.

Flowers, E. (1984). Musical sound perception in normal children and children with Down's Syndrome. *Journal of Music Therapy, 21*, 148–154.

Force, B. (1983). The effect of mainstreaming on the learning of nonretarded children in an elementary classroom. *Journal of Music Therapy, 20*, 2–13.

Ford, J. E. & Veltri-Ford, A. (1980). Effects of time-out from auditory reinforcement on two problem behaviors. *Mental Retardation, 18*, 299–303.

Ford, T. A. (1988). The effect of musical experiences and age on the ability of deaf children to discriminate pitch. *Journal of Music Therapy, 25*, 2–16.

Forsythe, J. L., & Jellison, J. A. (1977). It's the law. *Music Educators Journal, 64*(3), 30–35.

Foster, G., Yesseldyke, J., & Reese, J. (1975). I wouldn't have seen it if I hadn't believed it. *Exceptional Children, 41*, 469–473.

Fuchs, D., Fuchs, L. S., Dailey, A. M., & Power, M. H. (1985). The effects of examiners' personal familiarity and professional experience on handicapped children's test performance. *Journal of Educational Research, 78,* 141–146.

Fuchs, D., Fuchs, L. S., Power, M. H., & Dailey, A. M. (1985). Bias in the assessment of handicapped children. *American Educational Research Journal, 22,* 185–198.

Furman, C. E. (1986). A commentary on professional accountability: Preparing for the future. In K. Gfeller (Ed.), *Fiscal, Regulatory, and Legislative Issues for the Music Therapist* (pp. 15–16). Washington, D C: National Association for Music Therapy.

Garwood, E. C. (1988). The effect of contingent music in combination with a bell pad on enuresis of a mentally retarded adult. *Journal of Music Therapy, 25,* 103–109.

Gfeller, K. C. (1983). Musical mnemonics as an aid to retention with normal and learning disabled students. *Journal of Music Therapy, 20,* 179–189.

Gfeller, K. C. (1986). Music as a remedial tool for improving speech rhythm in the hearing impaired: Clinical and research considerations. *Journal of the International Association of Music for the Handicapped* (formerly *MEH Bulletin*), *2* (2), 3–19.

Gfeller, K. C., & Rath, L. B. (1990). The development and assessment of a music education curriculum for elementary level students with moderate retardation. *Journal of the International Association of Music for the Handicapped* (formerly *MEH Bulletin*), *5*(2), 3–22.

Giacobbe, G. A., & Graham, R. M. (1978). The responses of aggressive emotionally disturbed and normal boys to selected musical stimuli. *Journal of Music Therapy, 15,* 118–135.

Gibbons, A. C. (1983). Rhythm responses in emotionally disturbed children with differing needs for external structure. *Music Therapy, 3,* 94–102.

Gilbert, J. P. (1983). A comparison of the motor music skills of nonhandicapped and learning disabled children. *Journal of Research in Music Education, 31,* 147–155.

Grant, R. C., & LeCroy, S. (1986). Effects of sensory mode input on the performance of rhythmic perception tasks by mentally retarded subjects. *Journal of Music Therapy, 23,* 2–9.

Grant, R. C., & Share, M. R. (1985). Relationship of pitch discrimination skills and vocal ranges of mentally retarded subjects. *Journal of Music Therapy, 22,* 99–103.

Greene, R. J., Hoats, D. L., & Dibble, W. A. (1975). Generalization of the aversive effect of music distortion. *Psychological Records, 25,* 173–180.

Greenwald, A. M. (1978). The effectiveness of distorted music versus interrupted music to decrease self-stimulating behavior in profoundly retarded adolescents. *Journal of Music Therapy, 15,* 58–66.

Gregoire, M. (1984). Music as a prior condition to task performance. *Journal of Music Therapy, 21,* 133–145.

Grossman, S. (1978). An investigation of Crocker's music projective techniques for emotionally disturbed children. *Journal of Music Therapy, 15,* 179–184.

Gunsberg, A. (1988). Improvised musical play: A strategy for fostering social play between developmentally delayed and nondelayed preschool children. *Journal of Music Therapy, 25,* 178–191.

Haines, J. H. (1989). The effects of music therapy on the self-esteem of emotionally-disturbed adolescents. *Music Therapy, 8,* 78–91.

Hair, H. I., & Graham, R. M. (1983). A comparison of verbal descriptors used by TMR students and music therapists. *Journal of Music Therapy, 20,* 59–68.

Hairston, M. J. P. (1990). Analysis of responses of mentally retarded autistic and mentally retarded nonautistic children to art therapy and music therapy. *Journal of Music Therapy, 27,* 137–150.

Harding, C., & Ballard, K. D. (1982). The effectiveness of music as a stimulus and as a contingent reward in prompting the spontaneous speech of three physically handicapped preschoolers. *Journal of Music Therapy, 19,* 86–101.

Hedden, S. K. (1979). Dissemination of music education research: Are researchers the problem? *Council for Research in Music Education, 59,* 35–39.

Hill, J., Brantner, J., & Spreat, S. (1989). The effect of contingent music on the in-seat behavior of a blind young woman with profound mental retardation. *Education and Treatment of Children, 12,* 165–173.

Holloway, M. S. (1980). A comparison of passive and active music reinforcement to increase preacademic and motor skills in severely retarded children and adolescents. *Journal of Music Therapy, 17,* 58–69.

Hoskins, C. (1988). Use of music to increase verbal response and improve expressive language abilities of preschool language delayed children. *Journal of Music Therapy, 25,* 73–84.

Hughes, J. E., & Grice, P. (1986). Music therapy in the public schools: Developing a network of support at the state level. In K. Gfeller (Ed.), *Fiscal, Regulatory, and Legislative Issues for the Music Therapist* (pp. 45–47). Washington, DC: National Association for Music Therapy.

Hughes, J. E., Robbins, B. J., Smith, D. S., & Kinkade, C. F. (1987). The effect of participation in a public school choral music curriculum on singing ability in trainable mentally handicapped adolescents. *Journal of the International Association of Music for the Handicapped* (formerly *MEH Bulletin*), *2*(4), 19–35.

Humpal, M. (1991). The effects of an integrated early childhood music program on social interaction among children with handicaps and their typical peers. *Journal of Music Therapy, 28,* 161–177.

Humphrey, T. (1980). The effect of music ear training upon the auditory discrimination abilities of trainable mentally retarded adolescents. *Journal of Music Therapy, 17,* 70–74.

Hunter, L. L. (1989). Computer-assisted assessment of melodic and rhythmic discrimination skills. *Journal of Music Therapy, 26,* 79–87.

Individuals with Disabilities Education Act: 20 U. S. C. Chapter 33. (1991). Potomac, MD: EDLAW, Inc.

Jellison, J. A. (1979). The music therapist in the educational setting: Developing and implementing curriculum for the handicapped. *Journal of Music Therapy, 16,* 128–137.

Jellison, J. A. (1983). Functional value as criterion for selection and prioritization of nonmusic and music educational objectives in music therapy. *Music Therapy Perspectives, 1*(2), 17–22.

Jellison, J. A. (1985). An investigation of the factor structure of a scale for the measurement of children's attitudes toward handicapped peers within regular music environments. *Journal of Research in Music Education, 33,* 167–177.

Jellison, J. A. (1988). A content analysis of music research with handicapped children (1975–1986): Applications in special education. In C. K. Furman (Ed.), *Effectiveness of music therapy procedures: Documentation of research and clinical practice* (pp. 223–279). Washington, DC: National Association for Music Therapy.

Jellison, J. A., Brooks, B., & Huck, A. M. (1984). Structuring small groups and music reinforcement to facilitate positive interactions and acceptance of severely handicapped students in the regular music classroom. *Journal of Research in Music Education, 32,* 243–264.

Jellison, J. A., & Duke, R. A. (1994). The mental retardation label: Music teachers' and prospective teachers' expectations for children's social and music behaviors. *Journal of Music Therapy, 31,* 166–185.

Jellison, J. A., & Flowers, P. J. (1991). Talking about music: Interviews with disabled and nondisabled children. *Journal of Research in Music Education, 39,* 322–333.

Jellison, J. A., & Wolfe, D. E. (1987). Music educators' ratings of selected objectives for severely handicapped or gifted students in the regular music classroom. *Contributions to Music Education,* No. 14, 36–51.

Jones, R. E. (1986). Assessing developmental levels of mentally retarded students with the musical perception assessment of cognitive development. *Journal of Music Therapy, 23,* 166–173.

Jones, R. N., Mandler-Provin, D., Latkowski, M. E., & McMahon, W. M. (1987). Development of a reinforcement survey for inpatient psychiatric children. *Child & Family Behavior Therapy, 9,* 73–77.

Karper, W. B. (1979). Effects of music on learning a motor skill by handicapped and non-handicapped boys. *Perceptual & Motor Skills, 49,* 734.

Korduba, O. M. (1975). Duplicated rhythm patterns between deaf and normal hearing children. *Journal of Music Therapy, 12,* 136–146.

Kostka, M. J. (1993). A comparison of selected behaviors of a student with autism in special education and regular music classes. *Music Therapy Perspectives, 11,* 57–60.

Krout, R. E. (1986). Use of a group token contingency with school-aged special education students to improve a music listening skill. *Music Therapy Perspectives, 3,* 13–16.

Krout, R. E. (1987). Music therapy with multi-handicapped students: Individualizing treatment within a group setting. *Journal of Music Therapy, 24,* 1–13.

Larson, B. A. (1977). A comparison of singing ranges of mentally retarded and normal children with published songbooks used in singing activities. *Journal of Music Therapy, 14,* 139–143.

Larson, B. A. (1981). Auditory and visual rhythmic pattern recognition by emotionally disturbed and normal adolescents. *Journal of Music Therapy, 18,* 128–136.

Lathom, W. (1980). *Role of music therapy in the education of handicapped children.* Washington, DC: National Association for Music Therapy.

Lathom, W. (1982). Survey of current functions of a music therapist. *Journal of Music Therapy, 19,* 2–27.

Lathom, W., & Eagle, C. (Eds.). (1982). *Music therapy for handicapped children: Project monograph series.* Washington, DC : National Association for Music Therapy.

Lienhard, M. E. (1976). Factors relevant to the rhythmic perception of a group of mentally retarded children. *Journal of Music Therapy, 13,* 58–65.

Madden, N. A., & Slavin, R. E. (1983). Mainstreaming students with mild handicaps: Academic and social outcomes. *Review of Educational Research, 53,* 519–569.

Madsen, C. K. (1980). *Behavior modification and music therapy: A guide for working with the mentally retarded.* Washington, DC: National Association for Music Therapy.

Madsen, C. K. (1985). Research in music for the handicapped. *Journal of the International Association of Music for the Handicapped* (formerly *MEH Bulletin*), *1* (1), 25–28.

Madsen, C. K. (1986). Research and music therapy: The necessity for transfer. *Journal of Music Therapy, 22,* 50–55.

Madsen, C. K., Capperella-Sheldon, D. A., & Johnson, C. M. (1991). Use of the continuous response digital interface (CRDI) in evaluating music responses of special populations. *Journal of the International Association of Music for the Handicapped* (formerly *MEH Bulletin*), *6*(2), 3–15.

Madsen, C. K., & Darrow, A. A. (1989). The relationship between music aptitude and sound conceptualization of the visually impaired. *Journal of Music Therapy, 26,* 71–78.

Madsen, C. K., & Furman, C. E. (1984). Graduate versus undergraduate scholarship: Research acquisition and dissemination. *Journal of Music Therapy, 21,* 170–176.

Madsen, C. K., Moore, R. S., Dorow, L. G., & Womble, J. U. (1976). The use of music subject matter via television as reinforcement for correct mathematical responses. *Journal of Research in Music Education, 24,* 51–59.

Madsen, C. K., Smith, D., & Feeman, C. C. (1988). The use of music in cross-age tutoring within special education settings. *Journal of Music Therapy, 25,* 135–144.

Maranto, C. D., Decuir, A., & Humphrey, T. (1984). A comparison of digit span scores, rhythm span scores, and diagnostic factors of mentally retarded persons. *Music Therapy, 4,* 84–90.

McCarty, B. C., McElfresh, C. T., Rice, S. V., & Wilson, S. J. (1978). The effect of contingent background music on inappropriate bus behavior. *Journal of Music Therapy, 15,* 150–156.

McGivern, R. F., Berka, C., Languis, M. L., & Chapman, S. (1991). Detection of deficitis in temporal pattern discrimination using the Seashore Rhythm Test in young children with reading impairments. *Journal of Learning Disabilities, 24,* 58–62.

Merle-Fishman, C. R., & Marcus, M. L. (1982). Musical behaviors and preferences in emotionally disturbed and normal children: An exploratory study. *Music Therapy, 2,* 1–11.

Michel, D. M., Parker, P., Giokas, D., & Werner, J. (1982). Music therapy and remedial reading: Six studies testing specialized hemispheric processing. *Journal of Music Therapy, 19,* 219–229.

Miller, D. M. (1977). Effects of music-listening contingencies on arithmetic performance and music preference of EMR children. *American Journal of Mental Deficiency, 81,* 371–378.

Miller, L. (1987). Developmentally delayed musical savant's sensitivity to tonal structure. *American Journal of Mental Deficiency, 91,* 467–471.

Moore, R., & Mathenius, L. (1987). The effects of modeling, reinforcement, and tempo on imitative rhythmic responses of moderately retarded adolescents. *Journal of Music Therapy, 24,* 160–169.

Murphy, R., Doughty, N., & Nunes, D. (1979). Multielement designs: An alternative to reversal and multiple baseline evaluation strategies. *Mental Retardation, 17,* 23–27.

Myers, E. G. (1979). The effect of music on retention in a paired-associate task with EMR children. *Journal of Music Therapy, 16,* 190–198.

National Association for Music Therapy. (1952). Objectives of the National Association for Music Therapy. In E. G. Gilliland (Ed.), *Music Therapy 1951.* Washington, DC: Author.

National Association for Music Therapy. (1994). *NAMT member sourcebook 1994*. Silver Spring, MD: Author

Nicholas, M. J., & Gilbert, J. P. (1980). Research in music therapy: A survey of music therapists' attitudes and knowledge. *Journal of Music Therapy, 17*, 207–213.

Radocy, R. E. (1983). The research efforts—why we care. *Music Educators Journal, 69*, 29–31.

Reid, D. H., Hill, B. K., Rawers, R. J., & Montegar, C. A. (1975). The use of contingent music in teaching social skills to a nonverbal hyperactive boy. *Journal of Music Therapy, 12*, 2–18.

Reschly, D. J., & Lamprecht, M. J. (1979). Expectancy effects of labels: Fact or artifact? *Exceptional Children, 46*, 55–58.

Reynolds, M. C., Wang, M. C., & Walberg, H. J. (1986). The necessary restructuring of special and regular education. *Exceptional Children, 53*, 391–398.

Rider, M. S. (1977). The relationship between auditory and visual perception tasks employing Piaget's concept of conservation. *Journal of Music Therapy, 14*, 126–143.

Ritschl, C., Mongrella, J. & Presbie, R. J. (1972). Group time-out from rock and roll music and out-of-seat behavior of handicapped children while riding a school bus. *Psychological Reports, 31*, 967–973.

Rogers-Wallgren, J. L., French, R., & Ben-Ezra, V. (1992). Use of reinforcement to increase independence in physical fitness performance of profoundly mentally retarded youth. *Perceptual and Motor Skills, 75*, 975–982.

Rolison, M. A., & Medway, F. J. (1985). Teachers' expectations and attributions for student achievement: Effects of label, performance pattern, and special education intervention. *American Educational Research Journal, 22*, 561–573.

Roskam, K. (1979). Music therapy as an aid for increasing auditory awareness and improving reading skill. *Journal of Music Therapy, 16*, 31–42.

Schmidt, D. C., Franklin, R., & Edwards, J. S. (1976). Reinforcement of autistic children's responses to music. *Psychological Reports, 39*, 571–577.

Shehan, P. K. (1981). A comparison of mediation strategies in paired associate learning for children with learning disabilities. *Journal of Music Therapy, 18*, 120–127.

Slavin, R. E. (1986). Best-evidence synthesis: An alternative to meta–analytic and traditional reviews. *Educational Researcher, 15* (9), 5–11.

Society for Research in Music Education. (1993). Handbook of the society for research in music education. *Journal of Research in Music Education, 41*, 269–281.

Soraci, S., Jr., Deckner, C. W., McDaniel, C., & Blanton, R. L. (1982). The relationship between rate of rhythmicity and the stereotypic behaviors of abnormal children. *Journal of Music Therapy, 19*, 46–54.

Spencer, S. L. (1988). The efficiency of instrumental and movement activities in developing mentally retarded adolescents' ability to follow directions. *Journal of Music Therapy, 25*, 44–50.

Spitzer, S. (1989). Computers and music therapy: An integrated approach. *Music Therapy Perspectives, 7*, 51–54.

Spudic, T. J., & Somervill, J. W. (1978). The effects of musical stimulation on distractibility and activity level among retarded subjects. *Education & Training of the Mentally Retarded, 13*, 363–366.

Stainback, W., Stainback, S., & Forest, M. (1989). *Educating all students in the mainstream of regular education.* Baltimore: Paul H. Brooks Publishing.

Staum, M. J. (1983). Music and rhythmic stimuli in the rehabilitation of gait disorders. *Journal of Music Therapy, 20,* 69–87.

Staum, M. J. (1987). Music notation to improve the speech prosody of hearing impaired children. *Journal of Music Therapy, 24,* 146–159.

Staum, M. J. (1993). A music/nonmusic intervention with homeless children. *Journal of Music Therapy, 30,* 236–262.

Staum, M. J., & Flowers, P. J. (1984). The use of simulated training and music lessons in teaching appropriate shopping to an autistic child. *Music Therapy Perspectives, 1*(3), 14–17.

Steele, A. L. (1975). Three year study of a music therapy program in a residential treatment center. *Journal of Music Therapy, 12,* 67–83.

Steele, A. L. (1977). The application of behavioral research techniques to community music therapy. *Journal of Music Therapy, 14,* 102–115.

Steele, A. L. (1984). Music therapy for the learning disabled: Intervention and instruction. *Music Therapy Perspectives, 1*(3), 2–7.

Stratford, B., & Ching, E. Y. (1983). Rhythm and time in the perception of Down's syndrome children. *Journal of Mental Deficiency Research, 27,* 23–38.

Thaut, M. H. (1985). The use of auditory rhythm and rhythmic speech to aid temporal muscular control in children with gross motor dysfunction. *Journal of Music Therapy, 22,* 108–128.

Thaut, M. H. (1987). Visual versus auditory (musical) stimulus preferences in autistic children: A pilot study. *Journal of Autism and Developmental Disorders, 17,* 425–432.

Thaut, M. H. (1988). Measuring musical responsiveness in autistic children: A comparative analysis of improvised music tones sequences of autistic, normal, and retarded individuals. *Journal of Autism and Developmental Disorders, 18,* 561–571.

Thompson. K. P. (1986). The general music class as experienced by mainstreamed handicapped students. *Journal of the International Association of Music for the Handicapped* (formerly *MEH Bulletin*), *1*(3), 16–23.

Turnbull, H. R. (1993). *Free appropriate public education: The law and children with disabilities* (4th ed.). Denver, CO: Love Publishing Co.

United States Department of Education—Office of Special Education and Rehabilitative Services. (1993). *Fourteenth annual report to Congress on the implementation of P.L. 94–142.* Washington, DC: Author.

Velasquez, V. (1991). Beginning experiences in piano performance for a girl with Down syndrome: A case study. *Music Therapy Perspectives, 9,* 82–85.

Voeltz, L. M. (1982). Effects of structured interaction with severely handicapped peers on children's attitudes. *American Journal of Mental Deficiency, 86,* 380-390.

Voeltz, L. M., & Evans, I. M. (1983). Educational validity: Procedures to evaluate outcomes in programs for severely handicapped learners. *The Journal of the Association for the Severely Handicapped, 8,* 3–14.

Walmsley, R. P., Crichton, L., & Droog, D. (1981). Music as a feedback mechanism for teaching head control to severely handicapped children: A pilot study. *Developmental Medicine and Child Neurology, 23,* 739–746.

Warren, F. A. (1984). A history of the *Journal of Research in Music Education,* 1953–1965. *Journal of Research in Music Education, 32,* 223–242.

Wilson, C. V. (1976). The use of rock music as a reward in behavior therapy with children. *Journal of Music Therapy, 13,* 39–48.

Windwer, C. M. (1981). An ascending music stimulus program and hyperactive children. *Journal of Research in Music Education, 29,* 173–181.

Witt, A. E., & Steele, A. L. (1984). Music therapy for infant and parent: A case example. *Music Therapy Perspectives, 1*(4), 17–19.

Wolfe, D. E. (1980). The effect of automated interrupted music on head posturing of cerebral palsied individuals. *Journal of Music Therapy, 18,* 184–206.

Wolfe, D. E. (1982). The effect of interrupted and continuous music on bodily movement and task performance of third grade students. *Journal of Music Therapy, 19,* 74–85.

Wolfe, D. E., & Hom, C. (1993). Use of melodies as structural prompts for learning and retention of sequential verbal information by preschool students. *Journal of Music Therapy, 30,* 100–118.

Wylie, M. E. (1983). Eliciting vocal responses in severely and profoundly handicapped subjects. *Journal of Music Therapy, 20,* 190–200.

Zenatti, A. (1975). Melodic memory tests: A comparison of normal children and mental defectives. *Journal of Music Therapy, 12,* 41–52.

Appendix

RESEARCH WITH DISABLED AND NONDISABLED STUDENTS IN INTEGRATED
AND NATURAL SETTINGS: SUMMARIES OF VARIABLES,
DOCUMENTATION PROCEDURES, AND FINDINGS

SCHOOL

Music Achievement (Nondisabled)
Mainstreamed/Nonmainstreamed
Classrooms
(Force, JMT, 1983)

Circled answers to rhythm instrument in identification by name and loud or soft dynamic levels.
On/Off task ratings of classes.

Documentation: Behavioral Observation (Frequency; on/off task); Short Pencil and Paper Achievement Test

No significant differences in music test performance for nondisabled students in mainstreamed classroom (with 4 children with retardation) and a nonmainstreamed classroom. Nondisabled students in both classrooms increased test performance with instruction. Questionnaire responses were reported as similar for faculty in the schools of classrooms tested although data were not included. On/off task behavioral ratings were similar for the nonmainstreamed and mainstreamed classrooms.

Social Play Among Nondisabled Preschool Children and Preschool Children with Moderate Retardation (Gunsberg, JMT, 1988)

Duration of time engaged in social play.

Documentation: Behavioral Observation (Duration; social play); Narrative

Improvised music and lyrics were used to facilitate social play between disabled and nondisabled children in an early childhood special education program that employed reverse mainstreaming. Twelve children, three 4-year-old nondisabled children and nine children with moderate retardation aged 3 to 5½ participated in 1-hour of free play. During the play, four planned sequences of improvised music and lyrics were introduced to facilitate social play. Analysis of ten videotaped sessions showed that the improvised music play sustained social play episodes beyond durations predicted in the literature. Analysis also revealed widely varying play styles and skills within the same improvised music play session.

Social Interactions Among Children with Retardation and Their Typical Peers (Humpal, JMT, 1991)

Frequencies and mean percentages of selecting a partner from home site, alternative site, or either site. Teacher's rankings of the effectiveness of activities and benefits of integrated sessions.

Documentation: Behavioral Observation (Frequency; choosing partners); Questionnaire

Children from two different schools (15 nondisabled students attending a regular preschool and 12 students with retardation attending a special education preschool) met once weekly at the typical preschool for 15 integrated music sessions. Preliminary sessions were initiated for the purpose of preparing parents of all the children and the staff at the regular preschool. Nondisabled children were shown pictures of the disabled children who would be attending their school and efforts were made to promote positive ideas regarding the music mainstreaming program prior to beginning the sessions. The 15 music therapy sessions were designed to provide opportunities for social interaction and, in particular, choosing partners from the alternative site. Three pretest and three posttest observations were conducted during which children were instructed to "choose a partner." Posttest observations showed increases in the mean percentage of students who selected partners from the alternative site. Teachers and teacher assistants who observed the sessions completed questionnaires which confirmed the increases in interactions among the children. The teachers and assistants also provided the music therapist with ratings for the effectiveness of the different music activities in promoting interactions and identified benefits of the program (following group directives, positive self-concept, etc.). All of the staff agreed that the program had facilitated peer interaction and had fostered acceptance of differences among individuals.

Positive Interactions and Acceptance of Students with Severe Disabilities in the Regular Music Classroom (Jellison, Brooks, & Huck, JRME, 1984)

Mean percent of positive interactions (helping/reciprocal) and noninteractions (isolation/proximal) of disabled and nondisabled children in structured music conditions and free time. Written acceptance scores of nondisabled peers for disabled peers in music and nonmusic environments.

Documentation: Behavioral Observation (Frequency; types of social interactions); Rating Scales for Attitude Assessment (*Acceptance Scale*, Voeltz, 1982, and *Acceptance Within Music Scale*, Jellison, 1985)

Four levels of elementary music classes were observed for 13 weeks. Observations on 5-sec. intervals of a 30-minute class and a free time period following class were conducted for two integrated music classes per week. The frequency of positive interactions between students with severe retardation and multiple disabilities (*n*=26) integrated into the four regular music classrooms with chronological age peers (*n*=100) was higher when students had opportunities to interact in small groups than when placed in traditional large group settings only. Positive interactions were even higher when students had opportunities to interact in small groups and music was structured as a contingency for cooperation. Classes with the highest rates of positive interactions indicated significant positive change for acceptance of peers in music as well as nonmusic environments. Positive interactions generalized to free time settings. Results indicate that positive social interactions between nondisabled and disabled students in the integrated music classroom with increases in nondisabled students' acceptance are not a result of music classroom experiences and music instruction alone but the degree to which teaching conditions specifically structure classroom antecedents (opportunities) and reinforcement for social interaction.

Behaviors of Student with Autism in Special Education and Regular Music Classes. (Kostka, MTP, 1993)	Frequencies and percentages of arm flapping, body swaying, and appropriate participation in special education and regular education, class time, and for specific activities.

Documentation: Behavioral Observation (Frequency; selected behaviors)

A nine-year old boy with autism who was a member of a special education music class and who was included in a regular music class with his peers, was videotaped and observed three times in both classes over a time period of one month. Systematic observation procedures were used to collect data from six one-minute segments randomly selected from the beginning, middle, and end of the 35 minute classes for each of the six videotapes. Teachers identified two distracting behaviors, arm flapping and large circular upper body swaying, for observation. Additionally, the frequency of appropriate participation was observed. Frequencies were recorded within 10-second units for each minute. Although no significant differences were found, the data show that inappropriate and distracting flapping and swaying were less frequent for the student in the regular music class with fourth grade peers than in the special education music class. The behaviors did not vary significantly across beginning, middle, and end of the class time. Participation was slightly higher in the special education classroom. Significant differences across activities were not found although data show that the student demonstrated fewer inappropriate behaviors and attended more to listening activities in the regular classroom compared to singing, playing, or moving. The author concluded that being included in the regular classroom had a positive effect on the student's social behavior.

Basic Skills Improvement in Kindergarten Children through Cross-Age Tutoring within Special Education Settings and Attitudes and Behaviors of Tutors (Madsen, Smith, & Feeman, JMT, 1988)

Achievement scores for kindergarten students. Likert-type attitude measures of tutoring sessions by tutors and tutees. Narratives written by tutors. College student observation of videos of dyads and evaluation of characteristics of tutors and tutees using Osgood-type semantic differential.

Documentation: Achievement Test (*Leon Inventory of Kindergarten Entering Skills,* 1984); Semantic Differential (Evaluation of Students' Attributes); Likert-type Attitude Assessment; Narrative

Sixteen fourth or fifth grade students with learning and/or behavior disorders attending a special education class were selected to serve as tutors for kindergarten children who showed a learning deficit on standard academic basic skills tests. Sixteen kindergarten students were randomly assigned to the 16 tutors and 16 served in the control group. Older students agreed to be tutors after they participated in a music session, were interviewed, and were told that they could listen to their favorite music after each tutoring session combined with the possibility of earning their favorite cassette tape. Tutoring sessions were conducted for 16 sessions for 10 weeks. Assessment included pretest-posttest academic comparisons for the kindergarten subjects, daily assessment of student attitudes, and assessment of tutor/tutee behavioral interactions as viewed on videotape by adult professionals who were unaware of the students' behavioral histories or academic achievement. Results of the attitudinal assessments completed by each participant indicated that both tutor and tutee rated each of the 16 sessions as being very positive. A significant pre-posttest difference was found between the experimental and control groups, with the experimental group demonstrating a greater number of learned skills. Videotape analysis showed that older students, students that were labeled as having behavioral and/or learning problems, were judged to be somewhat gifted, quite on task, positive, socially appropriate, above grade level, and behaviorally normal by adults unaware of their histories. The younger students were judged to be somewhat disabled and below grade level, but mostly on task, positive, socially appropriate, and behaviorally normal. The development of apparently strong bonding between the tutor and tutee was indicated in the tutors' narratives.

Learning Activities, Student Behaviors in Mainstreamed General Music Class, (Thompson, JIAMH, 1986)

Frequency counts judging success, moderate, unsuccessful, involved, and distracted categories for disabled and nondisabled and class learning activities.

Documentation: Behavioral Observation (Frequency; successful participation)

Fourteen mainstreamed disabled and 14 nondisabled students in three different schools were observed for three general music class sessions. Observations were recorded every five seconds for coded behaviors. The most frequent classroom activity was "teacher talk" followed by singing activities. Verbal reinforcement, teacher criticism, teacher support comments, and student-student interaction were infrequent indicating low student-teacher interactions as well as student-student interaction. The author writes, "Considering the fact that nearly half of the classroom activities were 'teacher talking,' and 'success' was interpreted as looking at the teacher, one could assume that, if classtime were spent with more active involvement in music making, the difference in frequency of success between the two groups might have been even greater." Disabled students were reported to be as on-task as their nondisabled peers.

SCHOOL RELATED

School Bus Behavior
(McCarty, McElfresh, Rice, & Wilson, JMT, 1978)

Frequency of inappropriate bus including hitting, kicking, profane language, etc.

Documentation: Behavioral Observation (Frequency; appropriate/inappropriate behavior)

Teachers, administrators, and bus drivers determined that inappropriate behavior on the bus was a major problem. Contingent music was effective to decrease inappropriate bus behavior of children, aged 3–14, with emotional disorders. Observation of approximately 20 students on three buses each day for 29 days indicated decreases in inappropriate behavior for each of the three buses. Additional informal observations reported an increase in appropriate helping behaviors of older students toward younger students in reminding students of the rules for appropriate behavior. The study replicates findings of a similar study with children with retardation (Ritschl, Mongrella, & Presbie, 1972).

HOME AND SCHOOL

Music Learning/General/Instruments
(Steele, MTP, 1984)

Frequency of various communication patterns, motor development, conceptual ability, behavioral characteristics, and preferences for music and nonmusic activity. Assessment includes music/nonmusic skills of students as well as music preferences. Family and teachers included in collection of data.

Documentation: Behavioral Observation (Frequency/Rate; motor/verbal behaviors); Self-Report (Music Activity Preference)

The interweaving of a behavioral therapy approach with a sequential program of musical development intervention methods was used with elementary-aged children with learning disabilities. Several individual cases are presented. Examples of assessments are given for one child as well as assessments, procedures (development of performance skills at the piano and drums; advancing from the primer level of piano instruction and from rote skills to reading rhythmic notation for percussion instruments) and data for another child. Another example is given for a small group program including objectives, experiences, and procedures. Playing music in an ensemble with a brother was an effective bonus for one student. Parents and music teachers participated in the procedures and data collection. For example, referral given by the music therapist to a trumpet teacher, and assistance to the family in obtaining the support of the instrumental teacher at the student's elementary school. The student became a member of the band and used music to help secure "peer acceptance and recognition."

HOME

Responsiveness and interactions; Parental relationship with child
(Witt & Steele, MTP, 1984)

Frequencies of several behaviors involving interaction with parent and responding to toys and music materials.

Documentation: Behavioral Observation (Frequency; motor/verbal behaviors)

The music therapist assisted the mother to use music and music related activities and objects to interact with her 14-month-old child with multiple disabilities. At the conclusion of the 16 week period, significant improvement was indicated in the target behaviors of eye contact, purposeful reaching for objects, and response to her own name. The mother reported that the most important gain was the improvement the family felt in their ability to relate to their child in a helpful and meaningful way.

COMMUNITY

Social Behavior (Walking and car riding)
(Reid, Hill, Rawers, Montegar, JMT, 1975)

Percent of observation intervals of appropriate walking in the clinic; generalization data. Time sampling of socially accepted behavior per car ride.

Documentation: Behavioral Observation (Frequency; appropriate walking and car riding)

Contingent music was effective to increase appropriate car riding as well as social walking skills with an eight-year-old boy who was isolated, nonverbal, and had behavior problems. Social walking skills improved in the clinic, outside the clinic, and ultimately in a wider variety of situations (stores, parks, schools, etc.) with his mother and other persons. A remote control apparatus was developed for contingent music applications in a third experiment in the series. Sessions were conducted in the clinic, outside the clinic, and on car trips with the child. The authors write, "Following termination of the music-walking program, it was evident that (child's name) could be allowed to visit those places frequented by other children in normal socialization process which he had never experienced."

Shopping Behavior
(Staum & Flowers, MTP, 1984)

Frequency of inappropriate touching of merchandise, moving away from the therapist, and inappropriate verbalizations in simulated and natural environments.

Behavioral Observation (Frequency, inappropriate social behavior and verbalizations)

Simulated training and contingent music reinforcement with piano lessons were effective to teach shopping skills to a nine-year-old girl with autism. The behaviors were taught in a simulated shopping setting and were transferred to a community grocery store. Observations included assessment of music capabilities and interest and observations of the shopping skills during 11 days. Although music achievement was not of primary concern in the study, the child learned to read pitch names from staff notation and could play several simple melodies on the piano. The authors write, "It was apparent that [the child] could continue to progress in piano lessons either as a reward for other nonmusic behaviors or simply for the knowledge and enjoyment of music itself."

MUSIC THERAPY WITH CHILDREN WHO ARE DEAF AND HARD-OF-HEARING

Alice-Ann Darrow
Kate Gfeller

IT is estimated that 16 million Americans have a hearing loss. For these individuals, the primary impact of a hearing loss is on communication, understanding what others say and responding in an intelligible fashion. Communication is the basis of our social and cognitive being; without it, we are cut off from the world. The resulting isolation affects all psychological, social, and intellectual growth and development. The objectives then, for music therapy with clients who have a significant hearing loss, are related to communication: (1) auditory training; (2) speech production; and (3) language development of children who have a hearing loss.

Description of the Client Population

A number of terms have been used to describe persons with hearing loss. Some of those terms reflect the audiological condition or types or extent of hearing loss, while other terms have cultural or social significance. Let us first consider types of hearing loss:

Types of Hearing Loss

There are four types of hearing loss, each of which can result in different possibilities for remediation:

Conductive hearing losses are caused by diseases or obstructions in the outer or middle ear (the conduction pathways for sound to reach the inner ear). Conductive hearing losses usually affect all frequencies of hearing and do not result in severe losses. Because of this, a person with a conductive hearing loss usually is able to use a hearing aid with success.

Sensorineural hearing losses result from damage to the delicate sensory hair cells of the inner ear or the nerves which supply it. These hearing losses can range from mild to profound deafness. They often affect certain frequencies more than others, and this results in distorted sound perception even when the sound level is increased. The distortion accompanying some forms of sensorineural hearing loss is so severe that successful use of a hearing aid is impossible.

Mixed hearing losses are those in which there is a problem in the outer or middle ear and in the inner ear.

A central hearing loss is one resulting from damage or impairment to the nerves or nuclei of the central nervous system, either in the pathway to the brain or in the brain itself.

Classifications of Hearing Loss

Hearing Level Effect on the Clinical Environment

Slight loss (27 to 40 dB)	· May have difficulty hearing faint or distant speech. May experience some difficulty with language arts.
Mild loss (41 to 55 dB)	Understands conversational speech at a distance of 3 to 5 feet. May miss as much as 50% of conversation if not face-to-face. May have limited vocabulary and speech irregularities.
Moderate loss (56 to 70 dB)	Can understand loud conversation only. Will have difficulty in group discussions. Is likely to have impaired speech, limited vocabulary, and difficulty in language use and comprehension.
Severe loss (71 to 90 dB)	May hear loud voices about 1 foot from ear. May be able to identify environmental sounds. May be able to discriminate vowels, but not consonants. Speech and language likely to be impaired or to deteriorate.
Profound loss (91 dB or more)	More aware of vibrations than tonal patterns, Relies on vision rather than hearing as primary means of communication. Speech and language likely to be impaired or to deteriorate. Speech and language unlikely to develop spontaneously if loss is prelingual.

(Heward & Orlansky, 1988, pp. 259–260)

Onset of Deafness

Congenital deafness: when a person is born deaf.

Adventitious deafness: when deafness occurs sometime after birth usually as a result of an accident or illness.

Prelingual deafness: when deafness occurs before the acquisition of language (usually before three years of age). Such a person will have no language frame of reference when learning to speak, write, or speechread.

Postlingual deafness: when deafness occurs after the acquisition of language (usually after three years of age). In most cases, persons who have lost their hearing after this age have a relatively strong language base.

Related Terms

A number of terms have been used to describe those persons who have significant hearing losses. The term hearing impairment is a general term used to describe and encompass all types of hearing losses ranging from mild to profound. It is a term that is used in regulatory language related to the provision of educational services for children with disabilities, and as such, is the term that is commonly used in public school programs. It is important to realize, however, that there are persons within the deaf culture that reject this term. The word "impaired" is usually defined as "broken" or "defective" and persons who are deaf do not see themselves as "broken" or "defective." The deaf community has made great strides in recent years to depathologize their disability. The only true handicap related to deafness is being cut off from the usual means of acquiring and transmitting language. Within deaf culture, there are only two terms used to describe individuals with a hearing loss, deaf and hard-of-hearing (Padden & Humphries, 1988).

Deaf (with a capital "D"): people who share a language—American Sign Language—and a culture.

deaf (with a lower case "d"): individuals who are oral, or often those who lose their hearing adventitiously through illness, accidents, or old age. This group does not have access to the language, heritage, beliefs, and practices of Deaf people.

Hard-of-hearing: a condition where the sense of hearing is defective but functional for processing speech (usually with the help of a hearing aid).

Background Information Related to the Deaf Community

(This section was taken from Darrow, A. A. (in press). Music therapy and the deaf. In T. Wigram, R. West, & B. Saperston (Eds.), *A handbook of music therapy*. Chichester, West Sussex: Carden Publications Limited.)

Most individuals with severe to profound hearing losses communicate manually rather than orally. They regard this alternative form of communication as their only "difference." Consequently, one might understand their resentment in being considered a client in need of therapy, music or otherwise. Music therapists do not offer or provide services for other non-native speaking populations; solely on the basis of their communication status. The loss of hearing, however, has many implications for the develop of communication skills. It is during the process of acquiring communication skills that music therapists can contribute to the development of children who have a hearing loss.

The ability to adapt music therapy procedures to the learning characteristics and communication styles of individuals who are deaf and hard-of-hearing requires specialized preparation. There are some prerequisite skills and considerable background information that the music therapist must have in order to work successfully with these individuals. Background information in the following areas should be particularly helpful to the music therapist: speech and hearing science, audiology, aural habilitation, manual and oral communication methods, and the impact of hearing loss on speech, reading and language development. Probably no other area of information is more important, however, than deaf culture. Sensitivity to and respect for the culture of the deaf community is essential to working successfully with individuals who have hearing losses.

Deaf Culture

Culture has been defined as a way of life that differentiates a specific group of people. Deaf people in the United States have customs, mores, and institutions which differ from those of the hearing culture. Existing within and in continual relationship with the larger society, the deaf community adopts many of the characteristics of the hearing populations; yet, because language is the foundation of culture, the deaf community, which communicates in sign language, is also unique in many ways. "Taken as a whole, the deaf community emerges as a distinctive societal entity, marked by the satisfaction deaf people usually find in the company of each other" (Schein, 1978, p. 511).

The deaf population has grown, doubling its proportion of the total population in the last 40 years. The balance of adventitiously to congenitally deaf persons has shifted: a greater portion of the deaf population now is congenitally deaf. Changes in the nature of the deaf community are happening along with external events such as the practice of mainstreaming which dramatically reduced enrollment in residential schools. In the past, state schools for the deaf were the cornerstones and centers of the local deaf communities (Schein, 1978).

Other educational influences on the deaf community have been the practices of oral-only programs and the implementation (by hearing educators) of English sign systems, which differ greatly from American Sign Language, the language of the deaf community (Padden, 1980). Children with hearing losses who are educated by these sign systems and those who have oral skills only often find it difficult to communicate with other members of the deaf community. Because of these educational practices, children who have hearing losses are often caught between the hearing society and the deaf community, resulting in a lack of personal identity with either group (Sacks, 1989).

Political factors have also influenced the deaf community. In spring of 1988, after demonstrations, protests, and boycotts, Gallaudet University, the only university in the world for students who are deaf or hard-of-hearing, inaugurated its first deaf president. This was a pivotal moment in the history of the deaf community. The Gallaudet experience clearly demonstrated the power of advocacy and fueled the "deaf pride" movement. Legislative acts in the past 10 years have also influenced the deaf community by protecting their legal, personal, and educational rights (Kannapell, 1980; Prickett, 1989).

Though the deaf culture is a part of the larger society, it remains enigmatic to most of the hearing population. Knowing little about other cultures often results in ethnocentrism—the tendency to judge other cultures by the standards of one's own. This tendency has often been apparent in regard to the deaf community. Historically, the hearing have taken a paternalistic attitude toward the deaf; making decisions on their behalf for such important issues as speech instruction, the composition and use of various sign systems, as well as academic instruction and administration.

It is necessary for hearing professionals to recognize, be sensitive to, and respect the ways in which the deaf react to their societal environment. In deaf culture, subtle facial expressions and gestures often are used to communicate specific information such as comprehension or confusion. The deaf are also more physical when attempting to secure attention. They may stomp the floor or table, flicker lights, or grasp the individual with whom they are attempting to communicate. The deaf are also sometimes considered rude by hearing people because of their candid, straightforward manner. Their directness has been attributed to a desire to reduce the misunderstandings that have occurred throughout their lives due to problems in communication (Schmitz, 1990). Because of difficulty in using traditional telecommunication devices, the deaf are more apt to visit without calling. Acquiring knowledge of these and other cultural characteristics, which may differ or have alternative meaning from the hearing society, can avoid misunderstandings between music therapists and their clients who are deaf or hard-of-hearing. Until recently, information regarding deaf culture was primarily limited to those who lived within the culture. There are now several excellent resources on the deaf community and the social characteristics its people (Padden & Humphries, 1988; Sacks, 1989).

Communication Methods

In the United States, deaf persons also use a variety of methods and symbol systems for communication; these include:

American Sign Language—ASL is a natural language with its own grammar and syntax. It is a beautiful and graceful visual-gestural language created by deaf people and used widely in the United States. The signs in ASL are word-like units which have both concrete and abstract meanings. Signs are made by either one or both hands assuming distinctive shapes in particular locations and executing specified movements. The use of spatial relations, direction, orientation, and movement of the hands, as well as facial expression and body shift make up the grammar of ASL.

Fingerspelling—A manual alphabet is merely an alternative form of a written alphabet with hand shapes and positions corresponding to the letters of the written alphabet. In a very real sense, fingerspelling is "writing in the air." In a fingerspelling conversation, one person spells the message letter by letter to a second person who reads it and responds by spelling a reply. The use of fingerspelling as the primary mode of communication in combination with spoken English is known as the Rochester Method.

Manual Communication—The term "manual communication" includes a combination of sign language and fingerspelling used for both expressive and receptive communication. A number of manual communication systems combine sign language and fingerspelling with the grammar and syntax of standard English. There are four major systems in this group: (1) Seeing Essential English, (2) Signing Exact English, (3) Linguistics of Visual English, and (4) Signed English.

Oral Communication—This term denotes the use of speech and speech-reading as the primary means for the transmission of thoughts and ideas with deaf persons. Educators who believe in the Oral Communication philosophy, in their work with deaf children, emphasize, the teaching of speech and speech-reading (speech-reading) together with amplification and the use of whatever residual hearing individuals have.

Cued Speech—Cued Speech is a system of communication in which eight hand movements supplement the information being spoken. This is not a form of sign language. The hand "cue" is used to indicate, visually, the exact pronunciation of every syllable spoken. With Cued Speech, a person with hearing loss can see all the words a hearing person hears. It is a speech-based method of communication aimed at taking the guesswork out of speech-reading.

Simultaneous Communication—This term is used to denote the combined use of speech, signs, and fingerspelling. Receptively, an individual receives the message both by speech-reading what is being said and by reading the signs and fingerspelling simultaneously.

Total Communication—Total Communication is a philosophy of communication which implies acceptance, understanding, and use of all methods of communication to assist the deaf child in acquiring language and the deaf adult in understanding.

Historically, proponents of the various system have been at odds. There is increasing consensus that whatever system or method works most successfully for the individual should be used to allow the person who has a hearing loss access to clear and understandable communication.

The Use of Music in the Auditory Training of Children Who Are Deaf or Hard-of-Hearing

The role of auditory training is to teach the complex task of listening, a much more involved task than the physical act of hearing. The child who has a hearing loss must learn to use his/her residual hearing to interpret sounds, attach meaning to them, and develop listening rules, cues and strategies. Hearing children, through the auditory reception of sounds around them, appear to accomplish these tasks with relative ease. For children with hearing losses, the lack of normal auditory stimulation must be compensated for by additional training and practice. Music is a powerful medium through which listening skills can be taught and practiced. Music is generally more intense than conversational speech and employs many more frequencies than normal speech sounds, which is why children with even severe hearing losses are able to listen to and make aural discriminations about the musical sounds they hear. Music is also a powerful tool in the auditory training of children who are deaf and hard-of-hearing because it is an integral part of our environment, it is easily adapted to a child's age and musical preferences, and it is highly valued by most children.

The perception, interpretation, and performance of sound serve as the basis for both speech and music. The auditory perception of speech and music involves the ability to distinguish between different sounds, their pitches, durations, intensities, and timbres, and the ways in which these sounds change over time. Even the simplest kinds of sound in speech and music contain many common properties, though perhaps identified by different names. In music, reference is made to intonation, tempo, accent and rhythm. Speech counterparts are inflection or intonation, rate, stress, and rhythm or the temporal organization of speech sounds. These properties aid the listener's ability to interpret speech sounds and attach meaning to them.

Treatment Objectives in Auditory Training

The goal of auditory training is to enable children with hearing losses to make maximum use of the speech signal by developing residual hearing to the fullest extent possible. Appropriate placement in an auditory training program requires careful assessment of auditory, visual, combined auditory-visual, and language competencies (Van Tassel, 1981). In consultation with the child's audiologist, the music therapist should establish appropriate treatment objectives for individual clients. Objectives in the music therapy setting should include the following:

1. The detection (determining the presence or absence) of sound.
2. The discrimination of sound (determining whether sounds are the same or different).
3. The identification (recognition) of sound.
4. The comprehension (understanding) of sound.

(Erber & Hirsh, 1978)

Assessment Procedures in Auditory Training

The ultimate goal of auditory training is the comprehension of speech. There are many listening behaviors, however, that are a prerequisite to speech perception. Derek Sanders (1977) developed a hierarchy of auditory processing which should assist the music therapist in developing sequential objectives for the use of music in auditory training.

1. Awareness of Acoustic Stimuli
    Can the child demonstrate, with some observable behavior (e.g., the sign for "start" and "stop"), the initiation and termination of sound?
2. Localization
    Can the child find the sound source (radio, person speaking) when blindfolded?
    Can the child point in the direction of the sound source?
3. Attention
    Can the child track (follow) the sound source?
    Can the child take a step each time the drum is struck?
4. Discrimination between speech and nonspeech
    Can the child discriminate the tapping of a drum and speech?
    Can the child discriminate between singing and instrumental music?
5. Auditory Discrimination
    Can the child discriminate the timbre of different instruments?
    Can the child identify the entrance and exit of one instrument while others continue to play?
6. Suprasegmental Discrimination
    Can the child detect tempo changes in music and speech?
    Can the child detect accents in music or stressed syllables in words?
    Can the child detect changes of dynamics in music or intonation in speech (anger, surprise)?
7. Segmental Discrimination
    Can the child discriminate a changing target word within a single delivery sentence? (ex. Show me the *book*. Show me the *ball*. Show me the *bat*.)
8. Auditory Memory
    Can the child remember and name what instruments were played?
    Can the child remember isolated words from a song?
9. Auditory Sequential Memory
    Can the child remember the order in which instruments were played?
    Can the child remember the correct sequence of the lyrics? (ex. Which animal did we sing about first? Second? etc.)
10. Auditory Synthesis
    Can the child listen to a song and answer question about the lyrics? (ex. Puff was a magic . . . what?)
    Can the child follow the directions given in a song? (ex. You put your *right hand* in . . .)

There are a number of relatively uncomplicated speech perception tests that can be administered by the music therapist in order to obtain functional information regarding the child's hearing. These speech perception tests are:

1. Ling Five-Sound Test

    The Five-Sound Test described by Ling and Ling (1978) is an example of the way in which speech detection can be used to predict speech perceptual abilities. This test consists of five isolated phonemes (oo, a, ee, sh, and s), which are spoken to the child at a normal conversational level. The child simply indicates whether or not each sound is heard. According to Ling and Ling, children with measurable hearing at frequencies up to 100 Hz should be able to detect the three vowels; hearing through 2000 Hz should permit reception of the sh; and the s should be perceived if there is residual hearing at frequencies up to 4000 Hz.

2. Auditory Numbers Test (ANT)

    One widely used speech-sound test employed to assess suprasegmental discrimination is the (ANT) Auditory Numbers Test (Erber, 1980). The ANT was developed to assist in determining whether a young child with a hearing loss can perceive spectral aspects of speech or only gross temporal acoustic patterns. The stimulus materials for the ANT consist of the numbers 1 through 5. The test is given in two parts, an identification of the actual numbers as spoken and a detection of the number of "beats" present in a counting sequence. In the second part, the child is asked to identify the actual number spoken.

3. Children's Auditory Test (CAT)

    The Children's Auditory Test (Erber & Alencewicz, 1976) consists of four nouns in each of the three stress categories of monosyllabic, trochaic, and spondaic multisyllabic words. Trochaic are two-syllable words spoken with the accent on the 1st syllable (mother). Spondaic words are two-syllable words spoken with equal stress on both syllables (airplane). Response format is a closed set; the child points to the picture corresponding to each stimulus item as it is presented auditorily. The clinician records the child's responses in a confusion matrix. The results can then be analyzed for number of items correctly identified in terms of stress category. Stimulus words can easily be changed to ensure the child's familiarity with all items, making this a useful and versatile test.

4. Test of Auditory Comprehension (TAC)

    The TAC (Trammell et al., 1980) is a comprehensive test instrument designed for individual use with children who have hearing losses in assessing auditory functioning. Subtests one through four should be useful for the music therapist. They assess suprasegmental discrimination and word recognition; proceeding from gross discrimination between speech and nonspeech stimuli, discrimination among various speech phrases on the basis of prosodic features, to discrimination of mono- and multisyllabic words chosen from a primary noun lexicon.

5. Word Intelligibility by Picture Identification (WIPI)

With children whose receptive language ages are between 4 and 6, the Word Intelligibility by Picture Identification (WIPI) Test (Ross & Lerman, 1970) may be used. It consists of four lists of 25 monosyllabic words. Response format is a closed set of six stimuli. Children listen to the given word and point to the representative picture. The stimuli are minimally contrasting words (ex. mail, snail, sail, pail).

6. Minimum Auditory Capabilities (MAC)

The Minimum Auditory Capabilities (MAC) battery of tests was designed at the University of California in San Francisco in the department of otolaryngology (Owens, Kessler, Telleen, & Schubert, 1981). The object was to design a battery of tests which would lend consistency to the evaluation of cochlear implant clients at different centers. Full details of the test and tapes are available commercially. The MAC battery consists of 13 auditory tests and one speech-reading test. Twelve consist primarily of spoken materials and the tests are of graduated difficulty. In the first group of tests, the simplest is designed to see whether the client can differentiate a rising pitch from a falling pitch. Another test asks which word in a sentence is accented. The most important part of this first group of tests shows whether a client can distinguish between a voice and speech modulated noise. The tests take the form of multiple choice responses where the client is given a list of the possible answers and has to choose the correct one (closed list). A second group of tests requires identification of phonemes and also takes the form of multiple choice responses. The consonant items are designed to test whether nasality, voicing and glide features of speech may be detected. The spondee recognition test is a relatively easy speech recognition test because the client only has to make a selection from a closed list of four choices. The remaining tests in the battery are open response (open list) tests in which the client is required to describe the sound, word or sentence given. Fifteen environmental sounds are delivered for identification such as a car horn or a dog barking. A spondee recognition test uses 25 two-syllable words for the client to identify. An everyday sentence test employs sentences from a series developed at the Central Institute for the Deaf at St. Louis, Missouri. The two most difficult tests in the battery involve repetition of single words and identification of words in context. The final test involves a single speaker presenting the subject with sentences while sitting one meter in front of the client. Scores are compared with the amplification device turned on and off. This test is designed to test how much the device aids speech-reading.

Music Therapy Procedures

I. Detection of Sound

There are many ways in which children who have hearing losses can respond to the presence of sound. Some of these are:

1. The child begins to dance when the music is on and stops when the music is off.
2. The child makes a doll dance when the music is on and stops when it is off.
3. The child raises a hand when the music is on and puts it down when the music is off.

II. Auditory Discrimination

1. The child discriminates between loud and soft aural stimuli.

2. The child discriminates between fast and slow aural stimuli.
3. The child discriminates between long and short sounds.
4. The child discriminates between uneven and even rhythms.
5. The child discriminates between high and low pitches.

III. The Identification (Recognition) of Sound
1. The child recognizes and identifies the timbre of selected instruments.
2. The child recognizes and identifies selected words in the context of a song.
3. The child recognizes and identifies the names of familiar instruments.
4. The child recognizes and identifies the lyrics of a familiar song.
5. The child responds to his or her name.

IV. Auditory Comprehension
1. The child follows directions.
2. The child correctly answers questions in class.
3. The child summarizes the story told in a ballad.
4. The child points to a picture described orally.
5. The child places pictures in sequence based upon an oral story.

Criteria for Termination

Termination of auditory training is indicated if the client has reached the highest level of auditory processing, auditory synthesis or the comprehension of speech. Most individuals with hearing losses have considerable residual hearing. It is highly unlikely, however, that individuals with severe or profound losses will attain the goal of speech comprehension without the aid of speech-reading. For these clients, termination criteria may be set at other stages along the hierarchy of auditory processing. Termination may also be indicated if the assessment of music therapy procedures indicates that little improvement has been made over the course of six months to one year. In this case, the client's time may be better spent in other areas of rehabilitation such as speech-reading.

The Use of Music in the Speech Development of Children Who Are Deaf and Hard-of-Hearing

The acquisition of speech is controlled by the ear. We learn to speak by imitating the sounds of others. Imagine learning to speak a foreign language without the benefit of ever hearing it spoken, only seeing part of it (approximately one third) on someone's lips. Children whose hearing losses are congenital are additionally without the benefit of a reference language. It is some time before they realize words can control their environment and allow communication with others.

Because we learn to speak through imitation, speech perception and production are interrelated. Therefore, it is important to encourage the use of speech even while working on auditory training skills. Music therapists are generally not trained to also be speech therapists; however, there are objectives that can be incorporated into music therapy programs which will encourage the use of speech by children who have hearing losses.

Treatment Objectives for Speech Production

Treatment objectives in the music therapy setting should include the following:
1. Free Vocalization
2. Vocal Imitation
3. Rhythmic Vocalization
4. Vocal Phrasing
5. Vocal Dynamics

Assessment Procedures in Speech Production

The speech production skills of children with hearing losses must be assessed before appropriate objectives can be selected, remedial strategies can be implemented, and progress can be evaluated. Based upon the objectives given for speech production, the following nominal data can be collected:

1. The child . . .
   ___ does not vocalize
   ___ vocalizes on command
   ___ vocalizes spontaneously

2. The child . . .
   ___ does not imitate sound
   ___ imitates sounds on command
   ___ imitates sounds spontaneously

3. The child . . .
   ___ does not vary the speech rhythm
   ___ varies speech rhythm

4. The child . . .
   ___ breathes in the middle of words or phrases
   ___ breathes at the end of phrases

5. The child . . .
   ___ vocalizes only on a single pitch
   ___ varies vocal pitch

A panel of judges can evaluate speech samples collected from music therapy sessions based upon Subtelny's (1975) *Deaf Speech and Voice Diagnostic*:

NATIONAL TECHNICAL INSTITUTE FOR THE DEAF SPEECH AND VOICE DIAGNOSTIC

Intelligibility
1. Speech is completely unintelligible.
2. Speech is very difficult to understand—only isolated words or phrases are intelligible.

3. With difficulty the listener can understand about half the content of the message (intelligibility may improve after a listening period).
4. Speech is intelligible with the exception of a few words or phrases.
5. Speech is completely intelligible.

Pitch Register
If pitch register is judged to be below optimal, mark rating with a (–).
1. Cannot sustain phonation.
2. Much above or below optimal level.
3. Moderately above or below optimal level.
4. Slightly above or below optimal level.
5. Appropriate for age and sex.

Pitch Control
1. Cannot sustain phonation.
2. Noticeable breaks or fluctuations of large magnitude.
3. Noticeable breaks or fluctuations of small magnitude
4. Flat within limited speaking range.
5. Normal-satisfactory modulation of pitch.

Loudness
If loudness is judged to be below an appropriate level, mark rating with a (–).
1. Cannot sustain audible tone.
2. Much above or below appropriate level.
3. Moderately above or below appropriate level.
4. Slightly above or below appropriate level.
5. Speech is completely intelligible.

Loudness Control
1. Cannot sustain audible tone.
2. Noticeable breaks or fluctuations of large magnitude.
3. Noticeable breaks or fluctuations of small magnitude.
4. Flat within limited speaking range.
5. Normal-satisfactory modulation of intensity.

Rate
If rate is too rapid for efficient communication, mark rating with a (+).
1. Cannot control rate of syllable articulation.
2. Much too slow—labored, single syllable utterances. Rate definitely interferes with content of communication.
3. Moderately below optimal rate for efficient communication.
4. Slightly below optimal rate, but monitored well for clarity.
5. Normal.

Control of Air Expenditure During Speech
1. Severe problem—cannot coordinate respiration and phonation to sustain tone.
2. Marked excess or deficiency in air expenditure.
3. Moderate excess or deficiency in air expenditure.
4. Slight excess or deficiency in air expenditure.
5. Normal.

Breath Control
(Record average of three trials)
1. Maximum duration of sustained /s/ ___seconds.
2. Maximum duration of sustained vowel ___seconds.
3. Counts on one breath, number ____. (Provide count model three digits per second.) "Count as far as you can in one breath."
4. Number of words per minute in reading ____. (Record data from second trial.)

Prosodic Features—Blending, Stress and Inflection
1. Cannot evaluate.
2. Severe problem.
3. Moderate problem.
4. Mild problem.
5. Normal.

Voice Quality
Breathy, Weak, Lacking Clarity
1. Voice quality varies or is too weak to judge.
2. Severe breathiness.
3. Moderate breathiness.
4. Mild breathiness.
5. Normal quality.

Tense, Harsh
1. Vocal tension too great to sustain tone.
2. Severe tenseness.
3. Moderate tenseness.
4. Mild tenseness.
5. Normal quality.

Nasal Resonance
1. Resonance varies and cannot be judged.
2. Severe denasality or hypernasality.
3. Moderate denasality or nasality.
4. Mild denasality or nasality.
5. Normal resonance.

Pharyngeal Resonance
1. Resonance varies and cannot be judged.
2. Marked pharyngeal resonance.
3. Moderate pharyngeal resonance.
4. Mild pharyngeal resonance.
5. Normal resonance.

Mode of Communication
1. Uses writing instead of speech or manual communication.
2. Signs, fingerspells, and gestures without voice.
3. Signs and fingerspells frequently with voice.
4. Resorts to signing and fingerspelling occasionally during speech.
5. Uses oral communication habitually.

Boothroyd (1983) had identified several other speech intelligibility tests adopted by researchers concerned with the assessment of the speech production of children who are deaf or hard-of-hearing:

Hudgins Word Intelligibility Tests
Hudgins (1949) used groups of listeners who were previously unfamiliar with the speech of the deaf and gave them sufficient practice to reach a learning plateau. For linguistic structures he chose words in isolation. The subject under investigation read a phonetically balanced list of words, and the listener, without the support of context, tried to write down what he/she heard. Hudgins demonstrated a high correlation between scores obtained with isolated words and those obtained with sentences.

Magner Intelligibility Test
Magner (1972) chose to measure the intelligibility of words in sentence context. She wrote 600 sentences of roughly equal length, containing vocabulary and structures of the type used with deaf children in written language exercises. Each child reads six sentences which are then audited by six students attending a training program for teachers of the deaf. Intelligibility is measured as the percentage of words correctly identified.

Spontaneous Speech Samples
Ling and Milne (1981) reported a procedure in which samples of conversation are dubbed onto a listening tape and audited by persons previously unfamiliar with the speech of the deaf. Intelligibility score is the percentage of words correctly identified.

Music Therapy Procedures for Speech Production

The music therapist has many opportunities to encourage the vocalization of children who have hearing losses. Music programs for the deaf have traditionally centered around rhythm activities, with little attention given to singing or vocal training. Perhaps this emphasis has been developed because children who have hearing losses are not considered "singers" given their unusual voice quality. It would seem, however, that vocal training is precisely the type of training required to modify problems in speech pitch and intonation. Previous research (Darrow & Starmer, 1986) has shown that specific vocal training, vocal exercise, and singing songs in appropriately lower keys may help to modify the fundamental frequency and frequency range of the speech of children with hearing losses.

Many children who are deaf or hard-of-hearing are hesitant to use their voices. The music therapist must encourage and be accepting of any sound the child produces. If a child does not vocalize at first, spontaneous vocalization, such as laughter, must be evoked and reinforced. The vocalization should be followed by praise and reassurance.

The child should be allowed to feel the throat of the therapist. Then the child's hand should be placed on his/her own throat to encourage imitation. Once the child begins to imitate target speech patterns on the basis of auditory cues only, additional stimuli can be introduced into the music therapy sessions. Imitation based upon auditory cues only requires the child to perceive as well as produce the speech patterns correctly.

Once the child has learned the concept of imitation, the music therapist can progress to procedures which will incorporate objectives concerned with speech rhythm, phrasing, and intonation. These speech characteristics are taught through the following process:

*presentation of the stimuli
*perception of the stimuli
*productive response
*feedback on the productive response
*modification of the productive response
*appropriate productive response
*independent initiation of response
                 (Blackwell, 1983)

Criteria for Termination

Termination of speech therapy is indicated if the speech of the client with a hearing loss is easily understood by others. Though intelligible, the speech of these clients can often be further improved in the following areas: intonation, rhythm, rate, and quality. Therefore, music therapists may want to extend their goals beyond speech intelligibility. There are many factors involved in the acquisition of speech and speech-reading skills by those with hearing losses. Speech acquisition cannot be the isolated goal of the music therapist. It must be an integral part of other educational or rehabilitation programs in which the client is involved. Speech acquisition is without question a desirable goal; however, the music therapist may determine that it is not a very realistic goal for a particular client. In this case, goals may be directed toward alternative forms of communication such as American Sign Language or one of the signed English systems.

The Use of Music in the Language Development of Children
Who are Deaf and Hard-of-Hearing

A serious hearing loss, that is either congenital or is acquired before the development of speech, affects not only auditory processing and speech intelligibility; it also has an impact on language development. This impact is easier to understand when we recall that most children develop language informally through on-going exposure to and interaction with adults or older children who act as language models. Hearing children interact with and overhear their parents and older siblings who are competent language models in everyday activities such as dinner conversation, play time, during bedtime stories, or hearing parents talk to friends over the backyard fence. If the child has normal cognitive functioning, and has a rich language environment, he or she will master various communicative tasks in a relatively predictable order. For example, most children start to babble, then use one word utterance, two and three word sentences, and eventually complete sentences, including complex syntax and rich vocabulary.

Similarly, children whose parents are deaf and use American Sign Language have on-going exposure to that language system. Although the language is transmitted through hand gestures and facial and body markers rather than speech, both hearing or deaf children in the household develop language competency in that system in a very similar sequence as do hearing children who are regularly exposed to speech.

Language competency is compromised, however, if the child is hard-of-hearing, or if a deaf child who uses sign language is spending much of the time in an environment where only rudimentary or no sign language is used. A child who is hard-of-hearing may miss out on portions of conversation (especially when speech-reading is hampered), and therefore receive incomplete or imperfect models of language. Children who use sign language as their primary mode of communication, but who are not given ample opportunity to communicate with or observe fluent sign language models will not develop a rich internal or expressive language.

The result of inadequate or incomplete language models result in language development described as delayed, deviant, or different (Davis & Hardick, 1981; Schirmer, 1985). Particular characteristics include: reduced or improper vocabulary; slow progress in or misuse of syntactic skills; shorter, simpler sentence structure than that of peers; and diminished spontaneous interaction (Davis & Hardick, 1981; Heider & Heider, 1940; Pressnell, 1973; Quigley, Wilbur, Power, Montanelli, & Steinkamp, 1976; Schirmer, 1985). There is also concomitant delay in the development of academic skills (reading and writing) based on language competency (Davis & Hardick, 1981).

A home and educational environment where the communicative needs of the child are accommodated regularly can itself have a tremendous impact on language development. Good communication habits (Gfeller & Schum, 1994) that maintain clear interaction and enhance incidental exposure to language can help the child to experience fewer delays (for in-depth discussion of clear communication and how to repair communication breakdown, refer to Gfeller & Schum, 1994, which is listed in the related articles). However, direct and aggressive rehabilitation may also be necessary if serious language delays exist.

Because of the complex nature of language development, the primary responsibility for language remediation generally rests with the speech/language pathologist who has extensive background in normal and deviant or delayed language acquisition. However, because language development is so important to academic, social, and emotional development, it is an area that requires the coordinated efforts of the entire treatment team (speech-language pathologist or rehabilitation audiologist, deaf education teacher, child development coordinator, and music therapist). The music therapist should be in regular communication as she or he establishes treatment goals and objectives and develops interventions.

Before selecting music therapy as a potential intervention for language development, it is important to determine that the music therapist can communicate effectively in the child's major form of communication. For example, if the child uses American Sign Language, or Manually Coded English, the music therapist needs adequate command of the mode of communication to facilitate activities and to be able to comprehend the child's responses. This might be likened to a music therapist who goes to Mexico to work with Spanish-speaking children. Few of us could imagine trying to facilitate music therapy sessions in which a good language model is important if we had only had a few weeks of elementary Spanish classes!

While the focus of the music therapy sessions should be determined in cooperation with the treatment team, there are several music therapy goals that are most commonly the focus of treatment. They include: (a) increased and appropriate use of vocabulary, and (b) increased and appropriate use of spontaneous topic-related interaction.

Increased and Appropriate Use of Vocabulary

Determine the present level of vocabulary usage and comprehension. The initial step in this goal area is the determination of current functional level (baseline). The language pathologist may have already completed extensive assessment of vocabulary (both formal, such as the Peabody Picture Vocabulary Test–Revised, Dunn & Dunn, 1981, and informal assessment). In addition, the music therapist may wish to do some informal assessment of vocabulary that may be used specifically in the music therapy setting. Formal testing is often designed to identify improvements that occur in treatment in short increments of time. Therefore, such formal testing is more appropriately used for long-term evaluation than for determining progress on short-term objectives.

Select vocabulary words to be targeted in music therapy sessions. In cooperation with the speech-language therapist, select the vocabulary words to be targeted in music therapy activities. For example, there may be words that are important in science or social studies class, or there may be units of adjectives or polar opposites (fast/slow, loud/soft, happy/angry, etc.). In the first days of therapy, do a pre-test for these specific words to determine competence.

Design and implement activities that require exposure to and use of these vocabulary words. Activities such as signing to songs (songs in which the vocabulary is imbedded) and writing songs on topics that will use the vocabulary word provide opportunities for the children to use these words in spoken, signed, and written form. Vocabulary words can also be included in the fabric of activities in which children make music. For example, if you are working on the vocabulary associated with seriation or classification, the use of rhythm instruments such as large and small drums, round drums, square wood blocks, and the like can provide vivid experiential opportunities to associate these vocabulary words with objects. For example, the music therapist can pair the word with the object and later require the child to use the correct vocabulary in order to request the instrument of choice.

Increased and Appropriate Use of Spontaneous Topic-related Interaction

Determine the present level of interactive skills. A language sample can be taken through the use of videotape. Work with the speech-language pathologist to identify particular grammatical structures or skills that can be reinforced in music therapy sessions. There are two primary concerns: pragmatics, or the functional use of rules that govern communication, and social/emotional maturity. The following pragmatic behaviors may be tallied (+ or –) by using event recording:

1. The child attends (visually and/or auditorily) for the speaker's entire message or instruction.
2. The child makes maximal use of visual cues.
3. The child is able to follow a topic shift in conversation.
4. The child requests clarification if unsure or confused.
5. The child requests repetition when necessary.
6. The child fails to indicate non-understanding.
7. The child does not acknowledge comments.
8. The child attempts to repair broken communication.

          (Moeller, McConkey, & Osberger, 1983)

Discuss the specific criteria for each of these items with the speech-language pathologist, and collaborate on various cues or methods that you will use in sessions to encourage more effective pragmatic behaviors.

Spontaneous interaction is not only affected by pragmatics; it is also influenced by social and emotional maturity of the child (Meadow, 1980a). Therefore, the music therapist may want to evaluate social/emotional skills along with functional language use. Two easily used tests are: (a) the *Meadow/Kendall Social-Emotional/Assessment Inventory for Deaf Students (SEAI)*, 1980b, and (b) *Child Behavior Checklist*, 1981, by Achenback and Edelbrock.

Design and implement activities that permit opportunities to use those language skills. Remediation of language usually involves two major approaches: a grammatical language intervention approach, which focuses on structural aspects of language (syntax), and natural language intervention, which attempts to model natural language development through exposure to language models and ample opportunity for usage of language forms. Music therapists are more likely to contribute to language development through a natural language approach.

Music therapy has a variety of features that can be exploited in a natural language approach: (a) Music therapy often includes activities for small groups, most of those activities which require following directions, socialization and cooperation; (b) The common pairing of music and lyrics through song signing or song writing allows for the manipulation of written and spoken language in a motivating and unique context.

Extensive discussion of methodological procedures is beyond the scope of this chapter. More in-depth descriptions can be found in articles listed in the bibliography at the end of this chapter. In brief, there are several categories of activities that lend themselves readily to language development. (a) Participation in musical ensembles and other musical activities requires children to follow directions, take turns, listen to the comments of others, make requests, follow a train of thought, and many other important pragmatic and social skills. For example, in a small ensemble in which some participants play the tonic contrabass tone bar, others play the dominant note, and still others the subdominant, the therapist may inquire, "Who is first? Who is next? Who is last?" "Describe the instrument that you would like to play." The structure of the ensemble sets up ample opportunity for language usage. (b) Activities such as song signing or writing song lyrics are excellent opportunities to practice reading and writing written language. Songs can be selected because of the appropriateness of topic and language difficulty. Other songs can be adapted or songs can be written specifically for the purpose at hand. For example, if the children are trying to master the use of past tense, a song that talks about events long ago can present information in the past tense. One particular approach to song writing draws on the language arts classes; group members use the same basic steps to write songs. For greater detail, refer to chapters in the bibliography.

Language use can be facilitated through the activity as long as there is regular interaction between the therapist and the children. The therapist can function as a language model, using language at a level of difficulty developmentally appropriate for the group members. As the therapist introduces each activity, she or he can describe what will happen, label or describe new or novel objects or events, require the children to make requests in order to obtain materials of choice, and expect group members to attend to one another in conversations.

Progress in Therapy

The length and frequency of sessions, as well as the expected rate of development, will vary greatly depending on the individual's age and severity of hearing loss. In general, younger children benefit from shorter sessions (initially 15 to 20 minute sessions comprised of a series of short and varied activities), with length of sessions increased with greater maturity. Upper elementary students, for example, may function well in sessions of 45 to 60 minutes in length (once again, this total session may be comprised of several shorter activities).

The frequency of session is usually dependent upon the complete rehabilitation plan. Often, children with hearing losses have a variety of services such as speech training, auditory training, and special deaf education classes. Therefore, it is important to coordinate music therapy sessions with other educational and rehabilitative demands. The IEP committee can help to determine session frequency. One possibility is weekly or bi-weekly sessions.

Criteria for termination is less clear cut than might be found in some medical conditions that can be "cured." Mastery of language may be a life-long challenge. Termination of services is indicated if the child has achieved age-level skills in language development, or if documented assessment from music therapy intervention indicates no substantive improvement over the year, suggesting that alternative treatment forms might prove more beneficial.

Research on Music with Individuals Who are Deaf and Hard-of-Hearing

Amir, D., & Schuchman, G. (1985). Auditory training through music with hearing impaired preschool children. *Volta Review, 87*, 333–343.

This study investigated the effects of auditory training within a musical context on how severely to profoundly hearing-impaired preschool children use their residual hearing. Two groups of six children each were matched for age and level of hearing loss. The experimental group received 24 sessions of highly structured music therapy emphasizing rhythm and intensity dynamics. Four aspects of the children's auditory behavior were evaluated before and after the therapeutic intervention. A significant improvement was found in the children's ability to discriminate and recognize auditory stimuli. However, the lowest level in the hierarchy of auditory perception, detection, and the highest level, comprehension, were unaffected. These data suggest that group auditory training through music cannot replace training with speech and environmental sounds; however, this type of therapy may serve as a useful adjunct to other techniques for maximizing the use of residual hearing in hearing-impaired preschool children.

Baird, S. (1979). A technique to assess the preference for intensity of musical stimuli in young hard-of-hearing children. *Journal of Music Therapy, 6,* 6–ll.

The purpose of this study was to attempt to determine what decibel level of auditory stimuli (music) would maintain response in young hard-of-hearing children. In other words, an attempt was made to determine what decibel level of music each child preferred. The following questions were answered:
1. Will auditory stimuli (music) maintain key response in young hard-of-hearing children?
2. Which decibel level of music will maintain the longest duration of commitment for each child?

The study appeared to produce an accurate assessment of sound intensity preference for music. Music of specified intensity did maintain responding in all subjects.

Billugi, U., & Klima, E. S. (1972). The roots of language in sign talk of the deaf. *Psychology Today, 6*(1), 61–74, 76.

The authors advocate the use of songs with American Sign Language to reflect the type and mood of the text.

Coffman, D., Gfeller, K., Darrow, A. A., & Coffman, S. (1992). Computer-assisted comparison of melodic and rhythmic discrimination skills in hearing impaired and normally hearing children. *The Arts in Psychotherapy, 18,* 449–454.

The purpose of this study was to examine the feasibility of using *Toney Listens to Music,* a commercially-available computer program, in testing differences in the discrimination skills of normally hearing and hearing-impaired children on listening tasks involving changes in tempo, rhythm patterns, intervals, and simple melodies. The researchers also examined the effects of differential auditory histories of the hearing-impaired subjects. In this study, subjects were required to match one of two comparison patterns with stimulus pattern, a task considered more difficult than merely discriminating "same" or "different" patterns. Normally hearing subjects missed less than one item per task as a group (95% to 98% accuracy), displaying narrow ranges (1 to 3) and small standard deviations (0.46 to 1/07). These subjects appeared to do equally well across the four listening tasks, with a slight decrement in rhythm pattern perception. Hearing-impaired subjects, on the other hand, varied widely in performance, with range scores varying from 3 to 10 and standard deviations from 1.20 to 3.73. Mann-Whitney U tests between means of the normally hearing and hearing-impaired groups revealed significant differences in only the pitch perception tasks: interval discrimination ($p = .028$) and melody discrimination ($p = .049$). *Toney,* as an assessment device has some shortcomings, including: (a) the effect of wave form presentation on tonal and temporal perception, (b) the response of hearing aids to differential frequency ranges, (c) the limited number of items available on the test, and (d) *Toney's* use of feedback. In summary, although the appropriateness of *Toney* as an assessment tool is somewhat in doubt, the study does indicate the importance of exposure and access to musical experiences. Concerned music educators and music therapist will need to consider the best ways to adapt the listening experiences of their hearing-impaired children, adaptations that present material of a complexity appropriate to an individual's auditory history. The lack of difference in temporal perception between the two populations and the high overall performances of some subjects in this study suggest that children with hearing impairment can achieve at relatively high levels if suitable measures are undertaken.

Darrow, A. A. (1979). The beat reproduction response of subjects with normal and impaired hearing: An empirical comparison. *Journal of Music Therapy, 16*(2), 91–98.

The study was designed to examine the beat reproduction responses of normal and hearing-impaired subjects on the basis of four considerations: (a) auditory experience, (b) auditory involvement during stimulus presentation, (c) auditory deprivation, and (d) tempo. Data were analyzed for temporal deviation in auditory and tempo conditions. A two-way analysis of variance indicated a significant temporal deviation difference between normal and hearing-impaired subjects. A significant temporal deviation difference was also found among four selected tempi. Observation of data indicated group tendencies for fastness or slowness.

Darrow, A. A. (1984). A comparison of the rhythmic responsiveness in normal hearing and hearing-impaired children and an investigation of the relationship of the rhythmic responsiveness to the suprasegmental aspects of speech perception. *Journal of Music Therapy, 21*, 48–66.

The study had two major objectives: (1) to compare the rhythm responsiveness of normal hearing and hearing-impaired students on six subtests designed to measure beat identification, tempo change, accent as a factor in meter discrimination, melodic rhythm duplication, rhythm pattern duplication, and rhythm pattern maintenance; and (2) to investigate the relationship of rhythmic responsiveness in hearing-impaired students to the suprasegmental (i.e., nonlinguistic) aspects of speech perception that involve rhythm discrimination. Sixty-two hearing impaired and normal hearing public school students served as subjects. Ages ranged from 9 to 16 with a mean age of 12 years. Speech reception thresholds (SRT) for hearing-impaired subjects' better ear ranged from 35 dB to dB levels beyond the limits of the audiometer. The Test of Rhythm Responsiveness, recorded on a specially prepared tape, was used in conjunction with the Tap Master, a stereo cassette tape player with the capacity to provide a quantitative measurement of student response. The test tape was administered to hearing-impaired subjects through a portable audiometer at 35 dB above subjects' SRT. Results indicated that hearing impaired subjects performed as well or better than normal hearing subjects with regard to beat identification, tempo change, accent as a factor in meter discrimination, and rhythm pattern maintenance. However, a significant difference was found between the two groups concerning melodic rhythm duplication and rhythm pattern duplication. No significant difference was found among age levels or between males and females. The specific degree of hearing loss was not related to the test performance of hearing-impaired subjects with the exception of those designated profoundly hearing-impaired. Two additional speech perception tests were administered to hearing-impaired subjects, the Children's Auditory Test and the Auditory Numbers Test. These tests evaluated subjects' ability to discriminate suprasegmental features of speech perception that involve speech rhythm discrimination. Significant correlations were found between the rhythmic responsiveness subtests intended to measure beat identification, melodic rhythm duplication, and rhythm pattern maintenance performance, and both of the suprasegmental speech perception tests.

Darrow, A. A. (1987). An investigative study: The effect of hearing impairment on musical aptitude. *Journal of Music Therapy, 24*(2), 88–96.

Little attention has been given to the study of music perception and the hearing impaired. As a result, music education programs for the hearing impaired have been based on intuition and perhaps inappropriate generalizations from music education programs for normal hearing children. The present exploratory study investigated the way in which hearing impaired children perceive tonal and rhythmic music. The Primary Measures of Music Audiation (PMMA), a music aptitude test for young children, was individually administered to hearing impaired children, Grades 1–3 (*N*=28), through a portable audiometer at 35 dB above subjects' speech reception threshold. The PMMA data were analyzed via a post hoc comparison of means, standard deviations, test reliability, standard error of measurement, and standard error of a difference representing normal hearing children and those of the hearing impaired sample. Data suggested that hearing impairment may adversely affect music perception and consequently musical aptitude. Despite these findings, hearing impaired children should not be excluded from participation in music education activities. Suggestions are given for ways music educators and therapists may adapt and program for the special needs of their hearing impaired students.

Darrow, A. A. (1989). Music and the hearing impaired: A review of the research with implications for music educators. *Update: Applications of Research in Music Education, 7*(2), 10–12.

This article is a review of the research in music education and music therapy, up to 1989, with persons who have impaired hearing.

Darrow, A. A. (1989). Music therapy in the treatment of the hearing impaired. *Music Therapy Perspectives, 6,* 61–70.

The author prefaces her description of clinical practice of music therapy with hearing-impaired clients by comparing blindness and deafness. She writes that blindness is "an environmental handicap" while deafness is a social disorder that keeps one from people. The parameters of hearing impairment are listed along with variables which extend beyond the classifications. A six-point music therapy procedure in auditory training is listed, along with the use of music in speech development. Finally, the author recounts the controversy surrounding the form of language to be used with hearing-impaired children. Methods of communication are listed along with music therapy procedures in language development.

Assessments used in music therapy clinical practice with hearing-impaired clients both for auditory training and language development are appended to the paper.

Darrow, A. A. (1990). The effect of frequency adjustment on the vocal reproduction accuracy of hearing impaired children. *Journal of Music Therapy, 27*(1), 24–33.

The purpose of the present study was to examine the effect of frequency adjustment of auditory stimuli to accommodate individual audiological response curves on the vocal reproduction accuracy of hearing impaired children. Subjects in the present study were eight hearing impaired public school students in an oral education program. Classification of hearing losses ranged from moderately to severely hearing impaired. All subjects had participated in the regular school music program for at least 2 years. Subjects were asked to reproduce given pitches under two conditions: (a) normal listening conditions, and (b) with frequency adjustments made in the presentation of the stimulus pitches to accommodate individual audiological response curves. Frequency measurements of subjects' vocal response were compared to frequency measurements of each stimulus tone and a cents deviation score computed. Results of a *t* test for dependent measures indicated a significant reduction in cents deviation under Condition 2, frequency adjustments made in the presentation of stimuli according to subjects' audiological curves ($t = 4.96$, $df = 7$, $p < .01$). The data were further examined for differences in cents deviation based on sequence of pitches. Data were also examined for direction of deviation (above or below the stimulus pitch). Implications for music educators of hearing impaired students are discussed.

Darrow, A. A. (1991). An assessment and comparison of hearing impaired children's preference for timbre and musical instruments. *Journal of Music Therapy, 28*(1), 48–59.

The purpose of these two studies was to examine the timbre and music instrument preferences of hearing impaired children. In the first study, 34 children from a state school for the deaf served as subjects. After a 15–minute presentation of six selected instruments representing the string, woodwind, and brass families, subjects were taken individually into an observation room and allowed to play the instruments for 5 minutes. For the purposes of this study, "play" was defined as the physical manipulation of music instruments. The children's videotaped playing behaviors were analyzed for preference in the following ways: the order in which the instruments were selected, the amount of time spent playing each instrument, and a signed report of preference (the equivalent of verbal report for hearing children). Total playing time across all subjects indicated preference for the instruments in the following order: trumpet, clarinet, viola, trombone, violin, and flute. The data of individual subjects indicated, however, that more time was spent with the violin. Signed responses of subjects revealed that the violin and trombone were the most preferred instruments. Though agreement among the three measures of preference was not significant, the preference data have implications for clinical practice. Novelty and aural feedback appeared to be factors related to subjects' interest in specific instruments. The purpose of Study 2 was to examine hearing impaired children's preference for timbre without reference to a musical instrument. A test designed to measure an individual's preference for the tone quality of various instruments was administered to 21 hearing impaired children at a state residential school for the deaf. Results of the Instrument Timbre Preference Test (Gordon, 1984) indicated a group preference for the clarinet and sax/French horn timbres. Individual subject timbre preferences were also found. Data from this study corroborated previous studies which indicated that preferences are more apparent in older children and that preferences may have a cultural bias. Implications for music therapists and audiologists are also given.

Darrow, A. A. (1992). The effect of vibrotactile stimuli on the identification of pitch change by hearing impaired children. *Journal of Music Therapy, 29,* 103–112.

The purpose of the present study was to examine the effect of vibrotactile stimuli via the Somatron® on the identification of pitch change by hearing impaired children. The research question was: Can vibrotactile stimuli assist hearing impaired children in developing tonal concepts normally acquired by hearing children through the auditory channel? Seventeen hearing impaired students from a state school for the deaf served as subjects. Ten alternating patterns of octaves, perfect fifths, and major thirds, ascending and descending, were recorded in random order on audio tapes using a Yamaha synthesized PSR–90. Subjects were tested individually for identification of pitch change under two conditions: (a) use of auditory skills only, and (b) use of auditory skills supported by vibrotactile stimuli. Identification of pitch change was indicated by subjects' response on a mechanical auditory signal device. Audiotape recordings of subject data were analyzed for identification of pitch change. Data were recorded for correct and incorrect responses. Incorrect responses were omissions or indications of pitch change when no change occurred. Of the 17 subjects, 10 subjects identified more pitch changes under the use of auditory skills supported by vibrotactile stimuli condition. Four subjects identified more changes under the use of auditory skills only condition, and three subjects identified the same number of changes under both conditions. The data were further analyzed for identification differences occurring on the bases of number of beats preceding a change, size of the melodic interval or discrepancy in change, and age of subjects.

Darrow, A. A. (1993). The role of music in deaf culture: Implications for music educators. *Journal of Research in Music Education, 41,* 93–110.

The primary purpose of this study was to examine the role of music in the deaf culture and to relate the findings to current practices in music education programs for hearing-impaired students. Secondary purposes of the study were to accumulate data that would either substantiate or refute the writings of hearing authors regarding the value of music to the deaf, and to examine factors that determine deaf individuals' involvement with music. Data were collected by (a) a questionnaire sent to a random sample of deaf Americans from across the country, and (b) videotaped personal interviews with a random sample of deaf community members in a large Midwestern metropolitan area. Based on their primary language and socialization practices, respondents were identified as members of the deaf culture, members of the hearing culture, or those that interact within both cultures. A summary of the results indicates that (1) cultural identification is a strong influential factor in deaf individuals' involvement with music; (2) deaf individuals that do involve themselves with music do so in ways similar to hearing individuals; (3) musical activities enjoyed most by deaf individuals are singing/signing songs, listening to music, and moving or dancing to music; (4) most respondents believed that music instruction should be optional for deaf students; (5) certain factors related to family involvement with music and musical training seem to be indicators of the role music will play in the lives of deaf individuals; and (6) deaf individuals do not participate to the degree that hearing individuals do in most common ritual uses of music. Quotes from respondents and implications for music educators teaching hearing-impaired students are given.

Darrow, A. A., & Cohen, N. (1991). The effect of programmed pitch practice and private instruction on the vocal reproduction accuracy of hearing impaired children: Two case studies. *Music Therapy Perspectives, 9,* 61–65.

The purpose of the present studies was to examine the effect of programmed pitch practice via the Pitch Master® and private vocal instruction on the ability of children with hearing impairments to reproduce given pitches and pitch patterns vocally. The subject of the first study was a 12-year-old female with a severe hearing loss. A pitch practice program utilizing the vocalization tapes which accompany the Pitch Master®, an instrument developed by Temporal Acuity Products, Inc., to facilitate the internalization of singing as a kinesthetic response, was set up. The subject was pretested and posttested using a test tape specifically designed for the Pitch Master®. Results indicated a significant improvement ($p < .05$) in the subject's ability to match a given pitch between the pre- and posttest evaluation. Daily recorded data revealed similar vocal performance accuracy scores across all sessions. The subject of the second study was an 11-year-old girl with a profound hearing loss. A repeated measures design was implemented to examine the effect of private instruction on the subject's vocal reproduction accuracy. A two-part assessment toll employed to measure the subject's ability to reproduce twenty pitches was administered three times over a period of eight months. Final figures revealed at 26% improvement in vocal accuracy on part one and a 49% improvement in vocal accuracy on part two.

Darrow, A. A., & Gfeller, K. (1991). A study of public school music programs mainstreaming hearing impaired students. *Journal of Music Therapy, 28*(1), 23–39.

The purposes of this study were to examine (a) the status of public school music instruction for hearing impaired students, and (b) the factors that contribute to the successful mainstreaming of hearing impaired students in the regular music classroom. A questionnaire was developed with items concerning demographic information, educational preparation, extent of instructional and administrative support, the extent of instructional and administrative support, the extent to which musical and nonmusical goals are set by music educators, factors related to the successful mainstreaming of hearing impaired students, obstructions to mainstreaming, and activities and curricula successfully implemented in mainstreaming programs. Results of the study revealed the following: (a) more than half of all hearing impaired students attend regular music classes; (b) of those students not mainstreamed, less than half receive no music education in the self-contained classroom or otherwise; (c) many music educators are lacking in the educational preparation necessary for teaching hearing impaired students; (d) important instructional or administrative support is often not available; (e) several factors, such as lack of appropriate curricula or poor communication with other professionals, are identified as obstructions to the successful mainstreaming of hearing impaired students; (f) only 35% of the respondents reported that they have the same objectives for hearing impaired students as for normal hearing students; and (g) methodologies, materials, and activities were identified that were helpful in integrating hearing impaired students into the regular music classroom. Implications for public school music educators are cited.

Darrow, A. A., & Goll, H. (1989). The effect of vibrotactile stimuli via the Somatron®on the identification of rhythmic concepts by hearing impaired children. *Journal of Music Therapy, 26*(3), 115–124.

The purpose of the present study was to examine the effect of vibrotactile stimuli on the identification of rhythmic change by hearing impaired children. Twenty-nine hearing impaired students from a state school for the deaf served as subjects. Ten alternating patterns of eighth and sixteenth notes were recorded in random order on audio tapes using an electronic drum machine. Subjects were tested individually for identification of rhythmic change under two conditions: (a) use of auditory skills only, and (b) use of auditory skills supported by vibrotactile stimuli. Identification of rhythmic change by hearing impaired subjects was facilitated by supplementing auditory skills with vibrotactile stimuli. The data were further analyzed for differences occurring on the bases of sequence of change, number of beats per change, and age of subjects. These data revealed that, for all changes and number of beats per change, subjects identified a greater number of rhythmic changes under this condition. Suggestions are given for use of the data in the clinical setting.

Darrow, A. A., & Heller, G. N. (1985). William Wolcott Turner and David Ely Bartlett: Early advocates of music education for the hearing impaired. *Journal of Research in Music Education, 33*, 269–279.

This historical research study recognizes the early efforts of William Wolcott Turner and David Ely Bartlett on behalf of music education for the deaf. In an 1848 article in the *American Annals for the Deaf and Dumb,* these two pioneers showed that a hearing-impaired student could learn music and that sound reasons existed to support such an endeavor. The research confirmed both the authenticity and credibility of Turner and Bartlett's work, with biographical information on the two authors and a critical analysis of the contents of their article in light of subsequent research on music for the hearing impaired.

Darrow, A. A., & Starmer, G. J. (1986). The effect of vocal training on the intonation and rate of hearing-impaired children's speech: A pilot study. *Journal of Music Therapy, 23,* 194–201.

The purpose of the study was to examine the effect of vocal training on the fundamental frequency, frequency range, and speech rate (syllable per second) of hearing-impaired children's speech. Twenty-two hearing-impaired children from a state school for the deaf served as subjects. Hearing losses were classified as severely and profoundly hearing impaired. Subjects attended a 30–minute vocal training class twice weekly for 8 weeks. Students spent equal amounts of time per class session singing songs and participating in vocal exercises. Subjects were pretested and posttested speaking 10 common sentences, 5 questions, and 5 statements. Audio tape recordings of speech were analyzed via the Visi-Pitch for fundamental frequency, frequency range, and speech rate, and for intonation differences between statements and questions. Results indicated a significant reduction of fundamental frequency and a significant increase in frequency range following vocal training. No significant differences were found regarding speech rate or intonation differences between questions and statements.

Edwards, J. V. (1991). *The relationship of contrasting selections of music and human field motion (hearing impaired).* Unpublished doctoral dissertation, New York University.

This research was focused on the relationship between the experience of music and human field motion. The purpose of the researcher was to explicate the conceptual framework of Martha E. Rogers through an exploration of the environmental field phenomenon, music, and human field motion. Rogers postulates that environmental and human fields are characterized by waves of particular pattern which are integral with one another. Human field motion represents the experience of the continuous, dynamic patterning of the human and environmental fields. The premise of this study was derived from this conceptual framework. Music represents an environmental field phenomenon. Therefore, it is proposed that when individuals experience music, the human field manifests change. contrasting music selections represent different environmental fields. As the fields are integral with one another, contrasting music selections will manifest different human field motion. The environmental field of music is present whether or not an individual has auditory function. It is deduced that music manifests change in the human field motion of both hearing and hearing-impaired individuals. The hypotheses were: a tonal, polyrhythmic music selection with a distinct melody and harmony manifests a different human field motion than an atonal music selection with no traditional rhythm structure which is dissonant and without melody in hearing subjects; and a tonal, polyrhythmic music selection with a distinct melody and harmony manifests a different human field motion than an atonal music selection with no traditional rhythm structure which is dissonant and without melody in hearing impaired subjects. Fifty hearing and 50 hearing-impaired subjects experienced two contrasting music selections. Following each music selection, participants completed the Human Field Motion Test. the hypotheses were supported. A significant effect of music selection and human field motion for hearing and hearing impaired participants was found ($p < .01$). Additionally, the difference in the human field motion scores of hearing and hearing-impaired participants was highly significant ($p < .001$). Recommendations for future research include replicating the study using familiar music and different types of music. Further investigation of the human field motion of those who are hearing impaired would be of interest.

Eisenson, J., Kastein, S., & Schneiderman, N. (1958). An investigation into the ability of voice defectives to discriminate among differences in pitch and loudness. *Journal of Speech and Hearing Disorders, 23*(5), 577–582.

This study was designed to investigate the ability of persons diagnosed as having defective voices to discriminate among differences in pitch and loudness of musical tones. This investigation sought answers to the following questions: (1) How does the ability of voice defectives for loudness discrimination compare with that of an unselected population? (2) How does the ability of voice defectives for pitch discrimination compare with that of an unselected population? (3) Is the diagnosis of the voice disorder (functional or organic) related to the ability of the subject to discriminate among differences in pitch and loudness? (4) What changes can be found in these discrimination abilities of voice defectives after a period of voice therapy including ear-training for these variables of pitch and loudness? The procedures followed in analyzing the test scores were: (1) Experimental group scores on the subtests for pitch and loudness were compared to those of the control group and again to those of the original standardization group by means of the *t* test. (2) Two groups were selected from the total experimental number, according to the diagnosis of the voice disorder: one group with organic voice problems and the other with functional voice problems. Those with mixed diagnosis were not considered for this part of the study. There were 54 members in the functional group and 23 members in the organic group. The scores of the organic and functional groups were compared by means of the *t* test. (3) Fifteen of the subjects who had formed the experimental group were retested at the end of a 15–week course in voice improvement which emphasized procedures in training for discrimination for differences in pitch. The two sets of scores were compared by means of the *t* test appropriate for the purpose of comparing test and retest scores. Conclusions: (1) The voice defectives in this study were found to be significantly poorer than either the control group or the Seashore standardization group in pitch discrimination. The voice defectives were not significantly poorer than the other groups in loudness discrimination. (2) The results showed that there were no significant differences for either pitch or loudness discrimination between the functional and organic voice defective subgroups. (3) The group tested before and after completing a program of voice training emphasizing ear-training in pitch discrimination showed a significant gain in pitch discrimination. There was no significant gain in loudness discrimination.

Ford, T. A. (1985). *The effect of musical experiences and age on the ability of deaf children to discriminate pitch of complex tones.* (Doctoral dissertation, University of North Carolina, 1985).

The purpose of this research was to investigate the ability of deaf children to discriminate pitch of complex tones. The research was designed to study the effects of age and school musical experiences on pitch discrimination and to identify possible relationships between pitch discrimination and other variables, including hearing levels, academic achievement, and home music background. A pitch discrimination test was designed to measure the difference limen for frequency (DLF) at 250 and 500 Hz. Subjects (ages 6 to 9 and 11 to 12) were selected from two residential schools for the deaf; one school included music classes in the curriculum. Information regarding prior musical experiences was elicited from subjects' parents and classroom teachers via written questionnaires. Audiometric data and achievement levels were obtained from school records. Programs in *SPSSX* were used to analyze data. Subjects demonstrated great variability if DLF sizes. The DLFs on the 250 Hz subtest ranged from 17.5 Hz to greater than 103 Hz; the median DLF was 39.9 Hz. On the 500 Hz subtest, DLFs ranged from 26 Hz to greater than 205 Hz; the median DLF was 86.2. The results of two-way ANOVA did not reveal any statistically significant differences between subjects when grouped by age and school. There were moderate to high positive correlations between DLF and hearing levels among the young subjects; among older subjects, there was little or no correlation between DLF and hearing levels. A stepwise multiple regression identified the hearing level at 250 Hz to be the best predictor of DLF at 250 Hz and 500 Hz. Results suggest that deaf children may benefit from appropriate pitch-related activities. Implications for music educators include using music in lower registers, discriminating large changes of pitch, and allowing for language deficiencies through the use of concrete examples of pitch concepts and a variety of communication modes.

Ford, T. A. (1988). The effect of musical experience and age on the ability of deaf children to discriminate pitch. *Journal of Music Therapy, 25*(1), 2–16.

Ford investigated effects of school music experience, age, academic level, and gender on pitch discrimination (same-different task) at 250 and 500 Hz. Hearing-impaired subjects listened to paired pitches of either no change or changes ranging from a minor second to greater than an augmented fourth. Stimuli were presented over stereo earphones at the most comfortable level of loudness (MCL), which for these subjects ranged from 90 to 110 dB. Over 50 percent of subjects were able to discriminate a change of a minor third with 75 percent accuracy at both 250 and 500 Hz. Intervals smaller than a minor third proved difficult for hearing-impaired subjects, the same small frequency changes found in many items of the PMMA Tonal subtest. Ford found no differences for pitch discrimination due to age or music training, but discrimination proved more accurate at 250 Hz than at 500 Hz (.05). The researcher concluded that hearing-impaired children may benefit from listening activities (1) that are in an optimal pitch range (around B below middle C to an interval of a twelfth above middle C) and (2) that start with gross pitch differentiation, gradually reducing the size of the interval change. The study reported subject characteristics: IQ, age (6–9; 11–12), type of loss (sensorineural loss only), onset of loss (all subjects were congenitally or prelingually deafened), musical background (home environment), music education (schools for the deaf with and without a music curriculum), and status regarding multiple disabilities (subjects with multiple disabilities were excluded) [p. 621].

Ford, T. A., & Shroyer, E. H. (1987). Survey of music teachers in residential and day programs for hearing impaired students. *Journal of the International Association of Music for the Handicapped, 3*, 16–25.

A national survey of residential and day programs for hearing-impaired students (Shroyer & Ford, 1986) examined the extent that music instruction and activities are included in schools for hearing-impaired children. Sixty-one (50%) of the responding programs reported that there was no ongoing music instruction for students. When asked to indicate reasons for the absence of music in the curriculum, 34 (56%) of the respondents indicated "a lack of qualified personnel to teach music." This raises an interesting question regarding a definition of "qualified personnel," particularly since the implementation of extensive, organized music curricula in many programs for hearing-impaired students in relatively new. In addition, information regarding characteristics of music educators who teach in residential and day programs for hearing-impaired students had not been available.

Galloway, H. F., & Bean, M. F. (1974). The effects of action songs on the development of body-image and body-part identification in hearing-impaired preschool children. *Journal of Music Therapy, 11*, 125–134.

Studied the effect of music action songs on body-image and body-vocabulary development in hearing-impaired children in a preschool classroom. Body-image is defined as the child's awareness and knowledge of the physical and spatial characteristics of his own body; body vocabulary is defined as his identification of parts of his body upon request. Two girls and four boys under 6 years old, with hearing loss from profound to moderate, were the Ss. Results suggest that music may be useful in teaching selected concepts to hearing-impaired children.

Gfeller, K. E. (1986). Music as a remedial tool for improving speech rhythm in the hearing impaired: Clinical and research consideration. *Music Education for the Handicapped Bulletin, 2*, 3–19.

While several sources have advocated music to help the hearing impaired acquire more normalized speech rhythm and intelligibility, these recommendations are generally based on historically and intuitively accepted practices rather than research data. This study is a preliminary investigation into the efficacy of musical speech rhythm training. Nine hearing-impaired children participated in a musical speech rhythm program. Pre- and posttest speech samples were measured on the following factors: (a) intelligibility, (b) speech rate, (c) prosodic features, and (d) number of utterances per second. Individual responses indicate improved intelligibility and speech rate of 5 of 9 subjects, improved prosodic features in 6 of 9 subjects, and increased number of utterances in 7 of 9 subjects. Decline in most speech intelligibility factors for two of the subjects indicates that this approach is not appropriate in all cases. Recommendations for clinical application and further research based on this preliminary study are provided.

Gfeller, K. E. (1987). Songwriting as a tool for reading and language remediation. *Music Therapy, 6*(2), 28–38.

This article discusses the use of the Language Experience Approach in conjunction with song writing to aid reading, writing skills, and overall language development of children, including the deaf, who have difficulties in language arts. Methodological recommendations are provided.

Gfeller, K. E., & Darrow, A. A. (1987). Music as a remedial tool in the language education of hearing impaired children. *The Arts in Psychotherapy, 14,* 229–235.

This article provides methodological suggestions for using songwriting and song-signing to enhance language development of hearing impaired children.

Gfeller, K. E., & Lansing, C. R. (1991). Melodic, rhythmic, and timbral perception of adult cochlear implant users. *Journal of Speech and Hearing Research, 34,* 916–920.

This article examines the melodic, rhythmic, and timbral perception of postlingually deafened adults who are using two different types of prosthetic hearing devices (cochlear implant): the Nucleus, which uses speech feature extraction, and the Ineraid, which transmits an analog signal. Subjects included 18 postlingually deafened adults with CI experience. Evaluative measures included the Primary Measures of Music Audiation (PMMA) and an evaluative measure of various instrumental timbres. Performance scores on the PMMA were correlated with speech perception measures, music background, and subject characteristics. Results demonstrated a broad range of perceptual accuracy and quality ratings across subjects. On these measures, performance for rhythmic contrasts was better than for melodic contrasts independent of CI device. Trends in the patterns of correlations between speech and music perception suggest that particular structural elements of music are differentially accessible to CI users. Additionally, notable qualitative differences for ratings of musical instruments were observed between Nucleus and Ineraid users.

Gfeller, K. E., & Lansing, C. R. (1992). Musical perception of cochlear implant users as measured by the *Primary Measures of Music Audiation*: An item analysis. *Journal of Music Therapy, 29*(1), 18–39.

The purposes of this study were (a) to evaluate the Primary Measures of Music Audiation (PMMA) as a test of musical perception for postlingually deafened adult cochlear implant (CI) users; and (b) to report test outcome on the Rhythm and Tonal subtests of the PMMA. Correlations between PMMA scores and speech perception tasks were calculated. Subjects were 34 postlingually deafened adults with CI experience. Subject performance on the PMMA was analyzed to determine test usability and technical adequacy (reliability, item discrimination, and difficulty) for this particular population. Comparisons were made across two different implant types (Nucleus and Ineraid devices) and across Rhythm and Tonal subtests. The PMMA was found to be usable with minor adjustments. No significant differences in accuracy were found for the Rhythm or Tonal subtest across devices. However, CI (Nucleus and Ineraid) users were significantly more accurate on the Rhythm than the Tonal subtest ($p \le .001$). The mean difficulty for the Rhythm subtest was 84.93, while the mean difficulty for the Tonal subtest was 77.50. The mean discrimination indices were as follows: Rhythm subtest, .18; Tonal subtest, .28. The Tonal subtest contained a larger number of items within the satisfactory range for item difficulty and item discrimination. The strongest correlations between musical perception and speech perception were between the Tonal subtest and the speech perception measures of phoneme identification ($r = .45$) and accent recognition ($r = .46$).

Gilbert, J. P. (1983). A comparison of the motor music skills of non-handicapped and learning disabled children. *Journal of Research in Music Education, 31*(2), 147–155.

Complete reporting of subject selection criteria and types of specific disabilities is absent in this study of motor music skills. Only age and years of academic discrepancy are provided. Nevertheless, Gilbert's study also had notable strengths. The author reported impressive test-retest (.91 – .94), interjudge (.98 – .94), and internal consistency (.78 – .89) coefficients for her self-devised assessment tool. Further, details about test development were reported in a previous publication (Gilbert, 1979). Gilbert's findings are of practical interest to the music educator. In comparing musical motor skills of nondisabled and learning-disabled children, nondisabled children showed greater performance on the composite test score (.001). Given the heterogeneous nature of the learning-disabled population, it could be expected that the standard deviation for learning-disabled children would be greater than that for nondisabled children. In addition, significantly more erratic motor development over age among learning-disabled children compared with nondisabled peers (.02) is consistent with theories of immature or idiosyncratic neurological development reported in the special education literature.

Klajman, S., Koldeg, E., & Kowalska, A. (1982). Investigation of musical abilities in hearing-impaired and normal-hearing children. *Folia Phoniatrica, 34*, 229–233.

Compared musical abilities of 130 hearing-impaired children (aged 7–19 years) with the musical abilities of 104 hearing controls. The following parameters were investigated: sense of rhythm, sense of duration, direct memory of rhythm, pitch, melody, music memory, hearing of harmonies, and hearing of timbre. The 25 Ss from the hearing-impaired group who received the best scores were subjected to exercises designed to develop their musical ability over 3 months. After 3 months, these Ss were retested, and the results were analyzed statistically. Significant differences were found between the hearing-impaired Ss and the normal Ss for the frequency of occurrence of almost all parameters. Ss who received musical instruction showed significant improvements in articulation, speech rhythm, breath regularity, phonation, and in the frequency of occurrence and value of estimation of most of the parameters. A good ear for music was found in 50% of the hearing-impaired Ss and in 80% of the normal hearing Ss.

Korduba, O. M. (1975). Duplicated rhythm patterns between deaf and normal hearing children. *Journal of Music Therapy, 12*(3), 136–146.

In a test of the hypothesis that there would be no significant differences in the comparison of error scores in duplicated patterns, 15 deaf, and 15 normal hearing children were presented 20 stimuli patterns. Error scores, computed deviations from correct responses, were calculated on two measures; the accuracy of the number of beats, and the accuracy of the actual rhythm. Three one variable analyses of variance were performed, with results indicating that significant differences were found in the beat error scores of deaf and normal hearing Ss. No significant differences were found in rhythm error scores. Results also indicated a significant difference in combined beat error, rhythm error scores between the Ss. A Multivariate Discriminant Analysis was performed to determine which patterns contributed the greater variance to the reported results. Spearman's coefficient of rank correlation was calculated to test the relationship between the beat and rhythm error score variables between the Ss. The implications of the findings are discussed.

Kracke, I. (1975). Perception of rhythmic sequences by receptive aphasic and deaf children. *British Journal of Disorders of Communication, 10,* 43–51.

Three groups of carefully selected children, twelve with severe receptive aphasia, twelve with profound hearing loss and twelve unimpaired controls were given the task of discriminating between simple rhythmic sequences. The results of the aphasic children were very poor whereas the deaf and the control children did not differ significantly. The disability of the aphasics was found to transcend the auditory modality. Theoretical and practical implications of the findings are discussed.

Madsen, C. K., & Mears, W. G. (1965). The effect of sound upon the tactile threshold of deaf subjects. *Journal of Music Therapy, 2*(2), 64–68.

The purpose of this study was to determine (1) if sound vibrations on the skin have a significant effect upon the threshold of the tactile sense, and (2) what differences exist between tactile thresholds and selected intensity and frequency levels of sound. Based on the results of this study, it is indicated that (1) Sound vibration does have a significant effect upon the threshold of the tactile sense; (2) A 50–c.p.s. tone at both high and low pressure levels desensitizes the skin and raises the tactile threshold; and (c) A 5,000–c.p.s. tone at both high and low pressure levels seemed to sensitize the skin (although this was not statistically significant).

Raleigh, K. K., & Odom, P. B. (1972). Perception of rhythm by subjects with normal and deficient hearing. *Developmental Psychology, 7*(1), 54–61.

Deaf and normal-hearing subjects, 10 and 15 years old, performed a rhythm-reproduction task. The visual rhythm patterns varied in length and complexity. Interactions between hearing status and the three measures of performance, number of beats, duration estimation, and rhythm reproduction, suggested an explanation for the obtained data in terms of salience for different aspects of the rhythm patterns. There is a general suggestion of a developmental continuum of skills relating to rhythm perception, ranging from salience for beats at the younger ages to salience for rhythm in adolescents. The distributions of the deaf and hearing subjects in this study overlap somewhat on the age continuum.

Schulz, E., & Kerber, M. (1994). Music perception with the MED-EL implants. In I. J. Hochmair-Desoyer & E. S. Hochmair (Eds.), *Advances in cochlear implants* (pp. 326–332). Manz, Wien.

The purpose of this research was to investigate music perception of persons using a prosthetic hearing device called a cochlear implant (CI). In particular, this article examines one particular type of CI, the MED-EL. The study compared 7 normally hearing listeners and 8 MED-EL CI users on tasks of rhythmic, melodic, and timbral perception. Implant users showed better perception of temporal information than pitch information (as is expressed in discrimination and recognition of tunes or different musical instruments). This test is considered preliminary in nature given the small sample size, and relatively narrow universe of musical tasks tested.

Sposato, M. (1983). *Implications of maximal exploitation of residual hearing on curriculum planning in music education for hearing impaired children.* Unpublished doctoral dissertation, State University of New York, Buffalo.

The purpose of the study was to identify those aspects of the planning process which parallel the identified and accepted music curricular goals for hearing children to establish a valid curricular framework for future curriculum planning in music education for hearing impaired children. The problem of the study was to identify the necessary components of a broad, integrated curriculum plan in music education for hearing impaired children contingent upon the maximal exploitation of residual hearing. Disciplined inquiry, as a systematic investigation, was used to determine: the current status of music education for hearing impaired children, the audiological parameters relevant to the provision of appropriate amplification for the purpose of music education, and the acoustical parameters of an amplification system intended for use in music education. Extant curriculum designs/plans do not constitute valid curricular frameworks for providing an optimal music experience for hearing impaired children. Those involved in the planning process did not obtain as much pertinent information as possible about the students to be educated nor did they establish a framework to clarify the factors involved in the selection of learning experiences. The present absence of a specialized music curriculum for hearing impaired children based upon the use of residual hearing, arises from the lack of data and understanding of the impact of hearing on auditory reception/perception of music. It was concluded that until unresolved issues crucial to the development of a relevant curriculum plan in music education for hearing impaired children have been adequately explored, the development of specialized teaching techniques or methods to maximize the use of residual hearing for a listening experience in music for hearing impaired children would be of limited value. Although the study emphasized musical development of hearing impaired children, the results, conclusions, and recommendations are applicable to hearing impaired students of all ages.

Sterritt, G. M., Camp, B. W., & Lipman, B. S. (1966). Effects of early auditory deprivation upon auditory and visual information processing. *Perceptual and Motor Skills, 23*(1), 123–130.

Nine children with hearing losses and nine normal controls used a telegraph key to reproduce temporal patterns created by an above-threshold tone or by a flashing light. They hypothesis was confirmed that early auditory deprivation is associated with a deficit in later abilities to use above-threshold auditory information. To a lesser degree, Ss with hearing losses were inferior to normals in visual temporal pattern reproduction as well, suggesting that the effects of sensory deprivation are not limited to the deprived sensory modality.

Van Deventer, E. L. (1991). *Music therapy with hearing impaired children* (Afrikaans text). Unpublished doctoral dissertation, University of Pretoria, South Africa.

One of the most profound encumberments of hearing impairment is the inability to communicate through language. The impaired language development often contributes to a negative self-concept. This was assessed in a group of hearing impaired grade one pupils, by means of the Martinek-Zaichkowsky Self-Concept Scale and the Human Figure Drawings by Koppitz. The first perception that a child has of himself is his body image which together with his physical experiences leads to the development of his self-concept. Although the hearing impaired child cannot always distinguish the pitch and melody of the music, he or she can experience the rhythm kinesthetically or visually. A music therapy programme was developed to enhance the self-concept of hearing impaired children. The programme which ran over 12 sessions, focused on rhythm and body image. Statistical analysis confirmed the therapist and teachers' observations of improvement in self-concept of the pupils.

Williams, H. (1989). The value of music to the deaf. *British Journal of Music Education, 6*(1), 81–98.

This study discusses the deaf person's physical potential to perceive music, and also looks at the technical aids that can increase this capacity. A survey of educational approaches, ranging from preschool to adult education, reveals that the initial step of enjoyable noise-making links them all. Nonmusical benefits gained from musical involvement are outlined, and finally the issue of aesthetic appreciation is addressed. How much can music mean to a deaf person?

References

Achenbach, T., & Edelbrock, C. (1981). *Child behavior checklist—Direct observation form.* Burlington, VT: University of Vermont.

Blackwell, P. M. (1983). Training strategies in functional speech routines. In I. Hochberg, H. Levitt, & M. J. Osberger (Eds.), *Speech of the hearing impaired.* Baltimore, MD: University Park Press.

Boothroyd, A. (1983). Evaluation of speech. In I. Hochberg, H. Levitt, & M. J. Osberger (Eds.), *Speech of the hearing impaired.* Baltimore, MD: University Park Press.

Darrow, A. A. (1985). Music therapy for hearing impaired clients. In T. Wigram, B. Saperston, & R. West (Eds.), *The art and science of music therapy: A handbook* (pp. 363–384). Chur, Switzerland: Harwood Academic Publishers.

Darrow, A. A., & Starmer, G. J. (1986). The effect of vocal training on the intonation and rate of hearing-impaired children's speech: A pilot study. *Journal of Music Therapy, 23,* 194–201.

Davis, J., & Hardick, E. (1981). *Rehabilitative audiology for children and adults.* New York: John Wiley & Sons.

Dunn, L., & Dunn, L. (1981). *Peabody picture vocabulary test—revised.* Circle Pines, MN: American Guidance Service.

Erber, N. P., & Alencewicz, C. M. (1976). Audiological evaluation of deaf children. *Journal of Speech and Hearing Disorders, 41,* 256–257.

Erber, N. P., & Hirsh, I. J. (1978). Auditory training. In H. Davis & S. R. Silverman (Eds.), *Hearing and deafness.* Chicago: Holt, Rinehart and Winston.

Erber, N. P., (1980). Use of the Auditory Numbers Test to evaluate speech perception abilities of hearing-impaired children. *Journal of Speech and Hearing Disorders, 45,* 527–532.

Gfeller, K. E., & Schum, R. (1994). Requisites for conversation: Engendering social skills. In N. Tye-Murray (Ed.), *Let's converse: A "how-to" guide to develop and expand conversational skills of children and teenagers who are hearing impaired.* Washington, DC: Alexander Graham Bell Association.

Gilbert, J. P. (1979). Assessment of motoric music skill development in young children: Test construction and evaluation procedures. Psychology of Music, 7(2), 3-12.

Gordon, E. E. (1986). *Instrument timbre preference test.* Chicago: G. I. A. Publications.

Heider, H., & Heider, B. (1940). A comparison of sentence structure of deaf and hearing children. *Psychological Monographs, 52,* 42–103.

Heward, W. L., & Orlansky, M. D. (1988). *Exceptional children.* Columbus, OH: Merrill Publishing Co.

Hudgins, C. V. (1949). A method of appraising the speech of the deaf. *Volta Review, 51,* 597–601, 638.

Kannapell, B. (1980). Personal awareness and advocacy in the deaf community. In W. C. Stokoe (Ed.), *Sign language and the deaf community.* Silver Spring, MD: National Association for the Deaf.

Ling, D., & Ling, A. (1978). *Aural habilitation.* Washington, DC: A. G. Bell Association.

Ling, D., & Milne, M. (1981). The development of speech in hearing-impaired children. In F. Bess, B. A. Freeman, & J. S. Sinclair (Eds.), *Amplification in education.* Washington, DC: A.G. Bell Association.

Magner, M. E. (1972). *A speech intelligibility test for deaf children.* Northampton, MA: Clarke School for the Deaf.

Meadow, K. (1980a). *Deafness and child development.* Los Angeles: University of California Press.

Meadow, K. (1980b). *Meadow/Kendall social-emotional assessment inventory for deaf students.* Washington, DC: Gallaudet College.

Moeller, M., McConkey, A., & Osberger, M. (1983). Evaluation of the communication skills of hearing impaired children. *Audiology, 8(8),* 113–127.

Owens, E., Kessler, D. K., Telleen, C. C., & Schubert, E. D. (1981). The minimal auditory capabilities (MAC) battery. *Hearing Aid Journal, 9,* 34.

Padden, C. (1980). The deaf community and the culture of the deaf people. In W. C. Stokoe (Ed.), *Sign language and the deaf community,* Silver Spring, MD: National Association of the Deaf.

Padden, C., & Humphries, T. (1988). *Deaf in America: Voices from a culture.* Cambridge, MA: Harvard University Press.

Pressnell, L. (1973). Hearing impaired children's comprehension and production of syntax in oral language. *Journal of Speech and Hearing Research, 16,* 12–21.

Prickett, H. T. (1989). *Advocacy for deaf children.* Springfield, IL: Charles C. Thomas Publisher.

Quigley, S., Wilbur, R., Power, D., Montanelli, D., & Steinkamp, H. (1976). *Syntactic structures in the language of deaf children.* Champaign-Urbana: University of Illinois Press.

Ross, M., & Lerman, J. W. (1970). A picture identification test for hearing-impaired children. *Journal of Speech and Hearing Research, 13,* 44–53.

Sacks, O. (1989). *Seeing voices.* Berkeley, CA: University of California Press.

Sanders, D. A. (1977). *Auditory perception of speech.* Englewood Cliffs, NJ: Prentice-Hall, Inc.

Schein, J. D. (1978). The deaf community. In H. Davis & S. R. Silverman (Eds.), *Hearing and deafness.* New York: Holt, Rinehart, & Winston.

Schirmer, B. (1985). An analysis of the language of young hearing-impaired children in terms of syntax, semantics, and use. *American Annals of the Deaf, 130*(1), 15–19.

Schmitz, K. (1990). An explorer's guide to cultural understanding. *NTID Focus,* 26–29.

Subtelny, J. (1975). *Speech and voice characteristics of the deaf.* Rochester, NY: National Technical Institute for the Deaf.

Trammell, J. L., Farrar, C., Grancis, J., Owens, S. L., Schepard, D., Thies, T. L., Witlen, R. P., & Faist, L. H. (1980). *Test of auditory comprehension.* North Hollywood, CA: Foremost.

Van Tassel, D. J. (1981). Auditory perception of speech. In J. M. Davis, & E. J. Hardick (Eds.), *Rehabilitative audiology for children and adults* (pp. 13–58). New York: John Wiley & Sons.

MUSIC THERAPY WITH TRAUMATIC BRAIN-INJURED PATIENTS: SPEECH REHABILITATION, INTERVENTION MODELS AND ASSESSMENT PROCEDURES (1970–1995)

Mary S. Adamek
Iris M. Shiraishi

Introduction

TRAUMATIC brain injuries (TBI), whether caused by accident or disease, may have a profound effect on the affected individual's ability to communicate and perform daily activities of living. The National Head Injury Foundation (NHIF) states that approximately 700,000 Americans suffer head injuries each year, and of these, 10–13% will have injuries so severe that the recovery of a normal life is not possible. The NHIF goes on to state that this group of individuals is underserved, and less than 1% will receive rehabilitation services.

A brain injury includes any internally- or externally-caused trauma to the brain which impairs normal functioning. This includes closed head injuries caused by a quick back and forth "whipped" motion of the brain as in vehicular accidents or the "shaken baby" syndrome, as well as open head injuries where the assault is visible as in gun shot wounds. Other etiologies of brain injuries may include stroke, cardiac arrest, drowning, and other causes due to lack of oxygen to the brain, aneurysms, encephalitis, drug/alcohol abuse, or brain injuries before or during birth resulting in cerebral palsy.

The use of music to aid individuals in their rehabilitation processes has been documented in music therapy and other related literature. Stated goals include remediating speech/language deficits, improving gross and fine motor skills, alleviating depression, and increasing functional skills. Music has also been used to assess, evaluate and more effectively design comprehensive treatment programs.

The purpose of this study was to identify articles which describe the use of music therapy procedures in the treatment of individuals with traumatic brain injuries. This review will focus specifically on (1) music and speech/language rehabilitation, (2) intervention models and program descriptions, and (3) music-based assessment procedures related to traumatic brain injuries.

Method

Computer-assisted searches through databases ERIC, PsychLit, MEDLINE, and *Dissertation Abstracts*, in addition to manual searches through related reference lists were used to develop this literature review. The initial search revealed an extremely small number of articles which specifically addressed the rehabilitative needs of TBI patients (i.e., open- or closed-head injuries) through music therapy procedures. The search parameters were then widened to include selected articles related to the primary focus area. These articles represent a starting point for the development of TBI-specific program models and research topics.

The second search excluded those music therapy articles which examined procedures and outcomes involving, for example, brain-injured individuals whose primary music therapy focus was physical rehabilitation, or those with mental retardation, cerebral palsy, or visual disabilities. They are examined in depth in other literature reviews and will not be covered in this survey. Also not included in this survey will be those articles published before 1970. This body of literature consists largely of case studies and program descriptions and also appears in prior literature reviews (Cohen, 1994; Faiver, 1988) or listed in bibliographies (Galloway, 1975) and will therefore not be summarized here.

Twenty articles which either documented the use of music therapy procedures with brain-injured patients in case or experimental studies, or described specific music-based methodologies or rehabilitative/palliative programs were identified in the second search. Of these, the majority (12) focused on the use of music to assess or improve speech/language skills (see Table 1), while 9 studies described music therapy techniques/program models or assessment techniques.

Data-Based Literature

Speech Rehabilitation and Related Studies

Recovery of full speech functions after an injury to the brain may be a relatively slow process. This is due to the fact that speech is one of the most complex cortical activities (Tobis & Lowenthal, 1960). Apraxia, dysarthria, and aphasia are speech dysfunctions that are caused by brain damage. Apraxia is a disorder which affects the motor memory for speech articulation. A person with verbal apraxia might know what to say but cannot physically produce the correct sounds. Dysarthria, an articulation disorder, involves incoordination of the speech act. Dysarthria results from damage to areas in the brain that regulate speech movements, making it difficult for people with this damage to effectively control the motor movements involved in speech. Aphasia is a language disorder, caused by damage to the left hemisphere of the brain. A person suffering from expressive aphasia has difficulty producing meaningful words, phrases, and sentences. Receptive aphasia is the inability for a person to understand language (Miller, 1982).

Speech Rehabilitation Studies

Cohen (1988) recommended the use of rhythm in the treatment of right-brain injured patients to treat speech rate dysfunctions. Rhythms were implemented to decrease the rate of speech in an 18 year old patient with right-hemispheric damage, which caused dysarthria and Kluver-Bucy Syndrome. Rhythm was used as a monitoring device to slow down the subject's extremely fast

Table 1
Selected Data-based Studies Utilizing Music Therapy Techniques

STUDY	TYPE OF STUDY	DESIGN	SUBJECTS	MUSIC ACTIVITY	RESULTS
1. Albert, Sparks, & Helm (1973)	Descriptive	Case report	N=3; right-handed aphasic adults	MIT	Improved language skills
2. Cohen (1992)	Descriptive	Case studies-Repeated measures	N=8; neurologically impaired adults	Singing instruction	Improvement in some speech skills
3. Cohen (1988)	Descriptive	Case report-Reversal (ABACAC)	N=1; 18 yr. old patient with right hemisphere damage	Rhythmic training	Rate of speech decreased
4. Cohen & Ford (1995)	Experimental	Repeated measures	N=12; aphasic adults	Speech with rhythmic beat and singing	No differences found in speech content or error types; verbal only had highest intelligibility
5. Cohen & Masse (1993)	Experimental	Repeated measures, factorial design	N=32; adults with neurogenic communication disorders	Singing instruction, rhythmic instruction	Rate of speech improved; verbal intelligibility improved
6. Hunter (1989)	Experimental	Statistical	N=80; 40 adults with brain injury, 40 adults with no brain injury	Seashore Rhythm Test; Primary Measure of Music Audiation	Tests were equally effective in differentiating brain injured from nonbrain injured individuals
7. Krauss & Galloway (1982)	Descriptive	Pre- posttest	N=2; aphasic children	MIT	Improvement in some speech skills
9. Laughlin, Naeser, & Gordon (1979)	Experimental	Pre- posttest	N=5; aphasic adults	MIT	Length of syllable is important factor in MIT
10. Naeser & Helm-Estabrooks (1985)	Descriptive	Pre- posttest	N=25; non-fluent aphasic patients	MIT	Subjects with good response to MIT had lesions in Broca's area
11. Oepen & Berthold (1983)	Descriptive	Posttest only	N=34; adults with cerebral lesions	Rhythmic test	Early rhythmic training during rehab to increase motor & speech functions
12. Pirtle & Seaton (1973)	Experimental	Pre-/posttest, Statistical	N=30; neurologically impaired children aged 4-12 yrs.	Listening, moving, dancing, singing, playing instruments	Acquisition of music skills helped to develop communication skills
13. Sparks, Helm & Albert (1974)	Descriptive	Pre-/posttest	N=8; right handed patients with left hemisphere damage	MIT	Improved speech skills

speech. A reversal design (ABACAC) was used to determine effects of the treatment procedure. After a baseline period (A) melody and rhythm were introduced. The patient was asked to sing along with a tape ("Hey Jude" at m.m.=80) and tap the beat on her leg. Treatment C (functional speaking) was introduced after a return to baseline period. During this phase, the subject was asked to repeat sentences that were played on a tape recorder (m.m.=80) while tapping the beat on her leg. Results indicated a decrease of 11% in speech rate from the baseline when the melody and rhythm were used. The use of the rhythm (without melody) with functional speech caused a 28% decrease in the subject's rate of speech from the original baseline. The author cautioned that other variables, such as changes in medications and seizure activity, could have had an effect on the treatment results.

Group singing instruction was used to improve speech production of neurologically impaired persons with expressive speech dysfunctions (Cohen, 1992). A series of single case studies were used to determine the effectiveness of the group singing instruction on the subjects' speaking fundamental frequencies, speaking fundamental frequency variability, vocal intensity, rate of speech or verbal intelligibility. Group singing instruction was held three times per week, 30 minute sessions, for three weeks. Activities during the treatment phase consisted of physical exercises for relaxation purposes, vocal warm-ups and breathing exercises, rhythmic speech drills, and singing familiar songs.

Results indicated improvements in speaking of fundamental frequency variability, rate of speech, and verbal intelligibility. The singing instruction did not seem to affect the speaking fundamental frequency of the subjects.

Cohen and Masse (1993) examined the effects of singing and rhythmic interventions on the speech patterns of neurologically impaired individuals. The authors hypothesized that the singing and rhythmic interventions would improve the subjects' rate of speech, which would cause an improvement in the subjects' verbal intelligibility. They also looked at the influence of age, musical experience prior to the damage to the brain, and the type of neurological impairment on the subjects' speech. The 32 subjects were patients with neurogenic communication disorders residing in a chronic care facility. The subjects were randomly assigned to one of three groups: music therapy rhythmic instruction, music therapy singing instruction, and control group. The music therapy treatment groups met two times per week, in 30-minute sessions, for a total of nine weeks.

Results indicated significant differences between groups on the measure of verbal intelligibility. The singing group made the most progress, followed by the rhythm group. Both treatment groups improved, yet there were no significant differences found in speech rate between groups. The control group maintained a constant rate of speech throughout the study.

Cohen (1994) reviewed published articles that have been written dealing with the therapeutic application of singing to improve communication skills of persons with speech disorders. The author covered areas such as similarities between speech and song, Melodic Intonation Therapy, singing in the treatment of speech disorders in children, and singing in the treatment of speech disorders in persons with neurological impairments. The majority of the articles presented were written about persons with neurological impairments, although other client disabilities included mental retardation, hearing impairment, speech-delays, and children with interdental stigmatism. The author recommended that additional documentation and research be conducted on this topic, as the number of relevant articles per decade has increased minimally since the initial five articles that were published from 1953–1959.

Cohen and Ford (1995) examined the effect of musical cues on the nonpurposive speech of 12 neurologically impaired persons with aphasia. A repeated-measures design was used to determine the differences in the subjects' speech production when asked to produce the words to a familiar song with each of the three experimental conditions: verbal production only (speak the words to the song), verbal production with rhythm (speak the words to the song while listening to the rhythmic beat of a drum), and, verbal production with melody (sing the words to the song while the melody was being played). No significant differences were found between conditions in the subjects' speech content or error types, however, the subjects had significantly higher intelligibility with the verbal production only condition. These results may have been due to the severity of some the subjects' impairment and the short-term nature of the project. The researchers recommended excluding individuals with severe apraxia from future studies of this nature, and extending the project utilizing long-term treatment conditions.

Related Speech Studies

Fifteen children with neurological impairments affecting speech/communication participated in a study by Pirtle and Seaton (1973). The investigators sought to determine if intense music instruction (20" twice weekly for 6 months) in addition to regular classroom music instruction would result not only in musical growth, but in language growth as well. When compared with their controls, the children in the experimental group had significantly increased their scores ($p<.05-.001$) on the measures of intelligence, musical development, vocal integration and verbal comprehension. The control group, which had been continuing with the weekly classroom music group also had significantly increased their scores ($p<.05$) on measures of musical development and verbal comprehension. They concluded that music can help neurologically impaired children develop auditory discrimination, listening and attending skills.

Oepen and Berthold (1983) studied the disturbances of musical functions in 34 patients who had cerebral lesions. Of the 34 subjects, 12 showed right cerebral lesions and 22 showed left cerebral lesions. The examiners found that receptive rhythmic disturbances were found exclusively in the patients having left cerebral lesions. Two thirds of these patients also had motor aphasia. Based on the relationship between rhythmic impairment and motor aphasia, the authors suggested that rhythmic training be applied early in the rehabilitation treatment for these patients. This rhythmic training might include simple motor functions such as walking and tapping, and lead to phonation and articulation exercises in speech therapy. "It is thought that this kind of rhythm training in the sense of training of partial functions would improve the other not-trained functions, as known in mental rehabilitation" (p. 171).

The singing capacity of 24 right handed patients with Broca's aphasia was examined by Yamadori, Osumi, Masuhara, and Okubo (1977). Of the 24 subjects, 21 (87.5%) were able to produce the melody well, and 12 of these (57%) produced some accurate text words while singing. Sixteen of the 21 cases (76.2%) needed some cueing to initiate or to continue their singing. The researchers suggested that the right hemisphere is more responsible for melodic production than the left hemisphere, but the ability to initiate or to continue singing might be more related to left hemisphere functions.

Melodic Intonation Therapy

Melodic Intonation Therapy (MIT) is a structured language rehabilitative program for persons with aphasia. This program, first described by Albert, Sparks, and Helm (1973), uses short phrases and sentences that are embedded into melodic patterns. The phrases are intoned and rhythmically tapped out, syllable by syllable, by the patient and the therapist (Sparks & Holland, 1976). This hierarchical program begins with unison singing of the phrases by the patient and therapist. The successful patient eventually progresses to repetition of the sentence in normal speech prosody. The melodic aspects of the program are faded as the patient's expressive language improves.

Albert, Sparks, and Helm (1973) reported significant improvement in the expressive language ability in three right handed aphasic patients for whom other therapeutic approaches had failed. All three patients had extremely restricted expressive language skills, but had fair to good language comprehension abilities. The authors found that two other patients with severely limited language comprehension did not benefit from MIT.

Sparks, Helm, and Albert (1974) followed a preliminary observation of the effect of MIT on the speech of three aphasic patients with further information about MIT, procedures for facilitation and scoring MIT, and a discussion about candidacy for MIT. Eight right-handed patients who had suffered left hemisphere cerebral vascular accidents were subjects in this study. Six of the eight subjects made improvements in appropriate propositional language after MIT. The authors suggested that some nonlinguistic processing, including some components of melody, may be dominant in the right hemisphere of the brain. "Perhaps the most acceptable hypothesis at this time, then, to account for the efficacy of MIT is that increased use of the right hemispheric dominance for the melodic aspects of speech increases the role of that hemisphere in inter-hemispheric control of language, possibly diminishing the language dominance of the damaged left hemisphere" (pp. 313–314). A patient with a lesion in or around Broca's area might be a good candidate for MIT (Berlin, 1976).

Laughlin, Naeser, and Gordon (1979) investigated the effect of increased syllable duration on the phrase production performance of nonfluent aphasic subjects undergoing MIT. The five subjects were presented with phrases with three syllable durations, including non-intoned durations of less than 1.0 second per syllable, a modified MIT duration of 1.5 seconds per syllable, and a modified MIT duration of 2.0 seconds per syllable. Results indicated the subjects produced the most correct phrases at the longest MIT duration (2.0 seconds) and the least success at the regular non-intoned duration. Researchers determined that length of syllable is a important factor to consider when utilizing MIT techniques with nonfluent aphasic persons.

Naeser and Helm-Estabrooks (1985) investigated the relationship between the location of the lesion and good or poor response to MIT. Subjects with good response to MIT had lesions which involved Broca's area and/or white matter deep to that area and to the lower motor cortex area for the face. These subjects had no large lesions in Wernicke's area, the temporal isthmus, or the right hemisphere. Subjects who had a poor response to MIT had bi-lateral lesions, lesions in Wernicke's area, or lesions in the temporal isthmus. No statistical analysis of the language data was undertaken due to the small sample size.

Krauss and Galloway (1982) were the first to document the use of Melodic Intonation Therapy with language delayed (aphasic) children. Two children, both of whom served as their own control in this study, exhibited language delay and developmental apraxia. The subjects received two months of traditional speech and language therapy followed by two months of Melodic Intonation Therapy as a verbal systemic warm-up. The authors examined pre- and posttest gains in word-morpheme usage, five types of verbal tasks, articulation skills and auditory comprehension. Results of the study indicated significant improvements in phrase length, noun retrieval, and verbal imitation tasks. These findings are similar to previous findings when using Melodic Intonation Therapy with adults.

Some alterations of the Melodic Intonation Therapy protocol were necessary to facilitate the procedure with children for this study. Visual materials were used to cue the children and longer presentation of some materials was helpful in establishing intonation patterns. The authors suggested that therapists make adaptations of the basic Melodic Intonation Therapy adult protocol based on the individual needs of the child receiving the treatment.

Based on the results of this study, in order to be a viable candidate for Melodic Intonation Therapy a child should have fair to good auditory and social skills, a good attention span, and evidence of developmental apraxia. The child also should have already developed language, since Melodic Intonation Therapy is a retrieval and faciliatory vehicle for language.

Experiential Literature

The most relevant and recent literature specifically addressing the use of music in the rehabilitation of persons with TBI is in the form of program models and intervention descriptions. It is this body of literature, along with the previously cited data-based studies, that can provide guidance to clinicians and researchers in the development of more sophisticated treatment protocols and empirically based research.

A music-speech therapy protocol to improve verbalizations in patients with left hemispheric damage was reported by Rogers and Fleming (1981). This five-step progressive technique was developed by a music therapist and was based upon musical and therapeutic principles. The first step involved the use of a familiar carrier melody that could be used for embedding differing phrases. In addition to being a familiar melody, the carrier melody had to have melody, rhythm, and intervals that were as close as possible to conversational speech. "Yankee Doodle" was given as an example of a possible carrier melody. The five therapeutic steps of the program included: (1) teaching the patient to hum or sing the carrier melody; (2) adding phrases to the melody; (3) expanding the phrases to include expression of needs, greetings, etc.; (4) increasing the vocabulary by using a two note pattern; and (5) reducing and eliminating the melodic aspects of the protocol and substituting more complex verbal phrases. The authors found that this technique worked well in settings where groups of patients worked together and in settings where family involvement was encouraged during rehabilitation.

Lucia (1987) described a model of music therapy intervention for aphasic rehabilitation and motor rehabilitation for head trauma patients. A Music Therapy Vocal Skills group was developed to address the area of aphasia rehabilitation. A music therapy assessment which determined preserved music skills and speech communication deficits preceded participation in the group.

Music therapy strategies were chosen to facilitate the use of preserved right brain functions for singing. "The strategy involved a gradual withdrawing of melodic facilitations toward rhythmic chanting and question-answer responses with rhythmic and content structuring. These techniques find support in the earlier reported hypotheses of brain plasticity and the concept of developing new traces in the cerebral structures that increase the probability of the occurrence of subsequent correct verbal behavior" (p. 36).

The format for the Music Therapy Vocal Skills group included upper body relaxation exercises, developed by an occupational therapist, and vocal warm-ups. The vocal warm-ups consisted of diaphragmatic breathing exercises, vocalizing, singing familiar songs, and rhythmic speech drills. Music was also used in this program to enhance motor rehabilitation. The author designed a music-facilitated upper extremity exercise program in conjunction with registered occupational therapists. Music was paired with these exercises. It was hypothesized that the singing of premorbidly learned songs paired with the movement of the exercises might enhance the patients' learning of the desired range of motion patterns. This mnemonic approach was established for the 14 exercises in the series. The exercise series included shoulder exercises, wrist exercises, and neck exercises, all paired with particular songs.

The author noted that while this mnemonic song strategy was useful to some patients, it was confusing to other patients. This strategy was particularly successful with right hemiplegic patients with aphasia. It is likely that this strategy would be most helpful to people with bilateral brain damage or left frontal lobe damage, in which the singing centers of the right temporal lobe are left relatively without damage.

Claeys, Miller, Dalloul-Rampersad, and Kollar (1989) described the role of music and music therapy in a rehabilitation program for persons with traumatic brain injury. A transdisciplinary approach using music and other therapeutic modalities was developed to enhance the treatment program and to address the physical, emotional and spiritual needs of the clients. In this program description, the authors outline specific music therapy interventions according to the clients' classification on the Rancho Los Amigos Levels of Cognitive Functioning Scale. Interventions for clients functioning in the Ranchos levels I–III include stimulus alerting responses, vocalizations, and facial movements. Music is used to enhance exercise routines and to address speech therapy goals for clients functioning in the Ranchos levels IV–VI. Music therapy for clients at the higher levels (VII–VIII) included previously stated goal areas plus expanded interventions to elicit creative expression and socialization. The authors included the Rancho Los Amigos Scale, an adapted Rancho Los Amigos Scale, and a Music Assessment form for use with TBI clients.

Barker and Brunk (1991) described a Creative Arts Therapy Group as part of the treatment for patients with traumatic brain injury. This group was designed and facilitated by an art therapist and a music therapist. Using the media of art and music, the therapists addressed the functional skills of the individual patients. This program focused on helping the patients improve their social skills, in addition to providing the means for emotional outlet through the group activities and processing.

Group activities were divided into five categories: individual processes, partner projects, group efforts, seasonal activities, and community experience. The authors described the structure for a group, including several art and music activities that were utilized. The patients' behaviors and progress were documented using 11 therapist developed scales. Four of these 11 scales were listed in the article: identifies with art, social behavior, use of physical skills, and addresses personal issues.

The authors recommended that this type of group be undertaken jointly with a music therapist and an art therapist, rather than one therapist taking both roles. They also discussed the importance of being flexible with the length of sessions to address the individual needs and functioning levels of the patients.

O'Callaghan (1993) described several music therapy techniques which combined language and music as a way to stimulate neurological pathways of brain-damaged, terminally-ill patients. Musically supported counseling used patient-selected lyrics as an avenue towards self-reflection and exploration of feelings. Reminiscing through the music-based life review process aided patients in affirming and evaluating their life experiences. Musical performance and song writing helped patients increase their sense of achievement through self-expression and communication of feelings to others. Music-based family sessions enabled family members to reminisce and communicate with the patient through shared memories.

Music therapy techniques were used as part of an interdisciplinary treatment approach to promote independence in patients with brain injury (Gervin, 1991). A music therapist and an occupational therapist worked together using song lyrics during dressing to help cue the patient as to the sequence for successful dressing. The music therapist sang individually created lyrics for each patient, while the occupational therapist provided any necessary physical assistance. The goal of this program was to increase the patients' ability to dress independently, as measured by a decrease in the time needed for dressing and a decrease in the amount of caregiver involvement. This compensatory technique utilizing song lyrics was used until the patients' cognitive skills improved and was able to recall the sequential steps required for dressing.

The author gave two case examples of patient applications. Both patients were able to successfully use this procedure, and make gains in their abilities to dress independently. Patients who had deficits in initiation, sequencing, motor planning, and problem solving benefited the most using this procedure. This procedure was recommended for patients who function within levels IV and V of the Rancho Los Amigos Levels of Cognitive Functioning scale. At this level, a person needs some degree of assistance to perform self-care activities. Persons who exhibit noncompliant behavior or who have severe physical limitations would likely not benefit from this compensatory technique.

Goldberg, Hoss, and Chesna (1988) utilized music and imagery in psychotherapy to help a woman with brain damage work through her issues in the treatment of depression. An adapted form of Guided Imagery and Music was used to treat the patient's depression and emotional lability. The authors found that the patient did engage with the music and imagery, and was able to work throughout some personal issues. Although the long-term effects of this procedure are unknown, this case suggested that the use of music and imagery may be a viable approach in the psychotherapeutic treatment of individuals with brain damage.

Assessment

Hunter (1989) examined and compared the *Seashore Rhythm Test* (SRT) and the *Primary Measures of Music Audiation* (PMMA) as assessment tools in the measurement of auditory discrimination of brain-injured patients. Forty individuals with traumatic brain injuries were paired with 40 normal controls. Etiologies included blows to the head from falls or motor vehicle accidents. He found that both the SRT and the PMMA were equally effective in differentiating between brain- and nonbrain-injured patients. He did find, however, that the PMMA had a higher reliability than the SRT. Other factors cited which may or may not be influential in choosing one test over the other were cost, test length, and quality of the accompanying sound recordings.

A music therapy assessment for use with cerebrovascular accident patients was developed by Thompson, Arnold, and Murray (1990). This assessment was developed in collaboration with an occupational therapist, a physical therapist, and a neurologist. The authors suggested the importance of working with team members to develop a more comprehensive treatment approach. The assessment is organized into five domains: cognitive, motor, communication, social, and visual. The five domains are divided into subtest areas and are sequenced according to levels of functioning.

Music techniques are utilized throughout the assessment. These techniques involve activities such as naming instruments, discrimination of melodic and rhythmic patterns and use of keyboard and rhythm instruments. Music techniques are used extensively for assessment of the motor domain, and to a lesser extent, for assessment of the cognitive domain. In addition, non-music activities which can be easily facilitated by the music therapist are used throughout this assessment for all five domains.

The authors found that music can be interesting and motivating to the patient, which may result in an increased level of recovery. It may be necessary for individual music therapists to adapt some of the procedures of this assessment based on the needs and abilities of the individual patient.

Conclusion

The use of music therapy in the rehabilitation of patients with brain injuries can be effective in treatment of speech dysfunctions, the retraining of activities of daily living, and in the processing of social and emotional issues. Sacks and Tomaino (1991) state that damage to the nervous system's "internal natural music" can be transformed by external music.

The type and small number of articles describing music therapy procedures with traumatically brain-injured patients indicates its preliminary nature. The six articles directly related to music therapy with TBI patients as defined in this review are literature reviews and program descriptions (Barker & Brunk, 1991; Claeys, Miller, Dalloul-Rampersad, & Kollar, 1989; Faiver, 1988; Gervin, 1991; Lucia, 1987) and one assessment (Hunter, 1989).

The remaining literature reviewed consists of descriptive and experimental studies whose subjects include specified or unspecified brain impairments, including cerebrovascular accidents and neurological disorders and whose findings may (or may not) be generalized to the TBI population. That the largest body of data-based literature (Melodic Intonation Therapy) was developed by non-music therapists and for the most part published in sources not readily available to music therapists also underlines the need for the development of a solid research foundation in this area.

Individuals with traumatic brain injuries constitute an underserved population needing rehabilitative services that address the cognitive, communication, physical, social, and/or emotional changes that may accompany even mild head injuries. The sheer number of individuals suffering from traumatic brain injuries makes more urgent the need for empirically-based, well-designed studies that examine the efficacy of music therapy with this population.

References

Albert, M., Sparks, R., & Helm, N. (1973). Melodic intonation therapy for aphasics. *Archives of Neurology, 29*, 130–131.

Barker, V. L., & Brunk, B. (1991). The role of a creative arts group in the treatment of clients with traumatic brain injury. *Music Therapy Perspectives, 9*, 26–31.

Berlin, C. I. (1976). On: Melodic intonation therapy for aphasia by R. W. Sparks and A. L. Holland. *Journal of Speech and Hearing Disorders, 41*, 298–300.

Claeys, M. S., Miller, A. C., Dalloul-Rampersad, R., & Kollar, M. (1989). The role of music and music therapy in the rehabilitation of traumatically brain injured clients. *Music Therapy Perspectives, 6*, 71–77.

Cohen, N. (1988). The use of superimposed rhythm to decrease the rate of speech in a brain-damaged adolescent. *Journal of Music Therapy, 25*, 85–93.

Cohen, N. (1992). The effect of singing instruction on the speech production of neurologically impaired persons. *Journal of Music Therapy, 29*, 87–102.

Cohen, N. (1994). Speech and song: Implications for therapy. *Music Therapy Perspectives, 12*, 8–14.

Cohen, N., & Ford, J. (1995). The effect of musical cues on the nonpurposive speech of persons with aphasia. *Journal of Music Therapy, 32*, 46–57.

Cohen, N., & Masse, R. (1993). The application of singing and rhythmic instruction as a therapeutic intervention for persons with neurogenic communication disorders. *Journal of Music Therapy, 30*, 81–89.

Faiver, R. (1988). *Music therapy in rehabilitation of traumatically brain injured persons: Proposal for the application of an ecological model for therapeutic intervention.* Unpublished Master's Thesis, Michigan State University.

Galloway, H. (1975). A comprehensive bibliography of musical studies referential to communication development, processing disorders and remediation. *Journal of Music Therapy, 12*, 164–197.

Gervin, A. P. (1991). Music therapy compensatory technique utilizing song lyrics during dressing to promote independence in the patient with a brain injury. *Music Therapy Perspectives, 9*, 87–90.

Goldberg, F. S., Hoss, T. M., & Chesna, T. (1988). Music and imagery as psychotherapy with a brain damaged patient: A case study. *Music Therapy Perspectives, 5*, 41–45.

Hunter, B. C. (1989). *A comparison of the* Seashore Rhythm Test *and the* Primary Measures of Music Audiation *for auditory discrimination in traumatic brain-injured patients.* Unpublished dissertation, The University of Kansas, Lawrence.

Krauss, T., & Galloway, H. (1982). Melodic intonation therapy with language-delayed, apraxic children. *Journal of Music Therapy, 19*, 102–113.

Laughlin, S. A., Naeser, M. A., & Gordon, W. P. (1979). Effects of three syllable durations using the melodic intonation therapy technique. *Journal of Speech and Hearing Research, 22*, 311–320.

Lucia, C. (1987). Toward developing a model of music therapy intervention in the rehabilitation of head trauma patients. *Music Therapy Perspectives, 4*, 34–39.

Miller, S. (1982). Music therapy for handicapped children: Speech impaired (pp. 115–154). *Project Monograph Series*. Washington, DC: National Association for Music Therapy, Inc.

Naeser, M. A., & Helm-Estabrooks, N. (1985). CT scan lesion localization and response to melodic intonation therapy with nonfluent aphasia cases. *Cortex, 21*, 203–223.

O'Callaghan, C. C. (1993). Communicating with brain-injured palliative care patients through music therapy. *Journal of Palliative Care, 9*, 53–55.

Oepen, G., & Berthold, H. (1983). Rhythm as an essential part of music and speech abilities: Conclusions of a clinical experimental study in 34 patients. *Neurologie-et-Psychiatrie, 21*, 168–172.

Pirtle, M., & Seaton, K. (1973). Use of music training to activate conceptual growth in neurologically handicapped children. *Journal of Research in Music Education, 21*, 292–301.

Rogers, G. P., & Fleming, P. (1981). Rhythms and music in speech therapy for the neurologically impaired. *Music Therapy, 1*, 33–38.

Sacks, O., & Tomaino, C. (1991). Music and neurological disorder. *International Journal of Arts Medicine, 1*, 10–12.

Sparks, R., Helm, N., & Albert, M. (1974). Aphasia rehabilitation resulting from melodic intonation therapy. *Cortex, 10*, 313–316.

Sparks, R., & Holland, A. (1976). Method: Melodic intonation therapy for aphasia. *Journal of Speech and Hearing Disorders, 41*, 287–297.

Thompson, A., Arnold, J., & Murray, S. (1990). Music therapy assessment of the cerebrovascular accident patient. *Music Therapy Perspectives, 8*, 23–29.

Tobis, J., & Lowenthal, M. (1960). *Evaluation and management of a brain-damaged patient*. Springfield, IL: Charles C. Thomas.

Yamadori, A., Osumi, Y., Masuhara, S., & Okubo, M. (1977). Preservation of singing in Broca's aphasia. *Journal of Neurology, Neurosurgery and Psychiatry, 40*, 221–224.

USES OF MUSIC THERAPY
WITH MENTAL RETARDATION:
AN UPDATE OF A PREVIOUS ANALYSIS

Charles E. Furman
Amelia G. Furman

O VER the past two decades in the United States, there have been dramatic changes in the focus of services and in the settings where those services take place, for people with mental retardation. There have long been references throughout history to those who did not fit in due to lesser mental ability. The view that mentally retarded citizens were unable to look after their own affairs or to plan for their own futures prevailed until well into the early 1900s (Robinson & Robinson, 1976). In the mid-1900s it was recognized that retarded citizens could, to a certain degree, live fulfilling lives, make some of their important life decisions independently, and certainly live outside of institutions. The expectation today is that supportive services are provided to promote the acquisition of adaptive skills which will prepare individuals to live in the community within the limits of their handicapping conditions. Since the majority of people specified as mentally retarded fall into the range known as mild mental retardation, most retarded citizens live in homes, group homes or apartments with a prescribed level of assistance.

About Labels

One commonly used definition of retardation states that mental retardation refers to "significantly sub-average general intellectual functioning" existing concurrently with deficits in adaptive behavior and manifested during the developmental period before age 18. Retardation most often occurs accompanied by secondary handicapping conditions such as physical disabilities. There are varying degrees of mental retardation (MR), generally divided into categories based on intelligence test scores, which have an average score of 100 and a standard deviation of 15 or 16. Carter (1984) and many others have discussed these categories at length and they describe the population roughly as follows: (a) borderline retardation: 70–80; (b) mild or educable (EMR): 55–69; (c) moderate or trainable (TMR): 40–54; and (d) S/PMR: severe (25–39) and profound (below 25). Of note is that the I.Q. tests generally yield higher test-retest reliability at scores closer to the mean. That is, the lower the I.Q. score or the "more retarded" the individual, the greater the variability in the actual scores yielded when the assessment is completed by several psychologists. To differentiate *on the basis of scores alone*, then, between a moderately retarded client scoring, for instance, a 41 and a severely retarded client scoring a 38, becomes an arguable point. Intricacies of funding often require these categorical labels but the realities of planning therapeutic intervention usually involve the systematic observation (Madsen, 1981) of the impaired and nonimpaired behaviors of the clients to be served.

The estimated incidence rate for mental retardation is 3% of the population. While only 25% of the cases of mental retardation can be traced to specific biological causes, the ability of technology to pinpoint specific syndromes, such as Down Syndrome, has risen steadily since 1965.

With the movement toward deinstitutionalization during the 1980s, many more retarded citizens now live in semi-independent group homes/apartments within the community at large than ever before. The relatively few retarded clients remaining in institutions are mostly adults (78%) and are mostly functioning at the severe or profound levels (Hauber, Bruininks, Hill, Lakin, & White, 1982). This institutionalized population now largely represents clients having major treatment needs, often with a secondary diagnosis such as a behavior disorder, psychiatric condition or physical disability (Coates, 1987).

The majority of individuals having mental retardation fall into the range of mild mental retardation. Most of the special educational services provided for these people are administrated by the public schools. Federal law mandates equal education for the disabled, from age zero until the age of 21, which includes those having retardation. Since music is among the reinforcers found to be effective with this population, music therapy is one of the adjunctive services sometimes provided within a school program.

Method and Results

A survey of literature published in the last 25 years, 1970–1995, involving music and mental retardation was undertaken, with a manual library search and computer-assisted searches occurring concurrently. Most of the studies prior to 1970 were case studies/testimonials and frequently were the impetus for the more extensive and better controlled studies appearing later. The early studies and their respective methodologies often appear in the literature reviews and reference lists of the later articles and therefore details are not included in this chapter.

Of the more recent studies, those which tested or documented the results of music therapy procedures are listed in Table 1. An analysis including the target behaviors and the specific music techniques is shown later in Tables 2 and 3, respectively. These studies are hereafter referred to as Music Therapy Studies; music therapy procedures were employed with MR client(s) to affect behavior(s) which was/were ultimately nonmusic behaviors.

Other studies, while addressing music and/or retardation in some way, were not primarily concerned with music therapy issues, per se. Instead, these articles: offered advice on "how to" handle this particular population within the music therapy session; described the actual musical abilities and musical development of MR clients as compared with nonhandicapped peers; and advocated special music education for individuals having MR. These articles are hereafter referred to as Music Therapy-Related Articles. It is emphatically noted here that the development of actual musical skills in MR clients is very important and is often addressed by music therapists, but usually as a secondary concern. Since Music Educators National Conference officially declares "music for *every* child" as a goal within its mission statement and PL 94–142 absolutely mandates equal educational opportunity for the handicapped, music therapists are more frequently called upon to address music goals within IEP's or to act in a consulting role (Furman & Steele, 1982)

Table 1
Selected Data-based Studies Employing Music Therapy Procedures

Study	N	Design	Dependent Measure	Music Activity	Independent Variable
Allen & Bryant (1985)	2	multi-element	crying, sitting	I L	CM
Ayres (1987)	5	Pre/post	feeding time	G L	MB
Barmann, Croyle-Barmann, & McLain (1980)	1	Reversal	social skills	I L	CM
Becker (1983)	1	ABACAB	eye contact	I L	CM/DM
Bellamy & Sontag (1973)	4;7	Reversal	assembly	G L	CM
Bornstein & Smith (1976)	1	Reversal	self-stimulation	I L	CM
Borreson & Anderson (1982)	1	Case report	rumination	I L	CM
Cass (1975)	39	Reversal	assembly rate	G L	MB
Cassity (1978)	27	Statistical	social behaviors	G P	P
Cook & Freethy (1973)	1	AB	complaining	I P	CM
Cunningham (1986)	20	ABACACAB	vocalizations	G L	MB
Davis, Brady, Williams, & Burta (1992)	3	Multiple baseline	Vocational tasks	I L	MB, ME
Davis, Wiescler, & Hanzel (1983)	1	Multiple baseline	out-of-seat; rumination	I L	CM/VC
Decuir (1975)	16	Statistical	vocalizations	I P	ME
Dileo (1975)	16	Statistical	social behaviors	I P	MTE
Dorow (1975)	3	Multiple baseline	imitation	I L	MSR
Dorow (1976)	17	Reversal	math problems	I L	CM
Dorow & Horton (1982)	4;4	Reversal	activity levels	I L	MB

Table 1
Continued

Study	N	Design	Dependent Measure	Music Activity	Independent Variable
Ford & Veltri-Ford (1980)	2	Multiple baseline	social skills	I L	CM
Grant & LeCroy (1986)	30	Statistical	imitation	I L P	ME
Greenwald (1978)	4	AA'BAA'C	self-stimulation	I L	CM/DM
Gregoire (1984)	17	2 group AB/BA	number matching	I G L	ME
Groeneweg et al. (1988)	12	Repeated measures	sorting	G L	MB
Hill, Brantner, & Spreat (1989)	1	Reversal	sitting	I L	CM
Holloway (1980)	8	Multiple baseline	motor skills	I L P	CM
Humphrey (1980)	30	Statistical	auditory discrimination	I L	ME
James, Weaver, Clemens, & Plaster (1985)	24	Pre/post	motor skills	I L	ME
Johnson & Zinner (1974)	2	Reversal	color discrimination	I P	CM/P
Jorgenson (1974)	1	Multiple baseline	social behaviors	I L	CM
Jorgenson & Parnell (1970)	4	Reversal	social behaviors	G L	CM/MTE
Karper (1979)	71	Statistical	motor skills	G L	MB
Kaufman & Sheckart (1985)	20	Repeated measures	activity levels	I L	MB
Macurik (1979)	3	Reversal	posture	I L	CM
McClure et al. (1986)	1	Multiple baseline	self-stimulation	I L	CM

Table 1
Continued

Study	N	Design	Dependent Measure	Music Activity	Independent Variable
Metzler (1974)	30	Statistical	imitation	I G L	CM
Moore & Mathenius (1987)	8	Statistical	motor skills	I L P	ME
Myers (1979)	18	Statistical	recall	I L	ME
Reid, Hill, Rawers, & Montegar (1975)	1	Multiple baseline/ Reversal	social behaviors	I L	CM
Richman (1976)	30	Reversal	motor skills	I L	CM
Saperston (1973)	1	Case review	complaining	I P	P
Saperston, Chan, Morphew, & Carlsrud (1980)	16	Reversal	motor skills	I L	CM
Silliman & French (1993)	15	AB with control gr.	kicking task	I L	CM
Spencer (1988)	27	Pre/posttest with control	direction following	G P	ME
Tallon & Stangl (1980)	4	Reversal	self-stimulation	I L	MB
Tierney, McGuire, & Walton (1978)	12	Reversal	self-stimulation	G L	MB
Underhill & Harris (1974)	4	Reversal	imitation	I L	CM
Walker (1972)	6	2 groups	verbalizations	G L P	CM
Wentworth (1991)	25	Repeated measures	vocational task	G L	MB
Wylie (1983)	28	Statistical	vocalizations	I L P	ME

Music Activity: I = individual, G = group, L = listening, P = performing.
Variables: CM = contingent music, DM = distorted music, MB = music as background, ME = music as elicitor, MSR = music as secondary (conditioned) reinforcer, MTE = music in a token economy, P = performing, PS = physical stimulation, VC = verbal cue.

with music educators who may be less familiar with the additional considerations necessary when teaching music to MR students.

Music Therapy-Related Articles

The singing ranges of MR clients have been described in several articles (Dileo, 1976; Grant & Share, 1985; Larson, 1977; Myers, 1985). In general, the MR clients tested evidenced lower and narrower vocal ranges than their nonhandicapped counterparts. Larson (1977) also compared the ranges of published songbooks with the vocal ranges of the MR clients and found the songbooks to be pitched higher than the actual midpoint of the MR singers' ranges.

Several writers described successes with the implementation of various music courses for MR students. Methods and materials were described for presenting guitar (Cassity, 1977), piano (Silini, 1979), music enrichment (Wingert, 1972), rhythm bands (Wolpow, 1976) and handbells (Rubin, 1976). Wolpow (1976) detailed the addition of social approval in order to enhance the musical performance of his group of MR performers.

Aural perception of MR children has been described by Flowers (1984) and Lienhard (1976); Rider (1977) documented a significant and positive correlation between auditory and visual perception when 40 developmentally disabled subjects were tested. The verbal responses of 44 MR clients to music have been explored (Bokor, 1976); verbal responses have also been compared with nonhandicapped subjects (Hair & Graham, 1983; Jellison & Flowers, 1991). Hair and Graham found that, for the most part, the MR participants did not lack the vocabulary with which to describe musical events, but rather they failed to use the terms appropriately. Several other studies provided guidelines and described technology by which other general music-related skills could be evaluated or assessed (DiGiammarino, 1990; Hasselbring & Duffus, 1981; Jones, 1986; Wasserman, Plutchik, Deutsch, & Taketomo, 1973).

Specific approaches and techniques for use with MR clients within the music therapy setting have been suggested by various authors. The techniques presented included the application of: behavioral research techniques (Steele, 1977), the Premack principle (Talkington & Hall, 1970), an integrated "personified" approach (Stubbs, 1970), an integrated play therapy approach (Moreno, 1985), an integrated dance therapy approach (Bornell, 1984), an integrated day treatment approach (Wolfgram, 1978), and the Orff-Schulwerk approach (Ponath & Bitcon, 1972). Heyer, Downs, Kallay, and Magdinac (1986) described an approach whereby MR clients were prepared for audiology screening by preconditioning with music.

The effects of mainstreaming, which is one of the outcomes of the implementation of PL 94–142, have also been studied. Force (1983) examined the effects of mainstreaming on the nonretarded children in an elementary music class; Jellison, Brooks, and Huck (1984) observed the interactions and acceptance of handicapped students in an otherwise regular music classroom. Jellison and Duke (1994), in surveying music teachers and prospective music teachers, found them accepting of students with mental retardation. Both groups indicated a willingness to teach both social and music behaviors to such a student.

Music Therapy Studies

By far, the most frequently used music therapy procedure documented in the music therapy studies was that of contingent music. Usually, the contingent music activity, such as music listening, is awarded immediately following a desired response; this is often combined with the immediate withdrawal of the ongoing music activity when an undesired or inappropriate response occurs. In all but five of the studies which utilized contingent music, marked success was noted.

Allen and Bryant (1985) found that a contingent-interrupted music procedure was more effective than a contingent music procedure alone in reducing crying and increasing proper sitting behaviors in two MR children. A contingent-interrupted music procedure was also employed to decrease disruptions during bus-riding of an 8-year-old PMR girl (Barmann, Croyle-Barmann, & McLain, 1980). Contingent music was also successfully used to increase correct head posturing of three SMR clients (Macurik, 1979), to increase intelligible speech (Walker, 1972), and to increase assembly line production (Bellamy & Sontag, 1973).

Holloway (1980) used both active (playing instruments) contingent music and passive (listening) contingent music to increase preacademic skills of eight MR clients. Other preacademic skills improved by using contingent music activities include imitation (Underhill & Harris, 1974) and reaching/touching (Saperston, Chan, Morphew, & Carlsrud, 1980). Dorow (1976) demonstrated the effectiveness of contingent televised music lessons as reinforcement for correct mathematical responses of 17 EMR subjects.

Frequent goals for MR clients are the improving of socials skills and the elimination of self-stimulatory behaviors. Cook and Freethy (1973) used contingent hymn playing to eliminate complaining behavior of a single client. Becker (1983) used contingent distorted and undistorted music to shape eye contact. Appropriate walking and car-riding (Reid, Hill, Rawers, & Montegar, 1975) and appropriate participation and initiation (Jorgenson & Parnell, 1970) were all increased with the implementation of contingent music procedures. Rumination (Davis, Wieseler, & Hanzel, 1983), rocking (Steele & Jorgenson, 1971) and other stereotyped behaviors (Ford & Veltri-Ford, 1980; Jorgenson, 1974) were also successfully decreased with the implementation of contingent music procedures.

It is noteworthy that the five studies having equivocal results using a contingent music procedure (Bornstein & Smith, 1976; Borreson & Anderson, 1982; Greenwald, 1978; Metzler, 1974; Richman, 1976) have in common the severe/profound MR population. All authors commented that the low rate and inconsistency of responding by the subjects made implementation especially difficult and that it is not clear whether extremely low level MR clients are capable of comprehending the contingency being employed.

The use of music as background has been tested by many experimenters. This use of music was the second most frequent method tested in the studies listed in Table 1. We note that adding music to the environment represents probably the most passive use of music in therapy. The sound is not used contingently; rather, music is played and client behavior is observed independently. Given the characteristics of this population, that the immediacy of feedback and the repetition of new tasks are crucial, it is not surprising that mixed effectiveness has been reported. Ayres (1987) compared feeding times in a school cafeteria under differing sound environments and found that music was effective in reducing some of the difficulties of therapeutic feeding. Cunningham (1986) found differences in vocalizations when volume of background music was changed during group free discussion time; soft music yielded higher frequency in verbal interchange. Volume as well as proximity of auditory stimuli were shown to affect activity levels of eight clients in two experiments, though the changes were consistent within each subject but not across the group (Dorow & Horton, 1982). Auditory stimulation was paired with vestibular stimulation and the procedure produced significant gains in specified motor

Table 2

Studies Shown by Targeted Behaviors (Dependent Measures)

Dependent Variable	Studies
Social behaviors and eye contact	Barmann, Croyle-Barmann, & McLain, 1980
	Becker, 1983
	Cassity, 1978
	Davis, Wiesler, & Hanzel, 1983
	Dileo, 1975
	Ford & Veltri-Ford, 1980
	Jorgenson, 1974
	Jorgenson & Parnell, 1970
	Reid, Hill, Rawers, & Montegar, 1975
	Spencer, 1988
Self-stimulation and rumination	Bornstein & Smith, 1976
	Borreson & Anderson, 1982
	Davis, Wieseler, & Hanzel, 1983
	Greenwald, 1978
	McClure et al., 1986
	Steele & Jorgenson, 1971
	Tallon & Stangl, 1980
	Tierney, McGuire, & Walton, 1978
Motor skills	Holloway, 1980
	James, Weaver, Clemens, & Plaster, 1985
	Karper, 1979
	Moore & Mathenius, 1987
	Richman, 1976
	Saperston, Chan, Morphew, & Carlsrud, 1980
	Silliman & French, 1993
Activity levels/Assembly rate	Bellamy & Sontag, 1973
	Cass, 1975
	Davis, Brady, Williams, & Burta, 1992
	Dorow & Horton, 1982
	Kaufman & Sheckart, 1985
	Wentworth, 1991

Table 2
Continued

Dependent Variable	Studies
Verbalizing/Vocalizing	Cunningham, 1986
	Decuir, 1975
	Walker, 1972
	Wylie, 1983
Imitation	Dorow, 1975
	Grant & LeCroy, 1986
	Metzler, 1974
	Underhill & Harris, 1974
Discrimination	Humphrey, 1980
	Groeneweg et al., 1988
	Johnson & Zinner, 1974
Sitting, posture	Allen & Bryant, 1985
	Hill, Brantner, & Spreat, 1989
	Macurik, 1979
Complaining	Cook & Freethy, 1973
	Saperston, 1973
Math	Dorow, 1976
	Gregoire, 1984
Feeding time	Ayres, 1987
Crying	Allen & Bryant, 1985
Recall	Myers, 1979

Table 3
How Music Was Used in the Studies

Independent Variable	Studies
Contingent music	Allen & Bryant, 1985
	Barmann, Croyle-Barmann, & McLain, 1980
	Becker, 1983
	Bellamy & Sontag, 1973
	Bornstein & Smith, 1976
	Borreson & Anderson, 1982
	Cook & Freethy, 1973
	Davis, Wieseler, & Hanzel, 1983
	Dorow, 1976
	Ford & Veltri-Ford, 1980
	Greenwald, 1978
	Hill, Brantner, & Spreat, 1989
	Holloway, 1980
	Johnson & Zinner, 1974
	Jorgenson, 1974
	Jorgenson & Parnell, 1970
	Macurik, 1979
	McClure et al., 1986
	Metzler, 1974
	Reid, Hill, Rawers, & Montegar, 1975
	Richman, 1976
	Saperston, Chan, Morphew, & Carlsrud, 1980
	Silliman & French, 1993
	Steele & Jorgenson, 1971
	Underhill & Harris, 1974
	Walker, 1972
Music as background	Ayres, 1987
	Cass, 1975
	Cunningham, 1986
	Dorow & Horton, 1982
	Groeneweg et al., 1988
	James, Weaver, Clemens, & Plaster, 1985
	Karper, 1979
	Kaufman & Sheckart, 1985
	Richman, 1976
	Tallon & Stangl, 1980
	Tierney, McGuire, & Walton, 1978
	Wentworth, 1991

Table 3
Continued

Independent Variable	Studies
Music to elicit specified response	Davis, Brady, Williams, & Burta, 1992
	Decuir, 1975
	Grant & LeCroy, 1986
	Gregoire, 1984
	Humphrey, 1980
	Moore & Mathenius, 1987
	Myers, 1979
	Spencer, 1988
	Wylie, 1983
Performing/Leisure skill	Cass, 1975
	Cassity, 1978
	Johnson & Zinner, 1974
	Saperston, 1973
Music as secondary reinforcer	Dileo, 1975
	Dorow, 1975
	Jorgenson & Parnell, 1970
Distorted music	Becker, 1983
	Greenwald, 1978
With physical stimulation	James, Weaver, Clemens, & Plaster, 1985
With verbal cue	Davis, Wieseler, & Hanzel, 1983

skills of 24 subjects (James, Weaver, Clemens, & Plaster, 1985). Background music did not significantly produce a desired change in general activity level of PMR's (Kaufman & Sheckart, 1985), a reduction of self-stimulatory behavior of PMR clients (Tallon & Stangl, 1980; Tierney, McGuire, & Walton, 1978), or facilitation of repetitive motor skill performance such as might occur in a workshop setting (Cass, 1975; Karper, 1979; Richman, 1976). Vibrotactile stimulation paired with music via the Somatron® bed yielded small changes in levels of vocalization and in deep inhalation (Pujol, 1994). Similar to those studies reporting equivocal results with contingent music, the less effective studies employing background music as the tested procedure also largely had SMR or PMR clients as participants.

Music performance seemed to produce desirable changes in social skills in two studies. Saperston (1973) used music performance as an effective reinforcer in eliminating complaining behavior, including the client in defining and structuring a contract to facilitate treatment. Cassity (1978) indicated that performers scored higher on several social skills measures than their nonperforming counterparts; music performers were also compared with athletic performers. In a third study, Johnson and Zinner (1974) used music performance (bell-ringing) in a reversal and fading procedure with a color discrimination task which yielded substantial and positive changes but nonsignificance.

The effectiveness with which music functions to improve behavior seems directly related to its reinforcing properties, which seem to differ not only by level of retardation (results with S/PMR's are the least consistent) but also by individual reinforcement history, as one would expect in the normal population. Dileo (1975) successfully demonstrated reinforcing effects when music activities were used as backup reinforcers in a token economy with 16 MR clients working on social skills. Dorow (1975) showed overall increases in imitative behaviors when music was conditioned as a secondary reinforcer and paired with verbal approvals in 3 MR subjects.

Many therapists acknowledge using music activities as an effective and engaging means simply to elicit the behaviors targeted for shaping or for increase. Several experimenters have reported results associated with this use of music. Decuir (1975) and Wylie (1983) studied the effects of several instruments and vocal ensembles as stimuli for eliciting vocal responses in MR clients. Piano, and vocal ensemble and piano, were most effective respectively in eliciting highest duration of vocal responses in the two studies. Grant and LeCroy (1986) examined the pairing of tactile and visual stimuli with auditory stimuli to produce rhythmic imitation. Moore and Mathenius (1987) included modeling and tempo in their considerations for using music to elicit movement responses. Less promising results were obtained when music was used to affect recall in a paired-associate task (Myers, 1979), number matching (Gregoire, 1984), and auditory discrimination within an ear training task (Humphrey, 1980). In 1990, Hairston reported that retarded nonautistic children made greater developmental gains than autistic retarded children using both music therapy and art therapy over a 5-week treatment period.

Discussion

The reinforcing value of music has been demonstrated in a variety of music therapy studies. However, it is noted that the results of some studies seem directly related to the level of mental retardation and the number of actual therapy sessions. Music is not universally reinforcing, especially with severely and profoundly retarded individuals (Hanser, 1983). Music preference must be given the same or greater consideration as would be given the normal population when therapeutic interventions are devised and research studies are designed.

While there is an obvious need for replications of these music and MR studies, music therapists must also be prepared to move on to more sophisticated research as well. In addition to overall effectiveness, the optimum size of the music therapy group within which to achieve the greatest change, for instance, will be critical information for the determination and improvement of cost effectiveness.

Looking Ahead

The demographics of the mentally retarded population continue to change. We note that the developmentally disabled and the elderly populations continue to top the list of employment opportunities for music therapists nationwide. The national trends toward decentralization will undoubtedly dictate the provision of services as part of a community-based plan. It is rare today for mentally retarded persons to remain institutionalized throughout their lifetime. As Coates (1987) predicted, therapists are now expected to justify their treatment goals in terms of "ultimate goals." There is a greater push toward truly functional skills, even without all the desirable prerequisites, which will be ready for immediate in-community use. Our advances in medicine and technology also mean that we will continue to serve more clients at both extremes of the age continuum. Music therapy programs focusing on early intervention and on the elderly MR client will become more numerous as life expectancy increases. Music skills, for their own sake, are taking on greater importance as we search for appropriate and dignified leisure time activities which are immediately usable in the community.

As we face the 21st century, the music therapy profession must maintain its strong data base, which is more present in some areas of MR study than in others. Calculating the amount of desirable change, over time, with the MR population will not only enhance the accountability of the profession, but will provide information with which cost effectiveness can be determined and music therapy services can be provided.

References

Allen, L. D., & Bryant, M. C. (1985). A multielement analysis of contingent versus contingent-interrupted music. *Applied Research in Mental Retardation, 6,* 87–97.

Ayres, B. R. (1987). The effects of a music stimulus environment versus regular cafeteria environment during therapeutic feeding. *Journal of Music Therapy, 24,* 14–26.

Barmann, B. D., Croyle-Barmann, C., & McLain, B. (1980). The use of contingent-interrupted music in the treatment of disruptive bus-riding behavior. *Journal of Applied Behavior Analysis, 13,* 693–698.

Becker, I. L. (1983). Control of acquisition of eye contact by distorted and undistorted music stimuli. *Journal of Music Therapy, 20,* 132–142.

Bellamy, T., & Sontag, E. (1973). Use of group contingent music to increase assembly line production rates of retarded students in a simulated skilled workshop. *Journal of Music Therapy, 10,* 125–136.

Bokor, C. R. (1976). A comparison of musical and verbal responses of mentally retarded children. *Journal of Music Therapy, 13,* 101–108.

Bornell, D. G. (1984). Movement is individuality: An interabilities approach using dance taps. *Music Therapy, 4,* 98–105.

Bornstein, E., & Smith, D. W. (1976). Effect of visual and auditory stimuli on self-stimulatory behavior: A case study. *Research and the Retarded, 3,* 40–44.

Borreson, P. M., & Anderson, J. L. (1982). The elimination of chronic rumination through a combination of procedures. *Mental Retardation, 20*, 34–38.

Carter, S. A. (1984). Music therapy for mentally retarded children. In C. T. Eagle, Jr., & W. B. Lathom (Eds.), *Music therapy for handicapped children* (pp. 63–114). Lawrence, KS: AMS.

Cass, M. (1975). The effects of music on retarded individuals in a workshop setting. *Research and the Retarded, 2*, 18–23.

Cassity, M. D. (1977). Nontraditional guitar techniques for educable and trainable mentally retarded residents in music therapy activities. *Journal of Music Therapy, 14*, 39–42.

Cassity, M. D. (1978). Social development of TMR's involved in performing and nonperforming groups. *Journal of Music Therapy, 15*, 100–105.

Coates, P. (1987). "Is it functional?" A question for music therapists who work with the institutionalized mentally retarded. *Journal of Music Therapy, 24*, 170–175.

Cook, M., & Freethy, M. (1973). The use of music as a positive reinforcer to eliminate complaining behavior. *Journal of Music Therapy, 10*, 213–216.

Cunningham, T. D. (1986). The effect of music volume on the frequency of vocalizations of institutionalized mentally retarded persons. *Journal of Music Therapy, 23*, 208–218.

Davis, C., Brady, M., Williams, R., & Burta, M. (1992). The effects of self-operated auditory prompting tapes on the performance fluency of persons with severe mental retardation. *Education and Training in Mental Retardation, 27*, 39–50.

Davis, W. B., Wieseler, N. A., & Hanzel, T. E. (1983). Reduction of rumination and out-of-seat behavior and generalization of treatment effects using a non-intrusive method. *Journal of Music Therapy, 20*, 115–131.

Decuir, A. A. (1975). Vocal responses of mentally retarded subjects to four musical instruments. *Journal of Music Therapy, 12*, 40–43.

DiGiammarino, M. (1990). Functional music skills of persons with mental retardation. *Journal of Music Therapy, 27*, 209–220.

Dileo, C. L. (1976). The relationship of diagnostic and social factors to the singing ranges of institutionalized mentally retarded persons. *Journal of Music Therapy, 13*, 17–28.

Dileo, C. L. (1975). The use of a token economy program with mentally retarded persons in a music therapy setting. *Journal of Music Therapy, 12*, 155–160.

Dorow, L. G. (1975). Conditioning music and approval as new reinforcers for imitative behavior with the severely retarded. *Journal of Music Therapy, 12*, 30–39.

Dorow, L. G. (1976). Televised music lessons as educational reinforcement for correct mathematical responses with EMR's. *Journal of Music Therapy, 13*, 77–86.

Dorow, L. G., & Horton, J. J. (1982). Effect on the proximity of auditory stimuli and sung versus spoken stimuli on activity levels of severe and profoundly mentally retarded females. *Journal of Music Therapy, 19*, 114–124.

Flowers, E. (1984). Musical sound perception in normal children and children with Down's syndrome. *Journal of Music Therapy, 21*, 146–154.

Force, B. (1983). The effects of mainstreaming on the learning of non-retarded children in an elementary music classroom. *Journal of Music Therapy, 20*, 2–13.

Ford, J. E., & Veltri-Ford, A. (1980). Effects of time-out from auditory reinforcement on two problem behaviors. *Mental Retardation, 18*, 299–303.

Furman, C. E., & Steele, A. L. (1982). Teaching the special student: A survey of independent music teachers with implications for music therapists. *Journal of Music Therapy, 19,* 66–73.

Grant, R. E., & LeCroy, S. (1986). Effects of sensory mode input on the performance of rhythmic perception tasks by mentally retarded subjects. *Journal of Music Therapy, 23,* 2–9.

Grant, R.E., & Share, M. R. (1985). Relationship of pitch discrimination skills and vocal ranges of mentally retarded subjects. *Journal of Music Therapy, 22,* 99–103.

Greenwald, M. A. (1978). The effectiveness of distorted music versus interrupted music to decrease self-stimulative behaviors in profoundly retarded adolescents. *Journal of Music Therapy, 15,* 58–66.

Gregoire, M. A. (1984). Music as a prior condition to task performance. *Journal of Music Therapy, 21,* 133–145.

Groeneweg, G., Stan, E. A., Celser, A., MacBeth, L., & Vrbancic, M. I. (1988). The effect of background music on the vocational behavior of mentally handicapped adults. *Journal of Music Therapy, 25,* 118–134.

Hair, H. I., & Graham, R. M. (1983). A comparison of verbal descriptors used by TMR students and music therapists. *Journal of Music Therapy, 20,* 59–68.

Hairston, M. J. P. (1990). Analyses of response of mentally retarded autistic and mentally retarded nonautistic children to art therapy and music therapy. *Journal of Music Therapy, 27,* 137–150.

Hanser, S. B. (1983). Music therapy: A behavioral perspective. *Behavior Therapist, 6,* 5–8.

Hasselbring, T. S., & Duffus, N. A. (1981). Using microcomputer technology in music therapy for analyzing therapist and client behavior. *Journal of Music Therapy, 18,* 156–165.

Hauber, F. A., Bruininks, R. H., Hill, B. K., Lakin, K. C., & White, C. C. (1982). *National census of residential facilities: Fiscal year 1982* (Project Report No. 19). Minneapolis: University of Minnesota, Department of Educational Psychology.

Heyer, J. L., Downs, D. W., Kallay, V., & Magdinac, M. (1986). Music conditioning before pure-tone screening of severely and profoundly mentally retarded adults. *Journal of Music Therapy, 23,* 142–156.

Hill, J., Brantner, J., & Spreat, S. (1989). The effect of contingent music on the in-seat behavior of a blind young woman with profound mental retardation. *Education and Treatment of Children, 12,* 165–173.

Holloway, M. S. (1980). A comparison of passive and active music reinforcement to increase preacademic and motor skills in severely retarded children and adolescents. *Journal of Music Therapy, 17,* 58–69.

Humphrey, T. (1980). The effect of music ear training upon the auditory discrimination abilities of trainable mentally retarded adolescents. *Journal of Music Therapy, 17,* 70–74.

James, M. R., Weaver, A. L., Clemens, P. D., & Plaster, G. A. (1985). Influence of paired auditory and vestibular stimulation on levels of motor skill development in a mentally retarded population. *Journal of Music Therapy, 22,* 22–34.

Jellison, J. A., Brooks, B. H., & Huck, A. M. (1984). Structuring small groups and music reinforcement to facilitate positive interactions and acceptance of severely handicapped students in the regular music classroom. *Journal of Research in Music Education, 32,* 243–264.

Jellison, J. A., & Duke, R. A. (1994). The mental retardation label: Music teacher's expectations for children's social and music behavior. *Journal of Music Therapy, 31*, 166–185.

Jellison, J. A. & Flowers, P. J. (1991). Talking about music: Interviews with disabled and nondisabled children. *Journal of Research in Music Education, 39*, 322-333.

Johnson, J. M., & Zinner, C. C. (1974). Stimulus facing and schedule learning in generalizing and maintaining behaviors. *Journal of Music Therapy, 11*, 84–96.

Jones, R. E. (1986). Assessing developmental levels of mentally retarded students with the Musical Perception Assessment of Cognitive Development. *Journal of Music Therapy, 23*, 166–173.

Jorgenson, H. (1974). The use of a contingent music activity to modify behaviors which interfere with learning. *Journal of Music Therapy, 11*, 41–46.

Jorgenson, H., & Parnell, M. K. (1970). Modifying social behaviors of mentally retarded children. *Journal of Music Therapy, 7*, 83–87.

Karper, W. B. (1979). Effects of music on learning a motor skill by handicapped and non-handicapped boys. *Perceptual and Motor Skills, 49*, 734.

Kaufman, K. M., & Sheckart, G. R. (1985). The effects of tempo variation and white noise on the general activity level of profoundly retarded adults. *Journal of Music Therapy, 22*, 207–217.

Larson, B. A. (1977). A comparison of singing ranges of mental retarded and normal children with published songbooks used in singing activities. *Journal of Music Therapy, 14*, 139–143.

Lienhard, M. E. (1976). Factors relevant to the rhythmic perception of a group of mentally retarded children. *Journal of Music Therapy, 13*, 58–65.

Macurik, K. M. (1979). An operant device to reinforce correct head position. *Journal of Behavior Therapy and Experimental Psychiatry, 10*, 237–239.

Madsen, C. K. (1981). *Music therapy: A behavioral guide for the mentally retarded.* Lawrence, KS: National Association for Music Therapy.

McClure, J., Moss, R., Peters, J., & Kirkpatrick, M. (1986). Reduction of hand mouthing by a boy with profound mental retardation. *Mental Retardation, 24*, 219–222.

Metzler, R. K. (1974). The use of music as a reinforcer to increase imitative behavior in severely and profoundly retarded female residents. *Journal of Music Therapy, 11*, 97–110.

Moore, R., & Mathenius, L. (1987). The effects of modeling, reinforcement, and tempo on imitative rhythmic responses of moderately retarded adolescents. *Journal of Music Therapy, 24*, 160–169.

Moreno, J. J. (1985). Music play therapy: An integrated approach. *Arts in Psychotherapy, 12*, 17–23.

Myers, E. G. (1979). The effect of music on retention in a paired-associate task with EMR children. *Journal of Music Therapy, 16*, 190–198.

Myers, K. F. (1985). The relationship between degree of disability and vocal range, vocal midpoint, and pitch-matching ability of mentally retarded and psychiatric clients. *Journal of Music Therapy, 22*, 35–45.

Ponath, L. H., & Bitcon, C. H. (1972). A behavioral analysis of Orff-Schulwerk. *Journal of Music Therapy, 9*, 56–63.

Pujol, K. K. (1994). The effect of vibrotactile stimulation, instrumentation, and precomposed melodies on physiological and behavioral responses of profoundly retarded children and adults. *Journal of Music Therapy, 31*, 186–205.

Reid, D. H., Hill, B. K., Rawers, R. J., & Montegar, C. A. (1975). The use of contingent music in teaching social skills to a nonverbal, hyperactive boy. *Journal of Music Therapy, 12*, 2–18.

Richman, J. S. (1976). Background music for repetitive task performance of severely retarded individuals. *American Journal of Mental Deficiency, 81*, 251–255.

Rider, M. S. (1977). The relationship between auditory and visual perception on tasks employing Piaget's concept of conservation. *Journal of Music Therapy, 14*, 126–138.

Robinson, N. M., & Robinson, H. B. (1976). *The mentally retarded child*. New York: McGraw-Hill.

Rubin, B. (1976). Handbells in therapy. *Journal of Music Therapy, 13*, 48–53.

Saperston, B. (1973). The use of music in establishing communication with an autistic mentally retarded child. *Journal of Music Therapy, 10*, 184–188.

Saperston, B. M., Chan, R., Morphew, C., & Carlsrud, K. B. (1980). Music listening versus juice as a reinforcement for learning in profoundly mentally retarded individuals. *Journal of Music Therapy, 17*, 174–183.

Silini, F. C. (1979). A piano course for special adults. *Music Educators Journal, 65*, 72–79.

Silliman, L. M., & French, R. (1993). Use of selected reinforcers to improve the ball kicking of youths with profound mental retardation. *Adapted Physical Activity Quarterly, 10*, 52–69.

Spencer, L. S. (1988). The efficiency of instrumental and movement activities in developing mentally retarded adolescents' ability to follow directions. *Journal of Music Therapy, 25*, 44–50.

Steele, A. L. (1977). The application of behavioral research techniques to community music therapy. *Journal of Music Therapy, 14*, 102–115.

Steele, A. L., & Jorgenson, H. A. (1971). Music therapy: An effective solution to problems in related disciplines. *Journal of Music Therapy, 8*, 131–145.

Stubbs, B. B. (1970). A study of the effectiveness of an integrated personified approach to learning with trainable mental retardates. *Journal of Music Therapy, 7*, 77–82.

Talkington, L. W., & Hall, S. M. (1970). A musical application of Premack's hypothesis to low verbal retardates. *Journal of Music Therapy, 7*, 95–99.

Tallon, R. J., & Stangl, J. M. (1980). Environmental influences on self-stimulatory behavior. *American Journal of Mental Deficiency, 85*, 171–175.

Tierny, I. R., McGuire, R. J., & Walton, H. J. (1978). The effect of music on body rocking manifested by severely mentally deficient patients in ward environments. *Journal of Mental Deficiency Research, 22*, 255–261.

Underhill, K. K., & Harris, L. M. (1974). The effect of contingent music on establishing imitation in behaviorally disturbed retarded children. *Journal of Music Therapy, 11*, 156–166.

Walker, J. B. (1972). The use of music as an aid in developing functional speech in the institutionalized mentally retarded. *Journal of Music Therapy, 9*, 1–12.

Wasserman, N., Plutchik, R., Deutsch, R., & Taketomo, Y. (1973). A music therapy evaluation scale and its clinical application to mentally retarded adult patients. *Journal of Music Therapy, 10*, 64–77.

Wentworth, R. (1991). The effects of music and distracting noise on the productivity of workers with mental retardation. *Journal of Music Therapy, 28,* 40–47.

Wingert, M. L. (1972). Effects of a music enrichment program in the education of the retarded. *Journal of Music Therapy, 9,* 13–22.

Wolfgram, B. J. (1978). Music therapy for retarded adults with psychotic overlay: A day treatment approach. *Journal of Music Therapy, 15,* 199–207.

Wolpow, R. I. (1976). The independent effects of contingent social and academic approval upon the musical on-task and performance behaviors of profoundly mentally retarded adults. *Journal of Music Therapy, 13,* 29–38.

Wylie, M. E. (1983). Eliciting vocal responses in severe and profoundly mentally handicapped subjects. *Journal of Music Therapy, 20,* 190–200.